London
2011

A SELECTION
OF **RESTAURANTS** & **HOTELS**

Commitments

"This volume was created at the turn of the century and will last at least as long."

This foreword to the very first edition of the MICHELIN Guide, written in 1900, has become famous over the years and the Guide has lived up to the prediction. It is read across the world and the key to its popularity is the consistency of its commitment to its readers, which is based on the following promises.

→ Anonymous inspections

Our inspectors make regular and anonymous visits to hotels and restaurants to gauge the quality of products and services offered to an ordinary customer. They settle their own bill and may then introduce themselves and ask for more information about the establishment. Our readers' comments are also a valuable source of information, which we can then follow up with another visit of our own.

→ Independence

Our choice of establishments is a completely independent one, made for the benefit of our readers alone. The decisions to be taken are discussed around the table by the inspectors and the editor. The most important awards are decided at a European level. Inclusion in the Guide is completely free of charge.

→ Selection & choice

The Guide offers a selection of the best hotels and restaurants in every category of comfort and price. This is only possible because all the inspectors rigorously apply the same methods.

→ Annual updates

All the practical information, the classifications and awards are revised and updated every single year to give the most reliable information possible.

Consistency: The criteria for the classifications are the same in every country covered by the Michelin Guide.

→ And our aim...

...to do everything possible to make travel, holidays and eating out a pleasure, as part of Michelin's ongoing commitment to improving travel and mobility.

Dear reader

We are delighted to introduce the 2011 edition of the Michelin Guide for London.

We make this guide for you and value your opinions, so let us know what you think about this guide and about the restaurants we have recommended.

All the restaurants within this guide have been chosen first and foremost for the quality of their cooking. You'll find comprehensive information on 450 dining establishments within these pages and they range from gastropubs and neighbourhood brasseries to internationally renowned restaurants. The diverse and varied selection also bears testament to the rich and buoyant dining scene in London, with the city now enjoying a worldwide reputation for the quality and range of its restaurants.

You'll see that Michelin Stars are not our only awards – look out also for the Bib Gourmands. These are restaurants where the cooking is still carefully prepared but in a simpler style and, priced at under £28 for three courses, they represent excellent value for money.

As well as the restaurants, our team of independent inspectors has also chosen 50 hotels. These carefully selected hotels represent the best that London has to offer, from the luxurious and international to the small and intimate. All have been chosen for their individuality and personality.

Consult the Michelin Guide at www.viamichelin.com
and write to us at themichelinguide-gbirl@uk.michelin.com

Contents

● Where to **eat**

CENTRAL LONDON   27

How to use this guide

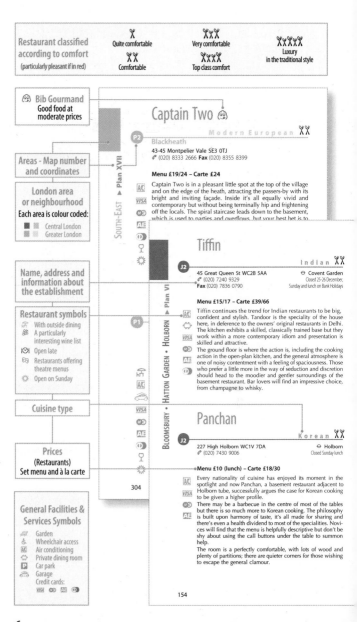

| Restaurant classified according to comfort (particularly pleasant if in red) | ✗ Quite comfortable ✗✗ Comfortable | ✗✗✗ Very comfortable ✗✗✗✗ Top class comfort | ✗✗✗✗✗ Luxury in the traditional style |

Bib Gourmand
Good food at moderate prices

Areas - Map number and coordinates

London area or neighbourhood
Each area is colour coded:
- Central London
- Greater London

Name, address and information about the establishment

Restaurant symbols
- With outside dining
- A particularly interesting wine list
- Open late
- Restaurants offering theatre menus
- Open on Sunday

Cuisine type

Prices
(Restaurants)
Set menu and à la carte

General Facilities & Services Symbols
- Garden
- Wheelchair access
- Air conditioning
- Private dining room
- Car park
- Garage
Credit cards:
VISA ⓂⒸ AE Ⓞ

Captain Two 🅰

Modern European ✗✗

P2 Blackheath

43-45 Montpelier Vale SE3 0TJ
☎ (020) 8333 2666 **Fax** (020) 8355 8399

Menu £19/24 – Carte £24

Captain Two is in a pleasant little spot at the top of the village and on the edge of the heath, attracting the passers-by with its bright and inviting façade. Inside it's all equally vivid and contemporary but without being terminally hip and frightening off the locals. The spiral staircase leads down to the basement, which is used to parties and overflows, but your best bet is to

SOUTH-EAST ▶ Plan XVII

Tiffin

Indian ✗✗

J2 45 Great Queen St WC2B 5AA
☎ (020) 7240 9329
Fax (020) 7836 0790

⊖ Covent Garden
Closed 25-26 December,
Sunday and lunch on Bank Holidays

Menu £15/17 – Carte £39/66

Tiffin continues the trend for Indian restaurants to be big, confident and stylish. Tandoor is the speciality of the house here, in deference to the owners' original restaurants in Delhi. The kitchen exhibits a skilled, classically trained base but they work within a more contemporary idiom and presentation is skilled and attractive.

The ground floor is where the action is, including the cooking action in the open-plan kitchen, and the general atmosphere is one of noisy contentment with a feeling of spaciousness. Those who prefer a little more in the way of seduction and discretion should head to the moodier and gentler surroundings of the basement restaurant. Bar lovers will find an impressive choice, from champagne to whisky.

BLOOMSBURY • HATTON GARDEN • HOLBORN ▶ Plan VI

Panchan

Korean ✗✗

J2 227 High Holborn WC1V 7DA
☎ (020) 7430 9006

⊖ Holborn
Closed Sunday lunch

Menu £10 (lunch) – Carte £18/30

Every nationality of cuisine has enjoyed its moment in the spotlight and now Panchan, a basement restaurant adjacent to Holborn tube, successfully argues the case for Korean cooking to be given a higher profile.

There may be a barbecue in the centre of most of the tables but there is so much more to Korean cooking. The philosophy is built upon harmony of taste, it's all made for sharing and there's even a health dividend to most of the specialities. Novices will find that the menu is helpfully descriptive but don't be shy about using the call buttons under the table to summon help.

The room is a perfectly comfortable, with lots of wood and plenty of partitions; there are quieter corners for those wishing to escape the general clamour.

304

154

Hotel classification according to comfort
(particularly pleasant if in red)

Quite comfortable

Comfortable

Very comfortable

Top class comfort

Luxury in the traditional style

Hotel symbols

39 rm Number of rooms
- Breakfast included (or not)
- ♦/♦♦ Prices for a single/double room
- ⅏ Quiet hotel
- ⅏O With restaurant
- ⅏ Swimming pool
- ⅏ Spa
- ⅏ Sauna
- ⅏ Tennis
- ⅏ Exercise room
- ⅏ Lift
- ⅏ Broadband connection
- ⅏ Wireless
- ⅏ Satellite TV
- ⅏ Equipped conference room

Map coordinates

⊖ Underground station

Agatha's

I2

15 Charlotte St W1T 1RJ
☎ (020) 7806 2000 **Fax** (020) 7806 2002

⊖ Goode Street

44 rm – ♦£247/282 ♦♦£347, ☐ £19 – 8 suites
⅏O **Hercule** (See restaurant listing)

Le Petit François ✿ ✿

G3

43 Upper Brook St W1K 7QR
☎ (020) 7408 0881
Fax (020) 7491 4387

⊖ Marble Arch
Closed Christmas-New Year, Sunday, Saturday
lunch and Bank Holidays – booking essential

Menu £48 – Carte £60/130

French ✕✕✕✕

In today's rush for the new and the novel, we sometimes forget about the jewels we already have. Le Petit François is guaranteed its own chapter when the history of British gastronomy is written and today, over forty years after it first opened in Chelsea, it's still maintaining its own high standards and respect for tradition. The service is unerringly professional; this is where any budding restaurateur should come if they want to learn how things are done 'properly' and one can observe the hierarchical structure from one's chair. The room retains a clubby and masculine feel but it also offers a palpable sense of history; those new to the restaurant are guided gently through its customs and politely reminded of its traditions.

The menu represents classic French cuisine and not just an English idea of French cuisine; a style of food which is becoming rarer by the day. A Soufflé Suissesse is rich enough to live on for days and the use of luxury items, from lobster to foie gras, would make Epicurus blanch. Those who prefer a lighter style, however, are not ignored.

First Course	*Main Course*	*Dessert*
• Hot foie gras and crispy duck pancake flavoured with cinnamon.	• Roast saddle of rabbit with crispy potatoes and parmesan.	• Bitter chocolate and praline 'indulgence'.
• Lobster mousse with caviar and champagne butter sauce.	• Whole roast John Dory with artichokes, olive oil mashed potato.	• Iced amaretto nougat with cherries cooked in red wine syrup.

...ion, within strolling distance of Soho, or ...own private screening room that attract ...h industry sorts and arty souls who have ...own, but the stimulating way in which it ...and the prevailing vibe.

...warehouse has been deftly transformed ...l and proves that comfort and design can ... that something good has come from ...g a combination of abstract art, sculpture ...rtists of the neighbouring Bloomsbury set, ...be also quite English in tone. The drawing ...ress-free areas, in contrast to the bustle of ...restaurant.

...bedrooms are one-off pieces of furniture ...rawer fabrics and fittings, all supported by ...amme of virtually constant refurbishment. ...enthusiastic and confident. The loft and ...l stir emotions of envy and desire or, if

MAYFAIR • SOHO • ST JAMES'S ▲ Plan II

WESTMINSTER ▲ Plan V

373

Area - Map number

Stars for good cooking
✿ to ✿ ✿ ✿

✿
Starred restaurant symbol

Sample menu for starred restaurant

41

A culinary history of London

London, influenced by worldwide produce arriving via the Thames, has always enjoyed a close association with its food, though most of the time the vast majority of its people have looked much closer to home for their sustenance.

Even as far back as the 2nd century AD, meat was on the menu: the profusion of wildlife in the woods and forests around London turned it into a carnivore's paradise, thereby setting the tone and the template. Large stoves were employed to cook everything from pork and beef to goose and deer. The Saxons added the likes of garlic, leeks, radishes and turnips to the pot, while eels became a popular staple in later years.

WHAT A LARK!

By the 13th century, the taste for fish had evolved to the more exotic porpoise, lamprey and sturgeon, with saffron and spices perking up the common-or-garden meat dish. Not that medieval tastes would have been considered mundane to the average 21st century diner: Londoners of the time would think nothing about devouring roasted thrush or lark from the cook's stalls dotted around the city streets. And you'd have been unlikely to hear the cry "Eat your greens!" In the 15th century the vegetable diet, such as it was, seemed to run mainly to herbs such as rosemary, fennel, borage and thyme.

As commercial and maritime success burgeoned in the age of the Tudors, so tables began to groan under the weight of London's penchant for feasting. No excess was spared, as oxen, sheep, boars and pigs were put to the griddle; these would have been accompanied by newly arrived yams and sweet potatoes from America and 'washed down' with rhubarb from Asia. People on the streets could 'feast-lite': by the 17th century hawkers were offering all sorts of goodies on the hoof.

FULL OF BEANS

All of this eating was of course accompanied by a lot of drinking. Though much of it took place in the alehouses and taverns - which ran into the thousands - by the 18th century coffee houses had become extraordinarily popular. These were places to do business as well as being convenient 'for passing evenings socially at a very small charge'.

Perhaps the biggest revolution in eating habits came midway through the 19th century when the first cavernous dining halls and restaurants appeared. These 'freed' diners from the communal benches of the cook-house and gave them, for the first time, the chance for a bit of seclusion at separate tables. This private dining experience was an egalitarian movement: plutocrats may have had their posh hotels, but the less well-off were buttering teacakes and scones served by 'nippies' at the local Lyons Corner House.

Influenced by post-World War II flavours brought in by immigrants from Asia, the Caribbean and Africa, Londoners can now enjoy an unparalleled cuisine alive with global flavours, while the worlds of food and drink have fused remarkably well in recent years with the growing excellence of the gastropub, which had its roots in the creative maelstrom of the capital.

C. Labonne / MICHELIN

Where to **eat**

Starred restaurants

Within this selection, we have highlighted a number of restaurants for their particularly good cooking. When awarding one, two or three Michelin Stars there are a number of factors we consider: the quality and compatibility of the ingredients, the technical skill and flair that goes into their preparation, the clarity and combination of flavours, the value for money and, above all, the taste. Equally important is the ability to produce excellent cooking not once but time and time again. Our inspectors make as many visits as necessary, so that you can be sure of the quality and consistency.

A two or three star restaurant has to offer something very special in its cuisine; a real element of creativity, originality or personality that sets it apart from the rest. Three stars – our highest award – are given to the very best.

Cuisines in any style and of any nationality are eligible for a star. The decoration, service and comfort have no bearing on the award.

Let us know what you think, not just about the stars but about all the restaurants in this guide.

The awarding of a star is based solely on the quality of the cuisine.

N: highlights those establishments newly promoted to one, two or three stars.

✿✿✿

Exceptional cuisine, worth a special journey.
One always eats here extremely well, sometimes superbly. Distinctive dishes are precisely executed, using superlative ingredients.

Alain Ducasse at The Dorchester	𝖃𝖃𝖃𝖃𝖃 34	Gordon Ramsay	𝖃𝖃𝖃𝖃 230

✿✿

Excellent cooking, worth a detour.
Skillfully and carefully crafted dishes of outstanding quality.

L'Atelier de Joël Robuchon	𝖃 95	The Ledbury	𝖃𝖃𝖃 251
Le Gavroche	𝖃𝖃𝖃𝖃 56	Marcus Wareing	
Hélène Darroze		at The Berkeley	𝖃𝖃𝖃𝖃 111
at The Connaught N	𝖃𝖃𝖃𝖃 60	Pied à Terre	𝖃𝖃𝖃 154
Hibiscus	𝖃𝖃𝖃 61	Square	𝖃𝖃𝖃𝖃 83

✿

A very good restaurant in its category.
A place offering cuisine prepared to a consistently high standard.

Amaya	𝖃𝖃𝖃 106	Nobu Berkeley St	𝖃𝖃 71
Apsleys (at Lanesborough Hotel)	𝖃𝖃𝖃𝖃 107	Petersham Nurseries Café N	𝖃 342
Arbutus	𝖃 37	Pétrus N	𝖃𝖃𝖃 116
L'Autre Pied	𝖃𝖃 126	Quilon	𝖃𝖃𝖃 117
Benares	𝖃𝖃𝖃 43	Rasoi	𝖃𝖃 237
Bingham Restaurant		Rhodes Twenty Four	𝖃𝖃𝖃 200
(at Bingham Hotel)	𝖃𝖃 340	Rhodes W1 (Restaurant)	𝖃𝖃𝖃𝖃 137
Chez Bruce	𝖃𝖃 347	River Café	𝖃𝖃 337
Club Gascon	𝖃𝖃 184	St John	𝖃 201
Galvin at Windows		Semplice	𝖃𝖃 79
(at London Hilton Hotel)	𝖃𝖃𝖃𝖃 55	Seven Park Place	
Galvin La Chapelle N	𝖃𝖃𝖃 307	(at St James's Hotel and Club) N	𝖃𝖃𝖃 80
Gauthier - Soho N	𝖃𝖃𝖃 57	Sketch (The Lecture Room	
The Glasshouse	𝖃𝖃 338	and Library)	𝖃𝖃𝖃 82
Greenhouse	𝖃𝖃𝖃 59	Tamarind	𝖃𝖃𝖃 84
Hakkasan	𝖃𝖃 150	Texture	𝖃𝖃 138
Harwood Arms	🍴 331	Tom Aikens	𝖃𝖃𝖃 238
Kai	𝖃𝖃𝖃 64	La Trompette	𝖃𝖃𝖃 327
Kitchen W8 N	𝖃𝖃 250	Umu	𝖃𝖃𝖃 87
Locanda Locatelli	𝖃𝖃𝖃 134	Viajante N	𝖃𝖃 300
Maze	𝖃𝖃𝖃 66	Wild Honey	𝖃𝖃 89
Murano	𝖃𝖃𝖃 69	Yauatcha	𝖃𝖃 91
Nobu (at The Metropolitan Hotel)	𝖃𝖃 70	Zafferano	𝖃𝖃𝖃 121

Bib Gourmand

Restaurants offering good quality cooking for less than £28
(price of a 3 course meal excluding drinks)

Al Duca	✗	35
Anchor and Hope	🍽	176
Bar Trattoria Semplice	✗	41
Benja	✗✗	44
Bocca di Lupo	✗	46
Bradley's	✗✗	274
Brown Dog	🍽	319
Cafe Spice Namaste	✗✗	310
Canton Arms N	🍽	309
Chapters	✗✗	301
Charlotte's Bistro N	✗	324
Comptoir Gascon	✗	185
Dehesa	✗	52
The Drapers Arms	🍽	289
500	✗	264
Galvin Café a Vin N	✗	306
Giaconda Dining Room	✗	148
Goldfish City N	✗	187
Great Queen Street	✗	149
Hereford Road	✗	163
Iberica N	✗✗	131
Malabar	✗	252
Mango and Silk	✗	329
Market	✗	265
Medcalf	✗	192
Metrogusto	✗✗	290
Morito N	✗	194
Polpo N	✗	74
Salt Yard	✗	155
Simply Thai N	✗	344
Terroirs	✗	100
Trullo N	✗	284
28°-50° N	✗	204
Zucca N	✗	209

Restaurants by Cuisine Type

American

Automat	✗	38

Asian

Champor-Champor	✗	181
Cicada	✗	182
Cocoon	✗✗	50
E and O	✗✗	247
Eight over Eight	✗✗	227
Goldfish	✗	269
Goldfish City	✗ 🏵	187
Great Eastern Dining Room	✗✗	287
Singapore Garden	✗✗	275
XO	✗✗	265

Beef specialities

Goodman	✗✗	54
Goodman City	✗✗	187
Hawksmoor	✗	306
Kew Grill	✗✗	336
Maze Grill	✗✗	65

British

Anchor and Hope	🏠 🏵	176
Bedford and Strand	✗	96
Bentley's (Grill)	✗✗✗	44
Bluebird	✗✗	220
Bumpkin (South Kensington)	✗	222
Bumpkin (North Kensington)	✗	246
Butlers Wharf Chop House	✗	180
Cat and Mutton	🏠	284
Corrigan's Mayfair	✗✗✗	51
Dean Street Townhouse Restaurant	✗✗	51
The Drapers Arms	🏠 🏵	289
Fat Badger	🏠	248
Great Queen Street	✗ 🏵	149
Harwood Arms	🏠 ❀	331
Hereford Road	✗ 🏵	163
Hix	✗	58
Hix Oyster and Chop House	✗	189
Inn the Park	✗	63
Magdalen	✗✗	191
Market	✗ 🏵	265
Medcalf	✗ 🏵	192
The National Dining Rooms	✗	68
Paradise by way of Kensal Green	🏠	271
Paternoster Chop House	✗	197
Prince of Wales	🏠	339
Quo Vadis	✗✗✗	76
Ransome's Dock	✗	323
Restaurant at St Paul's Cathedral	✗	199
Rex Whistler	✗✗	115
Rhodes Twenty Four	✗✗✗ ❀	200
Rivington Grill (Greenwich)	✗	304
Rivington Grill (Shoreditch)	✗	293
Roast	✗✗	199
Rules	✗✗	100
St John	✗ ❀	201
St John Bread and Wine	✗	308
Shepherd's	✗✗✗	119
Tate Modern (Restaurant)	✗	203
Victoria	🏠	330

Chinese

Baozi Inn	✗	40
Barshu	✗	41
Ba Shan	✗	42
China Tang	✗✗✗✗	49
Good Earth	✗✗	229
Hakkasan	✗✗ ❀	150
Kai	✗✗✗ ❀	64
Mao Tai	✗✗	332
Memories of China	✗✗	252
Min Jiang	✗✗✗	253
Mr Chow	✗✗	233
Pearl Liang	✗✗	164
Phoenix Palace	✗✗	135
Plum Valley	✗✗	73
Snazz Sichuan	✗✗	268
Yauatcha	✗✗ ❀	91

Eastern European

Baltic — 177

French

L'Absinthe — 271
Alain Ducasse at The Dorchester — 34
Almeida — 288
Angelus — 162
L'Atelier de Joël Robuchon — 95
Aubaine (Chelsea) — 216
Aubaine (Mayfair) — 38
L'Aventure — 127
Bar Boulud — 218
Bellamy's — 42
Belvedere — 245
Bibendum — 218
Bistro Aix — 266
Bistro K — 219
Bistrot Bruno Loubet — 177
Bleeding Heart — 147
Le Boudin Blanc — 46
Boundary — 292
Brasserie Roux — 47
Brula — 345
Le Cercle — 224
Chelsea Brasserie — 225
Chez Bruce — 347
Clos Maggiore — 97
Club Gascon — 184
Le Colombier — 226
Comptoir Gascon — 185
Coq d'Argent — 185
Galvin at Windows (at London Hilton Hotel) — 55
Galvin Bistrot de Luxe — 130
Galvin Café a Vin — 306
Galvin La Chapelle — 307
Gauthier - Soho — 57
Le Gavroche — 56
Gordon Ramsay — 230
Hélène Darroze at The Connaught — 60
Koffmann's — 110
The Ledbury — 251
Lobster Pot — 305

Luc's Brasserie — 190
Marcus Wareing at The Berkeley — 111
Mon Plaisir — 151
Morgan M — 282
1901 — 195
Notting Hill Brasserie — 253
Pearl — 153
La Petite Maison — 73
Le Pont de la Tour — 198
Racine — 236
The Restaurant at The Petersham — 341
Rhodes W1 (Restaurant) — 137
Roussillon — 118
Roux at Parliament Square — 118
Sauterelle — 202
Sketch (The Lecture Room and Library) — 82
Square — 83
Terroirs — 100
Tom's Kitchen — 239
Les Trois Garcons — 308
La Trouvaille — 86
28°-50° — 204
Le Vacherin — 317
Villandry — 139
Villandry Kitchen — 157
The Wallace — 140

Indian

Amaya — 106
Benares — 43
Bombay Brasserie — 220
Cafe Spice Namaste — 310
Chor Bizarre — 50
Chutney Mary — 226
The Cinnamon Club — 109
Cinnamon Kitchen — 183
Colony — 129
Dockmaster's House — 301
Eriki — 274
Imli — 62
Indian Zilla — 320
Indian Zing — 336
Kastoori — 344
Malabar — 252

17

Italian influences

Murano	ХхХ ✿	69
Petersham Nurseries Café	Х ✿	342

Italian vegetarian

Amico Bio	Х	176

Japanese

Aqua Kyoto	ХХ	36
Chisou	Х	49
Dinings	Х	130
Kiku	ХХ	63
Kiraku	Х	329
Matsuba	Х	341
Matsuri - St James's	ХХ	65
Nobu (at The Metropolitan Hotel)	ХХ ✿	70
Nobu Berkeley St	ХХ ✿	71
Roka	ХХ	155
Roka Canary Wharf	ХХ	303
Sake No Hana	ХхХ	77
Sumosan	ХХ	81
Sushi-Say	Х	277
Tsunami (Bloomsbury)	Х	156
Tsunami (Clapham)	Х	328
Umu	ХхХ ✿	87
Zuma	ХХ	240

Korean

Asadal	ХХ	146

Latin American

Floridita	ХХ	53

Lebanese

Fakhreldine	ХХ	53
Kenza	ХХ	189
Levant	ХХ	133
Noura Brasserie	ХХ	112

Malaysian

Awana	ХхХ	217

Mediterranean

Dehesa	Х ⊕	52

Harrison's	Х	318
Moro	Х	195
Ottolenghi	Х	291
Portal	ХХ	198
Salt Yard	Х ⊕	155
Sam's Brasserie	Х	326
Whitechapel Gallery Dining Room	Х	310

Modern

Charlotte's Bistro	Х ⊕	324

Modern European

Acorn House	Х	145
Arbutus	Х ✿	37
L'Autre Pied	ХХ ✿	126
Avenue	ХХ	39
Axis	ХхХ	96
Babylon	ХХ	245
Bank	ХХ	108
Bingham Restaurant (at Bingham Hotel)	ХХ ✿	340
Blueprint Café	Х	178
Bob Bob Ricard	ХХ	45
Bonds	ХхХ	179
The Botanist	ХХ	221
Bradley's	ХХ ⊕	274
Brasserie James	Х	318
Le Café Anglais	ХХ	163
Cafe at Sotheby's	ХХ	47
Cafe Luc	ХХ	128
Le Caprice	ХХ	48
The Chancery	ХХ	182
Chapters	ХХ ⊕	301
Charlotte's Place	Х	328
Clarke's	ХХ	247
Le Deuxième	ХХ	97
Devonshire Terrace	ХХ	186
Fellow	ⅡⅢ	291
Fifth Floor	ХхХ	228
Fig	Х	282
Forge	ХХ	98
Giaconda Dining Room	Х ⊕	148
The Glasshouse	ХХ ✿	338
Gordon Ramsay at Claridge's	ХхХ	58
High Timber	ХХ	188
Hix (Selfridges)	Х	131

Turkish

Vegetarian

Vietnamese

Restaurants with outside dining

Open late

Open on Sunday

Where to **eat** ▶ Open on Sunday

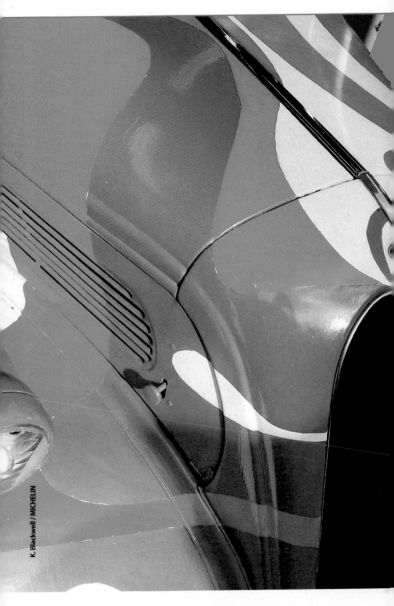

Central London

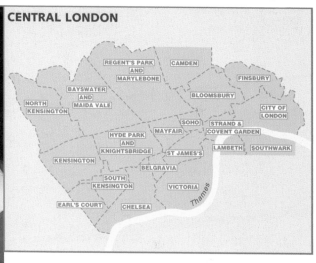

CENTRAL LONDON

Philippe Roy/MICHELIN

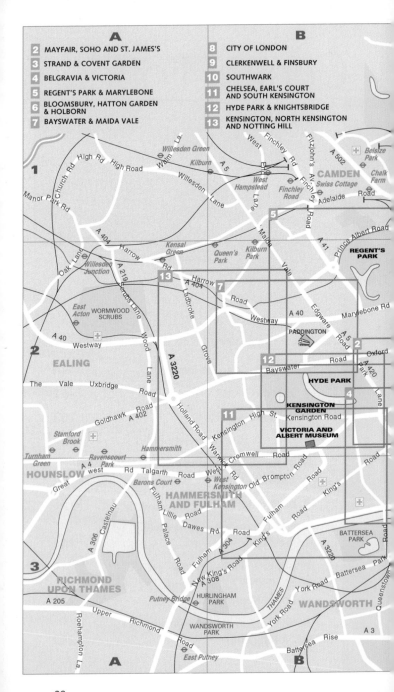

A

2 MAYFAIR, SOHO AND ST. JAMES'S

3 STRAND & COVENT GARDEN

4 BELGRAVIA & VICTORIA

5 REGENT'S PARK & MARYLEBONE

6 BLOOMSBURY, HATTON GARDEN & HOLBORN

7 BAYSWATER & MAIDA VALE

B

8 CITY OF LONDON

9 CLERKENWELL & FINSBURY

10 SOUTHWARK

11 CHELSEA, EARL'S COURT AND SOUTH KENSINGTON

12 HYDE PARK & KNIGHTSBRIDGE

13 KENSINGTON, NORTH KENSINGTON AND NOTTING HILL

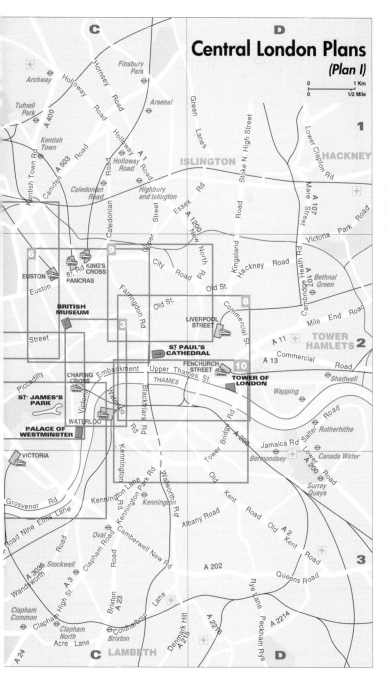

Central London Plans
(Plan I)

0 ___ 1 Km
0 ___ 1/2 Mile

Mayfair · Soho · St James's

There's one elegant dividing line between Mayfair and Soho - the broad and imposing sweep of **Regent Street** - but mindsets and price tags keep them a world apart. It's usual to think of easterly Soho as the wild and sleazy half of these ill-matched twins, with Mayfair to the west the more sedate and sophisticated of the two. Sometimes, though, the natural order of things runs awry: why was rock's legendary wild man Jimi Hendrix, the embodiment of Soho decadence, living in the rarefied air of Mayfair's smart 23 Brook Street? And what induced Vivienne Westwood, punk queen and fashionista to the edgy, to settle her sewing machine in the uber-smart Conduit Street?

Mayfair has been synonymous with elegance for three and a half centuries, ever since the Berkeley and Grosvenor families bought up the local fields and turned them into posh real estate. The area is named after the annual May fair introduced in 1686, but suffice it to say that a raucous street celebration would be frowned upon big time by twenty-first century inhabitants. The grand residential boulevards can seem frosty and imposing, and even induce feelings of inadequacy to the humble passer-by but should he become the proud owner of a glistening gold card, then hey ho, doors will open wide. Claridge's is an art deco wonder, while **New Bond Street** is London's number one thoroughfare for the most

chi-chi names in retailing. **Savile Row** may sound a little 'passé' these days, but it's still the place to go for the sharpest cut in town, before sashaying over to compact **Cork Street** to indulge in the purchase of a piece of art at one of its superb galleries. Science and music can also be found here, and at a relatively cheap price: the Faraday Museum in **Albemarle Street** has had a sparkling refurbishment, and the Handel House Museum in Brook Street boasts an impressive two-for-one offer: you can visit the beautifully presented home of the German composer and view his musical scores… before looking at pictures of Hendrix, his 'future' next door neighbour.

Soho challenges the City as London's most famous square mile. It may not have the money of its brash easterly rival, but it sure has the buzz. It's always been fast and loose, since the days when hunters charged through with their cries of 'So-ho!' Its narrow jumbled streets throng with humanity, from the tourist to the tipsy, the libertine to the louche. A lot of the fun is centred round the streets just south of **Soho Square,** where area legends like The Coach & Horses ('Norman's Bar'), Ronnie Scott's and Bar Italia cluster in close proximity. There's 80s favourite, the Groucho Club, too, though some of its lustre may have waned since a corporate takeover. The tightest t-shirts in town are found in **Old Compton Street,** where the pink pound jangles the registers in a

C. Barrely / MICHELIN

swathe of gay-friendly bars and restaurants. To get a feel of the 'real' Soho, where old engraved signs enliven the shop fronts and the market stall cries echo back to the 1700s, a jaunt along **Berwick Street** is always in vogue, taking in a pint at the eternally popular Blue Posts, an unchanging street corner stalwart that still announces 'Watney's Ales' on its stencilled windows.

Not a lot of Watney's ale was ever drunk in **St James's;** not a lot of ale of any kind for that matter. Champagne and port is more the style here, in the hushed and reverential gentlemen's clubs where discretion is the key, and change is measured in centuries rather than years. The sheer class of the area is typified by **Pall Mall's** Reform Club, where Phileas Fogg wagered that he could zip round the world in eighty days, and the adjacent **St James's Square,** which was the most fashionable address in London in the late seventeenth century, when dukes and earls aplenty got their satin shoes under the silver bedecked tables.

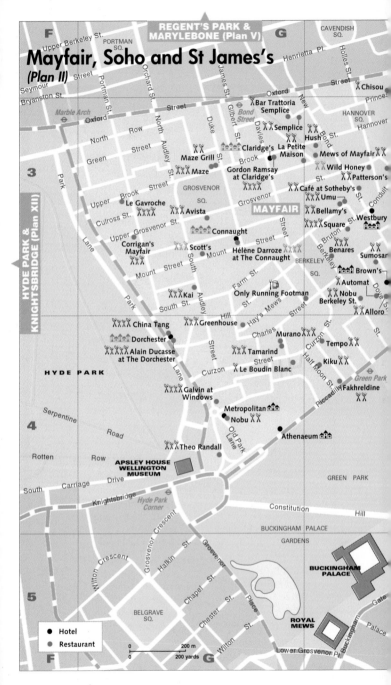

Mayfair, Soho and St James's
(Plan II)

REGENT'S PARK & MARYLEBONE (Plan V)

HYDE PARK & KNIGHTSBRIDGE (Plan XII)

CAVENDISH SQ.

Chisou

Bar Trattoria Semplice
Semplice
Hush
La Petite Maison
Mews of Mayfair
Wild Honey
Patterson's
Claridge's
Maze Grill
Maze
Gordon Ramsay at Claridge's
Café at Sotheby's
Umu
Bellamy's
Le Gavroche
Avista
Square
Westbury
Connaught
Corrigan's Mayfair
Scott's
Hélène Darroze at The Connaught
Benares
Sumosar
Brown's
Only Running Footman
Automat
Nobu Berkeley St.
Kai
Alloro
China Tang
Greenhouse
Murano
Tempo
Dorchester
Charles
Kiku
Alain Ducasse at The Dorchester
Tamarind
Le Boudin Blanc
Galvin at Windows
Fakhreldine
Metropolitan
Nobu
Athenaeum
Theo Randall

APSLEY HOUSE WELLINGTON MUSEUM

HYDE PARK

GREEN PARK

BUCKINGHAM PALACE GARDENS

BUCKINGHAM PALACE

ROYAL MEWS

BELGRAVE SQ.

● Hotel
● Restaurant

0 ___ 200 m
0 ___ 200 yards

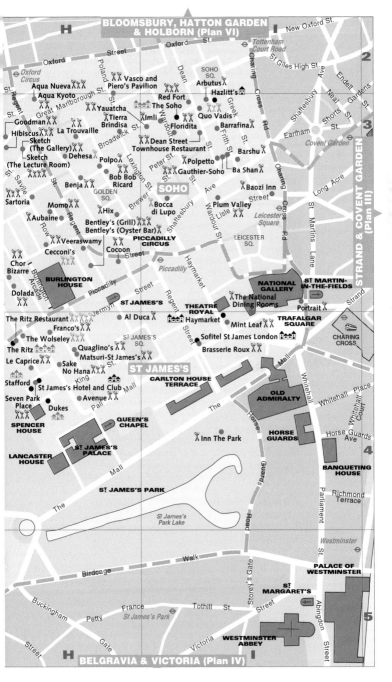

Alain Ducasse at The Dorchester ✿ ✿ ✿

French XXXXX

Park Ln. ✉ W1K 1QA
✆ (020) 7629 8866
e-mail alainducasse@thedorchester.com
www.alainducasse-dorchester.com

Menu £50/78

⊖ Hyde Park Corner
Closed 25 December dinner until
dinner 31 December,
22-25 April, 7-30 August,
Saturday lunch, Sunday and Monday

Alain Ducasse

Coco Chanel once said that "luxury must be comfortable, otherwise it is not luxury". The London outpost of über-chef Alain Ducasse's global empire is, without doubt, a sumptuous and extravagant affair. Patrick Jouin's design uses tans and creams, leather and wood, as well as 30,000 green silk buttons to reflect the colours of the park opposite. The tables are immaculately laid and the striking, semi-private Table Lumière is surrounded by a curtain of 4,500 fibre optics. Waiting staff are a sincere and eager lot, although sometimes impenetrable accents can make communication a little wearisome. The choice is between a set tasting menu, a seasonal menu and the à la carte, with which you can have both fish and meat courses. 16 chefs in the kitchen use the best available prime ingredients, half of which are from the British Isles, half brought over from France, to create supremely refined and sophisticated dishes that reflect Ducasse's lighter approach to gastronomy. An experience here may not come cheap - but then luxury never does.

First Course
- Roasted chicken and lobster with sweetbreads.
- Langoustine salad with coral jus.

Main Course
- Fillet of beef and foie gras Rossini with 'sacristain' potatoes.
- Scallops with ceps and potato gnocchi.

Dessert
- "Baba like in Monte-Carlo".
- Lime soufflé with Sichuan pepper sorbet.

Al Duca

H4

Italian ✗

4-5 Duke of York St. ✉ SW1Y 6LA
☏ (020) 7839 3090
e-mail alduca@btconnect.com
www.alduca-restaurant.co.uk

⊖ Piccadilly Circus
Closed 24 December-
4 January and Sunday

Menu £18/28

Al Duca has become as much a part of the fabric of St James's as many of the shirt makers who have made neighbouring Jermyn Street home over the years. It is also one of the those restaurants that manage the trick of appearing quiet one minute and full to the rafters the next without anyone noticing and this ensures that the atmosphere is never less than spirited. The serving team are a young, confident bunch and the manager knows who his regulars are. The menu is priced per course; there is plenty of choice and the cooking is crisp and confident, with plenty of well-priced bottles to match. The rib-eye with porcini mushrooms is a highlight. Prices are also pretty keen, especially for a restaurant in this neck of the woods.

Alloro

H3

Italian ✗✗

19-20 Dover St. ✉ W1S 4LU
☏ (020) 7495 4768
e-mail alloro@londonfinedininggroup.com
www.alloro-restaurant.co.uk

⊖ Green Park
Closed Christmas-New Year,
Saturday lunch
and Sunday

Menu £33/35

Alloro celebrated its 10th anniversary in 2010 and this comparative longevity owes much to its sensible prices, confident service and easy-to-eat Italian food. The current chef has been here for nearly half the restaurant's life; he comes from Piedmont and manages to sneak in a few specialties from his home region. The menu offers an appealing choice and nicely balanced selection, from a crisp chicory salad with bottarga to slow-cooked lamb shoulder, with all breads and pastas being made in-house. It's priced per number of courses taken; having all four represents the best value. Noise drifts in from the adjacent, boisterous baretto and so ensures that the atmosphere in the comfortable and urbane restaurant is always lively.

MAYFAIR, SOHO & ST JAMES'S ▶ PLAN II

Aqua Kyoto

H3

240 Regent St. (entrance on Argyll St.) ⊖ **Oxford Circus**
⊠ **W1F 7EB**
✆ (020) 7478 0540
e-mail reservation@aqua-london.com
www.aqua-london.com

Closed 25-26 December,
1 January and Sunday

Menu £17 (lunch) – Carte £34/54

[A/C]
[⊞]
[☺☺]
[VISA]
[M/C]
[AE]
[①]

Aqua London occupies all 17,000 square foot of the 5th floor of the former Dickins & Jones department store and boasts, along with a big bar and terrific terraces, two large restaurants. Aqua Kyoto is the more boisterous of the two, although getting to the table can be a drawn out affair, as you first give your name at the Argyll Street entrance, do so again when you get out of the lift, and only then are you handed over to the restaurant reception. However, Aqua Kyoto offers a fun night out, more so if you've come in a group – not just so you can compete with the noise, but also because the contemporary Japanese food is designed for sharing. Highlights include the eel teriyaki and the noodle dishes. Service means well but lacks direction.

Aqua Nueva

H3

240 Regent St. (entrance on Argyll St.) ⊖ **Oxford Circus**
⊠ **W1F 7EB**
✆ (020) 7478 0540
e-mail reservation@aqua-london.com
www.aqua-london.com

Closed 25-26 December,
1 January and Sunday

Menu £20 (lunch) – Carte £30/52

[A/C]
[⊞]
[☺☺]
[VISA]
[M/C]
[AE]
[①]

To reach the relative tranquillity of this Spanish restaurant, one first has to fight through the crowds enjoying a drink and a sense of exclusivity in Aqua Spirit, another part of this huge operation. Aqua Nueva feels more sophisticated than Aqua Kyoto with which its shares the 5th floor. It comes divided into two; the main room is more elegant and comfortable, but the tapas bar area, with its ceiling feature of 15,000 wooden beads, has more buzz and character and fills up first. The food comes in a stylised fashion that delivers the classic combinations of Spanish cuisine in original ways, although some subtle balances can get lost in the interpretation. The tapas, however, is more traditional and often features regional specialities.

Arbutus ✿

Modern European ✖

63-64 Frith St. ✉ W1D 3JW   ⊖ **Tottenham Court Road**
✆ (020) 7734 4545   Closed 25-26 December
e-mail info@arbutusrestaurant.co.uk   and 1 January –
www.arbutusrestaurant.co.uk   booking advisable

Menu £17 (lunch) – Carte £28/37

A/C
🍇
🎭
☼
VISA
MC
AE

Arbutus

MAYFAIR, SOHO & ST JAMES'S ▶ PLAN II

When a restaurant makes it look as easy as this, you know that
an enormous amount of work and experience have actually gone
into it. Arbutus has also proved an enormous success because
all its components dovetail together just so: the decoration is
relaxed and contemporary but seems to work in harmony with
the food; service is prompt and efficient but also bubbly and
affable; the cooking is intelligent and honest and the prices are
realistic and accessible. Despite the apparent simplicity of the
food on the plate, this is highly accomplished cooking which
demonstrates an inherent understanding of ingredients, textures
and flavours. Dishes are dictated by the seasonal availability
of their component parts and the skilled use of cheaper cuts
like tripe, tongue and trotters rather than luxury ingredients
highlights the kitchen's level of ability and also keeps prices
down-to-earth. Factor in a wine list that makes experimenting
with some serious wines an affordable practice and you have a
restaurant that deserves its success.

First Course

- Braised pigs head,
  ravioli of caramelised
  onions.
- Smoked eel with
  chorizo and rhubarb.

Main Course

- Rabbit with braised
  celery and shoulder
  cottage pie.
- Cod with
  caramelised endive
  and curly kale.

Dessert

- Crème caramel.
- Floating island with
  custard and pralines.

Aubaine

French

H3

4 Heddon St. ✉ W1B 4BS
✆ (020) 7440 2510
e-mail info@aubaine.co.uk
www.aubaine.co.uk

⊖ Oxford Circus
Closed Sunday dinner

Menu £19 (lunch) – Carte approx. £28

This is the newer sister to the Brompton Road original, although they've had to tweak it slightly: they tried a food counter but that didn't work and there is no boulangerie here as the area is less residential. Being surrounded by so many offices and shops in the vicinity means they do a brisk trade throughout the day and particularly during lunch; its corner position also affords it a two-sided outdoor terrace and there aren't many of them in Mayfair. The look is of a farmhouse as imagined by a townie; avoid the basement room as it's dull by comparison. With a selection of salads, grilled fish, steaks and a burger, the menus wouldn't look out of place in a bistro. For dessert, you choose from the presented patisserie selection.

Automat

American

H3

33 Dover St. ✉ W1S 4NF
✆ (020) 7499 3033
e-mail info@automat-london.com
www.automat-london.com

⊖ Green Park
Closed 25-26 December
and 1 January

Carte £39/50

Automat, an American-style brasserie, comes divided into three: the first section by the entrance is the least enticing as those waiting for tables will stand around near yours; the mid-section comes decked out in the style of a railway carriage and the third is undoubtedly where the action is. The open kitchen and noise bouncing of the white tiles creates quite a buzzy vibe. The menu could have come direct from NYC. You'll find chowder, cakes of the crab and cheese variety, burgers and steaks, although in portions more European than Stateside. Brunch here is the genuine article. Where the authenticity falls down is in the service which lacks that energetic confidence and relentless efficiency one usually finds across the 'pond'.

Avenue

Modern European ✗✗

7-9 St James's St. ✉ SW1A 1EE
✆ (020) 7321 2111
e-mail avenuereservations@danddlondon.com
www.theavenue-restaurant.co.uk

⊖ Green Park
Closed 25-26 December,
Saturday lunch
and Sunday

Menu £25 – Carte £28/57

Judging by the number of suited business types standing around the long bar this is clearly a good place to close deals. Its brash and boisterous atmosphere puts it in sharp contrast to the Gentlemen's Clubs that still populate St James's and the unsullied sheer whiteness of the place keeps everyone alert. The number of larger tables also makes it less suited to those hoping for a little intimacy. The cooking is crisp and fresh, from an all-encompassing menu that keeps its influences within Europe but also has a growing British element. There's everything from smoked salmon, fishcakes and blade of beef to burgers, bream and – to celebrate the deal – oysters and caviar. Service comes with an urgency which isn't always called for.

Avista

Italian ✗✗✗

Millennium Mayfair Hotel,
39 Grosvenor Sq ✉ W1K 2HP
✆ (020) 7596 3399
e-mail reservations@avistarestaurant.com
www.avistarestaurant.com

⊖ Bond Street
Closed Saturday lunch
and Sunday

Menu £23 (lunch) – Carte £28/66

Avista occupies the generous space within the Millennium Hotel that was previously farmed out to Brian Turner. Not only did they soften the room but they also added a separate street entrance which helps in establishing the restaurant's identity, despite the best efforts of the intrusively anodyne music. Veneto born Chef Michele Granziera, a Zafferano alumnus, has created a menu that traverses Italy and marries the rustic with the more refined. There are dishes designed for sharing as well as pre-starter 'snacks' if you really can't wait. The homemade pastas are a particular highlight, while the kitchen's creativity is given full rein on the 'Surprise' seven course menu which is available at dinner.

Baozi Inn

25 Newport Court ✉ WC2H 7JS ⊖ **Leicester Square**
☎ (020) 7287 6877 Closed 24-25 December

Carte £19/25

Further proof that Chinatown is shaking off its tired, touristy image comes in the shape of Baozi Inn. Granted, there's nothing particularly noteworthy about the predictable surroundings of red lanterns and chunky tables but the friendly staff are welcoming and eager to please and the food is generously sized. It's also hard to blow your budget, which is especially significant as they only take cash. The eponymous baozi, or steamed filled buns, are a good way to start, although one is certainly enough; dishes have a fiery Sichuan slant and you'll feel the force in the noodle soup. The peanut and rolled tofu skin salad makes a perfect, calming side dish. Only Chinese beer is served but that's the ideal accompaniment anyway.

Barrafina

54 Frith St. ✉ W1D 3SL ⊖ **Tottenham Court Road**
☎ (020) 7813 8016 Closed bank holidays –
e-mail info@barrafina.co.uk (bookings not accepted)
www.barrafina.co.uk

Carte £30/45 s

London has been a bit iffy about restaurants that don't take reservations but Barrafina is the likely candidate to buck that trend. This is the younger sibling to the Hart brothers' Fino restaurant and its success is down to its mix of satisfyingly unfussy and authentic tapas and a buzzy atmosphere. Seafood is a speciality and the fish displays an exhilarating freshness; the Jabugo ham is also well worth trying. Four dishes per person is about par and the choice varies from razor clams a la plancha and tuna tartar to grilled chorizo and lamb sweetbreads with capers. It all centres around a counter, with seating for 20, so be prepared to talk to your neighbour - another thing that's never caught on in the capital. Be sure to try one of the sherries.

Barshu

I3

28 Frith St. ✉ W1D 5LF
☎ (020) 7287 8822
e-mail headoffice@bar-shu.co.uk
www.bar-shu.co.uk

⊖ **Leicester Square**
Closed 24-25 December –
Booking advisable

Carte £24/35

Those who like their food with a kick won't be disappointed by Bar Shu as it features the fiery flavours of China's Sichuan Province. The menu, which looks more like a brochure, features a photo of each dish along with a chilli rating – a useful aid, as the staff can be a little reluctant to engage with customers. But it's not all mouth-numbingly hot and some of the dishes do display a more subtle balance of flavours. The legendary chillies and pepper are imported directly from China and, with the chef coming from the province too, authenticity is assured, particularly with the 'Five colour appetiser platter,' which includes duck tongues and pig intestines. Lots of carved wood and lanterns decorate the place; larger groups should head downstairs.

Bar Trattoria Semplice 🙂

G3

22 Woodstock St. ✉ W1C 2AR
☎ (020) 7491 8638
e-mail info@ristorantesemplice.com
www.bartrattoriasemplice.com

⊖ **Bond Street**
Closed 25-26 December,
Easter and bank holidays

Menu £17 (lunch) – Carte £23/36

Bar Trattoria Semplice was opened in 2008 by the same expert team behind Semplice which is just yards away. This is a simpler, more accessible but by no means inferior little sister. The tone is set by the old Berkel meat slicer by the entrance and the cheeses and cured meats above the bar. Oak-topped tables, creams and burgundies and a photo of a Tuscan dawn create a relaxed but bubbly room. The kitchen goes back to basics, with its emphasis on flavour and value. There's a giveaway set lunch menu and each month specialities from a different region of Italy, such as Piedmont or Lazio, feature. Desserts come from the trolley just like trattorie of old; wines are available in 500ml carafes and the bar has an easy, all day menu.

Ba Shan

I3

Chinese

24 Romilly St. ✉ W1D 5AH
✆ (020) 7287 3266
e-mail headoffice@bar-shan.co.uk

⊖ Leicester Square
Closed Christmas –
Booking advisable

Carte £16/26 s

Ba Shan is the third enterprise from the team who brought you Bar Shu and Baozi Inn. While this cosy place still has some Sichuan leanings, it mainly focuses on traditional styles from Northern areas and Henan province. Somewhat confusingly, there are two menus: one 'snack', the other 'home-style' - but just pick from both. Dry-wok dishes are plentiful and the guotie dumplings are their own take on a classic. Shaanxi flatbread 'sandwiches' or pork Chaoshou are a good way to start; noodles and vegetables come dressed with a provocative amount of chilli. Decoratively, it treads a fine line between cute and kitsch. There are three or four tables in each of the five rooms and service copes well with the constant influx of customers.

Bellamy's

H3

French XX

18 Bruton Pl. ✉ W1J 6LY
✆ (020) 7491 2727
e-mail info@bellamysrestaurant.co.uk
www.bellamysrestaurant.co.uk

⊖ Bond Street
Closed Saturday lunch,
Sunday and bank holidays,

Menu £29 – Carte £43/57

If Audrey Tautou ever opened a shop it would probably look a little like Bellamy's: it's sweet, petite and pretty. The counter doubles as the oyster bar but turn left and you'll find yourself in a roomy, ersatz French brasserie, complete with assorted Gallic posters and accented waiters. The menu covers all bases, from foie gras and caviar to duck rillettes and entrecôtes and the kitchen keeps to the classic techniques and combinations. The good value little set menu offers some financial sanctuary from the more robust prices on the à la carte, although the cover charge is an unwelcome anachronism. The lunchtime crowd are mostly male, suited and serious but dinner is more relaxed, while the mews location adds to the feeling of exclusivity.

Benares ✿

H3

12a Berkeley Square House ✉ W1J 6BS
✆ (020) 7629 8886
e-mail reservations@benaresrestaurant.co.uk
www.benaresrestaurant.com

⊖ **Green Park**
Closed 25 December
and 1 January

Menu £25 (lunch) – Carte £45/83

Benares

MAYFAIR, SOHO & ST JAMES'S ▶ PLAN II

When Benares reopened after an extended hiatus caused by a kitchen fire, it seemed that not a great deal had changed in its appearance although, apparently, much work did take place behind the scenes. One sparkly new addition, however, is the terrific Chef's Table with its floor to ceiling windows looking directly into the kitchen; the Sommelier's Table doesn't quite have the same cachet. Another difference came in the subtle evolution of Atul Kochhar's cooking. His dishes now appear a little simpler on the plate; the main ingredient takes centre stage, with the Indian spices adding interesting and complementary flavours but without being the dominant force. Those who want to experience as much of the cooking as they can are able to do so thanks to the Grazing menu, although those who don't care for too much modernity with their Indian food will find enough recognisable dishes to satisfy them. Much thought has also gone into the wine list and in choosing the right pairings for the food.

First Course

- Tandoor roasted pigeon with vanilla and beetroot.
- Lamb, chicken tikka and king prawn kebab platter.

Main Course

- Tiger prawns with asparagus and spring onions.
- Duck breast with star anise, cinnamon sauce and bean stir fry.

Dessert

- Strawberry jelly with black pepper and yoghurt parfait.
- Allspice brownie with salted pistachios.

Benja

H3

Thai ✕✕

17 Beak St ⊠ W1F 9RW
℘ (020) 7287 0555
e-mail info@krua.co.uk
www.benjarestaurant.com

⊖ Oxford Circus
Closed Sunday

Carte £25/39

AIC

VISA

M©

AE

⓪

Authentic Thai cooking and colourful, cosy surroundings are what draw plenty of customers to Benja. Dining is spread over a couple of floors in this converted townhouse; the green room with mirrors and carved lotus flowers is the most appealing but one can also eat in the intimate and alluringly red-hued basement Na Ga Bar. The serving team are all Thai and, when prompted, will offer sound advice on what to order. The kitchen offers true tastes of Thailand and the refreshing and interesting selection of salads come with varying degrees of spice. Choo chee dried red curry paste with king prawns, scallops and lychee is a speciality, as is stir-fried seafood with sweet chilli paste. Portions are ideal for sharing.

Bentley's (Grill)

H3

British ✕✕✕

11-15 Swallow St. ⊠ W1B 4DG
℘ (020) 7734 4756
e-mail reservations@bentleys.org
www.bentleys.org

⊖ Piccadilly Circus
Closed 25-26 December, 1 January,
Saturday lunch and Sunday

Carte £35/90

AIC

⌁

VISA

M©

AE

The beloved institution called Bentley's continues to enjoy its new lease of life. The green neon sign is still outside but these days the upstairs dining room has a contemporary feel with leather chairs, fabric covered walls and paintings of boats and fish for those who haven't twigged what's on the menu. One thing that will probably never change is the clubby feel and the preponderance of suited male customers. Seafood also remains the draw, with fish on the bone dissected at the table something of a house speciality. Much of the produce comes from St Ives and Looe in Cornwall and the freshness is palpable. Dover and Lemon soles feature strongly, as do oysters and soups whilst the breads and beef remind you that owner Richard Corrigan is Irish.

Bentley's (Oyster Bar)

Seafood ✗

H3

11-15 Swallow St. ✉ W1B 4DG
☎ (020) 7734 4756
e-mail reservations@bentleys.org
www.bentleys.org

⊖ Piccadilly Circus
Closed 25 December
and 1 January

Carte £29/85

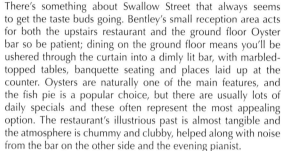

There's something about Swallow Street that always seems to get the taste buds going. Bentley's small reception area acts for both the upstairs restaurant and the ground floor Oyster bar so be patient; dining on the ground floor means you'll be ushered through the curtain into a dimly lit bar, with marbled-topped tables, banquette seating and places laid up at the counter. Oysters are naturally one of the main features, and the fish pie is a popular choice, but there are usually lots of daily specials and these often represent the most appealing option. The restaurant's illustrious past is almost tangible and the atmosphere is chummy and clubby, helped along with noise from the bar on the other side and the evening pianist.

Bob Bob Ricard

Modern European ✗✗

H3

1 Upper James St ✉ W1F 9DF
☎ (020) 3145 1000
e-mail reservations@bobbobricard.com
www.bobbobricard.com

⊖ Oxford Circus
Closed 25-26 December

Carte £26/49

"Taste is the enemy of creativeness" said Pablo Picasso. The creatively decorated Bob Bob Ricard was set up to compete with the traditional grand cafés and diners by serving anything to anyone at anytime. Your table could be getting stuck into beef Wellington while your neighbours are spooning an evening bowl of cornflakes – and no one raises an eyebrow. If your doctor has prescribed a diet of caviar and jelly then this place is ideal. Each table even has a button to press if you want more champagne. Don't get palmed off with a table by the entrance: to get the full, flamboyant effect of all the smoked glass and marble you need to be in the body of the restaurant. But spare a thought for the waiters in those bubblegum-pink waistcoats.

Bocca di Lupo ☺

I3

Italian ✗

12 Archer St. ✉ WID 7BB
✆ (020) 7734 2223
www.boccadilupo.com

Carte £19/39

⊖ **Piccadilly Circus**
Closed Christmas-
New Year and Sunday dinner –
Booking essential

Deservedly busy from the day it opened, Bocca di Lupo is one of the best things to have arrived in Soho since the espresso bar. But be sure to sit at the marble counter in front of the chefs rather than at one of the faux-distressed tables at the back – not only is the atmosphere here more fun but the food is often better as it hasn't hung around the waiters' station waiting to be delivered. Each item has its region of origin within Italy noted on the menu and is available in a large or smaller size. The flavours don't hang back and over-ordering in all the excitement is very hard to resist. Highlights include the veal and pork agnolotti, the poussin in bread, the suckling pig and tripe; but leave room for dessert too.

Le Boudin Blanc

G4

French ✗

5 Trebeck St. ✉ W1J 7LT
✆ (020) 7499 3292
e-mail reservations@boudinblanc.co.uk
www.boudinblanc.co.uk

⊖ **Green Park**
Closed 24-26 December

Menu £15 (lunch and early dinner) – Carte £32/44

Le Boudin Blanc fits perfectly into Shepherd Market: it's lively, atmospheric and doesn't take itself quite so seriously as some of the establishments who share its Mayfair postcode. It's essentially two houses knocked together and they've certainly managed to squeeze in plenty of tables over the two floors. Try to sit by the window on the ground floor as you'll be out of the path of the young French staff who run around at quite a pace. The menu provides a comforting read of French classics and country cooking from all regions. The snails are popular, as is the boudin blanc. The lunch prix fixe is a steal; there are daily specials on the board and the wine list ranges from quaffing wines of Languedoc to premier crus from Bordeaux.

Brasserie Roux

I4

8 Pall Mall ✉ SW1Y 5NG
☎ (020) 7968 2900
e-mail info@brasserieroux.com
www.brasserieroux.com

⊖ Piccadilly Circus

Menu £20 – Carte £21/45

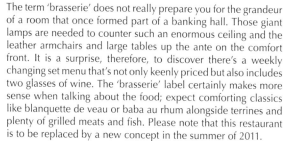

The term 'brasserie' does not really prepare you for the grandeur of a room that once formed part of a banking hall. Those giant lamps are needed to counter such an enormous ceiling and the leather armchairs and large tables up the ante on the comfort front. It is a surprise, therefore, to discover there's a weekly changing set menu that's not only keenly priced but also includes two glasses of wine. The 'brasserie' label certainly makes more sense when talking about the food; expect comforting classics like blanquette de veau or baba au rhum alongside terrines and plenty of grilled meats and fish. Please note that this restaurant is to be replaced by a new concept in the summer of 2011.

MAYFAIR, SOHO & ST JAMES'S ▶ PLAN II

Cafe at Sotheby's

H3

34-35 New Bond St. ✉ W1A 2AA
☎ (020) 7293 5077
e-mail ken.hall@sothebys.com
www.sothebys.com

⊖ Bond Street
Closed 24 December-4 January,
Saturday, Sunday and bank hoildays
– Booking essential – (lunch only)

Carte £26/35 s

It's usually the seasons that inform the menu of most restaurants but here at Sotheby's they change the style of the dishes according to the art being sold. For instance, experience has shown them that modern and Impressionist artists attract a diet-conscious crowd who like their salads, while the Old Masters appeal to those who favour a more substantial, well-lubricated lunch which ends with a proper pudding. The lobster sandwich is a perennial feature and the wine list is brief but appealingly eclectic. Occupying a cosy space just off the lobby of the auction house, this is a little gem of a restaurant which is smarter than the 'cafe' moniker would suggest. Service is well-judged and the many regulars are discreetly acknowledged.

Le Caprice

Modern European 𝖃𝖃

H4

Arlington House, Arlington St. ✉ SW1A 1RJ   ⊖ **Green Park**
☎ (020) 7629 2239   Closed 24-26 December and 1 January
e-mail reservation@le-caprice.co.uk
www.le-caprice.co.uk

Menu £20 (dinner) – Carte £29/53

A/C
🕙
🎭
☀
VISA
MC
AE
①

When a restaurant is described as an "institution" one thinks of somewhere stuffy, old and probably a little smelly. For more than 25 years Le Caprice has proved that a clubby, senior restaurant can actually be warm, fun and feverishly fashionable and the only anachronism here is the cover charge. The pianist and the long bar add a hint of old New York while the black and white décor and David Bailey photographs give it a certain timelessness. The position and size of your table will depend on the extent of your celebrity or patronage but the service is commendably democratic. Easy-eating is the order of the day and the appealing menu has everything from eggs Benedict to rump of veal. The Caesar salad and salmon fishcakes are permanent fixtures.

Cecconi's

Italian 𝖃𝖃𝖃

H3

5a Burlington Gdns ✉ W1S 3EP   ⊖ **Green Park**
☎ (020) 7434 1500   Closed 25 December –
e-mail giacomo@cecconis.co.uk   Booking essential
www.cecconis.com

Carte £27/45

🍴
A/C
🕙
☀
MC
AE

It's obviously a winning formula because Cecconi's are now popping up in various appropriately fashionable cities around the world. One can certainly see the appeal as they do feel like a private members club and even have a roped off VIP area to induce envy amongst those who find themselves insufficiently famous. The bar is the place to sit if you want to give the impression you're a regular who's often in for a quick bite; and if you are one such regular then you'll be assured of good service. The all-day menu offers a good selection of cicchetti, or small Italian tapas; prosciutto is sliced to order; the salads are popular at lunch and the classic, no-nonsense main courses are clearly prepared with care.

China Tang

Chinese 𝄢𝄢𝄢𝄢

Park Ln. ✉ W1A 2HJ
☏ (020) 7629 9988
e-mail chinatang@dorchesterhotel.com
www.thedorchester.com

⊖ Hyde Park Corner
Closed 25 December

Menu £15 (lunch) – Carte £40/70

Sir David Tang's atmospheric art deco inspired Chinese restaurant at The Dorchester Hotel is always a blur of activity, with noise spilling out from the large tables in the centre; regulars head for the library side, from where one can take in the whole room. In contrast to the sleek and decorative surroundings, the kitchen is a model of conservatism and rightly sticks to what it does best, namely classic Cantonese cooking. Peking duck and roasted meats are the highlights, but check out the chef's recommendations at the back of the menu too. The standard is good considering the numbers of customers and you can have dim sum in the striking bar for lunch or dinner. Apart from the set lunch menu, it isn't cheap – but it is fun.

Chisou

Japanese 𝄢

4 Princes St. ✉ W1B 2LE
☏ (020) 7629 3931
e-mail chisoujpr@aol.com
www.chisou.co.uk

⊖ Oxford Circus
Closed Christmas-New Year, Sunday and
bank holidays

Menu £15 (lunch) – Carte £25/43

Chisou proves that size should be no obstacle to providing good service so you'll find plenty of staff are on hand to guide you through the Japanese food. While it may be intimate, they are generous with the table size and spacing. The kitchen is headed up by a Japanese speaking Sri Lankan; he's often seen manning the sushi counter and has the owner's permission to source ingredients entirely on quality rather than cost restrictions. Specialities, from a menu that covers all points, include Tuna yukke, Gyu tataki (seared beef) and Hourensou (spinach) salad. There are some good value set lunch menus and next door is the useful 'Go Chisou,' where the growing local Japanese community go to get their Bento boxes.

Chor Bizarre

H3

Indian XX

16 Albemarle St. ✉ W1S 4HW   ⊖ Green Park
✆ (020) 7629 9802
e-mail chorbizarrelondon@oldworldhospitality.com
www.chorbizarre.com

Carte £32/47

No two tables are the same shape and the restaurant is decked out with an eccentric but strangely uplifting mix of old doors, curios, mismatched chairs and trinkets, which is all very appropriate as the name translates as "thieves' market". The menu is a long and chatty tome; each page is filled with dishes, explanations, drawings and anecdotes so it can take quite a while to work your way through it. The cooking is competent and consistent; Northern Indian dishes are the speciality but there is much to be said for ordering a thali and sharing the bounty on your silver platter. If only the staff could add more warmth and personality to proceedings instead of concentrating so much on speedy delivery from the kitchen.

Cocoon

H3

Asian XX

65 Regent St. ✉ W1B 4EA   ⊖ Piccadilly Circus
✆ (020) 7494 7600
e-mail reservations@cocoon-restaurants.com
www.cocoon-restaurants.com

Menu £25/50 – Carte £31/44

A quick glance at the menu would suggest a Japanese restaurant: sushi, sashimi, bento boxes and tempura all feature prominently and you may find yourself transfixed by the master craftsman behind one of the counters doing his thing with a very large knife. However, on closer investigation, you'll find dishes whose influences owe more to Korea, China and Thailand, while others are shaped more from the culinary zeitgeist. The common theme, though, is sharing, so ordering should be a group activity, and staff give good advice. The place seats 170 but is cleverly divided and the styling and décor are decidedly space-age. Lunches are relatively calm affairs with shoppers in for salads and Bento boxes. It all hots up big-time in the evenings.

Corrigan's Mayfair

B r i t i s h XXX

28 Upper Grosvenor St. ✉ W1K 7EH ⊖ Marble Arch
☎ (020) 7499 9943 Closed 25-26 December,
e-mail reservations@corrigansmayfair.com 1 January and
www.corrigansmayfair.com Saturday lunch

Menu £27 (lunch) – Carte £43/73

Richard Corrigan's flagship restaurant may have opened a couple of years ago but it feels as though it has been around for many years. It's comfortable, clubby yet quite glamorous and Martin Brudnizki's design includes some playful features, such as the feather-covered lamps that give a nod to the restaurant's forte, which is game. The menu is lengthy and the food largely a celebration of British and Irish cooking. It is also fiercely seasonal, which makes having the day's special always a worthwhile choice. This relatively straightforward style of cooking still requires care and precise timing but sometimes the kitchen takes its eye off the ball. Service is smooth and well organised but the anachronistic cover charge is an unwelcome sight.

Dean Street Townhouse Restaurant

B r i t i s h XX

69-71 Dean St. ✉ W1D 3SE ⊖ Tottenham Court Road
☎ (0207) 4341 775 Booking essential
e-mail info@deanstreettownhouse.com
www.deanstreettownhouse.com

Carte £22/40

As this Georgian house was once home to the bacchic Gargoyle Club, it's fitting that its incarnation is attracting clusters of pleasure-seeking celebrities. The designers have cleverly made this restaurant seem as though it's been here for years. The first thing you notice is the beautiful, long zinc-topped dark bar, although eating at one of the nearby tables does mean you're in danger of having someone sitting on your food, as this area does get packed. If you want a quieter spot, ask for the 'parlour' which is decorated just as its name suggests. The appealingly British menu includes retro dishes like prawns and avocado and mince with boiled potatoes; puddings are stout but satisfying. You can also come for afternoon or high tea.

51

Dehesa

Mediterranean ✗

25 Ganton St. ✉ W1F 9BP   ⊖ Oxford Circus
℘ (020) 7494 4170   Closed Christmas and Sunday dinner
e-mail info@dehesa.co.uk
www.dehesa.co.uk

Carte £20/30

Dehesa does now take bookings, except for lunch on Saturday, so there's no longer a need to get there quite so early. It's a few streets away from its sister restaurant, Salt Yard, and repeats the format of offering delicious Spanish and Italian tapas. The menu is not an exact copy but the bestsellers all feature: the pork belly with cannellini beans; courgette flowers with Monte Enebro and honey and the soft chocolate cake with Frangelico ice cream. They recommend 2-3 plates per person. Between 3pm and 5pm the kitchen takes a breather so the choice becomes ham on or off the bone, charcuterie and cheese. The drinks list is worthy of a visit in itself. Dehesa is a wooden area of Spain and home to Ibérico pigs who produce such great ham.

Dolada

Italian ✗✗

13 Albemarle St. ✉ W1S 4HJ   ⊖ Green Park
℘ (020) 7409 1011   Closed 23 December-6 January,
e-mail manager@dolada.co.uk   Saturday lunch and Sunday
www.dolada.co.uk

Menu £23 (lunch) – Carte £22/46

The owner bought the restaurant after falling in love with the receptionist; now that's amore. He then changed the name from Mosiaco to Dolada, in honour of his chef's family restaurant in Pieve d'Alpago. It's still a somewhat corporate-looking basement restaurant, with lots of marble, but the effusive welcome and confident service create a sociable spirit. The chef, liberated from serving local Venetian specialities back home, is clearly taken with the idea of cooking dishes from across Italy and introduces his own touches: his spaghetti carbonara is a deconstructed affair, where the egg, pasta, pancetta and pecorino sit separately in the bowl, waiting to be mixed. Dishes in his tasting menu display even greater originality.

Gauthier - Soho ❀

I3

French ✕✕✕

21 Romilly St ✉ W1D 5AF
℘ (020) 7494 3111
e-mail info@gauthiersoho.co.uk
www.gauthiersoho.co.uk

⊖ **Leicester Square**
Closed 21-30 August, Sunday,
lunch Saturday and
bank holidays

Menu £25/35

[A/C]
[⊡]
[🎭]
[VISA]
[MC]
[AE]

Gauthier Soho

Unlike many in his profession, Alex Gauthier is not a chef who changes jobs at the drop of a toque. Having spent 12 successful years at Roussillon, in 2010 he decided to go it alone and, together with his former head chef and sommelier, took over the 18C house in Soho that was previously home to Richard Corrigan. This charming, narrow house is spread over three floors and has been given a good lick of white emulsion, which they set off with large floral displays. The house does throw up certain operational challenges – for starters, a waiter needs to be as fit as a butcher's dog to cope with going up and down stairs all service – but it does also mean that the restaurant feels intimate and somehow secretive. Gauthier not only shuns the media spotlight but also avoids any culinary excesses; instead, his refined cooking emphasises natural, harmonious flavours, as his strength has always been his sourcing of great ingredients. The option is between having 3, 4 or 5 courses, from a choice of three dishes per course, or the seasonal set menu; having the full 5 courses is surprisingly easy.

First Course

- Truffle risotto with brown butter and Parmesan.
- Tomato cappelletti with herb velouté.

Main Course

- Roast red deer with pear and celeriac.
- John Dory with leeks and confit tomatoes.

Dessert

- Goose egg soufflé and chocolate custard.
- Cherry and chocolate with red wine jelly.

Gordon Ramsay at Claridge's

Modern European 🗡🗡🗡🗡

G3

Brook St. ✉ W1K 4HR
☎ (020) 7499 0099
e-mail reservations@gordonramsay.com
www.gordonramsay.com/claridges

⊖ **Bond Street**
Booking essential

Menu £30/70

As befits a restaurant within the sumptuous surroundings of Claridge's hotel, all is elegance and grandeur here. Sit in the main room as that is where the action is, although the Davies Room and The Salon on the raised level are better suited to the romantically inclined. The service is ceremonial and structured and the more confident members of the team really roll out the red carpet for their guests. It is clear that many come here for a celebration and this is reflected in the impressive selection of champagne on offer. The menu is faithful to the Gordon Ramsay formula of largely classical combinations with just a few embellishments to keep it fresh, although the cooking doesn't quite sparkle as it once did.

Hix

British 🗡

H3

66-70 Brewer St. ✉ WIF 9UP
☎ (020) 7292 3518
www.hixsoho.co.uk

⊖ **Piccadilly Circus**
Closed 25-26 December

Carte £27/55

Leaded, frosted windows similar to The Ivy hint at exclusivity within, as does the huge wooden door and the discreet name plaque. Once entry has been secured, one finds oneself in an enormous space with specially commissioned artwork from Damien Hirst, Sue Webster and Sarah Lucas, reflecting Mark Hix's close relationship with London's artists. Meanwhile, his menu reflects his passion for British recipes and ingredients, which translates as plenty of game in season, unusual cuts of meat, rediscovered classics and proper puddings. Portions aren't over-generous and side dishes are required which makes the bill rise quickly – and sometimes a dish doesn't quite deliver the promise of the menu. But it's a fun, inclusive place.

Greenhouse ✿

Innovative XXX

27a Hay's Mews ✉ W1J 5NY
☎ (020) 7499 3331
e-mail reservations@greenhouserestaurant.co.uk
www.greenhouserestaurant.co.uk

Menu £29/70

⊖ **Hyde Park Corner**
Closed 24 December-
4 January,
Saturday lunch,
Sunday and bank holidays

The Greenhouse

MAYFAIR, SOHO & ST JAMES'S ▶ PLAN II

The Greenhouse looks as fresh and contemporary as ever, thanks to regular reinvestment – and its terrific location in a charming mews adds to the somewhat clubby and exclusive feel. Antonin Bonnet trained under celebrated French chef Michel Bras and spent time as personal chef to Marlon Abela, whose restaurant this is. He is the kind of chef who is always looking at new techniques and approaches to cooking and his style leans towards artfully constructed dishes, where the main ingredient is subtly enhanced with contrasting textures and creative combinations. France provides the main influence but he is not afraid of using, for example, the occasional Moroccan spice or Asian twist. The restaurant has clear ambitions and this goes a long way in accounting for the number of loyal and supportive guests, although the kitchen can sometimes overreach itself in trying to be original. The wine list is one of the most comprehensive you'll come across and service is undertaken in a structured and formal manner.

First Course	*Main Course*	*Dessert*
• Calves sweetbreads with wild garlic and leeks.	• Lamb with artichokes, quinoa and lemon cream.	• "Snix" - chocolate, salted caramel and peanuts.
• Mackerel with blackcurrant, gooseberries and horseradish.	• Sea bass with vegetable and pancetta cocotte and crayfish bisque.	• Amalfi lemon tart with lime jelly and meringue.

Hélène Darroze
at The Connaught ✿ ✿

French XXXX

Carlos Pl. ✉ W1K 2AL
☎ (020) 3147 7200
e-mail dining@the-connaught.co.uk
www.the-connaught.co.uk

⊖ Bond Street
Closed 2 weeks August,
1 week January, Saturday lunch,
Sunday and Monday –
Booking essential

Menu £35/75

The Connaught

London's diverse and vibrant dining scene has had quite an influence on Hélène Darroze and although she insists it is France and her native region of Landes that informs her cooking, she also uses interesting flavours of a more international persuasion. In essence, the dishes appear relatively simple on the plate, even though their descriptions on the menu can be quite florid. She is keen to champion the high quality produce they use, much more of which now comes from within the UK. Bayonne ham sliced on their gleaming Berkel machine heralds the start of one's meal and delightful mignardises round things off. Dishes can be surprisingly robust and the presentation is often exquisite. Service is courteous and professional, and the staff also manage to inject personality into the proceedings. Meanwhile, the room itself is warm and elegant, thanks to India Mahdavi's clever softening of all that mahogany wall panelling. A small private dining room has been added adjacent to the wine cellar, two floors below.

First Course	Main Course	Dessert
• Foie gras with mild spices and dried fruit chutney.	• Scallops with tandoori spices and lemongrass.	• Strawberry and bay leaf panna cotta with lemon jelly.
• Lobster ravioli with carrot and confit citrus mousseline.	• Pigeon with coffee butter, quinoa and dates.	• Champagne rhubarb compote and meringue.

Hibiscus ⍟⍟

H3

Innovative XXX

29 Maddox St. ⊠ W1S 2PA   ⊖ **Oxford Circus**
℘ (020) 7629 2999   Closed 23 December-3 January,
e-mail enquiries@hibiscusrestaurant.co.uk   Sunday and Monday
www.hibiscusrestaurant.co.uk

Menu £30/75

Hibiscus

Now that his restaurant is firmly established on the circuit of pre-eminent Mayfair restaurants, chef-owner Claude Bosi can breathe a sigh of relief, content in the knowledge that his move from the pastoral surrounds of Ludlow to the metropolitan hotbed of competitiveness has been vindicated. But that's not to say he feels he's cracked it, because his cooking continues to develop and evolve. The breads and all the little extras such as the canapés and petit fours are executed with as much care as the main courses and there are an impressive selection of menus available, including a vegetarian option. The kitchen team are a well-drilled outfit; they may use the occasional Asian note to bring out the flavour of a particular ingredient but they also have a very solid classical base. Claude is also one of those 'chefs' chefs' so you'll often see a table of boys in ill-fitting suits sampling as much of the menu as they can manage while making mental notes. There is more of a sense of occasion to the atmosphere at weekends.

First Course

- Smoked sweetbreads with lettuce velouté.
- Mackerel with strawberry and celery salad.

Main Course

- Lobster with pork 'san choi bau' and hollandaise.
- Veal with white miso, aubergine and bonito jus.

Dessert

- Chocolate tart with basil ice cream.
- Apricot and sourdough parfait with Horlicks sorbet.

61

Hush

Modern European

8 Lancashire Ct., Brook St. ⊠ W1S 1EY
☎ (020) 7659 1500
e-mail info@hush.co.uk
www.hush.co.uk

⊖ Bond Street
Closed 25-26 December,
1 January and Sunday –
Booking essential

Carte £25/47

Hush celebrated its 10th anniversary in 2010 by doing what all restaurants should do – it listened to its customers. They, for example, liked the slick upstairs dining room but preferred the more accessible, brasserie-style menu from the ground floor room. The result was that this same menu is now served throughout the building. One can see the appeal: it offers straightforward classics, from burgers to risotto and salads to sausages as well as all-day favourites like eggs Benedict. Upstairs also has a stylish destination bar but the best seats are on the delightful courtyard terrace. Add in several private dining rooms and you have a hostess who is more air-traffic controller and staff who spend time rushing hither and thither.

Imli

Indian

167-169 Wardour St ⊠ W1F 8WR
☎ (020) 7287 4243
e-mail info@imli.co.uk
www.imli.co.uk

⊖ Tottenham Court Road
Closed 25-26 December
and 1 January

Menu £9 (weekday lunch)/13 – Carte £20/30

'Relatively timely food' may not sound quite as snappy as 'fast food' but Imli proves that, if you don't want to linger long over a meal, there are alternatives to multinationals. It may be an Indian restaurant but 'tapas' is the shorthand for dishes that are diminutive and involve sharing. The menu is short, well-priced and to the point; three dishes per person should suffice, although the hungry should go for the 'Taste of Imli'. The cooking is a combination of street food and some regional, particularly Northern Indian, influences; vegetarians will find themselves with plenty of choice. Where Imli has borrowed from the 'experts' is in its use of bright lighting and vivid colours to encourage a rapid turnover.

Inn the Park

I4

British ✗

St James's Park ✉ SW1A 2BJ
✆ (020) 7451 9999
e-mail info@innthepark.com
www.innthepark.com

⊖ **Charing Cross**
Closed 25 December

Carte £26/36

When the sun has a little spring warmth and the season's first asparagus has appeared, few restaurants can compete with Oliver Peyton's place in the park. Its eco-friendly credentials are such that it resembles a camouflaged bunker; approach from the east and you won't see it. The entrance can be a little confusing: to avoid the self-service section, head for the 'waiter service' reception. The terrace is terrific and quickly fills in summer. The menu makes much of its Britishness and uses many small suppliers. The kitchen does have a somewhat heavy hand that lessens the impact and service can also lack a little humour but, despite these shortcomings, the restaurant is worthy without being pious and the setting is glorious.

Kiku

H4

Japanese ✗✗

17 Half Moon St. ✉ W1J 7BE
✆ (020) 7499 4208
e-mail kikumayfair@kikurestaurant.co.uk
www.kikurestaurant.co.uk

⊖ **Green Park**
Closed 25 December, 1 January,
lunch Sunday and
bank holidays

Menu £20 (lunch) – Carte £29/55

Kiku is a traditional Japanese restaurant, which makes it something of a rarity these days. The menus are numerous and varied, offering sushi to assorted kaiseki, a selection of soba noodle dishes, salads and casseroles; the lunch time menus are very popular locally. Apart from the kaiseki set menus, the prices are not unreasonable when one considers the Mayfair location, the crisp and understated décor and the endearingly charming staff who can swiftly soothe the most cantankerous of diner. They are also on hand to offer sensible advice. The best place to sit is in the raised section at the back with its own sushi counter; here it's never quite so busy and you get to really appreciate the skills of the chefs.

Kai ⸙

65 South Audley St. ✉ W1K 2QU
☎ (020) 7493 8988
e-mail reservations@kaimayfair.co.uk
www.kaimayfair.co.uk

⊖ Hyde Park Corner
Closed 25-26 December and 1 January
– Booking essential

Menu £19 (lunch) – Carte £40/75

Kai

Displays of perfect, polished red apples – to represent the Chinese flag – along with oil paintings and antique mirrors add to the air of opulence, while the music is incongruously clubby. But what underpins the operation is chef Alex Chow's skilled kitchen. His extensive menu comes with a plethora of little anecdotes and stories which, although too long to read in company, do at least highlight the restaurant's overriding enthusiasm. Dishes come packed with clean flavours and equal care goes into preparing the classics as goes into the more innovative choices. Regulars, of which there are many, ensure that certain dishes can never be removed from the menu; these include the wasabi prawns, the Peking duck – which comes from Scotland – and the excellent pumpkin cream dessert. Prices can vary quite wildly, from the very costly Imperial Delicacies to the more reasonably priced poultry dishes. The restaurant is spread over two floors; the ground floor is where the action is. This being Mayfair means that the wine list is a serious tome.

First Course

- Wasabi prawns with mango and basil seeds.
- Aromatic crispy duck.

Main Course

- Sea bass with chickpeas, shallots and ginger.
- Sichuan chicken with cashew nuts.

Dessert

- Rice dumplings with ginger and honey wafers.
- Almond curd with fresh fruit.

Matsuri - St James's

H4

Japanese ✗✗

15 Bury St. ✉ SW1Y 6AL
✆ (020) 7839 1101
e-mail dine@matsuri-restaurant.com
www.matsuri-restaurant.com

⊖ **Green Park**
Closed 25 December
and 1 January

Menu £25 (lunch and early dinner) – Carte £25/44

A/C

Matsuri is now as much of a St James's stalwart as some of the galleries and gentlemen's outfitters that surround it. This original branch remains very traditional in feel and its longevity can be put down to its reliable food and sweet-natured service. You're escorted downstairs to one of the teppan-yaki tables, or alternatively you can sit at the sushi counter, where you'll find yourself presented with a plethora of menus. The food is largely traditional, which makes a nice change from the current fad of 'reinterpreting' Japanese cuisine, and the Scottish beef is the star of the theatrical teppan-yaki. Dinner doesn't come cheap but, thanks to the assorted set menus, lunch represents decent value.

VISA

MC

AE

①

Maze Grill

G3

Beef specialities ✗✗

10-13 Grosvenor Sq. ✉ W1K 6JP
✆ (020) 7495 2211
e-mail mazegrill@gordonramsay.com
www.gordonramsay.com

⊖ **Bond Street**

Menu £21 (lunch) – Carte £30/47

A/C

Use the Grosvenor Square entrance as it offers a little more charm than if one wanders in from the adjacent Marriott Hotel, for which this restaurant also acts as the breakfast room. But then again, this is less about glamour, more about just enjoying good quality beef. The assorted cuts, from Casterbridge grain-fed and Hereford grass-fed through to Creekstone prime USDA corn-fed and Wagyu, are brought to your table in their raw state for you to hear about their differing personalities. Your preferred steak is then given a blast in the super-hot broiler before being served on a wooden board. The sides and sauces are numerous, varied and individually priced so your wallet can also end up feeling a little tender.

VISA

MC

AE

①

65

Maze ✿

Innovative ✗✗✗

G3

10-13 Grosvenor Sq. ✉ W1K 6JP   ⊖ Bond Street
✆ (020) 7107 0000
e-mail maze@gordonramsay.com
www.gordonramsay.com

Menu £23 (lunch) – Carte £29/33

Such is the well-tuned nature of this Gordon Ramsay operation that a change of head chef and most of the kitchen brigade in 2010 made very little difference and the restaurant wisely adopted the adage 'If it ain't broke, don't fix it'. Maze remains the most original of the restaurants in the Ramsay stable and boasts the most buoyant atmosphere, thanks largely to the confident style of service and the glamour of the David Rockwell designed room – this is a restaurant where diners like to dress up and make an occasion of it. It has also always benefited from its close proximity to the US Embassy, which ensures that it gets busy from around 5.30pm. The kitchen produces diminutive but imaginative constructions that pack a punch but are also balanced and satisfying. While there's a high degree of originality and boldness, it also understands the importance of textural contrast and has a fundamental understanding of what goes with what. Around half of all customers have the tasting menu, which best demonstrates the kitchen's ability.

First Course	*Main Course*	*Dessert*
• Terrine of foie gras and smoked eel with apple and celery.	• Roast duck with pickled red endive and beetroot.	• Rice pudding with chocolate and an orange and thyme marmalade.
• Smoked mackerel, tartare and olive jelly.	• Hake in Parma ham with chorizo, pimento and squid.	• Lemon meringue, citrus curd and basil sorbet.

Mews of Mayfair

Modern European 🍴🍴

10-11 Lancashire Ct., Brook St. (first floor)
✉ W1S 1EY
☎ (020) 7518 9388
e-mail info@mewsofmayfair.com
www.mewsofmayfair.com

⊖ **Bond Street**
Closed 25-26 December,
Sunday dinner and
bank holidays

Menu £19 (lunch) – Carte £29/47

Mews manages that trick of being cool and bright in summer and warm and inviting in winter. The relative serenity of the pretty restaurant is in sharp contrast to the crowds in the narrow lane and busy cocktail bar below, while the private dining room on the next floor up is a very pleasant space. The menu is very appealing and sufficiently sensitive to the changing seasons, so expect venison in winter, spring lamb and summer fruit. Simpler dishes are also pepped up, so burgers come with an optional foie gras topping and fish and chips arrive with a wasabi tartare. Flavours are sometimes compromised by an over-eagerness to make dishes look pretty but prices are generally sensible and the atmosphere thoroughly civilised.

Mint Leaf

Indian 🍴🍴

Suffolk Pl. ✉ SW1Y 4HX
☎ (020) 7930 9020
e-mail reservations@mintleafrestaurant.com
www.mintleafrestaurant.com

⊖ **Piccadilly Circus**
Closed 25-26 December,
1 January,
lunch Saturday
and Sunday

Menu £18/20 – Carte £29/37

Indian restaurants come in a variety of guises these days: Mint Leaf is from the contemporary, slick and designery school. This vast subterranean space with its moody lighting can seat over 250 but it comes divided into seven different areas so you're never rattling around. There is also an enormous bar running the length of the room for those wanting to make a night of it. The menu is also quite a lengthy affair, with many choices available in small or larger sizes. The best bet is to share a few dishes such as the soft shell crab or jumbo prawns, and then have your own curry – the kitchen's strength. The serving team are a mixed bunch: some will explain dishes enthusiastically; others seem keener upselling drinks.

MAYFAIR, SOHO & ST JAMES'S ▶ PLAN II

Momo

H3

25 Heddon St. ✉ W1B 4BH
☏ (020) 7434 4040
e-mail info@momoresto.com
www.momoresto.com

⊖ **Oxford Circus**
Closed 25 December and
Sunday lunch

Menu £19 (lunch) – Carte £31/47

Lanterns, rugs, trinkets and music all contribute to the authentic Moroccan atmosphere that makes Momo such a fun night out. That being said, it's even more fun if you come with friends as tables of two can get somewhat overawed. The menu is divided into three: a somewhat expensive set menu, traditional dishes and Momo specialities. The traditional section is the best as here you'll find the classics from pastilla to tagines; the Momo specialities are more contemporary in their make-up. Whatever you order, you'll end up with a pile of couscous and enough good food to last the week. The wine list lacks affordable bottles but there's a great bar downstairs. If it weren't for the absence of cigarette smoke, you could be in Marrakech.

The National Dining Rooms

I3/4

Sainsbury Wing,
The National Gallery,
Trafalgar Sq ✉ WC2N 5DN
☏ (020) 7747 2525
e-mail enquiries@thenationaldiningrooms.co.uk
www.thenationaldiningrooms.co.uk

⊖ **Charing Cross**
Closed 25-26 December
and 1 January –
(lunch only and dinner Friday)

Menu £28 – Carte approx. £25

There's usually a queue but don't panic – it's either those wanting the bakery section or others realising they should have booked. Oliver Peyton's restaurant on the first floor of the National Gallery's Sainsbury Wing is a bright, open affair, enriched by Paula Rego's complex mural 'Crivelli's Garden.' Ask for a table by the window, not just for the views of Trafalgar Square but also because the other half of the room is darker and under the eaves of the early Renaissance on the floor above. The menu champions British cooking and produce; fish and cheeses are the highlight – pies and puds will write-off the afternoon. The set menu represents decent value and is popular with the customers, who resemble a bridge club up from Winchester for the day.

Murano ఇ

Italian influences 🍴🍴🍴

20 Queen St. ✉ W1J 5PP
✆ (020) 7495 1127
e-mail pa@angela-hartnett.com
www.angela-hartnett.com

⊖ **Green Park**
Closed 24 until dinner
31 December and Sunday

Menu £30/60

A/C
VISA
MC
AE
D

Murano

Angela Hartnett became her own boss at the end of 2010 when she bought the restaurant from Gordon Ramsay. The Murano style is most evident in the glassware and the swirls on the wall and, less obviously, in the ceiling light 'sculpture'. The room is a long and narrow one – ask for a table by the front window as they're slightly more packed in towards the back – while the creams and greens combine to create a luminous feel that becomes quite intimate when they lower the lights in the evening. Angela Hartnett has established her reputation through a fairly unique style of cooking that combines classical techniques with Italian influences. Stars of the show include the dried meats and the expertly rendered risottos and pasta dishes which predominantly feature as starters. Many ingredients come from within the British Isles and from wherever they are best, such as Cornish lamb or Scottish beef. Combinations are well-judged and flavours clear. Lunch represents very decent value and there's also a very appealing vegetarian menu.

First Course

- Apple, black pudding and octopus salad with chorizo oil.
- Sweetbreads with cauliflower and golden raisins.

Main Course

- Lamb with celery, olive purée, artichokes and garlic.
- Confit halibut with celeriac and crab vinaigrette.

Dessert

- Chocolate mousse with raspberry sorbet.
- Pistachio soufflé with chocolate sauce and macaroon.

Nobu ঞ

G4

Japanese ✗✗

19 Old Park Ln. ⊠ **W1Y 1LB**
✆ (020) 7447 4747
e-mail london@noburestaurants.com
www.noburestaurants.com

⊖ **Hyde Park Corner**
Closed 25-26 December
and 1 January –
Booking essential

Carte £37/68

◁
A/C
🎄
☼
VISA
M©
AE

Nobu

Nobu restaurants now number over twenty and are spread around the world, but this one was the first to open in Europe, back in 1997, and came not long after the original in Manhattan. The two London branches can be considered the pick of the bunch and much of the credit is down to the long-standing executive chef, Mark Edwards. He has also been responsible for introducing the Osusume menu, which is exclusive to London and is aimed at offering neophytes the opportunity to discover what makes the food – Japanese with South American influences – quite so interesting. The reason is that the flavours are unique, the combinations wholly complementary and the ingredients top-notch – it's little wonder the dishes have been plagiarised across the city. The enthusiasm of the staff is undimmed and while the restaurant is perhaps less obviously glitzy than its younger sibling, that does mean that the fashionable crowd here are a little less excitable. Those who don't have the time to visit can now simply pick up a lunch or pre-theatre bento box.

First Course

- Tuna sashimi salad with matsuhisa dressing.
- Beef tenderloin with ponzu and garlic chips.

Main Course

- Black cod with miso.
- Ume crusted lamb chops with pickled lotus root.

Dessert

- Chocolate bento box with green tea ice cream.
- Fuji apple crumble with peanut ice cream.

Nobu Berkeley St ✿

Japanese ✕✕

15 Berkeley St. ✉ W1J 8DY
☎ (020) 7290 9222
e-mail berkeleyst@noburestaurants.com
www.noburestaurants.com/berkeley

Carte £65/85

⊖ **Green Park**
Closed 25-26 December,
Saturday, Sunday and
bank holidays –
Booking essential

Nobu

As a general rule, if there are paparazzi outside a restaurant, then the talent inside is unlikely to be in the kitchen. But there are exceptions and Nobu Berkeley St is one of them. This is a restaurant that still does things properly, despite serving around 900 people each day. There are 45 chefs in the kitchen, 60% of whom are Japanese, and considerable care is taken with the food. Nobu tacos are a good way of getting things started and staff are well informed if you need help. Greatest hits like yellowtail sashimi, black cod with miso and shrimp tempura remain on the menu but each Nobu has some unique element and at Nobu Berkeley St it is the wood oven. The cabbage steak with truffles and lamb anti cucho miso are top sellers; the chocolate tart is catching the chocolate bento box in popularity. Lunch sees regular or deluxe bento boxes with organic juices. Anyone whose fame does not extend beyond their own home needs to book well in advance to get their desired time; although, if you're prepared to wait in the busy bar, it may be worth just pitching up.

First Course

- King crab claw tempura with butter ponzu.
- Crispy pork belly with spicy miso.

Main Course

- Black cod with miso.
- Duck breast with wasabi salsa.

Dessert

- Chocolate tart with sake kasu ice cream and chocolate sauce.
- 'Geisha's delight' with elderflower and sake.

Only Running Footman

GH3

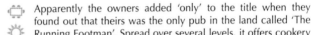

Gastropub 🍺📖

5 Charles St ✉ W1J 5DF   ⊖ Green Park.
✆ (020) 7499 2988
e-mail manager@therunningfootmanmayfair.com
www.therunningfootmanmayfair.com

Carte £26/35

Apparently the owners added 'only' to the title when they found out that theirs was the only pub in the land called 'The Running Footman'. Spread over several levels, it offers cookery demonstrations and private dinners along with its two floors of dining. Downstairs is where the action usually is, with its menu offering pub classics from steak sandwiches to fishcakes, but you can't book here and it's always packed. Upstairs is where you'll find a surprisingly formal dining room and here they do take reservations. Its menu is far more ambitious and European in its influence but the best dishes are still the simpler ones, with desserts a strength. You can't help feeling that you would be having a lot more fun below stairs, though.

Patterson's

H3

Modern European 🍴🍴

4 Mill St. ✉ W1S 2AX   ⊖ Oxford Street
✆ (020) 7499 1308   Closed 25-26 December,
e-mail info@pattersonsrestaurant.co.uk   Saturday lunch and Sunday
www.pattersonsrestaurant.com

Menu £23/45

A family moving from a small fishing village in the Scottish borders to the middle of Mayfair may sound like one of those dependable fish-out-of-water comedies, but that is exactly what the Pattersons did back in 2003, and theirs remains one of the few family-run restaurants in this part of town. Father and son in the kitchen still get much of the seafood from their erstwhile home and even supply a number of other restaurants. Their fairly extensive menus feature a lot of Scottish produce in general but it's the seafood that's generally best and the cooking influences come largely from within Europe. It's a deceptively large place, fresh and uncluttered in its decoration, but can still provide a fairly intimate setting.

La Petite Maison

54 Brooks Mews ⊠ W1K 4EG
℘ (020) 7495 4774
e-mail info@lpmlondon.co.uk
www.lpmlondon.co.uk

⊖ Bond Street
Closed 25-26 December

Carte £32/65 s

Packed from the moment it opened in 2007, La Petite Maison brings a little piece of Nice to Mayfair. The appeal is sunny French Mediterranean cooking and its healthy bounty of artichokes, lemons, olives, peppers and tomatoes. 'Food is served to help yourself' it proclaims, which translates as 'you may want to share,' but you don't have to, as the dishes are of normal size. However, with over 20 starters including pissaladière, sardines and squid, it may be worth ordering a few. The whole roast black-leg chicken with foie gras has proved a hit, as have the fish main courses. As one would expect, there's plenty of rosé on the wine list. Their slogan is 'Tous célèbres ici', which means lots of all-year tans and good tailoring.

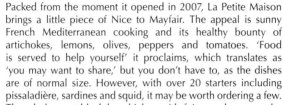

Plum Valley

20 Gerrard St ⊠ W1D 6JQ
℘ (020) 7494 4366
e-mail sooannliew@yahoo.co.uk

⊖ Leicester Square
Closed 24-25 December

Menu £38 – Carte £19/30

Is Chinatown finally casting off its tourist-trap reputation? Plum Valley is the latest venture with genuine aspirations to open in Gerrard Street and its contemporary styling gives the street a much-needed boost. The striking black façade makes it easy to notice, while flattering lighting and layered walls give the interior a dash of sophistication. The chef is from Chiu Chow, a region near Guangdong, and his menu is largely based on Cantonese cooking, with occasional forays into Vietnam and Thailand as well as the odd nod towards contemporary presentation. Dim sum is his kitchen's main strength which fits nicely with the all-day opening of the restaurant. If only those doing the service could muster the same levels of enthusiasm.

Polpetto

I3

Italian ✗

46 Dean St, (1st floor) ✉ W1D 5BG
✆ (020) 7734 1969
www.polpetto.co.uk

⊖ Leicester Square
Closed 25 December-1 January,
Sunday and bank holidays

Carte £16/22

VISA
MC
AE

The baby sister, or baby octopus, to Polpo is smaller and simpler and is located, somewhat incongruously, upstairs at The French House, a pub inexorably linked to Soho's literary and artistic communities. You can't book for dinner and there's nowhere to wait – they just take your mobile number and text you. It's just one small but thoughtfully designed room, with exposed brick, a tin ceiling, zinc tables and some red banquettes; the paper mat doubles as the menu. Choose a couple of cicheti, some bread, one vegetable, a meat and a fish dish and you'll have more than enough; pigeon saltimbocca or the soft shell crab are good. The small dishes are keenly priced; it's all great fun and is ideal for a quick bite before the theatre.

Polpo

H3

Italian ✗

41 Beak St. ✉ W1F 9SB
✆ (0207) 734 4479
www.polpo.co.uk

⊖ Oxford Circus
Closed 25 December-1 January,
Sunday dinner and bank holidays

Carte £12/20

A/C
🍽
VISA
MC
AE

Opening a Venetian bacaro in an 18C townhouse where Canaletto once lodged does seem providential and Polpo has indeed been packing them in since day one. The stripped-down faux-industrial look is more New York's SoHo than London's Soho, as is the no-reservation policy which means you'll probably have to wait. But the fun atmosphere and the appealing prices of the small plates will assuage any impatience you feel in waiting your turn. Order a couple of cicheti, like arancini or prosciutto, a plate of fritto misto, ham and pea risotto or Cotechino sausage along with a vegetable dish per person and you should leave satisfied; if you do over-order, it's not going to break the bank. Venetian wines, available by the carafe, complete the picture.

Portrait

Modern European ✗

National Portrait Gallery,
St Martin's Pl (3rd Floor)
✉ WC2H 0HE
✆ (020) 7312 2490
e-mail portrait.reservation@searcys.co.uk
www.searcys.co.uk

⊖ Charing Cross
Closed 24-26 December –
Booking essential –
(lunch only and dinner
Thursday-Saturday)

Menu £25 – Carte £29/37

Portrait is on the third floor of the Ondaatje wing of the National Portrait Gallery and is run by the Searcy's catering company. You needn't ask for a window seat because the views, of recognisable rooftops and Nelson standing proudly in Trafalgar Square, are just as good from any of the tables. Although open for breakfast and tea, this is principally a lunchtime operation, with dinner limited to Thursdays and Fridays - the nights of the gallery's extended opening hours. The à la carte menu keeps things relatively light and the influences mostly from Europe; there is a good value set menu at weekends. This is a useful spot, not only for gallery visitors but also for those attending matinee performances at the numerous theatres nearby.

MAYFAIR, SOHO & ST JAMES'S ▶ PLAN II

Quaglino's

H4

Modern European ✗✗

16 Bury St ✉ SW1Y 6AL
✆ (020) 7930 6767
e-mail quaglinos@danddlondon.com
www.quaglinos.co.uk

⊖ Green Park
Closed 25 December,
Sunday and bank holidays

Menu £20 – Carte £33/46

It's easy to forget the impact the iconic Quaglino's had when Sir Terence Conran reopened it back in the early '90s. It was big, bold and boisterous and getting a table could prove quite a challenge. But the smart crowd moved on and today much of that sparkle and glamour has gone. This is a restaurant that needs to be near capacity for there to be an atmosphere and, fortunately, current owners D&D are aware that the place needs reinvigorating and are pulling it up by the scruff of its neck. The menu may no longer look quite so original but there is still enough there to appeal to most, from the fruits de mer to the coq au vin. London needs glamorous restaurants like Quaglino's so let's hope it rediscovers its pizzazz.

Quo Vadis

British 🍴🍴🍴

13

26-29 Dean St. ✉ **W1D 3LL**
☏ (020) 7437 9585
e-mail info@quovadissoho.co.uk
www.quovadis.co.uk

⊖ **Tottenham Court Road**
Closed Sunday from 30 April-1 October
and bank holidays

Menu £20 (lunch) – Carte £29/33

A/C
VISA
MC
AE

Quo Vadis has been a Soho landmark since the 1920s and its renewal by the Hart brothers in 2008 ensured that it will be around for many years to come. The menu is of the instantly appealing variety and successfully evokes the classic British grill restaurant. Start with whitebait, razor clams or perhaps some pasta; follow with Hereford beef from the grill or roast turbot and finish with ginger cake or treacle tart. Or just come in for an omelette. Prices are fair, especially with the lunch and pre-theatre menus; and at least that cover charge includes an unlimited water supply. The frosted glass façade adds a dash of intrigue and the art deco elegance combined with a crisp, fresh feel provides suitably comfortable surroundings.

Red Fort

Indian 🍴🍴🍴

13

77 Dean St. ✉ **W1D 3SH**
☏ (020) 7437 2525
e-mail info@redfort.co.uk
www.redfort.co.uk

⊖ **Tottenham Court Road**
Closed 25 December, lunch Saturday,
Sunday and bank holidays –
booking advisable at dinner

Menu £20/40 – Carte £33/40

A/C
VISA
MC
AE

Dumpukht biyani (using Welsh lamb); monkfish tikka; tandoori jhinga (mildly spiced prawns) and baby aubergines with chilli are the signature dishes of this long-standing Indian restaurant, where the ingredients are top-notch and the rich sauces all made from scratch. The mango kulfi and the various homemade chutneys will also impress, while the menu gets subtly tweaked on a daily basis. The interior provides a sleek and understated homage to Lal Quila, the Red Fort in Delhi; the stone, imported from Rajasthan, combines with the waterfall to create quite a feature. The presence of plenty of managers ensures that service moves along nicely and the doorman is now back on watch. Akbar is the basement bar, with resident DJ.

The Ritz Restaurant

H4

Traditional XXXXX

150 Piccadilly ⊠ W1J 9BR
℡ (020) 7493 8181
e-mail rtizrestaurant@theritzlondon.com
www.theritzlondon.com

⊖ Green Park

Menu £39/48 – Carte £64/87 s

Dining at The Ritz is not just a mightily grand occasion but also provides a lesson in how things used to be done. The room is certainly unmatched in the sheer lavishness of its Louis XVI decoration; the table settings positively gleam thanks to all that polishing and there are probably more ranks to the serving team than in a ship's company. Little wonder they insist on jackets and ties. There's a plethora of menus: Ritz Classics could be saddle of Kentish lamb or roast sirloin; Ritz Traditions might include smoked salmon carved at your table or Dover sole filleted in front of you. For the full experience, have the six-course Sonata Menu, go at a weekend for a dinner dance and don't tell your bank manager.

Sake No Hana

H4

Japanese XXX

23 St James's St ⊠ SW1A 1HA
℡ (020) 7925 8988
e-mail reservations@sakenohana.com
www.sakenohana.com

⊖ Green Park
Closed 24-25 December
and Sunday lunch

Carte £20/60

As with most restaurants, things look a little different now than they did when the place opened. At Sake No Hana the idea of not offering wine along with the shochu and sake lasted about six months. The menu is also now considerably shorter. It is dominated by sashimi and sushi, after which one is expected to order a grilled dish and perhaps one of their 'special plates'- which could be fried tofu with bonito flakes – then end with some miso soup. Service can be hit and miss and whilst all that cedar wood goes some way towards hiding the ugliness of this '60s building, one does get the impression that this isn't yet the finished article as the overall experience can be a little lacklustre and quite expensive.

Sartoria

H3

20 Savile Row ✉ W1S 3PR   ⊖ **Green Park**
✆ (020) 7534 7000   Closed 24-25 December,
e-mail sartoriareservations@danddlondon.com   Sunday,
www.sartoriabar.com   Saturday lunch
     and bank holidays

Menu £24 – Carte £34/44

If you're going to have any restaurant occupying a prime site in Savile Row then it might as well be Italian as they know one or two things about tailoring themselves. Sartoria is an elegant, smartly dressed restaurant that always seems to exude a certain poise and self-assurance, along with a little charm. There are subtle allusions to tailoring in the decoration and the sofa-style seating in the middle of the room is very appealing. The à la carte menu is an extensive number and prices can quickly add up, but the cooking, which covers all parts of the country, is undertaken with care and it's apparent that the ingredients are top-notch. Service is also not lacking in confidence and is overseen by assorted suited managers.

Scott's

G3

20 Mount St ✉ W1K 2HE   ⊖ **Bond Street**
✆ (020) 7495 7309   Closed dinner 24, 25-26 December
www.scotts-restaurant.com   and 1 January

Carte £33/64

Scott's is one of those rare restaurants which is both fashionable and also has a palpable sense of history. As soon as you're through the door, you'll find the aroma and the bustle an enticing draw. Purportedly Ian Fleming's favourite restaurant, it still appeals to those whose faces we recognise and everyone looks as though they've dressed up for the occasion. The wood panelling is juxtaposed with modern art and the bar forms a striking centrepiece. The menu offers an enticing and varied choice, from caviar to razor clams, oysters to spider crabs and sea bass and turbot. The fish is cooked with skill and innate understanding. If only the taciturn staff could crack the occasional smile and add some personality to their efficiency.

Semplice ✿

Italian ✕✕

G3

9-10 Blenheim St. ✉ W1S 1LJ
✆ (020) 7495 1509
e-mail info@ristorantesemplice.com
www.ristorantesemplice.com

Menu £30 (lunch) – Carte £34/53

⊖ **Bond Street**
Closed 2 weeks Christmas,
Easter, Saturday lunch
and Sunday –
Booking essential at dinner

Semplice

The young owners' enthusiasm for their restaurant and their determination to uphold its reputation is palpable. As such, the chef-owner is intent on instilling in his brigade the importance of using good produce and the respect one should show it. Along with many ingredients imported directly from small, specialist suppliers in Italy, fresh fish arrives each day from Cornwall. The kitchen remains loyal to its north Italian roots and the main ingredient of each dish is allowed to shine. The Fassone carpaccio and the Milanese risotto with bone marrow are two choices that keep the many regulars particularly content, but those who are more trusting leave the decisions about what they'll eat to the kitchen. The gold waves, leather and lacquered ebony panels add a hint of luxury to the room, which takes on a more intimate feel in the evening. The lunch set menu allows newcomers the chance to experience Semplice without breaking the bank. Bar Trattoria Semplice is the simpler sibling a few yards away.

First Course

- Veal served with tonnata sauce.
- Artichoke salad with rocket and pecorino cheese.

Main Course

- Rabbit with glazed carrots and artichoke sauce.
- Hake with olive oil, peppers, courgette and squid.

Dessert

- Domori chocolate fondant.
- Apple fritters with cinnamon custard and apple jelly.

Seven Park Place ✿

H4 Modern European XXX

7-8 Park Pl. ✉ SW1A 1LS   ⊖ **Green Park**
☎ (020) 7316 1614   Closed Sunday and Monday – Booking
e-mail reservation@stjameshotelandclub.com   essential
www.stjameshotelandclub.com

Menu £30/45

A/C
VISA
MC
AE
①

St James's Hotel & Club

The problem facing the owners of the St James's Hotel when they converted it from a private club, was in operating within the limited amount of space available. Accordingly, this small restaurant is somewhat concealed at the end of a bar, through which one has to navigate. It's divided between two very contrasting rooms: the plush back room is the place to sit, as it holds just three large tables in its gilded setting; the outer room is not quite so intimate. The restaurant does, however, have a grown-up feel to it and the professional service team make everyone feel suitably relaxed. The hotel has also now got the right chef, cooking the right food. William Drabble made his name at Michael's Nook in Grasmere and Aubergine in Chelsea and his food has always displayed a sense of clarity, offering clean, unadulterated flavours. It is French at its base but the ingredients are decidedly British and mostly from more northerly parts, so expect lamb from the Lune valley, game from Cumbria and shellfish from the west coast of Scotland.

First Course

- Foie gras with roasted peaches and gingerbread.
- Scallops with Jerusalem artichoke purée and crispy bacon.

Main Course

- Lamb with garlic purée and rosemary jus.
- Sea bass with chard, mushrooms and red wine.

Dessert

- White chocolate parfait with cherries.
- Roasted pineapple with rum, ginger and lime.

Sketch (The Gallery)

H3

9 Conduit St. ✉ W1S 2XG
📞 (020) 7659 4500
e-mail info@sketch.uk.com
www.sketch.uk.com

⊖ Oxford Street
Closed 25-26 December, Sunday and bank
holidays – Booking essential – (dinner only)

Carte £35/63

A/C

📷⊘

VISA

MC

AE

Fund managers and footballers' wives flock to this lively, fun space, which transforms itself during the day into a gallery showing mostly video art, but even during dinner, lifestyle aphorisms are projected onto its white walls. The cocktail list is an essential element, while the food menu is international in its scope but in tune with the culinary zeitgeist in its constrained use of oil and dairy. Dishes come with plenty of flavour and colour and, as the staff are young, good-looking and fully conversant in the concept of up-selling, one needs to stand firm and politely decline their offer of a side dish because the main courses don't need them. It's loud, busy and it doesn't come cheap – but then exclusivity never does.

Sumosan

H3

26 Albemarle St. ✉ W1S 4HY
📞 (020) 7495 5999
e-mail info@sumosan.com
www.sumosan.com

⊖ Green Park
Closed bank holidays,
lunch Saturday and Sunday

Carte £53/97

As an unwelcome hangover from a time when all London restaurants were packed every night, you're still told more than once what time you're expected to leave before you've actually ordered anything and, for some of the staff, smiling is clearly considered far too uncool. This is a shame because Sumosan gets a lot of things right. Granted, some of the customers spend more time choosing their cocktail than their food but the kitchen does produce some interesting innovations and modern interpretations of Japanese flavours; the sushi and sashimi are particularly good and there is wide-ranging choice, from the rich duck with lingonberries to the subtle soft shell crab. If only the place could be a little less self-absorbed.

Sketch
(The Lecture Room & Library) ✿

French XXXX

9 Conduit St. (First Floor) ✉ W1S 2XG
℡ (020) 7659 4500
e-mail info@sketch.uk.com
www.sketch.uk.com

Menu £35 (lunch) – Carte £70/129

⊖ Oxford Street
Closed 25-30 December, last 2 weeks
August, Saturday lunch, Sunday,
Monday and bank holidays –
Booking essential

Sketch

Sketch was always designed as an ever-changing restaurant concept and, sure enough, there have been a few adjustments to proceedings in the Lecture Room and Library. The main difference is in the presentation of the food, most specifically with the main courses. In the past they came sub-divided into various equally sized components which arrived in a number of assorted vessels; now one plate dominates and is complemented by the other dishes that surround it. The quality of the ingredients, however, remains irreproachable and the room is as stunning as ever, with the odd quirky decorative touch adding to the general theatre of things. The wine list continues to dazzle, both in the array of French growths but also in the prices that sit alongside them. Another not quite so welcome change is that the serving team can sometimes cross the line from being confident into making guests feel lucky to have got a table. However, what remains constant is the sense of glamour, energy and vitality one experiences here.

First Course
- Langoustine 'addressed in five ways'.
- 'Perfume of the earth'.

Main Course
- Lamb with aubergine, tomato, ewe's milk cheese and spinach.
- John Dory, Parmesan gnocchi, shallots and artichoke.

Dessert
- Pierre Gagnaire's 'Grand Dessert'.
- Ricotta and chocolate millefeuille.

Square ✿ ✿

French ✕✕✕✕

6-10 Bruton St. ✉ W1J 6PU
☏ (020) 7495 7100
e-mail reception@squarerestaurant.com
www.squarerestaurant.com

Menu £35/75

⊖ **Green Park**
Closed 25 December, 1 January
and lunch Saturday,
Sunday and bank holidays,

The Square

MAYFAIR, SOHO & ST JAMES'S ▶ PLAN II

Philip Howard is one of the capital's more personable chefs and has been responsible for the development of a number of talented young chefs now cementing their own reputations in London. Despite being involved in Kitchen W8 in Kensington, he never took his hand off the tiller here at The Square. His food continues to be true to his classical roots yet he manages to bring in subtle modern influences without them jarring. The menu changes completely with the seasons but varies more in summer when certain ingredients are only available for short periods, although the regulars will never allow the removal of the two signature dishes of langoustine and lasagne of crab. The cheeseboard is now much improved and offers a selection of around 40 British and continental cheeses; it's worth asking as they don't 'sell' it as much as they could. They're also working on the service in an attempt to lighten it somewhat, especially for weekend visitors who are inclined to interact with the serving team more than corporate weekday diners.

First Course

- Langoustine with Parmesan gnocchi and truffle.
- Calves sweetbreads with truffled cauliflower and almonds.

Main Course

- Saddle of hare with tarte fine of celeriac and pear.
- John Dory with macaroni, chicken wings and chanterelles.

Dessert

- Brillat-Savarin cheesecake with passion fruit and mango.
- Rice pudding soufflé with chocolate ice cream.

Tamarind ❀

Indian 🗙🗙🗙

20 Queen St. ⊠ W1J 5PR
☏ (020) 7629 3561
e-mail manager@tamarindrestaurant.com
www.tamarindrestaurant.com

⊖ Green Park
Closed 25-27 December,
1 January, lunch Saturday
and bank holidays

Menu £19 (weekday lunch) – Carte £48/72

A/C
☼
VISA
MC
AE
◍

Tamarind

The earnest Alfred Prasad and his reinvigorated kitchen take familiar dishes and raise them to exceptional heights. The delicate and fragrant curries show particular care but also worthy of special mention are the tandoor chefs who produce, in considerable heat, specialities ranging from the delightfully light breads to kebabs of tender lamb. Spicing is subtle and brings out the natural flavours of the ingredients, whether that's the simmered chicken in the Adraki Murgh or the plump tiger prawns in the Kadhai Jhinga. Vegetable dishes are prepared with equal care and provide interesting counterpoints to the main dishes. The restaurant has always made the best of its basement location, albeit one that's in the heart of Mayfair. The smoked mirrors, gilded columns and copper-coloured chargers give the room a sophisticated veneer. Service is more polished and assured than in previous years and all these factors, plus the slight reduction in the prices of certain dishes, have made Tamarind as popular as ever.

First Course

- Spiced chickpeas and whole wheat crisps with mint chutney.
- Duck breast with peppers, tomato and chaat masala dressing.

Main Course

- Lamb cutlets marinated with garlic, papaya and fennel.
- Sea bass with curry leaves and coconut.

Dessert

- Mango kulfi.
- Poached pear with masala tea and ginger ice cream.

Tempo

Italian XX

54 Curzon St. ✉ W1J 8PG
☎ (020) 7629 2742
e-mail info@tempomayfair.co.uk
www.tempomayfair.co.uk

⊖ Green Park
Closed 24 December-3 January,
Sunday and bank holidays

Menu £22 (lunch) – Carte £29/50

Henry Togna, the affable and well-connected hotelier, took over a failing Italian restaurant, revamped it from top-to-toe and reopened it as Tempo in the summer of 2010. He adds a comforting presence to proceedings but is also wise enough to surround himself with an experienced team. The ground floor is cosy and neat, while the upstairs salon, where the small bar is located, is clubbier and a tad funkier. The main menu is an unobjectionable document and includes the popular cicchetti, or small plates. The cooking is executed with care and stays true to the principles of an Italian kitchen; a good selection of breads kick things off and the tagliolini with Cornish crab and the lemon tart have quickly become favourites.

Theo Randall

 Italian

1 Hamilton Pl, Park Ln. ✉ W1J 7QY
☎ (020) 7318 8747
e-mail reservations@theorandall.com
www.theorandall.com

⊖ Hyde Park Corner
Closed Saturday lunch,
Sunday and bank holidays

Menu £27 (lunch) – Carte £45/55

It may have taken a little longer to settle down than most pundits expected but now this large, contemporary restaurant on the ground floor of the InterContintental Hotel seems to have found its niche, and increased TV exposure for its eponymous chef has had a knock-on effect on business. Theo Randall's years at the River Café inform his cooking and, even now, a familiar dish like flourless chocolate cake can seem peculiarly out of context. The menu changes daily and loosely follows the formula of cooking more dishes from the north of Italy in winter and more southerly ones in the summer; the wood oven also plays a major role. As this is also a hotel dining room catering for all tastes, the wine list has something for everyone.

Tierra Brindisa

Spanish X

46 Broadwick St. ✉ W1F 7AF
✆ (020) 7534 1690
e-mail office@tierrabrindisa.com
www.brindisatapaskitchens.com

⊖ **Tottenham Court Road**
Closed Sunday –
Booking essential at dinner

Carte £18/30

For over twenty years Brindisa have been suppliers of the best Spanish produce so it was a logical decision to open a tapas bar, which they did in Borough Market back in 2004. The success of Tapas Brindisa led to this second venture, this time in the middle of Soho media-land. Tierra Brindisa is a slightly more structured affair, albeit one that is equally busy and bustling – but at least they take reservations. Again, this is all about the product which, thanks to the quality, doesn't need much doing to it – dishes are never overcrowded and flavours natural. There's a daily cazuela to satisfy the hungry and, owing to popular demand, suckling pig and shoulder of lamb come in larger sizes. Be sure to end with a Turrón mousse.

La Trouvaille

French XX

12A Newburgh St. ✉ W1F 7RR
✆ (020) 7287 8488
e-mail contact@latrouvaille.co.uk
www.latrouvaille.co.uk

⊖ **Oxford Circus**
Closed Monday dinner,
Sunday and bank holidays

Menu £21/35

Once you've found the entrance (avoid the more obvious corner door in the charming cobbled street) of this sweet and busy place, owned and enthusiastically run by a couple of northern Frenchmen, you'll be faced with a choice. You can either stay on the ground floor for platters of charcuterie or cheese and some splendid wines or, if you want something more substantial, you can head upstairs for 'Le Dining Room.' Here all is bright and appealing and they've added cushions to those clear plastic chairs. The set menus offer plenty of French classics; the best dishes are those with fewer of the modern embellishments and twists that the kitchen is prone to adding. The wines are almost exclusively organic and curiously all come from the south.

Umu ✿

14-16 Bruton Pl. ✉ W1J 6LX
℡ (020) 7499 8881
e-mail reception@umurestaurant.com
www.umurestaurant.com

⊖ Bond Street
Closed 24 December-
6 January, Saturday lunch,
Sunday and bank holidays

Menu £25 (lunch) – Carte £33/48

A/C
VISA
M©
AE
①

Umu

A new chef arrived here late in 2010, from Kyoto via Switzerland and New York, and his first task was to find ingredients to match the quality he had become used to back in Japan; so far, it is the Scottish langoustines that have bowled him over. The only other small change has been the creation of a table in the former wine cave – ideal for couples in the early throws of romantic entanglement but perhaps too much of a squeeze for parties of four. Otherwise, things remain the same. The hostess greets arrivals with enough enthusiasm to compensate for the somewhat po-faced persona of the waiting staff, from whom advice sometimes has to be coaxed. The menu consists of three pages of parchment – if you want the full experience head to one of the seasonally changing, multi-course kaiseki menus, although these have been adapted somewhat for western tastes. The perfect accompaniment, especially for the sashimi, is sake; not only is the list impressive in its depth and range but the charming female sommelier also offers thoughtful advice.

First Course

- Langoustine with amber tomato jelly, vinaigrette and caviar.
- Foie gras custard with brown crab and ginger sauce.

Main Course

- Pigeon with radish and egg yolk sauce.
- Eel kabayaki with steamed courgette.

Dessert

- Japanese tiramisu with matcha tea and sake.
- Yuzu cheesecake.

Vasco and Piero's Pavilion

Italian XX

H2/3

15 Poland St ✉ W1F 8QE
☎ (020) 7437 8774
e-mail eat@vascosfood.com
www.vascosfood.com

⊖ Oxford Circus
Closed Saturday lunch, Sunday and bank
holidays – Booking essential at lunch

Menu £20 (early dinner) – Carte lunch £27/38

This Soho institution celebrates its fortieth anniversary in 2011; if you ask them for the secret of their success the reply will be, "We just do what we believe in". That means a menu that changes twice a day, ingredients and influences from Umbria and simple but effective cooking, with homemade pasta a highlight. Service can sometimes lack a little enthusiasm but it does get the job done – it is not as if they don't care, more that their customers are often regulars who know the score, so why over-egg the pudding? The owners' confidence in their operation and their honest endeavours add to the grown-up feel. The restaurant, which was originally located in Oxford Street, remains fresh and bright.

Veeraswamy

Indian XX

H3

Victory House, 99 Regent St.
(entrance on Swallow St.) ✉ W1B 4RS
☎ (020) 7734 1401
e-mail veeraswarmy@realindianfood.com
www.realindianfood.com

⊖ Piccadilly Circus
Closed dinner 25 December

Menu £21 (lunch and early dinner) – Carte £34/49

The manager here knows not to come between a regular and their favourite table: some were first brought here by their grandparents and are now, in turn, introducing their own grandchildren to London's oldest surviving Indian restaurant, which dates from 1926. You'd be excused for thinking it might be a tad old-fashioned but Veeraswamy is anything but: it is awash with vibrant colours and always full of bustle. The Hyderabad lamb biryani may have been on the original menu but there are plenty of other dishes with a more contemporary edge. The meaty Madagascar prawns are a good way of kicking things off; slow-cooked lamb dishes are also done very well. There's a tasting menu available and desserts, prepared with a flourish, shouldn't be ignored.

Wild Honey ✿

12 St George St. ✉ W1S 2FB
✆ (020) 7758 9160
e-mail info@wildhoneyrestaurant.co.uk
www.wildhoneyrestaurant.co.uk

⊖ **Oxford Circus**
Closed 25-26 December
and 1 January

Menu £20 (lunch) – Carte £33/46

A/C
🎭
☼
VISA
MC
AE

Michelin

Wild Honey is all about relaxed and comfortable dining; the highly skilled cooking is a model of resourcefulness and the prices – when one considers the postcode and the quality of the food – are laudable. The kitchen proves that good – but not necessarily expensive – ingredients mean good food. The menus are hugely appealing and the seasonal ingredients are used at their peak; plates are never overcrowded and each component serves a purpose – there is nothing ostentatious here. The bouillabaisse and the wild honey ice cream are constants and the wine list is as magnanimous in its pricing as the menu, with all bottles available by the carafe. Like a talented sportsman, a lot of hard work and experience goes into making all this seem so easy. The fixed menu is a steal and there's now a short 'sweet and savoury' menu on offer for those who want an afternoon bite. Service is personable and unobtrusive and the atmosphere is far more animated than one would expect in a wood-panelled room that was once a private members club.

First Course

- Belly pork with snails, garlic and parsley.
- Smoked eel with mango and turnip.

Main Course

- Veal with gnocchi and young vegetables.
- Cod with razor clams, borlotti beans, tomato and sea greens.

Dessert

- Wild honey ice cream with crushed honeycomb.
- Cherry clafoutis with sour cherry ice cream.

The Wolseley

Modern European 𝕏𝕏𝕏

H4

160 Piccadilly ✉ W1J 9EB
☎ (020) 7499 6996
e-mail reservations@thewolseley.com
www.thewolseley.com

Carte £21/51

⊖ Green Park
Closed dinner 24 and 31 December,
25 December and
August bank holiday –
Booking essential

AC
🕐
☼
VISA
MC
AE
◎

Opened back in 2003, The Wolseley did not take long to earn iconic status, thanks to its stylish décor, celebrity following and smooth service. Its owners, Chris Corbin and Jeremy King, created a restaurant in the style of a grand European café, all pillars, arches and marble. Open from breakfast until late, the flexible menu offers everything from Austrian and French classics to British staples, so the daily special could be coq au vin or Lancashire hot pot. Pastries come from the Viennoiserie and lunch merges into Afternoon tea. So, one table could be tucking into Beluga caviar or a dozen oysters while their neighbours enjoy a salt beef sandwich or eggs Benedict. The large clock reminds you that there are probably others waiting for your table.

The sun is out – let's eat alfresco! Look for 🛆.

Yauatcha ⁣⊛

Chinese XX

15 Broadwick St ⊠ W1F 0DL
✆ (020) 7494 8888
e-mail mail@yauatcha.com
www.yauatcha.com

⊖ Tottenham Court Road
Closed 24-25 December

Carte £27/59

Yauatcha

MAYFAIR, SOHO & ST JAMES'S ▶ PLAN II

China and Britain: two countries inexorably linked through tea. If you want to see what this looks like in practice, then go along one afternoon to Yauatcha and witness a British institution given an Asian twist. The cakes, tarts and pastries are good too, although for that we have to thank a French pastry chef - and that's a whole different story. There is nowhere quite like Yauatcha: a dim sum restaurant that's so successful, where the food is so good and the surroundings so slick and stylish, that customers find it hard to be in and out in the allocated 1hr 45minutes. The trick is to spend time eating and chatting, rather than ordering so crack on with that bit. Around three dim sum per person followed by some sharing of noodles or a stir-fry should do the trick and, while you wait for it to arrive, have one of their terrific cocktails. Stand-out dishes are the Scallop Shumai, the Prawn Cheung Fun, the baked Venison Puff and the Kung Po Chicken; but don't ignore dessert, especially the roasted pineapple with praline parfait.

First Course

- Scallop shui mai with tobiko caviar.
- Crispy lamb with spring onion and sour plum dressing.

Main Course

- Spicy king soya wagyu beef.
- Cod with Chinese honey and wine.

Dessert

- Chocolate and raspberry delice with vanilla ice cream.
- Cola tart and marshmallow with lemon cream.

Strand · Covent Garden

It's fitting that Manet's world famous painting 'Bar at the Folies Bergère' should hang in the **Strand** within a champagne cork's throw of theatreland and Covent Garden. This is the area perhaps more than any other which draws in the ticket-buying tourist, eager to grab a good deal on one of the many shows on offer, or eat and drink at fabled shrines like J.Sheekey or Rules. It's here the names already up in lights shine down on their potential usurpers: celeb wannabes heading for The Ivy, West Street's perennially fashionable restaurant. It's here, too, that Nell Gwyn set up home under the patronage of Charles II, while Oscar Wilde revelled in his success by taking rooms at the Savoy.

The hub of the whole area is the piazza at **Covent Garden,** created by Inigo Jones four hundred years ago. It was given a brash new lease of life in the 1980s after its famed fruit and veg market was pulled up by the roots and re-sown in Battersea. Council bigwigs realised then that 'what we have we hold', and any further redevelopment of the area is banned. Where everyone heads is the impressive covered market, within which a colourful jumble of arts and crafts shops gels with al fresco cafés and classical performers proffering Paganini with your cappuccino. Outside, under the portico of St Paul's church, every type of street performer does a turn for the tourist trade. The best shops in Covent Garden, though, are a few streets north of the market melee, emanating out like bicycle spokes from Seven Dials.

For those after a more highbrow experience, one of London's best attractions is a hop, skip and *grand jeté* from the market. Around the corner in **Bow Street** is the city's famed home for opera and ballet, where fire – as well as show-stopping performances – has been known to bring the house down. The **Royal Opera House** is now in its third incarnation, and it gets more impressive with each rebuild. The handsome, glass-roofed Floral Hall is a must-see, while an interval drink at the Amphitheatre Café Bar, overlooking the piazza, is de rigeur for show goers. At the other end of the Strand the **London Coliseum** offers more opera, this time all performed in English. Down by Waterloo Bridge, art lovers are strongly advised to stop at **Somerset House** and take in one of London's most sublime collections of art at the Courtauld Gallery. This is where you can get up close and personal to Manet's barmaid, as well as an astonishing array of Impressionist masters and twentieth century greats. The icing on the cake is the compact and accessible eighteenth century building that houses the collection: real icing on a real cake can be found in a super little hidden-away café downstairs.

Of a different order altogether is the huge **National Gallery** at

AGE / PHOTONONSTOP

Trafalgar Square which houses more than two thousand Western European pieces (it started off with 38). A visit to the modern Sainsbury Wing is rewarded with some unmissable works from the Renaissance. It can get just as crowded in the capital's largest Gallery as in the square outside, so a good idea is to wander down **Villiers Street** next to Charing Cross station and breathe the Thames air along the Victoria Embankment. Behind you is the grand Savoy Hotel, which reopened in 2010 after major refurbishment;

for a better view of it, you can head even further away from the crowds on a boat trip from the **Embankment,** complete with on-board entertainment. And if the glory of travel in the capital, albeit on the water, has whetted your appetite for more, then pop into the impressively renovated Transport Museum in Covent Garden piazza, where gloriously preserved tubes, buses and trains from the past put you in a positive frame of mind for the real live working version you'll very probably be tackling later in the day.

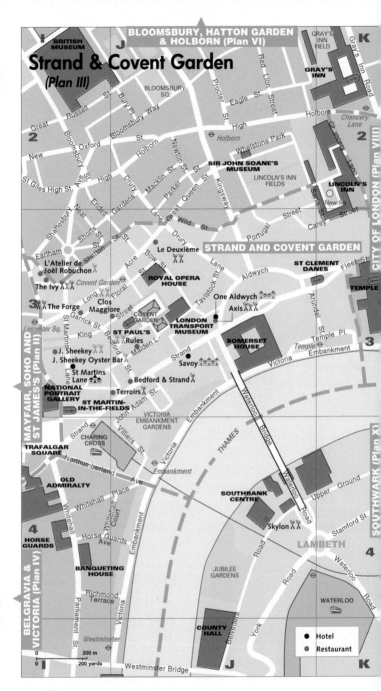

Strand & Covent Garden
(Plan III)

BLOOMSBURY, HATTON GARDEN & HOLBORN (Plan VI)

BRITISH MUSEUM

BLOOMSBURY SQ.

GRAY'S INN FIELD

GRAY'S INN

SIR JOHN SOANE'S MUSEUM

LINCOLN'S INN FIELDS

LINCOLN'S INN

STRAND AND COVENT GARDEN

Le Deuxième

ST CLEMENT DANES

TEMPLE

L'Atelier de Joël Robuchon

The Ivy

Covent Garden

ROYAL OPERA HOUSE

One Aldwych

Axis

The Forge

Clos Maggiore

COVENT GARDEN

LONDON TRANSPORT MUSEUM

SOMERSET HOUSE

ST PAUL'S

Rules

Savoy

J. Sheekey

J. Sheekey Oyster Bar

St Martins Lane

Bedford & Strand

Terroirs

NATIONAL PORTRAIT GALLERY

ST MARTIN-IN-THE-FIELDS

VICTORIA EMBANKMENT GARDENS

CHARING CROSS

THAMES

TRAFALGAR SQUARE

OLD ADMIRALTY

SOUTHBANK CENTRE

Skylon

LAMBETH

HORSE GUARDS

BANQUETING HOUSE

WATERLOO

JUBILEE GARDENS

COUNTY HALL

Westminster

Westminster Bridge

200 m
200 yards

● Hotel
● Restaurant

MAYFAIR, SOHO AND ST JAMES'S (Plan II)

BELGRAVIA & VICTORIA (Plan IV)

CITY OF LONDON (Plan VIII)

SOUTHWARK (Plan XI)

L'Atelier de Joël Robuchon ❀❀

13

13-15 West St. ✉ WC2H 9NE
☏ (020) 7010 8600
e-mail info@joelrobuchon.co.uk
www.joelrobuchon.co.uk

⊖ **Leicester Square**
Closed 25-26 December, 1 January,
Sunday and bank holidays

Carte £45/100

L'Atelier de Joël Robuchon

STRAND & COVENT GARDEN ▶ PLAN III

London's L'Atelier de Joël Robuchon differs from his other 'branches' dotted around the world's culinary hotspots by being two restaurants under one roof: on the ground floor is L'Atelier itself, with an open kitchen and large counter; upstairs is the monochrome La Cuisine, a slightly more structured, sleek and more brightly-lit affair with table seating. Apart from a few wood-fired dishes upstairs, the menus are largely similar. The cooking is artistic, creative and occasionally playful; it is technically very accomplished and highly labour intensive – there are over thirty chefs in the building – but it is never overworked and each dish is perfectly balanced, its flavours true and its taste exquisite. French is the predominant influence, supported by other Mediterranean flavours, and ordering a number of smaller dishes is the best way to fully appreciate Robuchon's craft and vision, although your final bill can be pretty lofty. Service is expertly timed and confident and sitting at the counter will give you some insight into this most polished of operations.

First Course

- Crispy langoustine fritters with basil pistou.
- Quail stuffed with foie gras and truffled mashed potatoes.

Main Course

- Rib of veal with girolles, fondant potatoes and braised sucrine.
- Red mullet with pissaladière and sauce vierge.

Dessert

- Cointreau soufflé with milk chocolate ice cream.
- Rum baba with mandarin marmalade and vanilla cream.

Axis

J3

Modern European 𝄪𝄪𝄪

1 Aldwych ✉ WC2B 4RH ⊖ Temple
☎ (020) 7300 0300 Closed Sunday and Monday
e-mail axis@onealdwych.com
www.onealdwych.com

Menu £20 – Carte £32/42

Expectation is everything and the spiral marble staircase leading down to this restaurant always adds a little excitement. The room, which must have one of the highest ceilings in London, is neatly laid out and service is well organised, if perhaps a little too formal for its own good. One wise decision was the moving of the bar to downstairs; this means there is always a little noise, even when the restaurant has a lull just after the theatre-goers have left. They have made the menu a little lighter by adding salads and a seafood section. More European influences now also sit alongside the British dishes, so you can have smoked salmon, salt beef and treacle sponge or scallops with chorizo, beef bourguignon and a crème brûlée.

Bedford & Strand

J3

British 𝄪

1a Bedford St ✉ WC2E 9HH ⊖ Charing Cross
☎ (020) 7836 3033 Closed 24 December-3 January,
e-mail hello@bedford-strand.com Sunday and bank holidays –
www.bedford-strand.com booking essential

Carte £27/38

Maybe it's the basement location or the discreet entrance, but Bedford & Strand has an almost secretive, clubby feel. The bar dominates proceedings although in a good way – you'll hear the laughter as you come down the stairs – and the character of the place makes you quickly forget about its subterranean location. Wine is given equal billing with the food; the list is sensibly laid out and there's plenty by the glass and carafe. The food menu complements it well and is appealingly to the point; highlights are the British classics like shepherd's pie, potted crab and treacle tart. The young staff make up in eagerness what they lack in direction; and the atmosphere is pleasantly unhurried, despite its proximity to scores of theatres.

96

Clos Maggiore

33 King St ✉ WC2E 8JD
☎ (020) 7379 9696
e-mail enquiries@closmaggiore.com
www.closmaggiore.com

⊖ Leicester Square
Closed lunch 24 December–
26 December

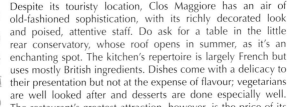

Menu £20 (lunch) – Carte £29/34

Despite its touristy location, Clos Maggiore has an air of old-fashioned sophistication, with its richly decorated look and poised, attentive staff. Do ask for a table in the little rear conservatory, whose roof opens in summer, as it's an enchanting spot. The kitchen's repertoire is largely French but uses mostly British ingredients. Dishes come with a delicacy to their presentation but not at the expense of flavour; vegetarians are well looked after and desserts are done especially well. The restaurant's greatest attraction, however, is the price of its lunch and pre-theatre menus – with an even greater choice at weekends – making this one of the hottest tickets in town. They also take very late bookings for post-theatre debriefing.

STRAND & COVENT GARDEN ▶ PLAN III

Le Deuxième

65a Long Acre ✉ WC2E 9JH
☎ (020) 7379 0033
e-mail info@ledeuxieme.com
www.ledeuxieme.com

⊖ Covent Garden
Closed 24-25 December

Menu £17 (lunch) – Carte £33/38

Don't think that because it's busy in the early evening before curtain-up in all the local theatres that's it's going to quieten down when all the early-diners have gone – it seemingly stays busy most of the evening, most nights. This certainly gives the room plenty of energy but it also means that this is the sort of place where, if you get the attention of the waiter or waitress, you'll want to be ready with your order so as not to waste the opportunity. The menu offers an extensive range of dishes, whose influences come largely from within Europe. In amongst the pastas and the salads are some fairly classic French dishes and this is where the kitchen's experience lies. Side dishes, though, can quickly bump up the bill.

Forge

I3

Modern European ✗✗

14 Garrick St ✉ WC2E 9BJ
✆ (020) 7379 1432
e-mail info@theforgerestaurant.co.uk
www.theforgerestaurant.co.uk

⊖ **Leicester Square**
Closed 24 December and
bank holidays

Menu £17/28 – Carte £31/38

For those who can't decide what they want to eat or at what time, there is The Forge. Open all day, every day, with last orders at midnight, it offers an exhaustive choice of dishes to satisfy both the late-riser and the early-reveller. Omelettes and oysters vie with snails and salads; there's a pasta section and main courses range from whole Dover sole to liver and bacon; so whether it's tournedos Rossini or a hamburger you're after, you'll probably find what you want. Waiters weave between tables and make up in confidence what they sometimes lack in direction. The décor mixes the old with the new and, while the front of the restaurant is more intimate, the back is more fun. There is a good value pre and post theatre menu.

The Ivy

I3

International ✗✗✗

1-5 West St ✉ WC2H 9NQ
✆ (020) 7836 4751
www.the-ivy.co.uk

⊖ **Leicester Square**
Closed 24-26 December and 1 January

Carte £27/52

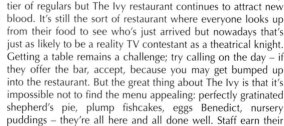

The members-only Ivy Club may have siphoned off the top tier of regulars but The Ivy restaurant continues to attract new blood. It's still the sort of restaurant where everyone looks up from their food to see who's just arrived but nowadays that's just as likely to be a reality TV contestant as a theatrical knight. Getting a table remains a challenge; try calling on the day – if they offer the bar, accept, because you may get bumped up into the restaurant. But the great thing about The Ivy is that it's impossible not to find the menu appealing: perfectly gratinated shepherd's pie, plump fishcakes, eggs Benedict, nursery puddings – they're all here and all done well. Staff earn their crust by frequently but discreetly re-laying the tables.

J. Sheekey

Seafood 🍴🍴

28-32 St Martin's Ct. ✉ WC2 4AL
📞 (020) 7240 2565
www.j-sheekey.co.uk

⊖ Leicester Square
Closed 25-26 December and
1 January – booking essential

Menu £26 (weekend lunch) – Carte £19/64

When one thinks of fashionable restaurants one usually thinks of the glossy and the new but J. Sheekey has been doing its thing since 1896 and its sense of Englishness and links to the theatre still draw a crowd. It helps that they also do fish and seafood rather well, by keeping it all simple. The reassuring sight of potted shrimps, fruits de mer, fishcakes, fish pies and Dover Sole all feature and can be followed by uncomplicated fruit tarts or chocolate puddings so you leave feeling immeasurably satisfied, although a little lighter in the wallet. There are five sections and if you're a regular or your name's been up in lights, then you'll be given a choice of table. Those tables are quite compact but that just adds to the bonhomie.

STRAND & COVENT GARDEN ▶ PLAN III

J. Sheekey Oyster Bar

Seafood 🍴

33-34 St Martin's Ct. ✉ WC2 4AL
📞 (020) 7240 2565
www.j-sheekey.co.uk

⊖ Leicester Square
Closed 25-26 December
and 1 January

Carte £23/35

And you can't even see the join. When the opportunity arose for J. Sheekey to expand next door, the obvious decision would have been to extend the restaurant which has, after all, been working well since 1896. Instead, they decided to create this terrific oyster bar – and for that we should all be grateful. There are four or five tables but you're much better off sitting at the bar as you can chat with the chaps behind it and, if you're on the far side, watch the chefs in action. The tablemat doubles as a menu, which offers the same high quality seafood as next door but at slightly lower prices. Along with favourites like oysters and the individual fish pie, come dishes designed for sharing such as the fruits de mer.

Rules

British XX

35 Maiden Ln. ⊠ WC2E 7LB
☎ (020) 7836 5314
e-mail info@rules.co.uk
www.rules.co.uk

⊖ Leicester Square
Closed 4 days Christmas –
booking essential

Carte £34/58

Some restaurants don't even last 1798 days; Rules opened in 1798, at a time when the French were still revolting, and has been a bastion of Britishness ever since. Virtually every inch of wall is covered with a cartoon or painting and everyone from Charles Dickens to Buster Keaton has passed through its doors. The first floor is now a bar; time it right and you'll spot some modern-day theatrical luminaries who use it as a Green Room. The hardest decision is whether to choose the game, which comes from their own estate in the Pennines, or one of their celebrated homemade pies. Be sure to leave room for their proper puddings, which come with lashings of custard - no wonder John Bull was such a stout fellow. It makes you proud.

Terroirs ⊛

French X

5 William IV St ⊠ WC2N 4DW
☎ (020) 7036 0660
e-mail enquiries@terroirswinebar.com
www.terroirswinebar.com

⊖ Charing Cross
Closed 24-27, 31 December, 1 January,
Sunday and bank holidays

Carte £20/33

The ground floor is as busy and as fun as ever but now you can also eat 'Downstairs at Terroirs', where the menu is slightly more substantial and there's a greater variety of cooking methods used; there are also dishes for two such as the roast Landaise chicken. Tables down here are a little bigger which makes that sharing easier and, despite being two floors down, it is more atmospheric. If you recognise the banquette seating it's because it comes from Mirabelle. Meanwhile, upstairs and downstairs share the same respect for flavoursome and satisfying French cooking, with added Italian and Spanish influences. The wine list is interesting, varied and well-priced. Service remains a mixed bag and can be of the headless chicken variety.

ViaMichelin

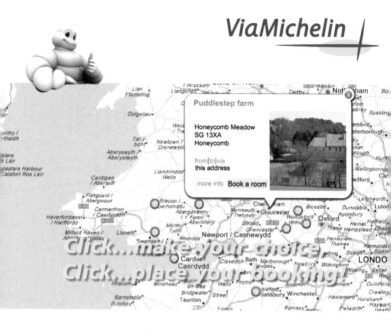

HOTEL BOOKING AT

www.ViaMichelin.com

Plan your route on-line with ViaMichelin to make the most
of all your trips. You can compare routes, select your stops at
recommended restaurants and learn more about any not-to-be-
missed tourist sites along your route. And…for peace of mind,
you can check real-time availability for 100,000 hotels around
the world (independents and chains). Simply specify your
preferences (parking, restaurant, etc) and place your booking
on-line.

- *No booking fee*
- *No cancellation fee*
- *Best available prices*
- *The option to filter and select hotels
from The Michelin Guide*

Belgravia · Victoria

The well-worn cliché 'an area of contrasts' certainly applies to these ill-matched neighbours. To the west, Belgravia equates to fashionable status and elegant, residential calm; to the east, Victoria is a chaotic jumble of backpackers, milling commuters and cheap-and-not-always-so-cheerful hotels. At first sight, you might think there's little to no common ground, but the umbilical cord that unites them is, strange to say, diplomacy and politics. Belgravia's embassies are dotted all around the environs of **Belgrave Square,** while at the furthest end of bustling Victoria Street stands **Parliament Square.**

Belgravia – named after 'beautiful grove' in French - was developed during the nineteenth century by Richard Grosvenor, the second Marquess of Westminster, who employed top architect Thomas Cubitt to come up with something rather fetching for the upper echelons of society. The grandeur of the classical designs has survived for the best part of two centuries, evident in the broad streets and elegant squares, where the rich rub shoulders with the uber-rich beneath the stylish balconies of a consulate or outside a high-end antiques emporium. You can still sample an atmosphere of the village it once was, as long as your idea of a village includes exclusive designer boutiques and even more exclusive mews cottages.

By any stretch of the imagination you'd have trouble thinking of **Victoria** as a village. Its local railway station is one of London's major hubs and its bus station brings in visitors from not only all corners of Britain, but Europe too. Its main 'church', concealed behind office blocks, could hardly be described as humble, either: **Westminster Cathedral** is a grand concoction based on Istanbul's Hagia Sophia, with a view from the top of the bell tower which is breathtaking. From there you can pick out other hidden charms of the area: the dramatic headquarters of Channel 4 TV, the revolving sign famously leading into New Scotland Yard, and the neat little Christchurch Gardens, burial site of Colonel Blood, last man to try and steal the Crown Jewels. Slightly easier for the eye to locate are the grand designs of **Westminster Abbey,** crowning glory and resting place of most of England's kings and queens, and the neo-gothic pile of the **Houses of Parliament.** Victoria may be an eclectic mix of people and architectural styles, but its handy position as a kind of epicentre of the Westminster Village makes it a great place for political chit-chat. And the place to go for that is The Speaker, a pub in Great Peter Street, named after the Commons' centuries-old peacekeeper and 'referee'. It's a backstreet gem, where it's not unknown for a big cheese from the House to be filmed over a pint.

visitlondon.com / MICHELIN

Winston Churchill is someone who would have been quite at home holding forth at The Speaker, and half a mile away in King Charles Street, based within the **Cabinet War Rooms** – the secret underground HQ of the war effort – is the Churchill Museum, stuffed full of all things Churchillian. However, if your passion is more the easel and the brush, then head down to the river where another great institution of the area, **Tate Britain,** gazes out over the Thames. Standing where the grizzly Millbank Penitentiary once festered, it offers, after the National Gallery, the best collection of historical art in London. There's loads of space for the likes of Turner and Constable, while Hogarth, Gainsborough and Blake are well represented, too. Artists from the modern era are also here, with Freud and Hockney on show, and there are regular installations showcasing upwardly mobile British talent. All of which may give you the taste for a trip east along the river to Tate Modern. This can be done every twenty minutes courtesy of the Tate-to-Tate boat service, which handily stops enroute at the London Eye, and, even more handily, sports eye-catching Damien Hirst décor and a cool, shiny bar.

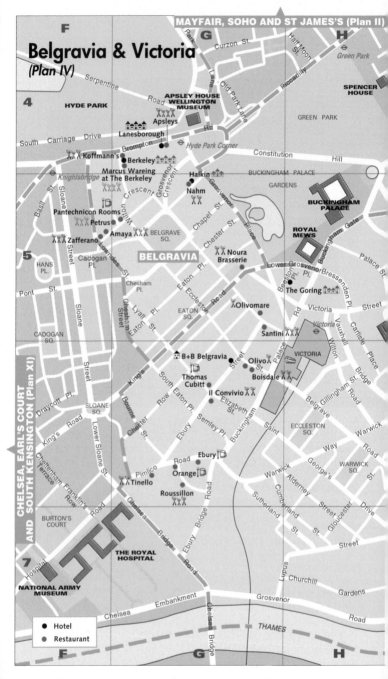

Belgravia & Victoria
(Plan IV)

F G H

Curzon St.

Half Moon St.

Green Park

SPENCER HOUSE

Piccadilly

Serpentine

Park Lane

Old Park Lane

4

HYDE PARK

APSLEY HOUSE
WELLINGTON MUSEUM

Apsleys

Lanesborough

GREEN PARK

South Carriage Drive

Brompton

Hyde Park Corner

Constitution Hill

Koffmann's

Berkeley

Marcus Wareing at The Berkeley

Knightsbridge

Halkin

Nahm

BUCKINGHAM PALACE GARDENS

BUCKINGHAM PALACE

Crescent

Grosvenor Crescent

Chapel St.

Chester St.

ROYAL MEWS

Buckingham Gate

Pantechnicon Rooms

Petrus

Zafferano

Amaya

BELGRAVE SQ.

BELGRAVIA

Wilton

Basil St.

Sloane St.

Cadogan Pl.

Lowndes St.

HANS PL.

Pont St.

Sloane

Chesham Pl.

Chesham Street

Lyall Pl.

Lyall St.

Eaton Pl.

Noura Brasserie

Lower Grosvenor Pl.

Bressenden Pl.

Palace St.

The Goring

Victoria

Carlisle Place

Street

CADOGAN SQ.

Eaton St.

Eccleston

EATON SQ.

Olivomare

Santini

Victoria

VICTORIA

Wilton Rd.

Bridge

Draycott Pl.

SLOANE SQ.

King's Road

Lower Sloane St.

Bourne St.

Chester St.

B+B Belgravia

Thomas Cubitt

Il Convivio

Olivo

Boisdale

St.

Elizabeth St.

Buckingham

Saint

Belgrave

Gillingham St.

ECCLESTON SQ.

Way

George's

WARWICK SQ.

Warwick Road

CHELSEA, EARL'S COURT AND SOUTH KENSINGTON (Plan XII)

King's Road

Cheltenham Terrace

Franklin's Row

South Eaton Pl.

Ebury

Semley Pl.

Ebury

Orange

Pimlico

Tinello

Roussillon

Alderney

Street

Gloucester

Cumberland St.

Drive

Sutherland St.

Warwick

BURTON'S COURT

Chelsea

Chelsea Bridge

Ebury Bridge Road

7

THE ROYAL HOSPITAL

Hospital

NATIONAL ARMY MUSEUM

Churchill

Gardens

Lindsay

Grosvenor

Road

Chelsea Embankment

Chelsea Bridge

THAMES

● Hotel
● Restaurant

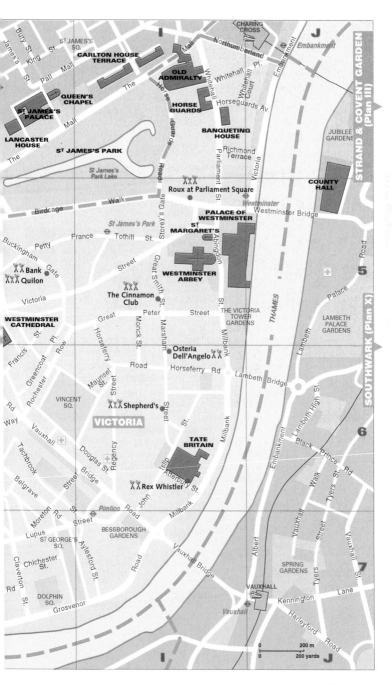

Amaya ✿

F5

Halkin Arcade, 19 Motcomb St
✉ SW1X 8JT
☎ (020) 7823 1166
e-mail amaya@realindianfood.com
www.realindianfood.com

⊖ **Knightsbridge**
Closed 25 December

Menu £25/39 – Carte £32/68

A/C

VISA

MC

AE

Amaya

Since its opening in 2004, Amaya has built up a tremendous following for the quality and consistency of its food. The tandoor, the tawa griddle and the sigri charcoal grill are all used to great effect and the spicing enhances the natural flavours of the ingredients. Dishes arrive as and when they are ready; to best experience the variety and range of the menu, order a number of small plates to share and then finish with a curry or biryani – or else plump for the Gourmet or Tasting menus where the selection has already been made for you. Seafood plays a large part, with rock oysters, grouper and prawns competing with the ever popular tandoori monkfish. The delicate and flavoursome lamb chops are another dish that almost everyone seems to order and one shouldn't ignore the imaginative vegetable dishes. The interior is suitably bright and colourful, with the raised section nearest the open kitchen offering the best seats. Service can be a touch muted at times; a possible consequence of the sheer volume of business.

First Course	*Main Course*	*Dessert*
• Tarragon and turmeric chicken tikka. • Tandoori wild prawns with tomato and ginger.	• Duck grilled with tamarind glaze. • Lemon sole with coconut and herb crust.	• Rose petal crème brûlée. • Pomegranate and mango granita.

Apsleys ✿

Hyde Park Corner ⊠ SW1X 7TA ⊖ Hyde Park Corner
℘ (020) 7333 7254
e-mail apsley@lanesborough.com
www.apsleys.co.uk

Menu £28/35 – Carte £51/80

The Lanesborough

BELGRAVIA & VICTORIA ▶ PLAN IV

Heinz Beck is a German-born chef responsible for some pretty exceptional Italian cooking in his restaurant La Pergola in Rome. Apsleys is very much his creation and he is actively involved in the operation, although he does have a head chef who is extremely committed and passionate about his craft. The sourcing of the finest ingredients is the starting point; vegetables are imported from Italy but meat and fish are from much nearer to home. Proving that not all Italian food has to be of the rustic, thrown-together variety, the cooking displays a deft, light touch and there are subtle hints of innovation, such as in one of the signature dishes, carbonara fagottelli. Designed by the ubiquitous Adam Tihany, the room is elegant and undeniably opulent, but its grandeur never intimidates, thanks largely to the assured serving team who are adept at putting their guests at ease. They are also well-versed in the menu and offer fuller explanations, which is just as well as the menu descriptions are understated to say the least.

First Course	*Main Course*	*Dessert*
• Potato agnolotti with lobster.	• Pigeon with pearl onions and mustard seed sauce.	• Chocolate dome with mint and sea salt ice cream.
• Fish crudo.	• Turbot in salt crust with pepper and potato terrine.	• Ricotta soufflé with passion fruit and chocolate.

Bank

H5

45 Buckingham Gate ✉ SW1E 6BS
✆ (020) 7630 6644
e-mail alison.berry@bankrestaurants.com
www.bankrestaurants.com

⊖ St James's Park
Closed Saturday lunch,
Sunday and bank holidays –
booking essential at lunch

Carte £34/49

Unlike certain financial institutions, this bank seems to know what it's doing. It occupies a generous space within the Crowne Plaza Hotel but, as it has its own street entrance, feels very much like a stand-alone restaurant. It's bright and breezy inside, with the long Zander bar running down the length of one wall and the conservatory overlooking a pleasant little courtyard garden. The menu is an international affair, with the kitchen travelling to all parts, but it's clearly laid out. Steaks are a popular choice; there are plenty of pasta dishes and whether you like your fish in a pie or cooked with Thai herbs, there's something for you. The biggest surprise is the thoroughly cheerful and unexpectedly enthusiastic service.

Boisdale

G6

15 Eccleston St ✉ SW1W 9LX
✆ (020) 7730 6922
e-mail info@boisdale.co.uk
www.boisdale.co.uk

⊖ Victoria
Closed 1 week Christmas, Saturday
lunch and Sunday

Menu £20 – Carte £30/64

Acres of tartan, whiskies galore, haggis, mash and neeps - Boisdale couldn't be more Scottish if it sang Scots Wha Hae and did the Highland Fling. Owner Ranald Macdonald bought various parts of the building at different times, hence the charmingly higgledy-piggledy layout. The original Auld restaurant is the more characterful; the Macdonald Bar has more buzz and nightly live jazz and a large cigar selection add to the masculine feel. The menu features plenty of Scottish produce, from Orkney herring to Shetland scallops, but the stand-outs are the four varieties of smoked salmon, followed by the 28-day aged Aberdeenshire cuts of beef. Ignore the lacklustre tomato and watercress garnish and just savour the quality of the meat.

The Cinnamon Club

Indian XXX

30-32 Great Smith St ⊠ SW1P 3BU
𝒫 (020) 7222 2555
e-mail info@cinnamonclub.com
www.cinnamonclub.com

⊖ St James's Park
Closed 1 January,
Sunday and bank holidays

Menu £22 – Carte £29/45

The Grade II listed former Westminster library may seem an unlikely setting for an Indian restaurant but it works surprisingly well. The shelves of books are still there on the mezzanine level of the large main room where the action is, although the smaller front room has better air-conditioning. There are two bars: the one downstairs is the livelier. A variety of menus are on offer and prices can get quite steep but the cooking clearly displays ambition and innovation. Many of the ingredients may be more European, like Herdwick lamb or Anjou pigeon, but the cooking techniques, colours and spices are resolutely Indian. Staff are on the ball, as you'd expect from somewhere serving over 200 people twice a day.

Il Convivio

Italian XX

143 Ebury St ⊠ SW1W 9QN
𝒫 (020) 7730 4099
e-mail comments@etruscarestaurants.com
www.etruscarestaurants.com

⊖ Sloane Square
Closed Christmas-New Year,
Sunday and bank holidays

Carte £34/50

If only passing by, you'll find yourself being drawn in by the appealing façade of this handsome Georgian townhouse – and there's usually an eager welcome to boot, whether you're a regular or first-timer. Inside is equally pleasant, with Dante's poetry embossed on the wall to remind you you're in an Italian restaurant and a retractable roof at the back, under which sit the best tables. All pasta is made on the top floor of the house; the squid ink spaghetti with lobster is a menu staple. Dishes are artfully presented but not so showy as to compromise the flavours. Artisanal cheeses are carefully selected and looked after, while service is confident and able. Using the private dining room allows you to imagine being the owner of the house.

Ebury

G6 Gastropub

11 Pimlico Rd ⊠ SW1W 8NA
✆ (020) 7730 6784
e-mail info@theebury.co.uk
www.theebury.co.uk

⊖ Sloane Square.
Closed 25-26 December

Menu £20 (lunch and early dinner) – Carte £30/45

A/C
☀
VISA
MC
AE
◐

Grab a passing waiter to get yourself seated otherwise they'll assume you've just come for a drink at the bar and will ignore you. Once you've got your feet under one of the low-slung tables, however, you'll find everything moves up a gear. This is a rather smart affair and provides an object lesson in how to draw in punters. That means a varied menu, from burger to black bream, assorted salads that show some thought, three vegetarian dishes and main courses that display a degree of originality. Add to that a conscientious kitchen, a wine list that offers plenty by the glass and carafe, and weekend brunch that goes on until 4pm and it's little wonder the place is always so busy. The waiters come with French accents and self-confidence.

Koffmann's

G4 French

Wilton Pl. ⊠ SW1X 7RL
✆ (020) 7235 1010
e-mail koffmanns@the-berkeley.co.uk
www.the-berkeley.co.uk

⊖ Knightsbridge

Menu £23 (lunch) – Carte £46/77

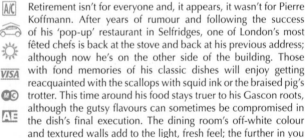

Retirement isn't for everyone and, it appears, it wasn't for Pierre Koffmann. After years of rumour and following the success of his 'pop-up' restaurant in Selfridges, one of London's most fêted chefs is back at the stove and back at his previous address; although now he's on the other side of the building. Those with fond memories of his classic dishes will enjoy getting reacquainted with the scallops with squid ink or the braised pig's trotter. This time around his food stays truer to his Gascon roots, although the gutsy flavours can sometimes be compromised in the dish's final execution. The dining room's off-white colour and textured walls add to the light, fresh feel; the further in you go, the better the table.

Marcus Wareing
at The Berkeley ⬩⬩

G4

Wilton Pl. ✉ SW1X 7RL   ⊖ Knightsbridge
✆ (020) 7235 1200   Closed Saturday lunch and Sunday
e-mail marcuswareing@the-berkeley.co.uk
www.marcus-wareing.com

Menu £38/75

A/C
⟨⟩
⟨⟩⟨⟩
VISA
MC
AE

Marcus Wareing at The Berkeley

BELGRAVIA & VICTORIA ▶ PLAN IV

There is nothing like a little competition amongst chefs, especially when it appears under the same roof. Thanks to the opening of Koffmann's on its north side, The Berkeley is now book-ended by two very good restaurants. On his side of the hotel, Marcus Wareing has put his separation from Gordon Ramsay well and truly behind him, delivering a formal dining experience involving confident and expertly constructed dishes. He is a chef who appreciates the importance of using the best quality of produce and, as such, will treat a carrot with as much respect as foie gras. His Prestige and Gourmand menus allow the diner to sample the full diversity of the cooking, which is mostly French in its influences and techniques but is not afraid of a little originality here and there. Desserts are a strength of the kitchen and, if you are one of those who likes to see how it's all done, then consider the Chef's Table, which is one of the best in town. Service is structured and deliberate, although a little more personality would not go amiss.

First Course	*Main Course*	*Dessert*
• Sweetbread, ginger and pineapple gastrique.	• Halibut with lobster, asparagus and almonds.	• Basil parfait with lemon caramel and sherbet.
• Langoustines with onion, pine and blueberries.	• Lamb with peas, peach and black olive.	• Granny Smith apple crème, spiced brioche and salted caramel.

Nahm

Thai XX

5 Halkin St. ✉ SW1X 7DJ
✆ (020) 7333 1234
e-mail res@nahm.como.bz
www.halkin.como.bz

⊖ Hyde Park Corner
Closed lunch Saturday and Sunday
– booking advisable

Menu £25/60 – Carte £40/50

AC

VISA

MC

AE

An appealing mix of copper tones, wood and candlelight, along with an understated hint of Asian design, allows the restaurant to blend effortlessly into the slick and stylish surroundings of the boutique Halkin hotel in which it is located. The Thai cuisine served here is based on Royal Thai traditions and the flavours and combinations of ingredients are authentic. However, the cooking has recently lost some of its essential vitality, which is one of the fundamental elements of Thai cuisine, and dishes can sometimes be let down by careless execution. Perhaps it was the opening of another Nahm in 2010, this time in Bangkok itself, that lead to the slight drop in the standard here at the original outpost.

Noura Brasserie

Lebanese XX

16 Hobart Pl. ✉ SW1W 0HH
✆ (020) 7235 9444
e-mail noura@noura.co.uk
www.noura.co.uk

⊖ Victoria

Menu £18/45 – Carte £24/39

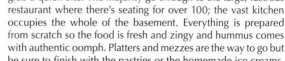

The Belgravia branch was the first of the Lebanese Noura restaurants to appear on these shores and such is its appeal that it's an all-day operation. You're greeted by the enticing sight of sweet, sticky pastries and it's here at the bar where you can grab a quick bite. The majority go through to the large, lustrous restaurant where there's seating for over 100; the vast kitchen occupies the whole of the basement. Everything is prepared from scratch so the food is fresh and zingy and hummus comes with authentic oomph. Platters and mezzes are the way to go but be sure to finish with the pastries or the homemade ice creams, the flavours of which could include rosewater or clotted cream. Staff have a certain seen-it-all insouciance.

Olivo

Italian 🍴

G6

21 Eccleston St ⊠ SW1W 9LX
📞 (020) 7730 2505
e-mail shayne@olivetorestaurant.com
www.olivorestaurant.com

⊖ **Victoria**
Closed lunch Saturday and
Sunday and bank holidays

Menu £25 (lunch) – Carte dinner £33/38

Olivo is one of those places that, despite the constant banging of the front door, the somewhat monosyllabic waitress and the permanently aloof manager, are always bursting with bonhomie. The restaurant is simply kitted out in blues and yellows and its infectious atmosphere is most evident at lunch. It celebrates all things Sardinian so start with a glass of Vernaccia and carta di musica bread and finish with a glass of Mirto after you've had the sebada cheese fritters for dessert. Lunch is set priced and dinner à la carte; both are nicely balanced and appealing affairs, with the 'spaghetti alla bottarga' being an unquestionable highlight. The wine list is concise but decent value and bottles can be bought at nearby Olivino.

Olivomare

Seafood 🍴

G5

10 Lower Belgrave St ⊠ SW1W 0LJ
📞 (020) 7730 9022
e-mail shayne@olivetorestaurant.com
www.olivorestaurants.com

⊖ **Victoria**
Closed bank holidays

Carte £36/39

Olivomare is a restaurant that makes you want to live by the sea and, looking at the produce in their shop next door, that sea would be the Tyrrhenian. The room's piscatorial decoration – a sort of Philippe Starck gone fishin' – works well, especially when it's so cleverly lit. The menu changes every fortnight and has a Sardinian base to it. The kitchen buys the freshest fish, treats it with respect and uses traditional recipes. The fritto misto is excellent; razor clams and octopus have quite a following and the spaghetti with bottarga or half a lobster are favourites too. Be sure to end with gelato, which is also available in the shop, Olivino. Service would be better if they took their blinkers off and looked around more.

Orange

Gastropub 🍺

37-39 Pimlico Rd ⊠ SW1W 8NE   ⊖ Sloane Square.
℘ (020) 7881 9844
e-mail reservations@theorange.co.uk
www.theorange.co.uk

Carte £23/26

🔆 The Belgravia-Victoria-Pimlico quarter is clearly working for
the team behind The Thomas Cubitt and Pantechnicon Rooms
VISA because their latest pub, The Orange, is within shouting distance
of their other two and appears to be equally busy. There are a
🅜🅒 couple of differences: this pub has bedrooms, nicely decorated
🅐🅔 and named after the local streets, and the food is a little more
down-to-earth and family-friendly. Pizza in the bar from their
wood-fired oven is always a popular choice; there's Film Night
on Mondays and, unusually, the first floor restaurant is noisier
than the bar. The building's stucco-fronted façade may be quite
grand but the colonial feel inside and the particularly friendly
service create a pleasantly laid-back atmosphere.

Osteria Dell' Angolo

Italian 🍴🍴

47 Marsham St. ⊠ SW1P 3DR   ⊖ St. James's Park
℘ (020) 3268 1077   Closed 24-31 December,
e-mail osteriadell-angolo@btconnect.com   Saturday lunch,
www.osteriadellangolo.co.uk   Sunday and bank holidays

Menu £15/20 – Carte £29/42

A/C In over 30 years in London, Claudio Pulze has opened more
than 50 restaurants so you could say he knows what he's
 doing. One of his most recent ventures is this Italian restaurant
opposite the Home Office which is altogether smarter than the
VISA name suggests. It's bright and sunny inside, with a front bar;
🅜🅒 larger groups should ask for tables 14 or 15. The enthusiastic
team is run by an effusive manager who recognises all his
🅐🅔 regulars. There is a subtle Tuscan element to the cooking but
 the kitchen is also prone to adding a little playfulness or doing
a little reinterpreting of the classics. Pastas and breads, made
downstairs, are very good. The wine list is well-priced and
includes a decent choice by the glass.

Pantechnicon Rooms

Gastropub

10 Motcomb St ⊠ SW1X 8LA
℘ (020) 7730 6074
e-mail reservations@thepantechnicon.com
www.thepantechnicon.com

⊖ Knightsbridge

Carte £30/45

The name 'Pantechnicon' either refers to a large removal wagon or the antique repository which once sat on Motcomb Street until it was destroyed by fire in the 1870s. It's no clearer inside, as you'll find both sepia photos of assorted removal vehicles as well as a painting depicting the fire. But one thing is certain: this is the antithesis of a spit 'n' sawdust pub. The ground floor is first-come-first-served and is always lively but upstairs is an altogether more gracious affair, designed for those who like a little formality with their pheasant. The cooking is traditional but with a twist. Oysters are a perennial; there's a decent salad selection and they set their stall by the traceability of their mature Scottish steaks.

BELGRAVIA & VICTORIA ▶ PLAN IV

Rex Whistler

British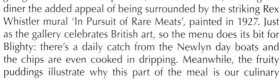

Tate Britain, Millbank ⊠ SW1P 4RG
℘ (020) 7887 8825
e-mail britain.restaurant@tate.org.uk
www.tate.org.uk/britain/eatanddrink

⊖ Pimlico
Closed 24-26 December –
booking essential –
(lunch only)

Menu £20 – Carte £33/40

Galleries everywhere are finally seeing the value of having a decent restaurant but the one here at Tate Britain has been going since 1972. It's a spacious, masculine room, offering the diner the added appeal of being surrounded by the striking Rex Whistler mural 'In Pursuit of Rare Meats', painted in 1927. Just as the gallery celebrates British art, so the menu does its bit for Blighty: there's a daily catch from the Newlyn day boats and the chips are even cooked in dripping. Meanwhile, the fruity puddings illustrate why this part of the meal is our culinary crowning glory. The wine list is truly excellent: it is intelligently laid out, full of gems and has over 80 half bottles, many of which are from wines rarely seen in halves.

Pétrus ✿

Modern European 𝓧𝓧𝓧

1 Kinnerton St. ✉ SW1X 8EA ⊖ Knightsbridge
✆ (020) 7592 1609 Closed 25 December and Sunday
e-mail petrus@gordonramsay.com
www.gordonramsay.com/petrus

Menu £25/55

Michelin

Following his divorce from Marcus Wareing, Gordon Ramsay
came away with custody of the name Pétrus and he has used
the appellation for this smart Belgravia restaurant, opened in
2010, in challengingly close proximity to the premises of his
former protégé. It's attractively decorated in understated tones
of silver, oyster and – to add warmth and as a nod to the name
– claret. Tables are immaculately dressed and service is under
the watchful eye of an experienced team who never let things
get too reverential. Downstairs is the 'show' kitchen with its
horseshoe shaped chef's table, for those whose enjoyment of
a meal is sharpened by watching a large brigade of chefs – in
this case around 14 – beavering away in front of them. Sceptical
diners should initially try lunch, when they'll find a set menu
that won't break the bank. There are also vegetarian and chef's
menus alongside the appealing à la carte of French-based
dishes. In a break with tradition and in a nod to Thomas Keller,
the cheese trolley is replaced by a single cheese offered as a
'savoury pudding'.

First Course
- Langoustine tail with
  watercress soup and
  confit potato.
- Foie gras with confit
  and smoked duck,
  pear carpaccio and
  cardamom caramel.

Main Course
- Beef fillet and shin
  with celeriac and
  Barolo sauce.
- Halibut with braised
  fennel and a citrus
  coriander sauce.

Dessert
- Chocolate sphere
  with milk ice cream
  and honeycomb.
- Pineapple with
  coconut panna
  cotta, lime and chilli
  syrup.

Quilon ✿

H5

41 Buckingham Gate ✉ SW1E 6AF
✆ (020) 7821 1899
e-mail info@quilonrestaurant.co.uk
www.quilon.co.uk

⊖ St James's Park
Closed Saturday lunch

Menu £22/39 – Carte dinner £34/57

Quilon

BELGRAVIA & VICTORIA ▶ PLAN IV

The flower-filled window boxes and the mellow lighting draw you in while an effusive welcome reassures you that you've made the right choice. Chef Sriram Aylur and his brigade are a committed and enthusiastic lot who understand the importance of consistency in their cooking. Their menu is influenced by India's southwest coast and changes with the seasons. Much of the produce is from the UK but spices are imported from India and ground in the kitchen. Fish is naturally a strength, whether in a broth, a curry or roasted in a plantain leaf, and, as in Kerala, there are plenty of vegetarian dishes. The kitchen's light touch is evident while the spicing is assured and balanced and rice and breads are prepared with equal care. It is also clear that the serving team enjoy a good relationship with the kitchen – which is not something that happens in all restaurants –so one can happily mix and match starters or even have smaller sized main courses if one requires a little flexibility. The room is quite large but one never feels at sea.

First Course	*Main Course*	*Dessert*
• Spiced oysters and lentils with onion relish.	• Koondapur halibut curry and tamarind gravy.	• Spiced dark chocolate and hazelnut mousse.
• Smoked mushroom and soya bean chop.	• Pistachio lamb with chilli and spices.	• Appam rice pancake.

Roussillon

French XXX

16 St Barnabas St ⊠ SW1W 8PE
℘ (020) 7730 5550
e-mail michael.lear@roussillon.co.uk
www.roussillon.co.uk

⊖ Sloane Square
Closed Christmas-New Year,
Saturday lunch and Sunday

Menu £35/60

A/C
88
VISA
MC
AE

Even the most dependable restaurants eventually change. In 2010, Roussillon had to face the upheaval caused by the departure of their longstanding chef, and it may take a while for it to find its feet once again. However, it has always had a loyal local following who also appreciated that their 'hidden jewel' kept itself below the fashion radar. The amount of menu choice remains largely unchanged but the cooking is now less French in its influence and therefore somewhat at odds with the restaurant's name; it is instead more creative – if slightly lacking in the clarity and balance which were once its hallmarks. The restaurant itself remains unchanged in its decoration and retains a comfortable, grown up and understated feel.

Roux at Parliament Square

French XXX

RICS, Parliament Sq. ⊠ SW1P 3AD
℘ (020) 7334 3737
e-mail roux@rics.org
www.rouxatparliamentsquare.co.uk

⊖ Westminster
Closed Christmas-New Year,
Saturday and Sunday

Menu £30/55

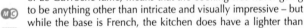

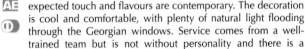

In this part of Westminster, chartered surveyors and Members of Parliament have never been faced with a plethora of restaurants from which to choose, but the opening of Roux at Parliament Square has helped fill the void. Knowing that the Roux is Michel, of Le Gavroche fame, means that the cooking was never going to be anything other than intricate and visually impressive – but while the base is French, the kitchen does have a lighter than expected touch and flavours are contemporary. The decoration is cool and comfortable, with plenty of natural light flooding through the Georgian windows. Service comes from a well-trained team but is not without personality and there is a particularly attractive private dining room in the library.

Santini

Italian ✗✗✗

29 Ebury St ✉ SW1W 0NZ   ⊖ Victoria
℘ (020) 7730 4094   Closed 1 January, Easter, 23-27 December,
e-mail santini@santini-restaurant.com   lunch Saturday and Sunday
www.santini-restaurant.com

Menu £25 (dinner) – Carte £29/54

Like many of its bronzed customers, Santini really comes into its own in the summer: the white walls and marble flooring are crisp and cooling and the terrace must be one of the largest around. Family-owned since 1984, it has never been the cheapest Italian around but then this was never the sort of place that pretended to be accessible to all and the service is decidedly old-school; the type that intimidated you when you were young. But the food, with its mild Venetian accent, is very good. Homemade pastas are excellent and the zabaglione is a gloriously rich concoction. Further evidence of the restaurant's self-belief is in the number of times its name appears in dishes, so you can follow insalata Santini with branzino Santini.

BELGRAVIA & VICTORIA ▶ PLAN IV

Shepherd's

British ✗✗✗

Marsham Ct., Marsham St. ✉ SW1P 4LA   ⊖ Pimlico
℘ (020) 7834 9552   Closed bank holidays –
e-mail admin@langansrestaurants.co.uk   booking essential
www.langansrestaurants.co.uk

Menu £38

Looking at the number of shiny pates and pin-striped suits that pile into Shepherd's for lunch you'd be forgiven for thinking that 'Blair's Babes' never left much of a legacy. This is a classic, old-school blokey institution that could show some of those new restaurants a thing or two. For starters, it runs on wheels and gives the punters what they want. The atmosphere is animated throughout, but the booths are the best places to sit. The menu is a combination of classic dishes and brasserie favourites but your best bet is to head for those bits of the menu that read like a UKIP manifesto – the fiercely British specialities, like the daily roast or the Dover Sole, followed by an indulgent dessert like a sponge pudding.

Thomas Cubitt

Gastropub

44 Elizabeth St ⊠ SW1W 9PA
℘ (020) 7730 6060
e-mail reservations@thethomascubitt.co.uk
www.thethomascubitt.co.uk

⊖ Sloane Square.
Booking essential

Carte £30/45

The Thomas Cubitt is a pub of two halves: on the ground floor it's perennially busy and you can't book which means that if you haven't arrived by 7pm then you're too late to get a table. However, you can reserve a table upstairs, in a dining room that's a model of civility and tranquillity. Here, service comes courtesy of a young team where the girls are chatty and the men unafraid of corduroy. Downstairs you get fish and chips; here you get pan-fried fillet of brill with oyster beignet and truffled chips. The cooking is certainly skilled, quite elaborate in its construction and prettily presented. So, take your pick: upstairs can get a little pricey but is ideal for entertaining the in-laws; if out with friends then crowd in downstairs.

Tinello

Italian ✗✗

87 Pimlico Rd ⊠ SW1W 8PH
℘ (020) 7730 3663
e-mail info@tinello.co.uk
www.tinello.co.uk

⊖ Sloane Square
Closed 24 December-2 January and Sunday
– booking essential at dinner

Carte £32/37

Italian restaurants have always thrived in this neighbourhood but it's no bad thing for a newcomer to shake things up and that's exactly what Tinello is doing. It is run by two Italian brothers, Max and Federico, who previously worked as sommelier and head chef respectively at Locanda Locatelli. The majority of the menu leans on their native Tuscany for inspiration and this is especially evident in the tempting antipasti or 'small eats' section. Pasta is exemplary and main courses ooze confidence. Service is undertaken with a refreshing earnestness and the sleek restaurant is spread over two floors; the ground floor is more fun, but if you are downstairs you do get to see the kitchen in action through the glass windows.

Zafferano ✿

Italian 🍴🍴🍴

F5

15 Lowndes St ✉ SW1X 9EY
✆ (020) 7235 5800
e-mail info@zafferanorestaurant.com
www.zafferanorestaurant.com

⊖ **Knightsbridge**
Closed Christmas-New Year –
booking essential

Carte £36/65

A/C

VISA
MC
AE

BELGRAVIA & VICTORIA ▶ PLAN IV

Zafferano

Such is the enduring nature of Zafferano's popularity that it is always busy, almost from the moment they unlock the front door each day. We all like a bit of bustle and bonhomie in a restaurant and this place doesn't disappoint, although the waiters do have a propensity to charge around as though their pants are on fire. If you favour less frenzy then ask to sit in the smaller end room. The deli may not have worked but the bar has proved a big success - regulars sometimes just pop in there for a plate of pasta. In fact, a plate of pasta should be ordered wherever you're sitting as it is a real strength of the kitchen, which operates under the expert guidance of Andy Needham who proves that Yorkshire doesn't just produce great cricketers. His menus provide an object lesson in how to satisfy your customers: they are reassuringly recognisable yet also seasonal and are supplemented with a few daily specials. The assured cooking ensures that natural flavours are to the fore. The wine list also continues to grow, with the recent addition of more choice from southern parts.

First Course	*Main Course*	*Dessert*
• Cured pork in figs, mozzarella in carrozza.	• Pappardelle with lamb ragu and pecorino cheese.	• Chocolate fondant with gianduia chocolate ice cream.
• French beans and cuttlefish salad with olives.	• Monkfish with courgettes and sweet chilli.	• Cherry and almond tart with vanilla ice cream.

Regent's Park · Marylebone

The neighbourhood north of chaotic Oxford Street is actually a rather refined place where shoppers like to venture for the smart boutiques, and where idlers like to saunter for the graceful parkland acres full of rose gardens and quiet corners. In fact, Marylebone and Regent's Park go rather well together, a moneyed village with a wonderful park for its back garden.

Marylebone may now exude a fashionable status, but its history tells a very different tale. Thousands used to come here to watch executions at Tyburn gallows, a six hundred year spectacle that stopped in the late eighteenth century. Tyburn stream was covered over, and the area's modern name came into being as a contraction of St Mary by the Bourne, the parish church. Nowadays the people who flock here come to gaze at less ghoulish sights, though some of the inhabitants of the eternally popular Madame Tussauds deserved no better fate than the gallows. South across the busy Marylebone Road, the preponderance of swish restaurants and snazzy specialist shops announces your arrival at **Marylebone High Street.** There are patisseries, chocolatiers, cheese shops and butchers at every turn, nestling alongside smart places to eat and drink. At St Marylebone Church, each Saturday heralds a posh market called Cabbages & Frocks, where artisan food meets designer clothing in a charming garden. Further down, the century old Daunt Books has been described as London's most beautiful bookshop: it has long oak galleries beneath graceful conservatory skylights. Close by, the quaintly winding Marylebone Lane boasts some truly unique shops like tiny emporium The Button Queen, which sells original Art Deco, Victorian and Edwardian buttons. In complete contrast, just down the road from here is the mighty **Wigmore Hall,** an art nouveau gem with great acoustics and an unerringly top-notch classical agenda that can be appreciated at rock-bottom prices. Meanwhile, art lovers can indulge an eclectic fix at the **Wallace Collection** in **Manchester Square,** where paintings by the likes of Titian and Velazquez rub shoulders with Sevres porcelain and grand Louis XIV furniture.

Regent's Park – an idyllic Georgian oasis stretching off into London's northern suburbs - celebrates its two hundredth birthday in 2011. Before architect John Nash and his sponsor The Prince Regent gave it its much-loved geometric makeover, it had been farming land, and prior to that, one of Henry VIII's hunting grounds. His spirit lives on, in the sense that various activities are catered for, from tennis courts to a running track. And there are animals too, albeit not roaming free, at **London Zoo,** in the park's northerly section. Most people,

C. Eymenier / MICHELIN

though, come here to while away an hour or two around the boating lake or amble the Inner Circle which contains **Queen Mary's Gardens** and their enchanting bowers of fragrant roses. Others come for a summer sojourn to the Open Air Theatre where taking in a performance of 'A Midsummer Night's Dream' is very much *de rigueur*. The Regent's Canal provides another fascinating element to the park. You can follow its peaceful waters along a splendid walk from the **Little Venice** houseboats in the west, past the golden dome of the **London Central Mosque,** and on into the north-west confines of Regent's Park as it snakes through London Zoo, before it heads off towards Camden Lock. On the other side of Prince Albert Road, across from the zoo, the scenic glory takes on another dimension with a climb up Primrose Hill. Named after the grassy promontory that sets it apart from its surrounds, to visitors this is a hill with one of the best panoramas in the whole of London; to locals (ie, actors, pop stars, media darlings and the city set) it's an ultra fashionable place to live with pretty Victorian terraces and accordingly sky-high prices. Either way you look at it (or from it), it's a great place to be on a sunny day with the breeze in your hair.

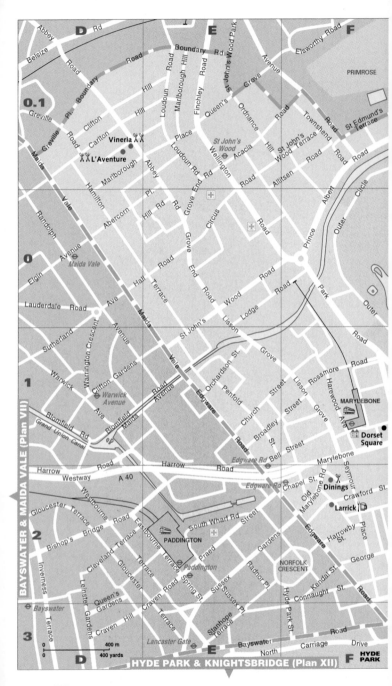

D Rd

Abbey

Belsize

Road

Boundary

Road

Boundary Rd

Loudoun Road

Marlborough Hill

Finchley Road

Queen's

Grove

St John's Wood Park

Avenue

Elsworthy Road

PRIMROSE

Greville Pl.

Boundary

Greville Road

Clifton

Carlton

Hill

Hill

Ordnance

Townshend Road

St Edmund's Terrace

Road

Maida

Maida Vale

Vineria ✕✕

✕✕ L'Aventure

Marlborough

Abbey Pl.

Place

Loudun Rd

Wellington

St John's Wood

Acacia

St John's Wood Terrace

St John's Wood Road

Road

Allitsen

Prince

Albert

Cicle

Outer

Hamilton

Abercorn

Hill Rd

Rd

Grove End Rd

Circus

Road

Randolph

Avenue

Maida Vale

Grove

End

Road

Wood

Road

Road

Park

Outer

Elgin

Hall

Terrace

Road

Lodge

Lisson

Prince

Lauderdale

Road

Ave

Maida

St John's

Grove

Rossmore

Road

Harewood

Sutherland

Warrington Crescent

Avenue

Warwick

Clifton Gardens

Warwick Avenue

Blomfield

Rd

Blomfield

Maida

Orchardson St.

Penfold

Church

Broadley

Lisson

Grove

Street

Street

Street

MARYLEBONE

Ave

Avenue

Road

Edgware

St.

Dorset Square

Grand Union Canal

Bell

Marylebone

Harrow

Westway

Road

Harrow

Road

A 40

Edgware Rd

Edgware Rd

Chapel St.

Old Marylebone Rd

Seymour

Crawford St.

Dinings ✕

Larrick 🏠

Gloucester Terrace

Bishop's

Bridge

Road

Eastbourne Terrace

South Wharf Rd

PADDINGTON

Praed

Street

Gardens

Edgware

NORFOLK CRESCENT

Harrowby St.

Place

George

Westbourne

Cleveland Terrace

Gloucester

Terrace

Paddington

Spring St.

Sussex

Radnor Pl.

Hyde Park St.

Kendal St.

Connaught St.

Road

Inverness

Bishop's

Queen's Gardens

Leinster Gardens

Craven Hill

Craven Road

Terrace

Sussex

Stanhope Terrace

Lancaster Gate

Bayswater North

Carriage

Drive

HYDE PARK

Bayswater

Terrace

0   400 m

0   400 yards

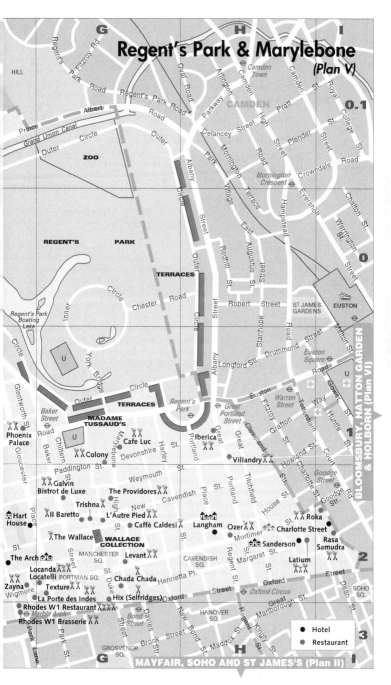

Regent's Park & Marylebone

(Plan V)

G **H** **I**

HILL

Regents Park Rd
Fitzroy Rd
Regent's Park Road
Albert
Prince
Grand Union Canal
Outer Circle
ZOO
Outer
Circle

Oval Road
Arlington Road
Camden High
Parkway
Delancey Street
Park Village
CAMDEN
Camden Town
Pratt Street
Plender Street
Crowndale Road
Mornington Crescent
Camden St.
Royal College St.
Eversholt Street
Chalton St.
Wellington St.

0.1

REGENT'S PARK

TERRACES

Inner Circle
Regent's Park Boating Lake

Chester Road

Albany Street
Village
Redhill St.
East Augustus St.
Hampstead Road
Mornington Terrace

Robert Street
ST JAMES GARDENS

O

EUSTON

York Bridge
U
Outer Circle
TERRACES

Stanhope Street
Drummond Street
Longford Str.
Euston Road
Euston Square

Melton St.
Gower St.
Huntle
Cour.

BLOOMSBURY, HATTON GARDEN & HOLBORN (Plan VI)

Glentworth St.
Circle
Baker Street
Road
Chiltern St.
Baker St.
Marylebone
Paddington St.
Devonshire St.
Harley St.
Portland St.
Great Portland Street
Regent's Park
Warren Street
Great Portland Street

Fitzroy St.
Grafton St.
Cleveland St.
Tottenham Court Rd
Gower St.
U

Goodge Street
Howland St.

1

✗✗ Phoenix Palace

✗✗ Galvin Bistrot de Luxe
Trishna ✗
✗ Il Baretto
✗ The Wallace

Cafe Luc ✗
✗✗ Colony
Weymouth St.
The Providores ✗✗
Cavendish Place
New St.
L'Autre Pied ✗✗
✗ Caffè Caldesi
Langham
MANCHESTER SQ.
WALLACE COLLECTION

Iberica ✗
Villandry ✗✗

Titchfield St.
Mortimer St.
Goodge Str.
✗✗ Roka
Charlotte Street
Sanderson ●
Rasa Samudra ✗✗

✗ Hart House ●

✗ The Arch ●
Locanda ✗✗✗
Zayna ✗✗
Locatelli
Texture ✗✗
Wigmore St.
La Porte des Indes ●
Rhodes W1 Restaurant ✗✗✗✗
Marble Arch
Rhodes W1 Brasserie ✗✗

Portman St.
Duke St.
Levant ✗✗
Chada Chada
Henrietta Pl.
CAVENDISH SQ.
Margaret St.
Ozer ✗✗
Latium ✗✗✗

Regent Street
Oxford Circus
Mortimer Ho.

Dean St.
SOHO SQ.

2

Park Lane
GROSVENOR SQ.
Bond Street
Brook Street
Davies St.
HANOVER SQ.
Maddox St.
Oxford Street
Great Marlborough St.
Kingly St.

Hix (Selfridges)
Oxford St.

● **Hotel**
● **Restaurant**

3

G **H** **I**
MAYFAIR, SOHO AND ST JAMES'S (Plan II)

125

L'Autre Pied ✿

G2

5-7 Blandford St. ✉ W1U 3DB
✆ (020) 7486 9696
e-mail info@lautrepied.co.uk
www.lautrepied.co.uk

⊖ Bond Street
Plan V

Menu £21 (lunch) – Carte £39/60

A/C
VISA
MC
AE

L'Autre Pied

Marcus Eaves is a confident young chef who has an instinct for flavour and texture. His cooking displays ambition and a hefty dose of originality but while some dishes may be quite elaborate in their construction he knows when enough is enough. The 'other foot' may well be the sparkly Pied à Terre but L'Autre Pied is certainly no diffusion line – it just continues the current trend for serving damn good food in surroundings that are refreshingly free from pomp or ceremony. In fact, if anything, the service is still slightly too stiff and could do with a degree or two more personality. Otherwise, this feels just like a genuine neighbourhood restaurant, albeit one with better cooking than most and with prices that are pretty friendly when one considers the talent in the kitchen. The à la carte is not overly long and is joined by a couple of tasting menus. Meats are handled confidently, especially game, and fish often arrives with some burly accompaniments. Meanwhile, the Valrhona chocolate mousse has virtually established its own fan club.

First Course

- Raviolo of veal and chorizo with shellfish bisque.
- Glazed snails with smoked bacon and beignets.

Main Course

- Roast pork with croquette of spiced pig's head.
- Lemon sole with Morteau sausage and girolles.

Dessert

- Baked Alaska, elderflower and vanilla cream.
- Cherries with chocolate brownie and pistachio ice cream.

L'Aventure

French

3 Blenheim Ter ✉ NW8 0EH
✆ (020) 7624 6232
e-mail laventure@live.co.uk

Menu £20/40

⊖ St John's Wood
Plan V
Closed first week January, last 2 weeks
August, Saturday lunch and Sunday

Tailor-made for anyone with a sound grasp of French wishing to impress a date - the menu is written entirely in French so politely decline the waiter's offer of a quick translation and wait for the admiring looks. What's more, if it's a warm day, you'll be sitting in the enchanting front terrace where the shrubs are covered in twinkly lights. This is a charming neighbourhood restaurant with a cosy and warm interior, owned and run by the delightful Catherine who'll make you feel you're being unfaithful if you don't return. The set menu is good value at lunch but pricier at dinner when the well-heeled locals come out. Expect the French bourgeois classics, from artichoke salad to rack of lamb and an ile flottante to finish.

Il Baretto

Italian

43 Blandford St. ✉ W1U 7HF
✆ (020) 7486 7340
e-mail info@ilbaretto.co.uk
www.ilbaretto.co.uk

Carte £21/46

⊖ Baker Street
Closed 24-26 December

Arjun Waney, the man behind Roka, Zuma and La Petite Maison, here gives Italy a go. The site had been Italian for a while and came complete with the wood-fired oven which is undoubtedly the star of the show. The ground floor wine bar doubles as a reception/holding area for the main basement room which comes with reclaimed brick walls and terracotta tiled flooring; the open kitchens somehow compensate for the lack of windows. Look for dishes marked in red on the extensive menu, such as the succulent lamb cutlets or the whole sea bass as they are cooked in the wood-fired oven or on the robata grill. Unless you're sticking to pizza, the final bill can be more than expected. Staff are in black and display varying degrees of commitment.

Cafe Luc

Modern European 🍴🍴

G1

50 Marylebone High St ✉ W1U 5HN   ⊖ Regent's Park
☎ (020) 7258 8595
e-mail info@cafeluc.com
www.cafeluc.com

Menu £16 – Carte £24/35

AC | 🎭 | ☀ | VISA | MC | AE | ①

London has always liked a good brasserie and now Marylebone High Street has one of its own to go with all its other restaurants and cafés. The surprisingly spacious Cafe Luc opened mid 2010 and appears to take its cue from The Wolseley in its 'grand European café' look. It's enthusiastically run and the dark leather banquettes, bar and clusters of lights give it a comfortable yet reassuringly authentic feel. It's also family-owned, and the family in question founded the Le Pain Quotidien international chain so they should know what they're doing. The menu has something for everyone and offers a host of brasserie and continental classics, although sometimes it feels as though the cooking is a little overwhelmed by the surroundings.

Caffé Caldesi

Italian 🍴

G2

118 Marylebone Ln. (1st floor) ✉ W1U 2QF   ⊖ Bond Street
☎ (020) 7487 0754   Closed 25-26 December
e-mail caffe@caldesi.com   and 1 January
www.caldesi.com

Menu £17 (lunch) – Carte £26/40

AC | ☀ | VISA | MC | AE

Simpler is often better but that doesn't always mean cheaper. Caffe Caldesi began as the informal relation to the now closed Caldesi further down the road by offering a more relaxed environment. The ground floor of this converted corner pub is the all-day café-bar part of the operation with the main restaurant upstairs. Here you'll find a bright and colourful room with a very genial atmosphere. The cheeses may be Tuscan but otherwise there's no single dominant Italian region on the menu. Instead it offers a selection of satisfying and earthy dishes, with the home-made pastas particularly good. Plates arrive with appetisingly simple presentation and flavours are bold and balanced, but you may find that the final bill is a little more than you were expecting.

Chada Chada

Thai 🍴

16-17 Picton Pl. ✉ W1U 1BP
☎ (020) 7935 8212
e-mail enquiry@chadathai.com
www.chadathai.com

⊖ Bond Street
Closed Sunday and bank holidays

Carte £19/47

[A/C]
[VISA]
[MC]
[AE]
[D]

The welcome may occasionally be a little timid, the decoration relatively featureless and the tables don't have space for too many dishes but Chada Chada retains a sense of authenticity that eludes the plethora of chain restaurants which surround James Street. The menu has been spruced up a little and offers a comprehensive tour around all parts of Thailand. The main course involves choosing your main ingredient, such as prawn or duck, and then deciding on the best accompaniments. The kitchen does the familiar well, which makes sense as it has a regular following who know what they like. It also doesn't hang around in sending forth the dishes which not only come in generous proportions but are also competitively priced.

Colony

Indian 🍴🍴

8 Paddington St ✉ W1U 5QH
☎ (020) 7935 3353
e-mail enquiries@colonybarandgrill.com
www.colonybarandgrill.com

⊖ Baker Street

Menu £20 – Carte £26/42

[A/C]

☀
[VISA]
[MC]
[AE]

At first glance, with its chilled music and extensive cocktail list, Colony would appear to be more of a lounge bar. But look closely and you'll see people are doing more than just snacking; venture further in and you'll even find some laid up dining tables. This is an outpost belonging to Atul Kochhar, of Benares fame, and the food bears the hallmarks of his contemporary style of Indian cooking, albeit in smaller sizes and without quite reaching the same heights. Flavours from others countries such as the Caribbean or East Africa also get a look-in and some dishes pack quite a punch. Four of the tasting plates should be more enough for two; the grill and the tandoor are most used and it's definitely worth coming for a lunchtime thali.

Dinings

F2

22 Harcourt St. ✉ W1H 4HH
✆ (020) 7723 0666
e-mail dinings@live.com
www.dinings.co.uk

⊖ **Marylebone**
Closed lunch Saturday and Sunday
– booking essential

Carte £31/43

VISA
Ⓜ◎
ᴀᴇ
⊙

The smiling chefs greet you from behind the sushi counter which acts as a prompt to the girls in the basement to rush upstairs and escort you back down below. The idea behind Dinings is to resemble an after-work Japanese izakaya, or pub, and this they achieve. Staff outnumber guests and their service is endearingly sweet, while comfort levels are modest – chairs are built for purpose rather than comfort. The atmosphere is chummy and music loud. The young owner has come from Nobu-land and the food calls itself 'Japanese tapas'; shorthand for small plates of diligently prepared dishes, similar in style to his alma mater in its mix of traditional and modern but without the lofty price tag. Puddings are more your classic French variety.

Galvin Bistrot de Luxe

G2

66 Baker St. ✉ W1U 7DJ
✆ (020) 7935 4007
e-mail info@galvinrestaurants.com
www.galvinrestaurants.com

⊖ **Baker Street**
Closed 25-26 December
and 1 January

Menu £18/20 (early dinner) – Carte £32/51

A/C
🎭
☼
VISA
Ⓜ◎
ᴀᴇ

Despite the enormous success of Galvin La Chapelle in The City, brothers Chris and Jeff Galvin have never taken their eyes off the ball here at their eponymous 'bistrot de luxe' in Baker Street. Regulars still flock here for the clubby, relaxed atmosphere and the traditional French food, which may look simple on the plate but is carefully constructed behind the scenes. The emphasis is very much on flavour; the kitchen's understanding and appreciation of ingredients, and the classic combinations in which they are used, really comes through. The menu has enough variety to satisfy those happy to indulge but those with one eye on the cost should come for lunch or before 7pm if they want to take advantage of a good value fixed menu.

Hix (Selfridges)

Modern European ✗

Mezzanine Fl, Selfridges, 400 Oxford St ⊖ Bond Street
✉ W1A 1AB
✆ (020) 7499 5400
e-mail reservations@hixatselfridges.co.uk
www.hixatselfridges.co.uk

Carte £25/40

A/C

☼

VISA

MC

AE

◑

It comes as no surprise to learn that this outpost of Mark Hix's expanding group, found on the mezzanine floor of Selfridges overlooking the designer handbags, is an altogether daintier affair that his muscular Chop House in Clerkenwell. It mirrors the opening hours of the store so breakfast kicks things off at 9.30am and the champagne bar offers refuelling opportunities throughout the day. Lunch comes with the buzz generated by the promise of some post-prandial shopping, although the affordable wine list could make this a risky proposition. The cooking is a little lighter and more European than his other restaurants and there are also more salads; but it does share their philosophy of serving unadorned food using home-grown ingredients.

Iberica 😊

Spanish ✗✗

195 Great Portland St ✉ W1W 5PS ⊖ Great Portland Street
✆ (020) 7636 8650 Closed Sunday dinner –
www.ibericalondon.co.uk booking advisable at dinner

Menu £22 (weekday lunch) – Carte £15/32

A/C

☐

VISA

MC

If you want an idea of how seriously this large operation, dedicated to Spanish 'food and culture', takes the sourcing of its ingredients, then wander into the deli and try resisting the Iberico hams with their ruby meat and creamy fat. It's even easier to get carried away by the appealing menu in the ground floor bar, although portion sizes are larger than one expects and prices can vary quite considerably. Flavours are punchy and satisfying and highlights include the squid and octopus dishes, along with the slow-cooked cockerel rice. Those after a fuller experience should consider pre-ordering the Segovian lamb or the suckling pig and if you want a more intimate and slightly more structured meal then book on the mezzanine floor.

Larrik

F2

Gastropub

32 Crawford Pl ⊠ W1H 5NN
☎ (020) 7723 0066
e-mail info@thelarrik.com
www.thelarrik.com

⊖ Edgware Road.
Closed 25 December

Carte £20/27

☼
VISA
⓶❿
AE

Its airy feel and capable service means that The Larrik has always been popular with larger groups and now, thanks to the obvious ambition of the owner, it's attracting plenty more customers for the quality of its food; so it's no surprise to find the place packed by 1pm on a daily basis. Try to sit at the front where it's brighter and more fun. Freshly made and substantial salads, a luxurious chicken liver parfait, plump salmon and haddock fishcakes with hollandaise and rewardingly rich desserts like chocolate brownies confirm a kitchen that's well grounded in the basics and aware of what people want from a pub. Add regularly changing real ales and you have a pub that's set to be part of the local landscape for some time to come.

Latium

H2

Italian XXX

21 Berners St. ⊠ W1T 3LP
☎ (020) 7323 9123
e-mail info@latiumrestaurant.com
www.latiumrestaurant.com

⊖ Oxford Circus
Closed 10 days Christmas, Saturday
lunch, Sunday and bank holidays

Menu £20/33

A/C
VISA
⓶❿
AE
⓪

The last revamp made it brighter and more contemporary but such is the loyalty of its followers that a simple lick of paint would have been enough. There's now a window into the kitchen for those who like to know where their food comes from, and a chef's table for those who want to watch them at it. Tables by the entrance are given away first but it's worth asking to be seated further in; you'll almost certainly be accommodated as staff are a friendly and considerate bunch. The chef-owner is from Lazio, hence the name, so expect cooking that is free from over-elaboration. Recipes from across Italy also feature and many use British ingredients. The good value lunch menu changes weekly and homemade ravioli is the speciality.

Levant

L e b a n e s e XX

Jason Ct., 76 Wigmore St. ✉ W1U 2SJ
℘ (020) 7224 1111
e-mail reservations@levant.co.uk
www.levant.co.uk

Menu £28 – Carte £20/40

⊖ Bond Street
Closed 23-29 December
and 1 January –
(dinner only and
lunch Saturday-Sunday)

The enticing scent of joss sticks and hookah pipes, belly dancing and pumping Arabic beats mean that Levant is guaranteed to provide a more exotic dining experience than most restaurants. Its basement location, lanterns and low-slung bar add further to the mystique and, as with anywhere offering a hint of spice, diners adopt the principle of safety in numbers and come in larger groups. With all these elements, it is almost a surprise to discover that equal care and enthusiasm has gone into the food. The kitchen uses good ingredients to create satisfying Lebanese dishes ideal for sharing. Avoid the more expensive set menus and head for the à la carte, with its appealing selection of falafel, pastries, char-grills and slow-roasted specialities.

Ozer

T u r k i s h XX

5 Langham Pl., Regent St. ✉ W1B 3DG
℘ (020) 7323 0505
e-mail ozer@ozer.co.uk
www.ozer.co.uk

Menu £19/23 – Carte £21/42

⊖ Oxford Circus

Huseyin Ozer may have built the successful Sofra chain but Ozer is clearly where his heart lies. His passion and pride in Turkish and Ottoman cuisine is clear for all to see – anyone who prints on their menu an offer to replace any dish not enjoyed must feel confident about his kitchen. The hot and cold meze is the main attraction here, especially the platters which represent good value. The crusty bread and hummus is almost a meal in itself and the borek, kofte and the skewered and chargrilled meats are all done well. There's an occasional modern twist and any overeating can be justified by considering just how healthy this cuisine is. The large front bar gets as packed as ever and the restaurant itself has just as many devotees.

REGENT'S PARK & MARYLEBONE ▶ PLAN V

Locanda Locatelli ❀

G2

Italian 𝗫𝗫𝗫

8 Seymour St. ✉ W1H 7JZ
✆ (020) 7935 9088
e-mail info@locandalocatelli.com
www.locandalocatelli.com

⊖ **Marble Arch**
Closed 25-26 December

Carte £41/60

A/C
🍾
☼
VISA
MC
AE
⓪

Locanda Locatelli

When your clientele is made up of lots of buffed and shiny people then it is important that you're looking pretty good yourself. So every year the cherry wood is given a fresh coat of varnish and the tan leather seating gets a good clean and this keeps the room looking dapper and slick. Despite the vicissitudes of fashion, Locanda Locatelli has remained an ever popular choice for the cognoscenti, thanks largely to the excellence of the cooking. The large serving team in their black shirts and white ties may look like they've just come from a Sicilian wedding, but they get the job done with alacrity and efficiency. The menu offers around ten dishes per section so there is enough choice for everyone, even those with food allergies. Pasta is a perennial highlight, especially the risotto and gnocchi, and desserts, which always include the toothsome tiramisu and tart of the day, are expertly rendered with flair and care. Thinly sliced calf's head makes an interesting start, while unfussy presentation allows the quality of fish to really shine.

First Course
- Chestnut tagliatelle with wild mushrooms.
- Char-grilled squid with chilli and garlic.

Main Course
- Veal Saltimbocca.
- Roast monkfish with walnut and caper sauce.

Dessert
- Degustation of Amedei chocolate.
- Prune financier with coconut ice cream.

Phoenix Palace

F1

Chinese ✗✗

5 Glentworth St. ⊠ NW1 5PG
☎ (020) 7486 3515
e-mail info@phoenixpalace.co.uk
www.phoenixpalace.co.uk

⊖ Baker Street
Booking advisable at dinner

Menu £25 – Carte approx. £28

You have to admire the ambition of the owners of Phoenix Palace, because despite the fact that their place can already seat over 100 people, they are still hoping to open an extension. To take it all in, sit in the raised section where you'll find polished wood, pretty lanterns and larger groups of families or friends creating what is clearly a contented atmosphere. Try to ignore the sheer number of different dishes on the vast menu, especially those involving kangaroo and ostrich. This is Cantonese cooking and the rotisserie meats are a specialty – some of which do need to be pre-ordered. Crab with chilli sauce served with a crispy Peking bun is a favourite, while the extensive dim sum during the day draws in plenty of Hong Kong businesspeople.

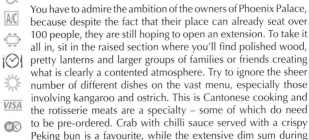

La Porte des Indes

F2

Indian ✗✗

32 Bryanston St ⊠ W1H 7EG
☎ (020) 7224 0055
e-mail london.reservation@laportedesindes.com
www.laportedesindes.com

⊖ Marble Arch
Closed 25-26 December and 1 January

Menu £36 – Carte £36/56

The façade gives little away but step in and you'll be instantly transported to what looks like the set from the latest Bollywood movie. Spread over two floors, La Porte des Indes really is vast and it's decorated in a spectacularly unrestrained display of palms trees, murals and waterfalls. The equally exuberant Jungle Bar is a popular place to kick off the evening. The menu offers something for everyone, including specialities from Pondicherry and others influenced by French India. Vegetarians are particularly well catered for and cookery demonstrations are held regularly for those wishing to learn more about Indian food. For those after a memento of their meal here, there is a little shop in the entrance lobby.

REGENT'S PARK & MARYLEBONE ▶ PLAN V

135

The Providores

G2

109 Marylebone High St. ✉ W1U 4RX
℘ (020) 7935 6175
e-mail anyone@theprovidores.co.uk
www.theprovidores.co.uk

⊖ **Bond Street**
Closed Christmas-New Year

Carte £36/57

'Marylebone Village' offers so many restaurants and cafés that it's becoming a destination in itself. Included in the roll call is this fusion restaurant within a former Edwardian pub. The warmth of the staff and the general buzz hit you immediately in the ground floor Tapa Room, where tables and tapas are shared. Upstairs is a slightly more sedate room but the staff are equally charming. Here all dishes come in starter size to "minimise food envy" and allow for sharing; three courses plus a dessert should suffice. There is no doubting the quality of the ingredients, although sometimes there's a flavour or two too many on the plate. The wine list champions New Zealand. Bookings are needed upstairs; downstairs, it's first-come-first-served.

Rhodes W1 Brasserie

F3

Great Cumberland Pl. ✉ W1H
℘ (020) 7616 5930
e-mail brasserie@rhodesw1.com
www.rhodesw1.com

⊖ **Marble Arch**

Menu £21 (lunch) – Carte £27/44

They've got their work cut out filling a space as big as this, because it does need to be close to capacity to get the atmosphere going. That said, the serving team do keep themselves busy and genuinely look after their customers. It's actually better to approach it from the lobby of the hotel than its separate street entrance which leads you through the equally large bar. The menu content differs little between lunch and dinner except for the Express lunch for those on the run: you get starter, main course and dessert all on one plate. Gary Rhodes's signature dishes like salmon fishcakes are all in evidence, but so are other more European influences so expect risotto, Greek salads, osso bucco, crab bisque and the like.

136

Rhodes W1 (Restaurant) ✿

F3

Cumberland Hotel, Great Cumberland Pl.
✉ W1H 7DL
📞 (020) 7616 5930
e-mail restaurant@rhodesw1.com
www.rhodesw1.com

⊖ Marble Arch
Closed 2 weeks in summer,
Saturday lunch, Sunday and
Monday – booking advisable

Menu £25/50

Rhodes W1

There are just twelve tables and when you book one it's yours for however long you want it – this isn't the sort of restaurant where they try to re-lay your table while you're ordering coffee. Kelly Hoppen's design is about texture and warmth, with crystal chandeliers hanging seductively over each table. The atmosphere is unexpectedly relaxed too, thanks largely to the staff who are a confident lot, who know what they are talking about and are ready with a smile. Gary Rhodes may be best known as a champion of British traditions and recipes but here more of the influences come from across the Channel. Whether the cooking techniques are French or the ingredients from more southerly parts, what does remain steadfastly Rhodesesque is the uncluttered and crisp presentation, the complementary flavour combinations and the ease of eating. The food is also quite masculine and some of the starters in particular are appealingly robust. The set menu is purely for the trusting and the brave as you are not told beforehand of its contents.

First Course

- Scallops with braised oxtail and blood orange.
- Confit of rabbit with carrot and tamarillo.

Main Course

- Pigeon with foie gras, chicory and pickled blackberries.
- Monkfish with aubergine purée, fennel and shellfish emulsion.

Dessert

- Pistachio cake with apricot and tarragon ice cream.
- Honeycomb mousse with lemon purée and chocolate.

Texture ✤

Innovative 🍴🍴

G2

34 Portman St. ✉ W1H 7BY
📞 (020) 7224 0028
e-mail info@texture-restaurant.co.uk
www.texture-restaurant.co.uk

⊖ Marble Arch
Closed Christmas-New Year,
2 weeks August,
Sunday and Monday

Menu £22 (lunch) – Carte £43/51

A/C

VISA

M C

AE

Texture

Chef-owner Agnar Sverrisson and his business partner Xavier
Rousset, who trained as a sommelier, have steadily gone about
creating an exceedingly good restaurant. The Champagne bar
at the front has become a destination in itself and is separated
from the restaurant by a large cabinet so you never feel too
detached from it. The high ceilings add a little grandeur and the
service is very pleasant, with staff all ready with a smile. Agnar's
cooking is a little less showy than when Texture opened in 2007
and is all the better for that; you feel he's now cooking the food
he wants to cook rather than the food he thought he should be
cooking. Iceland is his country of birth so it is no surprise to find
lamb, cod (whose crisp skin is served with drinks), langoustine
and skyr, the dairy product that nourished the Vikings. There's
considerable technical skill and depth to the cooking but dishes
still appear light and refreshing and, since the use of cream and
butter is largely restricted to the desserts, you even feel they're
doing you good.

First Course

- Salmon graflax with horseradish and rye bread.
- Pigeon with sweetcorn, shallot and bacon popcorn.

Main Course

- Icelandic salted cod with barley and shellfish jus.
- Duck with butternut purée and five spice spring roll.

Dessert

- White chocolate mousse with cucumber and dill.
- Quince and fennel cake with citrus and spice ice cream.

Trishna

G2

15-17 Blandford St. ✉ W1U 3DG   ⊖ Baker Street

✆ (020) 7935 5624   Closed 25-29 December and 1-4 January

e-mail info@trishnalondon.com

www.trishnalondon.com

Menu £16/35 – Carte £29/39

Trishna has added much to Marylebone's already interesting foodie quarter, despite its dodgy acoustics and service that can sometimes go AWOL. Those familiar with the Mumbai original will find the cooking here a little more subtle as less butter and garlic are used. The emphasis is firmly on fish and seafood and the dishes come with both wine and beer pairing suggestions. They have substituted the Indian species for domestic varieties and dishes are for sharing – this is the sort of food which makes you want to roll up your sleeves. Stand-outs include the gloriously rich Cornish brown crab and the crisp Isle of Wight plaice with pea and mint. Avoid the à la carte and head for the more reasonably priced 8 course tasting menu.

Villandry

H1

170 Great Portland St ✉ W1W 5QB   ⊖ Regent's Park

✆ (020) 7631 3131   Closed Christmas, New Year and

e-mail contactus@villandry.com   Sunday dinner

www.villandry.com

Carte £25/47

It's almost a whole food village here as they've got most areas covered, from morning coffees to late drinks, snacks and plates of charcuterie to full meals. As such, it's worth coming in through the Great Portland entrance so as to walk past all the bounteous produce, rather than the Bolsover Street entrance which takes you straight into the restaurant. It has an appealing farmhouse-in-the-city kind of feel. The menu is quite extensive and its thrust is mostly French; there's a daily-changing plat du jour and a shellfish section but, in among the onion soups, cassoulets and terrines, you might also find roast beef or a steak and ale pie. Bargain-hunters will be familiar with the Villandry outpost at Bicester Village.

REGENT'S PARK & MARYLEBONE ▶ PLAN V

139

Vineria

Italian XX

1 Blenheim Ter. ⊠ NW8 0EH
📞 (020) 7328 5014
e-mail london@vineria.it
www.vineria.it

⊖ St John's Wood
Plan V
Closed Monday

Menu £20 (lunch) – Carte £27/37

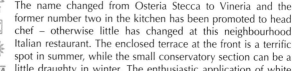

The name changed from Osteria Stecca to Vineria and the former number two in the kitchen has been promoted to head chef – otherwise little has changed at this neighbourhood Italian restaurant. The enclosed terrace at the front is a terrific spot in summer, while the small conservatory section can be a little draughty in winter. The enthusiastic application of white emulsion gives the main room a bright, clean feel. Service can sometimes be a little anxious. The menu covers all points of the country and the pasta section is one not to be ignored. Prices on the à la carte may seem quite high, especially in comparison to the good value lunch menu, but all dishes come fully garnished so there are no side orders to bump up that final bill.

The Wallace

French X

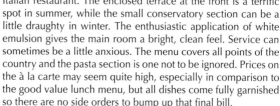

Hertford House, Manchester Sq ⊠ W1U 3BN
📞 (020) 7563 9505
e-mail reservations@thewallacerestaurant.com
www.thewallacerestaurant.com

⊖ Bond Street
Closed 24-27 December –
(lunch only and
dinner Friday-Saturday)

Carte £26/35

Away from the bustle of Marylebone High Street sits Hertford House and the Wallace Collection of 18C and 19C paintings. Go past the Canalettos on the ground floor and through the French doors and you'll find yourself in a huge glass-roofed courtyard. The restaurant takes up most of the space, although there's also an all-day café. The menu is largely French in influence and cooking is done ably enough. There's a popular fruits de mer section and terrines are the speciality, ranging from foie gras to pork rillettes. Mains are never too heavy and cheeses are kept in good order. There may occasionally be larger parties in but the size of this atrium means there's room for everyone. Staff make up in alacrity what they lack in personality.

Zayna

F2

25 New Quebec St. ✉ W1H 7SF   ⊖ Marble Arch
✆ (020) 7723 2229
e-mail info@zaynarestaurant.co.uk
www.zaynarestaurant.co.uk

Menu £25/30 – Carte £30/40

A/C
⌖
☼
VISA
MC
AE

When a restaurant is named after the owner's daughter you know there's going to be a lot of love around. Zayna reflects the personality of Riz Dar who spent his formative years around Kashmir and Punjab and whose first job was in his father's restaurant in Pakistan. It's no surprise then to find a menu of North Indian and Pakistani delicacies. It comes divided according to cooking method, from the pan, grill, tawa or oven; but look out for the refined street food using offal. He is passionate about produce: spices are roasted and ground in house and only halal meat and free-range chicken are used. Dishes come packed with flavour, although the final bill can quickly mount up. The ground floor is the more elegant of the two rooms.

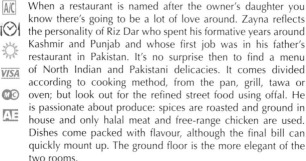

Good food without spending a fortune? Look for the Bib Gourmand 😊.

REGENT'S PARK & MARYLEBONE ▶ PLAN V

Bloomsbury · Hatton Garden · Holborn

A real sense of history pervades this central chunk of London. From the great collection of antiquities in the British Museum to the barristers who swarm around the Royal Courts of Justice and Lincoln's Inn; from the haunts of Charles Dickens to the oldest Catholic church in Britain, the streets here are dotted with rich reminders of the past. Hatton Garden's fame as the city's diamond and jewellery centre goes back to Elizabethan times while, of a more recent vintage, Bloomsbury was home to the notorious Group (or Set) who, championed by Virginia Woolf, took on the world of art and literature in the 1920s.

A full-on encounter with **Holborn** is, initially, a shock to the system. Coming up from the tube, you'll find this is where main traffic arteries collide and a rugby scrum regularly ensues. Fear not, though; the relative calm of London's largest square, part-flanked by two quirky and intriguing museums, is just round the corner. The square is **Lincoln's Inn Fields,** which boasts a canopy of characterful oak trees and a set of tennis courts. On its north side is **Sir John Soane's Museum,** a gloriously eccentric place with twenty thousand exhibits where the walls open out like cabinets to reveal paintings by Turner and Canaletto. On its south side, the Hunterian Museum, refitted a few years ago, is a fascinating repository of medical bits and pieces. Visitors with a Damien Hirst take on life will revel in the likes of animal digestive systems in formaldehyde, or perhaps the sight of half of mathematician Charles Babbage's brain. Others not so fascinated by the gory might flee to the haunting silence of **St Etheldreda's church** in Ely Place, the only surviving example of thirteenth-century Gothic architecture in London. It survived the Great Fire of 1666, and Latin is still the language of choice.

Contemplation of a different kind takes centre stage in the adjacent **Hatton Garden.** This involves eager-eyed couples gazing at the glittering displays of rings and jewellery that have been lighting up the shop fronts here for many generations, ever since the leafy lane and its smart garden environs took the fancy of Sir Christopher Hatton, a favourite of Elizabeth I. After gawping at the baubles, there's liquid refreshment on hand at one of London's most atmospheric old pubs, the tiny Ye Old Mitre hidden down a narrow passageway. The preserved trunk of a cherry tree stands in the front bar, and, by all accounts, Elizabeth I danced the maypole round it (a legend that always seems more believable after the second pint).

Bloomsbury has intellectual connotations, and not just because of the writers and artists who frequented its townhouses in the twenties. This is where the University of London has its headquarters, and it's also home

C. Eymenier / MICHELIN

to the **British Museum,** the vast treasure trove of international artefacts that attracts visitors in even vaster numbers. As if the exhibits themselves weren't lure enough, there's also the fantastic glass-roofed Great Court, opened to much fanfare at the start of the Millennium, which lays claim to being the largest covered public square in Europe. To the north of here by the Euston Road is the **British Library,** a rather stark red brick building that holds over 150 million items and is one of the greatest centres of knowledge in the world. Meanwhile,

Dickens fans should make for the north east corner of Bloomsbury for the great man's museum in **Doughty Street:** this is one of many London houses in which he lived, but it's the only one still standing. He lived here for three years, and it proved a fruitful base, resulting in Nicholas Nickleby and Oliver Twist. The museum holds manuscripts, letters and Dickens' writing desk. If your appetite for the written word has been truly whetted, then a good tip is to head back west half a mile to immerse yourself in the bookshops of Great Russell Street.

143

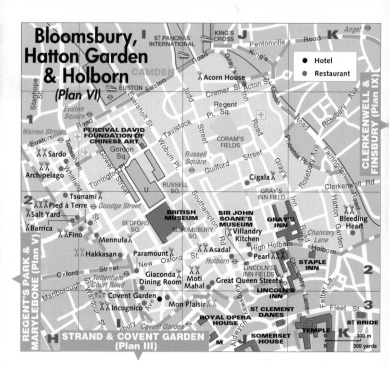

Bloomsbury, Hatton Garden & Holborn
(Plan VI)

144

Acorn House

JO

Modern European 🍴

69 Swinton St. ✉ WC1X 9NT
☎ (020) 7812 1842
e-mail bookings@acornhouserestaurant.com
www.acornhouserestaurant.com

⊖ King's Cross
Closed Saturday lunch and
bank holidays

Menu £25 (dinner) – Carte £22/32

|A/C|
☼
VISA
MC
AE

However worthy the principles of a restaurant – and this restaurant has many worthy principles – the proof must always be in the pudding and fortunately at Acorn House that pudding tastes good. This is a joint venture between the Terence Higgins and Shoreditch Trusts and was London's first eco-friendly training restaurant. They buy local and organic, use renewable 'green' electricity, purify their water, compost waste and recycle. Their menu is teasingly understated, with just the mainstays of the dishes listed. What you get is healthy, generously proportioned, flavoursome seasonality on a plate, using a variety of culinary influences; who can resist kicking off with a rhubarb Bellini? The room has a bright, café-style feel.

Archipelago

H1

Innovative 🍴🍴

110 Whitfield St. ✉ W1T 5ED
☎ (020) 7383 3346
e-mail info@archipelago-restaurant.co.uk
www.archipelago-restaurant.co.uk

⊖ Goodge Street
Closed Saturday lunch, Sunday and
bank holidays

Carte £27/40

VISA
MC
AE
⓪

Bored with beef? Tired of chicken? How about zebra? Or crocodile? Not only is the gloriously oddball Archipelago unlike any other restaurant in London but tales of your meal can also be used to frighten small children. 'Exploring the exotic' is their slogan although 'eating the exotic' would be more exact: the menu reads like an inventory at an omnivore's safari park and the place itself is like an eccentric Oriental bazaar that's running out of space. Several dishes are given an Asian twist and side dishes include the 'Love-bug salad' made with locusts and crickets. For dessert, try the chocolate covered scorpion; they now use smaller ones as they are, apparently, 'tastier'. It's all great fun and certainly memorable.

Asadal

J2

227 High Holborn ✉ WC1V 7DA
✆ (020) 7430 9006
e-mail info@asadal.co.uk
www.asadal.co.uk

⊖ Holborn
Closed 25-26 December, 1 January
and Sunday lunch

Menu £12 (lunch) – Carte £13/20

A/C

VISA

MC

AE

If it was any nearer Holborn Tube station you'd need an Oyster card to get in. But head down the stairs and you'll soon be oblivious to what's going on at street level, thanks to a comfortable room which is divided up and kitted out with lots of wood. Those unfamiliar with Korean food will find that, by and large, the menu explains itself, since many of the dishes have had their photo taken. One thing to note is that the more there are in your party the better as sharing is the key. Kimchi provides the perfect starter; there's plenty of seafood but the stars of the show are the hotpots and the barbecues where meats are cooked on the hotplate on the table. The young staff appear to have been hired for their efficiency rather than their personalities.

Barrica

H2

62 Goodge St ✉ W1T 4NE
✆ (020) 7436 9448
e-mail info@barrica.co.uk
www.barrica.co.uk

⊖ Goodge Street
Closed Sunday and bank holidays
– booking essential

Carte £20/23

A/C

VISA

MC

AE

If the zeitgeist is epitomised by informality and sharing then it's little wonder that tapas bars are sprouting up all over the place. Barrica opened in close proximity to a couple of well established competitors but manages to hold its own. You'll have to fight through the after-work group at the front to get to the tables and noise levels can overawe at times, but the food is good and the atmosphere fun. The menu is sensibly laid out and supplemented by daily specials. Highlights include braised veal cheeks, duck rillettes and marinated sardines. Cured meats hang above the bar and the cosy room is warm and intimate. If you haven't got a booking, you may get a counter seat or else you can try the Spanish way of eating standing up.

Bleeding Heart

Bleeding Heart Yard (off Greville St.)   ⊖ Farringdon
⊠ EC1N 8SJ   Closed 24 December-4 January,
✆ (020) 7242 8238   Saturday and Sunday – booking essential
e-mail bookings@bleedingheart.co.uk
www.bleedingheart.co.uk

Carte £26/41

Dickensian tales of murder and intrigue still haunt the wonderfully evocative Bleeding Heart Yard, while contented bankers and modern day industrialists sit in its candlelit and atmospheric restaurant, feasting on classic French cuisine. Weekly changing set menus sit alongside the fairly pricey à la carte, which comes written in French and English, and well-drilled French staff exhibit a fair degree of personality. The kitchen can sometimes overcomplicate dishes so you're better off going for the more traditional choices with their relative simplicity. The wine list is a splendid affair and the owners have their own estate in New Zealand. If you want something altogether less formal then cross the Yard for the bistro.

Cigala

54 Lamb's Conduit St. ⊠ WC1N 3LW   ⊖ Russell Square
✆ (020) 7405 1717   Closed 24-26 December and
e-mail tasty@cigala.co.uk   Easter – booking essential
www.cigala.co.uk

Menu £18 (lunch) – Carte £21/43

Cigala and Lamb's Conduit are a perfect fit; grab an outside table in summer and watch the world go by on this part-pedestrianised street. However, it is inside where you'll find the infectious vibe. The menu is cleverly divided, one side being tapas and/or starters, and main courses on the other, so you can choose to have lots of dishes, order a bigger dish – or go for an even bigger one like the paella for two which takes half an hour. The tapas are particularly good, especially the salt cod fritters, Padrón peppers and the morcilla blood sausage. The exclusively Spanish wine list has some little gems on it and the prices are commendably down to earth. The young Spanish girls serving display varying degrees of enthusiasm.

Fino

12

33 Charlotte St.
(entrance on Rathbone St.)
✉ W1T 1RR
✆ (020) 7813 8010
e-mail info@finorestaurant.com
www.finorestaurant.com

⊖ Goodge Street
Closed Saturday lunch
and Sunday

Menu £18 (lunch) – Carte £28/44

VISA
_MC_
_AE_

Fino's basement location and discreet entrance engender in its clientele that warm, satisfyingly smug feeling of being 'in the know'. The place remains fresh and vital and, while it is more formally structured than most restaurants offering tapas, the atmosphere is always lively and the crowd pleasingly mixed. Start with a sherry and some coquetas while you scour the sensibly laid out menu. The young staff all know what's on offer and the more effort you put in with them the more they'll be inclined to offer guidance. Then order a bottle of Albariño and dig in; seafood is a delight, especially the squid from the plancha. Dishes are easy to share and, as in life, the more people in your party the greater will be your enjoyment.

Giaconda Dining Room

12

9 Denmark St. ✉ WC2H 8LS
✆ (020) 7240 3334
e-mail paulmerrony@gmail.com
www.giacondadining.com

⊖ Tottenham Court Road
Closed 2 weeks August, Easter, Saturday,
Sunday and bank holidays –
booking essential

Carte £24/28

_A/C_
VISA
_MC_
_AE_

In the shadow of Centrepoint lies a frayed little area that's 'not quite Soho.' Here you'll find Denmark Street - London's own historic Tin Pan Alley – which is home to the Giaconda Dining Room. Aussies Paul and Tracey Merrony have a small but perfectly formed little place; spartanly decorated, busy from day one and great fun. Paul describes his cooking as "Frenchy, with day trips to Italy," which translates on the plate as confident, gutsy, no-nonsense and immeasurably satisfying. Tripe; steak tartare; pork sausage stew; risotto; a deconstructed pig's trotter and a daily changing fish or grilled dish special - there's something for everyone and, with most wine bottles in the £20s, it's all done at a credit-crunch busting price.

Great Queen Street 🎭

British 🍴

32 Great Queen St ✉ WC2B 5AA ⊖ Holborn
☎ (020) 7242 0622 Closed Christmas, New Year, Sunday dinner
e-mail greatqueenstreet@gmail.com and bank holidays –
booking essential

Carte £25/32

This is one of those restaurants that are perfect on a cold winter's night, with its candlelight, burgundy coloured walls, busy atmosphere and, most importantly, its heart-warming food. Its popularity does mean that service can sometimes need a prompt but there is no doubting the staff's enthusiasm for the food they serve. The menu descriptions are unapologetically concise but then dishes come equally unembellished. There's little difference between what constitutes a starter or main course and there's always a daily special or two. Highlights are the shared dishes such as the roast chicken crown or the shoulder of lamb, but offal is also done very well. Wine is served in tumblers and the list is thoughtfully put together.

Incognico

Modern European 🍴🍴

117 Shaftesbury Ave. ⊖ Tottenham Court Road
✉ WC2H 8AD
☎ (020) 7836 8866
e-mail incognicorestaurant@gmail.com
www.incognico.com

Menu £20/25 – Carte £31/38

Incognico, somewhat ironically, deserves to be better known, and not just as a well-placed pre-theatre spot. It is a comfortable and smartly dressed restaurant, the dark wood lending a masculine, clubby feel. It is also enthusiastically run, although service can sometimes be a little too formal and solicitous for its own good. As soon as you sit you're assailed somewhat with a plethora of assorted menus – there's a menu of the day, a specials menu and the somewhat expensive à la carte. The kitchen looks towards both France and Italy for inspiration; the former has greater influence but the Italian dishes are executed with greater aplomb. Dishes come pleasingly understated in presentation and flavours are nicely balanced.

Hakkasan ✿

12

8 Hanway Pl. ⊠ W1T 1HD
𝄞 (020) 7927 7000
e-mail mail@hakkasan.com
www.hakkasan.com

⊖ Tottenham Court Road
Closed 24-25 December

Carte £43/95

VISA

Hakkasan

The subterranean Hakkasan remains as cool and seductive as ever and its popularity shows no sign of slowing. Despite the size and general bustle, it is actually possible to have quite an intimate experience here, thanks to the clever lighting and good acoustics. However, service can be a little hit and miss and depends largely on who your waiter is and their levels of enthusiasm although it does generally get better when the room reaches capacity. Lunchtime dim sum is a real highlight, although they sometimes appear curiously reluctant to offer you that particular menu. There are 20 chefs in the kitchen, many of whom are, like the head chef, from Singapore. The extensive menu is laid out clearly and logically, although there can be a marked difference in price between similar sounding dishes. Cantonese remains the starting point but the kitchen adds its own signature of inventiveness to give the dishes zip and the flavours depth. One thing the waiting staff do get right is telling you when you've unwittingly but understandably succumbed to over-ordering.

First Course	Main Course	Dessert
• Crispy duck salad with pine nuts and shallot. • Steamed Peking dumplings.	• Grilled sea bass with honey. • Stir-fried rib of beef with red wine.	• 'Chocolate textures'. • Buttermilk bavarois with grapefruit and rosemary syrup.

Mennula

Italian ✗

10 Charlotte St. ✉ W1T 2LT ⊖ Goodge Street
☎ (020) 7363 2833 Closed Saturday lunch and
www.mennula.com bank holidays

Menu £20 (lunch) – Carte £27/43

Those who still mourn the passing of Passione, which occupied this space for quite some time, will be pleased to find in its place another Italian restaurant, this time with a Sicilian accent. The enthusiastically run Mennula shows that there's more to this region than cannoli and cassata by offering a varied selection of specialities, from arancini to spaghetti with sardines, and pasta cake. The name means 'almond' and they make several appearances, whether served smoked with your drinks or to accompany the lamb. The set lunch and early evening menus are attractively priced. The place is quite compact, which means that one larger table can dominate the room, but it's bright and crisply decorated; try to snare one of the three booths.

BLOOMSBURY, HATTON GARDEN & HOLBORN ▶ PLAN VI

Mon Plaisir

French ✗✗

19-21 Monmouth St. ✉ WC2H 9DD ⊖ Covent Garden
☎ (020) 7836 7243 Closed Christmas and New Year, Sunday
e-mail monplaisirrestaurant@googlemail.com and bank holidays
www.monplaisir.co.uk

Menu £17 (lunch) – Carte £29/38

Mon Plaisir couldn't be more French if it wore a beret and whistled La Marseillaise. But because this institution has been around since the 1940s, and under the current ownership since the 70s, it can also give one an unexpected but palpable sense of old London. It's divided into four rooms, all of which have slightly different personalities but share that Gallic theme; even the bar was reportedly salvaged from a Lyonnais brothel. Service may lack some of the exuberance of the past but that's just down to the relative lack of experience of the current serving team. All the authentically tasting classics are on offer, from snails to terrines, duck to coq; the set menu represents good value while the à la carte can be a little pricey.

Moti Mahal

J2

45 Great Queen St. ✉ WC2B 5AA
📞 (020) 7240 9329
e-mail reservations@motimahal-uk.com
www.motimahal-uk.com

⊖ Holborn
Closed 25-27 December,
1-2 January, Saturday lunch
and Sunday

Carte £43/58

To get the most out of your visit to Moti Mahal, order dishes from the menu which follows the path of the Grand Trunk Road, built in the 16C and stretching the 2500km from Bengal to the North West of India and the Pakistan border. This journey also takes little detours along the way to include specialities cooked on a clamp grill and there is no distinction between starters and main courses – just order a selection to share with your table. There is also a 'classics' menu for those who insist on only ordering dishes with recognisable names. The flavoursome cooking is done with care and service is conscientious and endearing. The restaurant is split between a bright and busy ground floor and a more intimate basement level.

Paramount

I2

Centre Point, 101-103
New Oxford St. (31st Floor)
✉ WC1A 1DD
📞 (020) 7420 2900
e-mail info@paramount.uk.net
www.paramount.uk.net

⊖ Tottenham Court Road
Closed 25 December
and Sunday

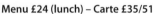

Menu £24 (lunch) – Carte £35/51

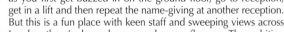

Restaurants with great views usually hope you'll spend so much time gawping out of the window that you won't notice the quality of the cooking. But Paramount, on the 32nd floor of the iconic Grade II listed Centre Point building, is owned by experienced restaurateur Pierre Condou and he has invested in a decent kitchen team. Getting to the restaurant can be a little laborious as you first get buzzed in on the ground floor, go to reception, get in a lift and then repeat the name-giving at another reception. But this is a fun place with keen staff and sweeping views across London; there's also a champagne bar one floor up. The ambition of the kitchen is shown by the presence of a tasting menu; cooking is surprisingly elaborate and the ingredients are good.

Pearl

French XXX

252 High Holborn ⊠ WC1V 7EN ⊖ Holborn
✆ (020) 7829 7000
e-mail info@pearl-restaurant.com
www.pearl-restaurant.com

Closed last 2 weeks August, Christmas,
Saturday lunch,
Sunday and bank holidays

Menu £29/58

A room as grand as this has to be busy otherwise the tables feel a little cast adrift. This former banking hall is within what was once Pearl Assurance's HQ; its high ceiling, chandeliers and columns certainly add some grandeur to proceedings but they clearly didn't make life easy when it came to adding the lighting. Waiting staff come dressed in black and are an enthusiastic, well-drilled bunch who do a good job ensuring that the surroundings don't become the main event. Chef Jun Tanaka, who pulls in plenty of the customers himself thanks to his television appearances, offers a menu high in originality but grounded in a classical French base. The wine list is a particularly impressive tome in both its depth and variety.

Rasa Samudra

Indian XX

5 Charlotte St. ⊠ W1T 1RE ⊖ Goodge Street
✆ (020) 7637 0222
e-mail info@rasarestaurants.com
www.rasarestaurants.com

Closed 25 December, 1 January and
Sunday lunch

Menu £23/30 – Carte £18/29

It still shines like a beacon on Charlotte Street, thanks to its shocking pink hue, and it is forever busy regardless of what time you arrive for dinner. The front room fills first but the back rooms are slightly more intimate. Service can be somewhat disorganised but the staff are so well meaning and eager to please that no one gets particularly grouchy about it. The menu specialises in the food of India's southwest region of Kerala so expect fish, creamy coconut dishes and plenty for vegetarians. The Meen curry, made with roasted coconut and tamarind, is a highlight. The homemade chutneys and pre-meal snacks are also worth ordering – and don't ignore the madhuram or desserts, which will certainly fill you up if you weren't already.

BLOOMSBURY, HATTON GARDEN & HOLBORN ▶ PLAN VI

Pied à Terre ✿✿

Innovative 𝕏𝕏𝕏

34 Charlotte St ✉ **W1T 2NH**
✆ (020) 7636 1178
e-mail info@pied-a-terre.co.uk
www.pied-a-terre.co.uk

Menu £30/72

⊖ **Goodge Street**
Closed last week December, first week
January, Saturday lunch, Sunday and
bank holidays

VISA
Ⓜ©
AE

Pied a Terre

David Moore may be spending less time here in the restaurant
as he continues his bourgeoning TV career and also looks after
their other place, L'Autre Pied; but Shane Osborn is a chef who
eschews the limelight in favour of getting on with what he likes
doing best – cooking. That doesn't mean he is cocooned in his
own world – he still spends time seeing what competitors are
up to by sharing thoughts and ideas with other chefs around
the country. The restaurant is very much the senior member in
Charlotte Street but this is still somewhere with ambition and a
will to improve. It is certainly not the most spacious place around
and when customers are assailed by staff at the beginning it
can feel a little claustrophobic but things do subsequently calm
down. The cooking may appear quite elaborate on the plate
but there is no jostling of flavours. Certain dishes, such as the
seared and poached foie gras starter and the bitter chocolate
tart dessert enjoy a perennial presence on the menu. The set
lunch menu represents decent value.

First Course	Main Course	Dessert
• Foie gras in Sauternes consommé, smoked bacon and red onion.	• Pigeon with liquorice purée, caramelised endive and caramel.	• Honey poached apricot, almond financier and vanilla ice cream.
• Ravioli of suckling pig and poached lobster.	• Turbot with cockles, pistachio and mango.	• Chocolate tart, stout ice cream and macadamia cream.

Roka

37 Charlotte St ✉ W1T 1RR
☎ (020) 7580 6464
e-mail info@rokarestaurant.com
www.rokarestaurant.com

⊖ Goodge Street
Closed 24- 26 December and
1 January

Carte approx. £38

Roka has one of those appealingly perceptible pulses that only really busy, well-run restaurants enjoy. It attracts a handsome crowd although they don't just come to glory in their mutual attractiveness but to share food that's original, easy to eat and just as pretty as they are. The kitchen takes the flavours, delicacy and strong presentation standards of Japanese food and adds its own contemporary touches. The menu can appear bewildering but just skip the set menus and order an assortment from the various headings; ensure you have one of the specialities from the on-view Robata grill. Sometimes too many dishes can arrive at once but the serving team are a friendly and capable bunch and they'll ease up on the delivery if you ask.

Salt Yard

54 Goodge St. ✉ W1T 4NA
☎ (020) 7637 0657
e-mail info@saltyard.co.uk
www.saltyard.co.uk

⊖ Goodge Street
Closed Christmas and New Year,
Saturday lunch, Sunday and
bank holidays

Carte £25/35

The ground floor is the more boisterous and you'll feel like you're in the middle of a fun party; downstairs is better if you don't know your dining companion that well, although it too is full of life. This is all about tapas, although not just about Spanish tapas. One side of the menu has bar snacks, charcuterie and cheese but after ordering some olives or boquerones, turn over and you'll find three headings: Fish, Meat and Vegetable – one plate of each per person should do it. Unusual dishes, like braised gurnard with smoked Jersey Royals, sit alongside more traditional pairings like duck breast with parsnip purée. Prices are excellent; sharing is encouraged and service, young and sincere. Spain and Italy dominate the wine list.

Sardo

H1

45 Grafton Way ✉ W1T 5DQ
☎ (020) 7387 2521
e-mail info@sardo-restaurant.com
www.sardo-restaurant.com

⊖ **Warren Street**
Closed Christmas, Saturday lunch and
Sunday

Carte £26/34

A/C
VISA
MC
AE
DC

Sardo always looks warm and inviting, especially as it stands on one of Bloomsbury's somewhat less hospitable streets. Inside is simplicity itself, with plain white walls and a minimum amount of decorative embellishment but the atmosphere is one of general bonhomie, thanks to a plethora of regulars and the young, friendly service. The highlights of the menu are dishes whose roots lie in Sardinia such as the rich bottarga; the salsiccia is also very robust, but desserts such as panna cotta also reveal the kitchen's lightness of touch. There's plenty of homemade pasta, three or four daily seasonal specials and tasty baskets of bread for which you will be charged. The first two pages of the wine list also celebrate the Italian island.

Tsunami

H2

93 Charlotte St. ✉ W1T 4PY
☎ (020) 7637 0050
e-mail westend@tsunamirestaurant.co.uk
www.tsunamirestaurant.co.uk

⊖ **Goodge Street**
Closed 24-26 December, 1 January,
Saturday lunch
and Sunday

Menu £15 (lunch) – Carte £21/40

A/C
VISA
MC
AE

You'll never find anyone from Clapham in Nobu or Roka because they always insist they have their own cheaper version in Tsunami. Now we all have the opportunity of seeing what they mean, thanks to their second branch here in the West End. Appropriately enough, it is at the less showy end of Charlotte Street but is prettily decorated with lacquered walls and a floral motif, with colour changing lights and lounge music. Staff have good intentions but do tend to go missing at crucial moments but the contemporary Japanese food is carefully prepared and the menu covers all points and includes plenty of originality. Seafood, whether grilled, as tempura or a sashimi salad, is a highlight and plenty can be shared without breaking the bank.

Villandry Kitchen

French ✗

95-97 High Holborn ✉ **WC1V 6LF**
✆ (020) 7242 4580
e-mail holborn@villandrykitchen.com
www.villandry.com

⊖ Holborn
Closed 25-26 December and
1 January

Carte £21/34

This is the third and most recent addition to the Villandry group and gives all the surrounding chain restaurants in Holborn a run for their money. It aims to attract customers from early morning to late evening, offering everything from a breakfast menu to assorted charcuterie, from children's menus and pizzas to comforting French classics – and all at a fair price, where service is not automatically added. There's a good selection of wine by glass and carafe, including a decent house wine from Languedoc. The place is too big to be considered a bistrot and its somewhat austere layout means that the noise bounces around, but it does have an appealingly rustic and honest feel. Service is friendly, if at times a little overconfident.

The sun is out – let's eat alfresco! Look for 🏠.

Bayswater · Maida Vale

There may not appear to be an obvious link between Maida Vale and Italy, but the name of this smart area to the west of central London is derived from a battle fought over two hundred years ago in Southern Italy, and the most appealing visitor attraction in the neighbourhood is the charming canalside **Little Venice.** To stroll around here on a summer's day brings to mind promenading in a more distant European clime; it's hard to believe that the ear-shattering roar of the Westway is just a short walk away. South of this iconic elevated roadway – a snaking route out from Marylebone to the western suburbs – is Bayswater, a busy area of imposing nineteenth century buildings that's the epicentre of London's Middle Eastern community.

During its Victorian heyday, **Bayswater** was a grand and glamorous address for affluent and elegant types who wanted a giant green space (Hyde Park) on their doorstep. The whole area had been laid out in the mid 1800s, when grand squares and cream stuccoed terraces started to fill the acres between Brunel's curvy Paddington station and the park. But during the twentieth century Bayswater's cachet nose-dived, stigmatised as 'the wrong side of the park' by the arrivistes of Knightsbridge and Kensington. Today it's still a backpacker's paradise: home to a bewildering number of shabby tourist hotels,

bedsits and B&Bs, converted from the grand houses. But this tells only a fraction of the modern story, because the area is undergoing a massive facelift that will transform it forever. The hub of this makeover is the **Paddington Basin,** a gigantic reclamation of the old Grand Union Canal basin in the shadow of the rail terminus. From a ramshackle wasteground, it's now a shimmering zone of metal, steel and glass, a phantasmagoria of blue chip HQs, homes, shops and leisure facilities. Even the barges have been turned into permanently moored 'retail opportunities'. Tree-lined towpaths along the perimeter complete the picture of a totally modern waterscape.

Lovers of the old Bayswater can still relish what made it famous in the first place: radiating out from **Lancaster Gate,** away from Hyde Park, is a web of streets with handsome squares and tucked-away mews, and it still retains pockets of close-knit communities, such as Porchester Square, west of Paddington station. Meanwhile, the 'cathedral' of the area, Whiteleys shopping centre in **Queensway**, remains a pivotal landmark, as it has been for more than a century. Just beyond Whiteleys heading away from central London, **Westbourne Grove** is still reassuringly expensive, or at least the bit that heads determinedly towards Notting Hill. But the wind of change has rustled other parts of the

S. Ollivier / MICHELIN

neighbourhood: Connaught Street has evolved into a villagey quarter of boutiques, galleries and restaurants, while, further west, Craven Hill Gardens is the height of chic, courtesy of The Hempel, a boutique hotel.

Little Venice pretty much acts as a dividing line between Bayswater and Maida Vale. Technically, it's the point where the Paddington arm of the Grand Union Canal meets the **Regent's Canal,** but the name, coined by poet Robert Browning who lived close by, has come to encompass the whole area just to the north of the soaring Westway. Narrow boat moorings vie for attention alongside

the cafés and pubs that mercifully lack the frantic high street buzz so typical of their kind away from the water's edge. The permanently moored boats were here a long time before those upstarts at Paddington Basin. This is where you can find old-time favourites including a floating art gallery and a puppet theatre barge, and all overseen by the Warwick Castle pub, a stalwart of the area that's a minute's walk from the canal. Suitably refreshed, a wander round the residential streets of Maida Vale is very pleasant, dominated by the impressive Edwardian blocks of flats that conjure up a distinctive well-to-do scene.

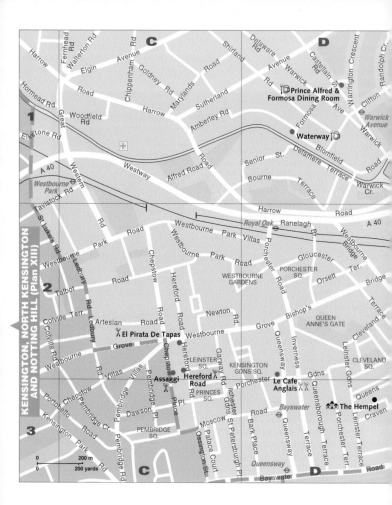

Prince Alfred & Formosa Dining Room

Waterway

Royal Oak

El Pirata De Tapas

Assaggi

Hereford Road

Le Cafe Anglais

The Hempel

0   200 m
0   200 yards

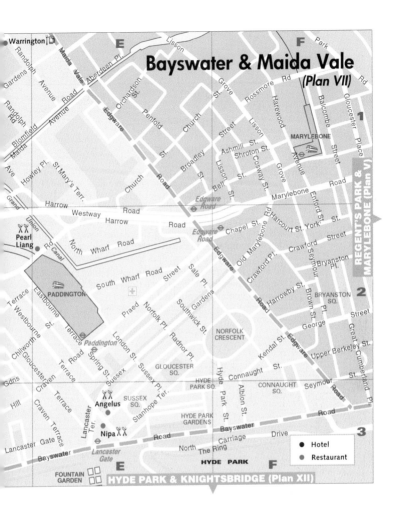

Bayswater & Maida Vale
(Plan VII)

Warrington

REGENT'S PARK & MARYLEBONE (Plan VI)

MARYLEBONE

Pearl Liang

PADDINGTON

NORFOLK CRESCENT

Angelus

Nipa

HYDE PARK SQ.

HYDE PARK GARDENS

CONNAUGHT SQ.

BRYANSTON SQ.

GLOUCESTER SQ.

SUSSEX SQ.

●	Hotel
●	Restaurant

HYDE PARK

FOUNTAIN GARDEN

HYDE PARK & KNIGHTSBRIDGE (Plan XII)

161

Angelus

E3

French 🍴🍴

4 Bathurst St. ✉ W2 2SD
☎ (020) 7402 0083
e-mail info@angelusrestaurant.co.uk
www.angelusrestaurant.co.uk

⊖ Lancaster Gate
Closed 24 December-2 January

Menu £30 (lunch) – Carte £34/56

A/C

VISA

MC

AE

This 19C former pub, with its Murano chandeliers and art nouveau mirrors, has a warm and inclusive feel, and much of the credit for that goes to its very hospitable owner, Thierry Tomasin, who knows all his regulars and has put together an equally committed team. Along with the front restaurant, there is a surprisingly large sitting area at the back. Thierry has resisted the temptation to put in more tables, although with the downstairs area and a chef's table in the kitchen he probably has enough. The cooking style is French with British ingredients and he has a 'proper' kitchen which does the right things at the right time of year: who could resist braised ox cheek on a cold winter's night? Equal thought has gone into the wine list.

Assaggi

C2

Italian 🍴

39 Chepstow Pl., (above Chepstow pub)
✉ W2 4TS
☎ (020) 7792 5501
e-mail nipi@assaggi.demon.co.uk
www.assaggi.com

⊖ Bayswater
Closed 2 weeks Christmas, Sunday and
bank holidays – booking essential

Carte approx. £47

A/C

VISA

MC

①

Assaggi has always been about simplicity, from the pared-down surroundings of this room above a pub to the handwritten bill at the end. The cooking has also always been about honest flavours and quality produce but the creeping hand of complacency has seen some of the shine come off; dishes that were once full of vitality now seem duller in comparison and the kitchen appears to have lost a little of its verve and panache. This is a pity because Assaggi has always been a spirited and inclusive restaurant and has shown that good food need not be accompanied by great ceremony. Regulars, kissed on the way in and the way out, may treat the place like their local trattoria, but the prices represent a special night out for most of us.

Le Café Anglais

Modern European ⅩⅩ

8 Porchester Gdns. ⊠ W2 4BD
☏ (020) 7221 1415
e-mail info@lecafeanglais.co.uk
www.lecafeanglais.co.uk

⊖ Bayswater
Closed 25-26 December
and 1 January

Menu £22/25 – Carte £26/46

AC
☼
VISA
MC
AE
O

The terminal blandness of Queensway received a boost back in 2007 when Rowley Leigh, formerly of Kensington Place, opened this vast brasserie within Whiteley's, the Grade II listed shopping centre. His place shares the same conviviality and culinary accessibility as 'KP' but on a bigger scale and with better acoustics. The art deco styling, leather banquettes and big windows may reflect Whiteley's 1911 roots but it's still best to take the lift up from the side entrance. Allow extra time for reading: the menu offers a huge range of brasserie classics, ranging from rabbit rillettes and parmesan custard to the daily specials and meats turning slowly on the rotisserie. The wine list is resolutely Old World.

Hereford Road ☺

British Ⅹ

3 Hereford Rd. ⊠ W2 4AB
☏ (020) 7727 1144
e-mail info@herefordroad.org
www.herefordroad.org

⊖ Bayswater
Closed 25-26 December and 1 January
– booking essential

Menu £16 (weekday lunch) – Carte £23/29

AC
☼
VISA
MC
AE
O

Hereford Road is, first and foremost, a local restaurant. Lunch is a relaxed affair, with the room brightened by the large domed skylight, while dinner is the livelier feast, where everyone gives the impression that they walked here. Owner-chef Tom Pemberton is often the first person you see as the open kitchen is by the entrance – this was once a butcher's shop. He is an acolyte of St John and his cooking shares the same principles but not the same prices. So expect seasonal, British ingredients in very tasty dishes devoid of frippery. Offal is handled with aplomb and dishes designed for two, such as the shoulder of lamb or the whole oxtail, are so good you won't actually want to share them. Staff are enthusiastic and articulate.

Nipa

E3

Thai ✗✗

Lancaster Ter. ⊠ W2 2TY
✆ (020) 7551 6039
e-mail nipa@lancasterlondon.com
www.niparestaurant.co.uk

⊖ Lancaster Gate
Closed Saturday lunch and Sunday

Menu £29/32 – Carte £26/37

A/C
VISA
MC
AE
①

You'll find Nipa to be a little oasis of calm and hospitality, once you've made it up to the first floor of the Royal Lancaster and sidestepped the businessmen on their laptops in the adjacent lounge. Its teak panelling and ornaments are all imported from Thailand and they've done a convincing job of replicating the original Nipa in Bangkok's Landmark Hotel – if anything, it's even a little smarter. The menu is comprehensive, with a mix of the recognisable blended with more regional specialities. Dishes are marked 1-3 in chillies for their respective heat, come in decent sizes and the harmonious blend of flavours and textures successfully delivers what the aromas promise. Set menus are at the back and provide a convenient all-round experience.

Pearl Liang

E2

Chinese ✗✗

8 Sheldon Sq., Paddington Central
⊠ W2 6EZ
✆ (020) 7289 7000
www.pearlliang.co.uk

⊖ Paddington

Menu £25 – Carte £25/44

A/C
⟨⟩
☼
VISA
MC
AE

Pearl Liang is a largely windowless restaurant which, depending on your opinion of the corporate development that is Paddington Central, may be a good or bad thing. The interior of this large Chinese restaurant is also kept pretty business-like, both in the type of clientele it attracts and the style of service it provides them with. The kitchen delivers the promises of the menu and no more, but those menus are quite varied, from the 'Jade', 'Pearl' and 'Diamond' set menus to the extensive à la carte which blends the classics and more unusual choices, like jellyfish with sesame, pig's trotter and drunken chicken. Dishes from other Asian countries creep onto the menu but it's best to stick to the Chinese specialities.

El Pirata De Tapas

C2

115 Westbourne Grove ⊠ W2 4UP   ⊖ Bayswater
✆ (020) 7727 5000
e-mail info@elpiratadetapas.co.uk
www.elpiratadetapas.co.uk

Menu £10 (lunch) – Carte approx. £25

Spanish restaurants and tapas-style eating satisfy our appetite for a shared, less structured dining experience and El Pirata is no exception. It's spread over two floors, although you wouldn't want to be the first table downstairs, and is decorated in a contemporary yet warm style. The staff give helpful advice on a menu that is quite lengthy but helpfully divided up into sections, from charcuterie to fish, croquettes to vegetarian, meat to paellas; there are also a couple of appealing and balanced set menus and the pricing structure is far from piratical. The kitchen shows respect for traditional flavours but is not afraid of trying new things or adding a note of playfulness to some dishes. A good place to come with friends.

Prince Alfred & Formosa Dining Room

D1

5A Formosa St ⊠ W9 1EE   ⊖ Warwick Avenue.
✆ (020) 7286 3287
e-mail princealfred@youngs.co.uk
www.theprincealfred.com

Carte £21/35

Original plate glass, panels and snugs make The Prince Alfred a wonderful example of a classic Victorian pub. Unfortunately, the eating is done in the Formosa Dining Room extension on the side but at least it's a lively room with capable cooking. There's a rustic theme running through the menu, with a strong British accent, so traditionalists will enjoy the fish pie, potted trout, steak and ale pie and calves liver but there are also risottos, parfaits and terrines for those of a more European bent. The open kitchen is not averse to sprucing up some classics, for example your burger arrives adorned with foie gras and truffles. Prices are realistic, even with a charge made for bread, and the friendly team cope well under pressure.

Warrington

G a s t r o p u b

93 Warrington Cres ✉ W9 1EH   ⊖ Maida Vale.
📞 (020) 7592 7960   Closed lunch Monday-Wednesday
e-mail thewarrington@gordonramsay.com
www.gordonramsay.com

Menu £22 (lunch and early dinner) – Carte £20/30

AC

VISA

MC

AE

The British pub appears to be steadily breaking up into two rival camps: there's the traditional pub, where you can stand at the bar with a sausage roll in one hand and a pint in the other; and the modern one, where you're given a table and someone serves you pork belly and a glass of Pinot Noir. The joy of The Warrington is that both types are available under one roof. The wood-panelled ground floor with its friezes and mosaic is full of atmosphere and the menu here includes fish pie and bangers. Upstairs is altogether smarter and the mood a little more subdued. Here the menu is much more sophisticated, as you'd expect from a Gordon Ramsay restaurant, although it's still commendably British and could include braised duck or pan-fried bream.

Waterway

G a s t r o p u b

54 Formosa St ✉ W9 2JU   ⊖ Warwick Avenue.
📞 (020) 7266 3557
e-mail info@thewaterway.co.uk
www.thewaterway.co.uk

Menu £17 (lunch) – Carte £30/45

Strictly speaking, The Waterway is not really a pub but it does always have lots of people standing outside with drinks in their hands. To see it at its best you have to arrive by narrowboat as the terrific canalside terrace is one of its great selling points. The dining area is beyond the bar and has a nicely balanced menu. For starters expect squid, scallops or risotto; main courses could include beef Bourguignon or duck breast with okra and dishes are executed with a certain degree of vim. There are more accessible choices available too, especially on the terrace, like the house burger, Caesar salad and rib-eye steak. The young team of servers can sometimes place too much emphasis on functionality at the expense of personality.

City of London · Clerkenwell Finsbury · Southwark

Say what you like about London, **The City** is the place where it all started. The Romans developed this small area – this square mile – nearly two thousand years ago, and today it stands as the economic heartbeat of not only the capital, but the country as a whole. Each morning it's besieged with an army of bankers, lawyers and traders, and each evening it's abandoned to an eerie ghost-like fate. Of course, this mass exodus is offset by the two perennial crowd-pullers, **St Paul's** and the **Tower of London**, but these are both on the periphery of the area, away from the frenetic commercial zone within. The casual visitor tends to steer clear of the City, but for those willing to mix it with the daytime swarm of office workers, there are many historical nuggets hidden away, waiting to be mined. You can find here, amongst the skyscrapers, a tempting array of Roman ruins, medieval landmarks and brooding churches designed by Wren and Hawksmoor. One of the best ways of encapsulating everything that's happened here down the centuries is to visit the Museum of London, on London Wall, which tells the story of the city from the very start, and the very start means 300,000 BC.

For those seeking the hip corners of this part of London, the best advice is to head slightly northwest, using the brutalist space of the **Barbican Arts Centre** as your marker. You're now entering **Clerkenwell**. Sliding north/south through here is the bustling and buzzy **St John Street,** home to some of the funkiest eating establishments and gastropubs in London, their proximity to **Smithfield** meat market giving a clue as to much of the provenance. Clerkenwell's revivalist vibe has seen the steady reclamation of old factory space: during the Industrial Revolution, the area boomed with the introduction of breweries, print works and the manufacture of clocks and watches. After World War II decline set in, but these days city professionals and loft-dwellers are drawn to the area's zeitgeist-leading galleries and clubs, not to mention the wonderful floor-to-ceiling delicatessens. Clerkenwell is home to The Eagle, one of the city's pioneering gastropubs and still a local favourite, brimming over with newspaper journalists (it's near The Guardian offices). It even has its own art gallery upstairs. Meanwhile, the nearby **Exmouth Market** teems with trendy bars and restaurants, popular with those on their way to the perennially excellent dance concerts at Sadler's Wells Theatre.

The area was once a religious centre, frequented by monks and nuns; its name derives from the parish clerks who performed Biblical mystery plays around the Clerk's Well set in a nunnery wall. This can be found in **Farringdon Lane** complete with an exhibition explaining all. Close by in St John's

C. Eymenier / MICHELIN

Lane is the 16C gatehouse which is home to the Museum of the Order of St John (famous today for its ambulance services), and chock full of fascinating objects related to the Order's medieval history.

Not too long ago, a trip over London Bridge to **Southwark** was for locals only, its trademark grimness ensuring it was well off the tourist map. These days, visitors treat it as a place of pilgrimage as three of London's modern success stories reside here. **Tate Modern** has become the city's most visited attraction, a huge former power station that generates a blistering show of modern art from 1900 to the present day, its massive turbine hall a must-see feature in itself. Practically next door but a million miles away architecturally is Shakespeare's **Globe,** a wonderful evocation of medieval showtime. Half a mile east is the best food market in London: **Borough Market.** Foodies can't resist the organic feel-good nature of the place, with its mind-boggling number of stalls selling produce ranging from every kind of fruit and veg to rare-breed meats, oils, preserves, chocolates and breads. And that's just for hors-d'œuvres…

169

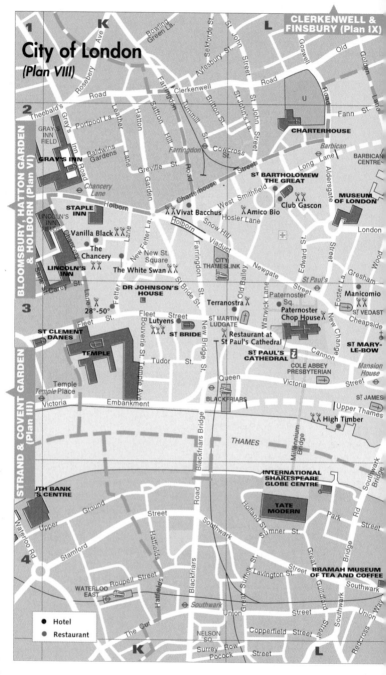

City of London
(Plan VIII)

CLERKENWELL & FINSBURY (Plan IX)

BLOOMSBURY, HATTON GARDEN & HOLBORN (Plan VI)

STRAND & COVENT GARDEN (Plan III)

GRAY'S INN FIELD

GRAY'S INN

Chancery Lane

STAPLE INN

LINCOLN'S INN FIELDS

Vanilla Black

The Chancery

LINCOLN'S INN

The White Swan

New Square

DR JOHNSON'S HOUSE

28°-50°

Lutyens

Bouverie St.

ST CLEMENT DANES

TEMPLE

Temple Place

Temple Place

Victoria

Embankment

Vivat Bacchus

Amico Bio

Club Gascon

ST BARTHOLOMEW THE GREAT

CHARTERHOUSE

BARBICAN CENTRE

MUSEUM OF LONDON

London

Gresham

Manicomio

ST VEDAST

Cheapside

ST MARY-LE-BOW

Mansion House

ST JAMES

Upper Thames

High Timber

Terranostra

ST MARTIN LUDGATE

ST BRIDE

CITY THAMESLINK

Restaurant at St Paul's Cathedral

Paternoster Chop House

Paternoster Sq.

ST PAUL'S CATHEDRAL

COLE ABBEY PRESBYTERIAN

Victoria

Cannon

BLACKFRIARS

THAMES

Blackfriars Bridge

Millennium Bridge

Southwark Bridge

INTERNATIONAL SHAKESPEARE GLOBE CENTRE

TATE MODERN

SOUTH BANK'S CENTRE

WATERLOO EAST

Southwark

BRAMAH MUSEUM OF TEA AND COFFEE

NELSON SQ.

● Hotel

● Restaurant

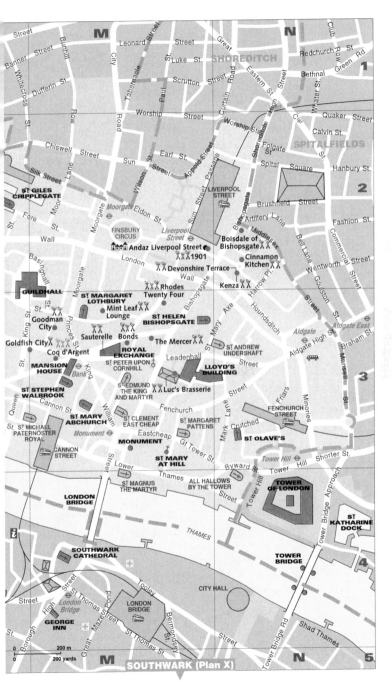

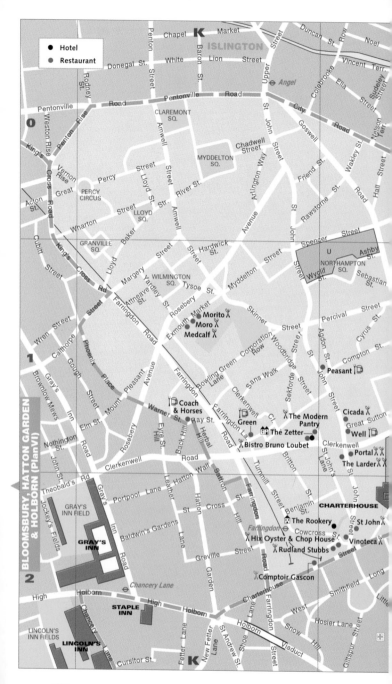

Hotel
Restaurant

K — Market — Street — Duncan — St. — Row — Noel
Chapel ISLINGTON
Penton — White — Baron — Lion — Street — Upper — St. — Vincent — Terr.
Donegal St. — Colebrooke — Ella — Sudeley Terr.
Rodney St. — Angel — City — Road — Nelson Terr.
Pentonville — Road — Pentonville — Road — Goswell
Weston Rise — King's — CLAREMONT SQ. — John — St.
Penton Rise — Chadwell Street — Arlington Way — Friend St. — Wakley St.
Vernon Rise — Amwell — MYDDELTON SQ. — Rawstorne — St. — Hall — St.
Percy — Street — Street — River St. — Spencer — Street
Great — PERCY CIRCUS — Lloyd St. — Str. — Amwell — U — Ashby St.
Cross — Street — LLOYD SQ. — NORTHAMPTON SQ. — Sebastian St.
Acton St. — Wharton — Baker — Myddelton — Wyclif — St.
Cubitt — GRANVILLE SQ. — Hardwick St. — Spencer — Street
Street — Lloyd — Margery — WILMINGTON SQ. — Tysoe St.
Wren — Street — Yardley St. — Rosebery — Skinner — Street — Percival — Cyrus St.
Calthorpe — Farringdon — Exmouth Market — **Morito** — Corporation Row — Compton St.
Gough — Road — **Moro** — **Medcalf** — Woodbridge Street — **Peasant**
Phoenix — Mount Pleasant — Bowling Green Lane — Sans Walk — Sekforde Street — John — St. — **Cicada**
Elm St. — Warner — **Coach & Horses** — Clerkenwell — Cl. — **The Modern Pantry** — Great Sutton
Nothington — Rosebery — Gray St. — **Green** — **The Zetter** — **Well**
John St. — Eyre St. — Hill — Herbal — Back — **Bistro Bruno Loubet** — Clerkenwell — **Portal**
Clerkenwell — Saffron — Britton — St John's Lane — **The Larder**
Theobald's Rd — Portpool — Lane — Leather — Hatton — Turnmill Street — CHARTERHOUSE
GRAY'S INN FIELD — Cross — St. — Benjamin — St.
Jockey's Fields — Baldwin's Gardens — **The Rookery** — **St John**
GRAY'S INN — Hatton — Farringdon — Cowcross — **Vinoteca**
John St. — Greville — Street — **Hix Oyster & Chop House** — Street
Garden — **Rudland Stubbs**
Chancery Lane — **Comptoir Gascon** — Smithfield — Long
High — Holborn — High — Holborn — West — Hosier Lane
STAPLE INN — Holborn — Snow
LINCOLN'S INN FIELDS — Chancery — Fetter — New Fetter — St Andrew St. — Holborn — Viaduct — Glitspur Street
LINCOLN'S INN — Lane — Lane — K — Cursitor St.

BLOOMSBURY, HATTON GARDEN & HOLBORN (Plan VI)

0

1

2

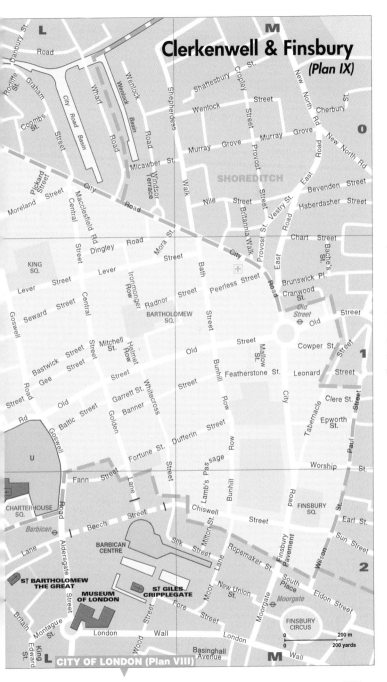

Clerkenwell & Finsbury
(Plan IX)

SHOREDITCH

KING SQ.

BARTHOLOMEW SQ.

CHARTERHOUSE SQ.

Barbican

BARBICAN CENTRE

St BARTHOLOMEW THE GREAT

MUSEUM OF LONDON

St GILES CRIPPLEGATE

FINSBURY SQ.

FINSBURY CIRCUS

Moorgate

CITY OF LONDON (Plan VIII)

0   200 m
0   200 yards

173

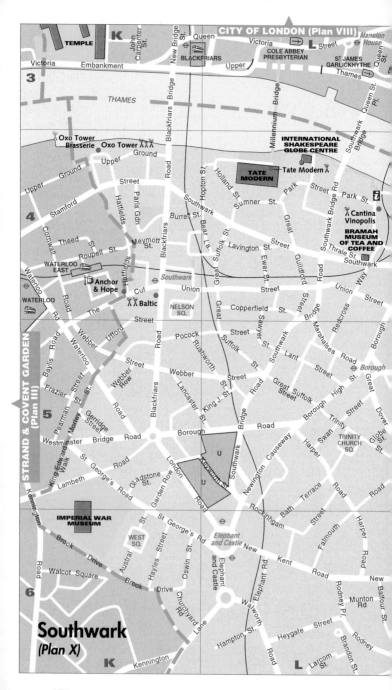

TEMPLE

John Carpenter St.

New Bridge St.

Queen Victoria

Mansion House

Street

BLACKFRIARS

COLE ABBEY PRESBYTERIAN

ST JAMES GARLICKHYTHE

Victoria Embankment

Upper Thames

Queen St.

3

THAMES

Blackfriars Bridge

Millennium Bridge

Southwark Bridge

Queen St.

Oxo Tower Brasserie

Oxo Tower

Ground

INTERNATIONAL SHAKESPEARE GLOBE CENTRE

Southwark Bridge Rd

Upper

Upper

Ground

Street

Hopton St.

Holland St.

Park Street

TATE MODERN

Tate Modern

Park St.

Cantina Vinopolis

Stamford

Hatfields

Paris Gdn

Southwark

Sumner St.

Great

Southwark Bridge Rd

BRAMAH MUSEUM OF TEA AND COFFEE

4

Cornwall

Theed

Roupell St.

St.

Burrel St.

Bear La.

Great Suffolk St.

Lavington St.

Street

Guildford

Thrale St.

Southwark

Waterloo

Hatfields

Meymott St.

Blackfriars

Ewer St.

Road

Union

WATERLOO EAST

Anchor & Hope

The Cut

Southwark

Union Street

Union Street

Street

WATERLOO

Baltic

NELSON SQ.

Great

Copperfield St.

Sawyer St.

Marshalsea Road

Redcross

Street

Waterloo Rd

Bayliss Road

Webber

Ufford

Street

Pocock

Rushworth

Great Suffolk St.

Southwark

Lant Street

Borough

Frazier St.

Street

Webber Row

Blackfriars

Webber Street

Lancaster St.

King J. St.

Street

Great Suffolk Street

Borough High St.

Trinity Street

Swan St.

Dover St.

5

Pearman St.

Morley St.

Gerridge Street

Road

Borough Road

Bridge

TRINITY CHURCH SQ.

Globe St.

Westminster Bridge Road

King Edward Walk

St George's Road

Gladstone St.

Garden Row

London Road

Borough Road

Southwark Bridge Road

Newington Causeway

Harper

Trinity

U

U

Lambeth

IMPERIAL WAR MUSEUM

St George's Road

Bath

Terrace

Rockingham

Falmouth

Harper Road

Road

St George's St.

Hayles Street

Oswin St.

Elephant and Castle

New Kent Road

WEST SQ.

Elephant and Castle

Kent Road

Munton Rd

Kennington

Brook Drive

Walcot Square

Austral St.

Brook Drive

Churchyard Rd

Elephant Rd

Walworth

Hampton St.

Heygate Street

Rodney Pl.

Brandon St.

Rodney

New

Road

Larcom St.

Southwark
(Plan X)

Kennington

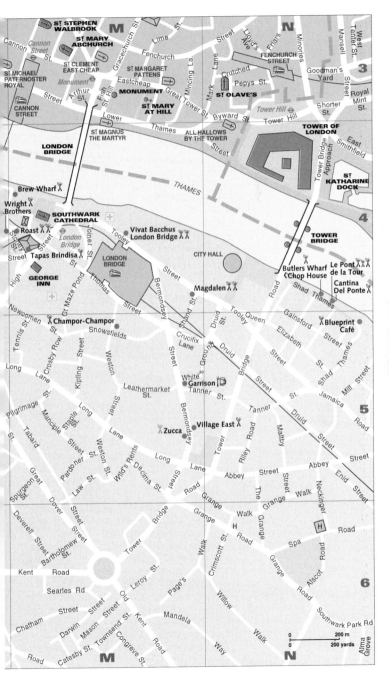

ST STEPHEN
WALBROOK

ST MARY
ABCHURCH

Cannon
Cannon Street
Street
St.

ST CLEMENT
EAST CHEAP

ST MICHAEL
PATERNOSTER
ROYAL

Monument

CANNON
STREET

Lime St.

Lloyd's Ave.

Street

Fenchurch

Gracechurch St.

FENCHURCH
STREET

Friars

Minories

Mansell

West
Tenter St.

3

Crutched

Fenchurch

ST MARGARET
PATTENS

Eastcheap

Mincing La.

Mark
Lane

Pepys St.

ST OLAVE'S

Goodman's
Yard

Street

Royal
Mint
St.

Arthur St.

MONUMENT

ST MARY
AT HILL

Lower
Thames

Great Tower St.

Byward

Tower Hill

St.

Tower Hill

Shorter
St.

TOWER OF
LONDON

East
Smithfield

ST MAGNUS
THE MARTYR

LONDON
BRIDGE

ALL HALLOWS
BY THE TOWER

Street

THAMES

Tower Bridge Approach

ST
KATHARINE
DOCK

Brew Wharf ✗

Wright ✗
Brothers

Roast ✗

SOUTHWARK
CATHEDRAL

London
Bridge

Joiner St.

Tooley

Vivat Bacchus
London Bridge ✗✗

CITY HALL

TOWER
BRIDGE

Tapas Brindisa ✗

St.
Street

GEORGE
INN

High

Gt. Maze Pond

LONDON
BRIDGE

Thomas

Street

Street

Bermondsey

Magdalen ✗✗

Butlers Wharf ✗
Chop House

Shad Thames

Le Pont ✗✗✗
de la Tour

Cantina
Del Ponte ✗

Newcomen

✗ Champor-Champor

St.

Snowsfields

Tennis St.

Crosby Row

Kipling Street

Weston

Leathermarket
St.

Island St.

Druid

Crucifix
Lane

Tooley

Queen

Druid

Bridge

Street

Street

Gainsford

Elizabeth

St.

Shad Thames

✗ Blueprint
Café

Jamaica

Mill Street

5

Long
Lane

Pilgrimage
St.

Tabard
St.

Manciple
Long Street
Lane

Staple
St.

Pardoner St.

Weston St.

Bermondsey

White's ■ Garrison
Tanner

St.

Tanner

St.

Druid

Street

Jamaica

Road

Spurgeon
St.

Law. St.

Wild's Rents

Decima St.

✗ Zucca

Village East ✗

Tower

Long
Lane

Riley
Road

Abbey

The

Street

Grange

Walk

Neckinger

Street

Abbey

Street

Enid Street

Deverell
Street

Dover
Street

Street

Bridge

Grange

Walk

Grange

Road

H
Road

Spa

H

Road

Road

Alscot

Kent

Road

Bartholomew
St.

Tower

Crimscott
St.

Page's

Willow

Grange

Road

Southwark Park Rd

6

Searles Rd

Leroy St.

Chatham

Street

Darwin
Street

Mason
Street

Old
Street

Townsend
Kent
St.
Road

Mandela

Walk

Way

Alma
Grove

Road

Catesby St.
Congreve St.

M

N

0   200 m
0   200 yards

M

N

Amico Bio

L2

Italian vegetarian ✗

44 Cloth Fair ✉ EC1A 7JQ
✆ (0207) 6007 778
e-mail info@amicobio.co.uk
www.amicobio.co.uk

⊖ Barbican
Closed 25 December, Saturday lunch,
Sunday and bank holidays

Carte £17/21 s

A/C
VISA
MC

Opening a vegetarian restaurant just yards from Smithfield Market may seem like a grand ironic gag but a dish of the baked red peppers with capers and olives could turn the most committed of carnivores. This simple little Italian place is owned by an experienced chef and his cousin and all their organic produce comes from their family farm in Capua. The menu changes as the produce comes and goes so don't be surprised if a dish suddenly runs out. The cooking is light and fresh with combinations of flavours that remain true to the chef's upbringing in Campania. He's happy to engage with his customers so it's worth asking for his recommendations. Photos of the farm adorn the walls and prices are unimpeachably generous.

Anchor & Hope 😊

K4

British 🍺

36 The Cut ✉ SE1 8LP
✆ (020) 7928 9898
e-mail anchorandhope@btconnect.com

**Menu £30 (lunch Sunday) –
Carte £22/35**

⊖ Southwark.
Closed 2 weeks at Christmas,
Easter, May and August
bank holidays, Sunday dinner
and Monday lunch –
(bookings not accepted)

VISA
MC
①

The Anchor & Hope is still running at full steam and its popularity shows no sign of abating. It's not hard to see why: combine a menu that changes with each service and is a paragon of seasonality, with cooking that is gutsy, bold and wholesome, and you end up with immeasurably rewarding dishes like suckling kid chops with wild garlic, succulent roast pigeon with lentils or buttermilk pudding with poached rhubarb. The place has a contagiously congenial feel and the staff all pull in the same direction; you may spot a waiter trimming veg or a chef delivering dishes. The no-reservation policy remains, so either get here early or be prepared to wait – although you can now book for Sunday lunch, when everyone sits down at 2pm for a veritable feast.

Baltic

Eastern European ✗✗

74 Blackfriars Rd ✉ SE1 8HA
✆ (020) 7928 1111
e-mail info@balticrestaurant.co.uk
www.balticrestaurant.co.uk

⊖ Southwark
Closed 24-26 December – booking
advisable at dinner

Menu £15/18 – Carte £22/34

Baltic celebrates ten years in 2011 and is as busy as ever, serving over 100 diners every night. The façade may have faded over time but the atmosphere inside is as contagious as ever, as the noise from the bar competes with the clatter from the large dining area at the back. Just kick back, order a vodka and get down to choosing from the menu. If you don't know your pierogi from your pelmeni, don't panic – most of the staff are Polish so help is at hand. Starters include soups such as botwinka and zurek; blinis come with all the toppings and meat dishes outnumber fish choices 2 to 1. Just be sure you're wearing your eating-boots because portions are big and dishes are packed with flavour. There's jazz on Sunday nights.

Bistrot Bruno Loubet

French ✗

St John's Sq., 86-88 Clerkenwell Rd.
✉ EC1M 5RJ
✆ (020) 7324 4455
e-mail eat@bistrotbrunoloubet.com
www.bistrotbrunoloubet.com

⊖ Farringdon
Booking advisable

Carte £26/36

The original Bistrot Bruno's heyday in Soho was around 1994, at a time when London house prices were struggling to recover, England were no-shows at the World Cup and Silvio Berlusconi was Italy's prime minister. So 2010 seemed as good a time as any for Bruno Loubet to return to the capital after his sojourn in Australia. He did surprise a few people by pitching up in Clerkenwell, at the trendy Zetter hotel, but it's a good fit for his satisfying and rustic cooking. There is actually more depth and sophistication to the food than the menu suggests and it's not exclusively French: a little Asian spicing or Moroccan flavour can find their way in too. The room is bright; the staff unhurried and the clientele self-assured.

Blueprint Café

N5

Design Museum, Shad Thames,
Butlers Wharf ⊠ SE1 2YD
℘ (020) 7378 7031
e-mail blueprintcafe@danddlondon.com
www.danddlondon.com

⊖ London Bridge
Closed Sunday dinner

Menu £20 – Carte £22/36

You'll find Blueprint Café at the less frenzied end of Shad
Thames, sitting proudly in its elevated position above the Design
Museum. Lunch is the more relaxed affair, when you can take
advantage of the retractable windows and the views of the
comings and goings on the river, thanks to the binoculars placed
on each table. Long standing chef Jeremy Lee, who despite
doing more telly work these days is still often at the stove, has
long been a champion of British produce and his simple, yet
informed, technique is evident in dishes like beetroot salad with
horseradish, hare and beef pie and steamed ginger pudding
with custard. Do ensure you order vegetables as dishes arrive
unadorned and as understated as the menu suggests.

Boisdale of Bishopsgate

N2

Swedeland Crt., 202 Bishopsgate
⊠ EC2M 4NR
℘ (020) 7283 1763
e-mail info@boisdale-city.co.uk
www.boisdale.co.uk

⊖ Liverpool Street
Closed 23 December-
2 January, Saturday, Sunday
and bank holidays

Carte £27/55

It's easy to miss and the ground floor is a popular spot for those
who like some champagne and oysters on their way home; but
follow the tartan carpet down to the relative calm of the cosy
and characterful restaurant, complete with live music. That
carpet was a clue as this is all about Scotland. Admittedly some
of the Scottish accents are as unconvincing as Mel Gibson's but
there is no denying that the food is the real thing. The large menu
is made up of plenty of Scottish specialities and reminds us just
how spectacular the produce is north of the border. Salmon,
shellfish, beef and, of course, haggis are the perennial favourites
but so are the daily specials of game, fish and assorted pies.
You'll leave with an urge to hike somewhere.

Bonds

Modern European XXX

 M3

5 Threadneedle St. ✉ EC2R 8AY ⊖ Bank
☎ (020) 7657 8088 Closed Saturday and Sunday
e-mail bonds@theetongroup.com
www.theetoncollection.com

Menu £18/20 – Carte £27/53

Bonds repays the investment of its customers by providing plenty of interest, in both the menu choice and the surroundings. This former banking hall dates from the 1850s and its marble, pillars and panelling make it a grand old room in which to house a restaurant. The cooking is equally bold and the experienced kitchen produced well-versed dishes that are unfussy and keep their roots largely within Europe. Slow-cooking is a popular technique and is used with veal shin, rump of lamb and pork belly, while fish from Newhaven is handled deftly. Service is up to speed at lunch; dinner is less frenzied, when the lower lighting helps create a more intimate atmosphere. The cocktail list makes the adjacent bar worth visiting.

Brew Wharf

Traditional X

M4

Brew Wharf Yard, Stoney St ✉ SE1 9AD ⊖ London Bridge
☎ (020) 7378 6601 Closed Christmas-New Year, Sunday and
e-mail vinum@vinopolis.co.uk bank holidays
www.brewwharf.com

Menu £24 – Carte £22/33

Needless to say, anywhere with the word 'brew' in the title is not somewhere for a romantic evening. But if you're on a night out with a few friends then this has all the ingredients: a large screen showing sport in the bar, real ales from the restaurant's own microbrewery, bottled beers imported from everywhere from Cuba to Kenya, and the sort of food that's ideal with a pint. Don't bother messing around the starters; head straight for the main courses of steak and ale pie, liver and bacon, pork belly or confit of duck. Even the platters for two don't let up: one includes spring rolls, kebabs, fishcakes and chips. It's all well organised; you can order your own cask for your group and they hold their own beer festival in October.

Butlers Wharf Chop House

British 🍴

N4

36e Shad Thames, Butlers Wharf
✉ SE1 2YE
✆ (020) 7403 3403
e-mail bwchophouse@dandddlondon.com
www.chophouse.co.uk

⊖ **London Bridge**
Closed 1-2 January

Menu £22 (lunch) – Carte £28/43

VISA   MC   AE   ①

"Location, location, location" as every estate agent has said. A little summer sunshine and few restaurants in London can rival Butlers Wharf's delightful spot on the river. However, those terrace tables can't be booked – just join the queue at the bar. The menu reads like a roll-call of Britishness: expect potted shrimps, prawn cocktail, grilled lemon sole with Jersey Royals and the classic mixed grill. While the kitchen doesn't always quite deliver on the promise of the menu, dishes are generally satisfying. Seasonal offerings, such as the long list of strawberry dessert creations in June, are usually worth exploring. Levels of noise and general merriment are high and staff just about cope with the high numbers of customers.

Cantina Del Ponte

Italian 🍴

N4

36c Shad Thames, Butlers Wharf
✉ SE1 2YE
✆ (020) 7403 5403
e-mail cantinareservations@dandddlondon.com
www.cantina.co.uk

⊖ **London Bridge**
Closed 25-27 December

Menu £15/19 – Carte £27/38

A refurbishment a few years back made this Italian stalwart a little darker and more atmospheric, although they wisely kept the mural. The best tables on a summer's day remain those on the riverside terrace under the bright orange awning. The menu was also tweaked: it was out with the pizzas and in with a greater degree of authenticity. The focus is on appealing and flavoursome dishes and the set menu, which is available until 7pm, represents very good value. The à la carte offers an appealing selection, from recognisable standards to others displaying greater originality. Those flavours are well defined and portions are bigger than expected. The wine list covers all of Italy and there's a good choice by the glass.

Cantina Vinopolis

No.1 Bank End ✉ SE1 9BU
✆ (020) 7940 8333
e-mail cantina@vinopolis.co.uk
www.cantinavinopolis.com

⊖ London Bridge
Closed 25-26 December

Menu £30 – Carte £23/39

Southwark is becoming something of a Utopia for today's gastronauts. Food supplies can be garnered at the wonderful Borough Market and oenologists will find relief and fulfilment at Vinopolis, the wine merchant and museum. Cantina Vinopolis is the wine attraction's public restaurant and is housed under vast, magnificent Victorian arches that lend a palpable sense of history and atmospherics to the whole place. The exposed kitchen offers a menu that flits between continents and, as one would expect, the wine list offers an interesting and correspondingly diverse selection with many well priced bottles. The styling and comforts are simple and uncomplicated and the service is smoothly effective.

Champor-Champor

62-64 Weston St. ✉ SE1 3QJ
✆ (020) 7403 4600
e-mail mail@champor-champor.com
www.champor-champor.com

⊖ London Bridge
Closed 1 week Christmas,
1 week Easter,
Sunday and bank holidays –
(dinner only)

Menu £32

It's no surprise that Champor-Champor celebrated its tenth birthday in 2010 as it has always managed to beguile diners with its quirky, colourful decoration, the warm service it extends to its regulars and its authentic cooking that delivers quite a punch. Booking is vital but then they do go to the trouble of putting little name cards on each table. Be sure to ask for the second room as it has more artefacts, better lighting and a very romantic mezzanine. The food is rooted in Malay traditions, with just a flick of modernity. Great homemade banana bread gets things going; main courses arrive in big bowls with rich and creamily spiced sauce or carefully judged broths, depending on the season; ice creams are also made in-house.

The Chancery

K2

9 Cursitor St ✉ EC4A 1LL   ⊖ Chancery Lane
✆ (020) 7831 4000   Closed 24-27 and 31 December,
e-mail reservations@thechancery.co.uk   Saturday lunch and Sunday
www.thechancery.co.uk

Menu £35

A/C
VISA
MC
AE
D

Surrounded by the law courts, The Chancery, open only during the week, provides the perfect spot for that last meal of freedom or for celebrating an acquittal. It is the sister restaurant to The Clerkenwell Dining Room and the bright main room benefits from the large picture windows and understated decoration. This is room in which to reserve your table, rather than the basement which can lack something in atmosphere. Service is sufficiently fleet of foot and efficient to reassure those with an eye on the adjournment. The cooking also comes suitably well-judged and is modern in style but underpinned by a solid understanding of the ingredients. The wine list has some well-chosen bottles under £25.

Cicada

L1

132-134 St John St. ✉ EC1V 4JT   ⊖ Farringdon
✆ (020) 7608 1550
e-mail cicada@rickerrestaurants.com
www.rickerrestaurants.com

Menu £18/30 – Carte £23/50

VISA
MC
AE
D

You'll need to book ahead to guarantee a table at this busy, noisy and infectiously entertaining Pan-Asian restaurant, which was the first in Will Ricker's London-wide chain. The semi-booth seating and open style kitchen add to the general drama and the bar is more than just an addendum to the restaurant. A pot of knives, forks and chopsticks on each table allow you to decide just how authentic you want the experience to be. The varied and lengthy menu changes often but perennial favourites like chilli salt squid are constants. The Chinese element is quite strong and dim sum forms a large part but there's also more Japanese influence than in the other branches, which comes in the form of sashimi, maki rolls and tempura.

Cinnamon Kitchen

Indian XX

9 Devonshire Sq. ✉ EC2M 4YL
℘ (020) 7626 5000
e-mail info@cinnamon-kitchen.com
www.cinnamon-kitchen.com

⊖ Liverpool Street
Closed 1 January, Saturday lunch,
Sunday and bank holidays

Menu £18/19 – Carte £23/33

Having successfully established Westminster's Cinnamon Club and made it a popular choice with those who run the country, the team behind it opened a second branch here in the City, to appeal to those who own, or once thought they owned, the country. This is all about contemporary Indian dining: the cooking is creative and original, the surroundings light and unobtrusive and the service keen and sprightly. The menu bears little resemblance to the usual Indian fare and includes ingredients like quinoa, red deer and scallops. The arresting presentation doesn't come at the expense of the punchy flavours. The grill section is worth exploring and enthusiastic amateur cooks should position themselves at the Tandoor Bar to watch all the action.

Coach & Horses

Gastropub 🍺

26-28 Ray St ✉ EC1R 3DJ
℘ (020) 7837 1336
e-mail info@thecoachandhorses.com
www.thecoachandhorses.com

⊖ Farringdon.
Closed 24 December-3 January,
Easter, Saturday lunch,
Sunday dinner and bank holidays

Menu £16 (Sunday lunch) – Carte £20/29

This is one of those small, warm and cosy pubs that provide such a welcome retreat on a winter's night. Restored rather than renovated, its wood panelling, engraved windows and mirrors add to the traditional feel. There are also vestibules at both entrances – a rare sight as most pubs removed them to create more space. Diners have their own area separated by a wooden partition but there is also a back room which adjoins the terrace. The kitchen keeps things as British and straightforward as they can; even the charcuterie board contains home-cured Wiltshire ham with piccalilli. Dishes could include devilled crab, smoked haddock fish pie, and apple and almond crumble; all prepared with care, sensibly proportioned and fairly priced.

CITY OF LONDON, CLERKENWELL, FINSBURY & SOUTHWARK ▶ PLANS VIII-IX-X

Club Gascon ❀

French 🍴🍴

L2

57 West Smithfield ✉ EC1A 9DS
📞 (020) 7796 0600
e-mail info@clubgascon.com
www.clubgascon.com

⊖ Barbican
Closed Christmas and New
Year, Saturday lunch, Sunday and bank
holidays – booking essential

Menu £28 (lunch) – Carte £37/57

A/C
❀
VISA
MC
AE

Club Gascon

The rich bounty of France's southwest region is celebrated in the bourgeoning empire of Pascal Aussignac and Vincent Labeyrie but their pre-eminent creation remains Club Gascon. The restaurant is now over a decade old but some subtle changes have prepared it for the next chapter. The colour-coordinated redesign has allowed the original marble to become more of a feature and the cooking has also developed. Traditional dishes such as cassoulet and the like are now available at their 'comptoir' nearby and this in turn allows the energetic Aussignac – who even creates the dramatic floral displays himself – to be a little more daring in the kitchen here. The southwest remains his greatest influence but these days he pushes a little at the boundaries. The size of the portions has also grown slightly, although the seasonal menu, with or without suggested wine pairings, is often the best way to go. Service always begins well but can sometimes wobble a little when the room reaches capacity, but it is very hard to leave Club Gascon without feeling a little better about life.

First Course

- White pudding gnocchi with asparagus and sea urchin jus.
- Duck hearts with asparagus and pea shoots.

Main Course

- Coconut glazed black cod with white port and winkle risotto.
- Charolais beef variations with caviar and ox sauce.

Dessert

- Rhubarb and custard sweet foie gras with vanilla.
- Praline ganache with chocolate and macadamia nuts.

Comptoir Gascon 😊

K2

61-63 Charterhouse St. ✉ EC1M 6HJ
✆ (020) 7608 0851
e-mail info@comptoirgascon.com
www.comptoirgascon.com

⊖ Farringdon
Closed Christmas and New Year,
Sunday and Monday –
booking essential

Carte £15/30

[A/C]
[VISA]
[MC]
[AE]

This buzzy restaurant should be subsidised by the French Tourist Board as it does more to illustrate one component of Gascony's famed douceur de vivre – sweetness of life – than any glossy brochure. The wines, breads, foie gras, duck and cheeses all celebrate SW France's reputation for earthy, proper man-food. The menu is divided into 'mer', 'vegetal' and 'terre'; be sure to order duck, whether as rillettes, confit or in a salade Landaise. After these big flavours, it'll come as a relief to see that the desserts, displayed in a cabinet, are delicate little things. The prices are also commendable; even the region's wine comes direct from the producers to avoid the extra mark-up. There's further booty on the surrounding shelves.

Coq d'Argent

M3

1 Poultry ✉ EC2R 8EJ
✆ (020) 7395 5000
e-mail coqdargent@danddlondon.com
www.coqdargent.co.uk

⊖ Bank
Closed Christmas, bank holidays,
Saturday lunch and
Sunday dinner – booking essential

Menu £28 (lunch) – Carte £44/58

[A/C]

[VISA]
[MC]
[AE]

Resembling the bow of a ship, Coq d'Argent stands in a commanding position on the top floor of a striking building, from where one can gaze imperiously over the Square Mile. The restaurant itself is slick and stylish; service is on the ball and the cooking is mostly French but with contemporary elements. The large chilled fish counter is appealing and there are plenty of luxurious ingredients on offer, including a caviar list, to entice anyone out celebrating a deal; those whose budgets have constraints will appreciate the better value lunch menu. But it is not just the food that attracts visitors up here: the bar, terrace and fantastic formal garden are great after-work spots or venues for private parties.

Devonshire Terrace

N2

Devonshire Sq. ✉ EC2M 4WY
✆ (020) 7256 3233
e-mail info@devonshireterrace.co.uk
www.devonshireterrace.co.uk

⊖ **Liverpool Street**
Closed Saturday, Sunday and
bank holidays

Carte £28/41

Devonshire Terrace is all about flexibility. Not only is it open from 7am until 11pm, but the idea is to create your own main course by choosing the sauce and the side dishes to accompany your tiger prawns, veal chop, fishcakes or other brasserie-style offering. For those who would no sooner create their own main course than offer to help wash-up can choose salad or pastas dishes which come fully dressed. Apart from the two terraces, one of which is an all-year affair within the atrium, try to snare one of the booths in the bright restaurant with its high ceiling and open kitchen. The elephant motif? This was once an ivory store for the East India Company and the restaurant sponsors an elephant in South Africa.

Garrison

M5

99-101 Bermondsey St ✉ SE1 3XB
✆ (020) 7089 9355
e-mail info@thegarrison.co.uk
www.thegarrison.co.uk

⊖ **London Bridge.**
Booking essential at dinner

Menu £14 (early dinner) – Carte £30/40

'Sweet' is not an adjective that could apply to many of London's pubs but it does seem to fit The Garrison. The service has a certain natural charm and the place has a warm, relaxed vibe, while its mismatched style and somewhat vintage look work well. Open from 8am for smoothies and breakfast, it gets busier as the day goes on – and don't bother coming for dinner if you haven't booked. Booth numbers 4 and 5, opposite the open kitchen, are the most popular while number 2 at the back is the cosiest. The menu has a distinct Mediterranean flavour; salads dominate the starters and steaks and braised meats sit alongside pasta and fresh fish options. Puddings are more your classic pub variety. The owners' other place, Village East, is just down the street.

Goldfish City

A s i a n ✗

L/M3

46 Gresham St. ✉ EC2V 7AY
✆ (020) 7726 0308
e-mail geoffleong@gmail.com
www.goldfish-resaturant.co.uk

Menu £23/30 – Carte £23/37

⊖ Bank
Plan VIII
Closed Saturday, Sunday and
bank holidays –
booking advisable

A/C

VISA

M©

AE

Having wowed the notoriously picky hordes of Hampstead with their first Goldfish, a second branch was opened here on the edge of The City in 2010. It's spread over three floors and the décor is soothing and discreet, with walls of Chinese symbols and fretwork alongside an aquarium of the eponymous fish. An appealing selection of attractively priced steamed dim sum pulls in the punters at lunch. The à la carte menu is balanced and not overlong and mixes the classic with the more modern. Fish is clearly a strength of the kitchen and, whilst it is a little more expensive than the other choices, the steamed sea bass with soy sauce is a stand-out dish. Helpful and smartly dressed staff are on hand and make sensible recommendations.

Goodman City

B e e f   s p e c i a l i t i e s

M3

11 Old Jewry ✉ EC2R 8DU
✆ (020) 7600 8220
e-mail info@goodmanrestaurants.com
www.goodmanrestaurants.com

Menu £18 (lunch) – Carte £26/63

⊖ Bank
Closed Saturday and Sunday

A/C

VISA

M©

AE

The Mayfair branch proved such a success that the opening of a second steakhouse was inevitable. For it, they chose the more appropriate setting of a semi-industrial looking space in The City, perfect for this incontestably macho style of food. Steaks are obviously the stars of the show: the corn-fed USDA beef is imported a tonne at a time and wet-matured for 60 days; the Scottish and Irish beef is grass fed. Competitive eating from suited City types mean that steaks weighing an impressive 700grammes are the most popular; the meats are cut to order in the kitchen using a band saw. Commendably – and perhaps unusually for a steakhouse – equal care goes into the other dishes, whether that's calamari to start, or a sorbet at the end.

Green

K1

Gastropub

29 Clerkenwell Gn ✉ EC1R 0DU   ⊖ Farringdon.
℘ (020) 7490 8010
e-mail info@thegreenec1.co.uk
www.thegreenec1.co.uk

Carte £21/30

29 Clerkenwell Green dates from 1580 and had become a tavern by 1720. It's therefore fitting that, after decades being used firstly as offices and then as a restaurant, The Green is now back to being known as a pub. Appetising and imaginative bar snacks like hog shank on toast are to be had in the ground floor bar, but the intimate upstairs is where the real eating goes on. Here you'll find an appealing menu of fresh, seasonal ingredients which might include Devon crab, Cornish mackerel, Wiltshire trout or Suffolk pork. The traditional fish pie is a favourite of many and the puds on the blackboard continue the British theme. Lunches get pretty busy with those wearing suits but dinner is more relaxed and the clientele in less of a hurry.

High Timber

L3

Modern European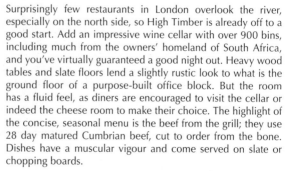

8 High Timber St. ✉ EC4V 3PA   ⊖ Mansion House
℘ (020) 7248 1777   Closed 25-26 December, Saturday, Sunday
e-mail info@hightimber.com   and bank holidays
www.hightimber.com

Menu £19 (lunch) – Carte £24/51

Surprisingly few restaurants in London overlook the river, especially on the north side, so High Timber is already off to a good start. Add an impressive wine cellar with over 900 bins, including much from the owners' homeland of South Africa, and you've virtually guaranteed a good night out. Heavy wood tables and slate floors lend a slightly rustic look to what is the ground floor of a purpose-built office block. But the room has a fluid feel, as diners are encouraged to visit the cellar or indeed the cheese room to make their choice. The highlight of the concise, seasonal menu is the beef from the grill; they use 28 day matured Cumbrian beef, cut to order from the bone. Dishes have a muscular vigour and come served on slate or chopping boards.

Hix Oyster and Chop House

L2

36-37 Greenhill Rents ✉ EC1M 6BN   ⊖ Farringdon
✆ (0207) 017 1930   Closed 25-26 December, 1 January,
e-mail chophouse@restaurantsetcltd.co.uk Saturday lunch and
www.hixoysterandchophouse.co.uk   bank holidays

Carte £29/60

Utilitarian surroundings, seasonal British ingredients, plenty of offal and prissy-free cooking: this may sound like a description of St John but is in fact the solo venture of Mark Hix, the chef who made The Ivy more than just a celebrity love-in. Smithfield Market seems an appropriate location for a restaurant that not only celebrates Britain's culinary heritage with old classics like rabbit brawn, nettle soup and beef and oyster pie but also reminds us of our own natural bounty, from sand eels and asparagus, whiting to laver bread. It's also called an Oyster & Chop House for a reason, with four types of oyster on offer as well as plenty of meat, including Aberdeen beef aged for 28 days and served on the bone.

Kenza

N2

10 Devonshire Sq. ✉ EC2M 4YP   ⊖ Liverpool Street
✆ (020) 7929 5533   Closed Saturday lunch, Sunday and
e-mail info@kenza-restaurant.com   bank holidays
www.kenza-restaurant.com

Menu £12 – Carte £26/37

The newly regenerated Devonshire Square may not appear that mysterious but descend the stairs down into Kenza and you'll be transported into the exotic Levant. The name, Arabic for 'treasure,' is well chosen and the floor tiles, lamps, carvings, colourful candles and satin cushions were all imported from Morocco. Moroccan and Lebanese cooking are the two main influences; the choices include samboussek pastries, kibbeh parcels, pureés and chargrills. There are also 'feast' menus for larger parties and the cooking is accurate and authentic; finish with theatrically poured mint tea and baklava. There's belly dancing, pumping music and large tables but the kitchen proves that a party atmosphere and good food are not mutually exclusive.

The Larder

L1

91-93 St John St. ✉ EC1M 4NU
☏ (020) 7608 1558
e-mail info@thelarderrestaurant.com
www.thelarderrestaurant.com

⊖ Farringdon
Closed 23 December-3 January and
Sunday

Menu £18 (lunch) – Carte £25/37

A/C

An appropriate name as there is bounty galore. On one side is the bakery with plenty of artisanal breads and cakes. The restaurant, meanwhile, is one of those large, semi-industrial places with exposed brick and pipes and an open kitchen at the back. This kind of hard-edged space can push up the decibels but that's part of its appeal. Think modern European comfort food, from moules marinière to roast salmon with pumpkin ravioli, but alongside the halloumi you might find Lancashire cheese and next to the chicken breast with Puy lentils could be a Barnsley chop, so the Union flag is raised occasionally (the owners are from Liverpool). A side dish to accompany the main course is recommended and some thought has gone into them.

VISA

MC

AE

Luc's Brasserie

M3

17-22 Leadenhall Market ✉ EC3V 1LR
☏ (020) 7621 0666
e-mail info@lucsbrasserie.com
www.lucsbrasserie.com

⊖ Bank
Closed 25 December-4 January,
Saturday, Sunday, bank holidays,
dinner Friday and Monday –
booking essential at lunch

Menu £19 – Carte £29/41

VISA

Go into Leadenhall Market and look up – that's Luc's Brasserie, a restaurant which first appeared in the late 1890s and was reinvigorated and re-launched in 2006. The top floor is fairly sedate but the main room- from where you can admire the Victorian splendour of the market – is where the action is. The menu is an unapologetic paean to all things French, from snails to steak tartare, confit of duck to crème brûlée. The kitchen wisely sticks to conventional and classic recipes and it's easy to see why ties are quickly loosened. Staff do their bit by getting on with things but do so with a smile. As one would expect, the mood relaxes somewhat on the three nights they open for dinner, when a fixed price menu is also available.

MC

AE

Lutyens

Modern European 🍴🍴🍴

K3

85 Fleet St. ✉ EC4Y 1AE   ⊖ St Paul's
☎ (020) 7583 8385   Closed 24 December-4 January and
e-mail info@lutyens-restaurant.com   bank holidays
www.lutyens-restaurant.com

Menu £40 (dinner) – Carte £38/57

Having built one restaurant empire, Sir Terence Conran appears to have embarked on creating another. Lutyens opened in 2009 following the success of Boundary, and boasts that unmistakeable Conran look: timeless and effortless good looks mixed with functionality. He also found another building of note: the restaurant is within what was the HQ of Reuters and is named after its architect, Sir Edwin. The menu is an appealing Anglo-French affair, with an assortment of classics ranging from parfaits and fruits de mer to Dover sole and roast grouse, along with dishes from the rotisserie; sushi even makes an incongruous appearance. Service is clued-up but perhaps a little more formal than it needs to be. There's a busy bar on the Fleet Street side.

Magdalen

British 🍴🍴

M4

152 Tooley St. ✉ SE1 2TU   ⊖ London Bridge
☎ (020) 7403 1342   Closed Christmas and New Year, 2 weeks
e-mail info@magdalenrestaurant.co.uk   August, Saturday lunch,
www.magdalenrestaurant.co.uk   Sunday and bank holidays

Menu £19 (lunch) – Carte £28/36

The cooking aromas have an immediate Pavlovian effect as you enter: Magdalen is the restaurant of choice for hungry locals looking for large portions and big flavours. The kitchen is a clever one: super sourcing and direct contact with farmers take care of the ingredients, the cooking is full of technique without being showy and influences are thoroughly British. Rump of Longhorn beef is a favourite; the treacle tart is spot on and the lunch menu is a steal. The wine list has been thoughtfully put together by someone who clearly also eats the food. Staff are kept busy but rarely take their eye off the ball. The restaurant is divided between two floors; upstairs is more convivial, downstairs more intimate.

Manicomio

L3

Italian 🍴

6 Gutter Ln. ✉ EC2V 8AS
℘ (020) 7726 5010
e-mail gutterlane@manicomio.co.uk
www.manicomio.co.uk

⊖ St Paul's
Closed 24 December-3 January,
Saturday, Sunday and
bank holidays

Menu £20 (early dinner) – Carte £33/51

[A/C]
[VISA]
[MC]
[AE]

This sibling to the King's Road branch opened in the summer of 2008 and is on the first floor of a Norman Foster-designed building. On the ground floor is the deli/café while the bar is kept separately on the top floor, away from the restaurant which makes a nice change in this part of town. The owners' other business is importing Italian produce so they know their cipollas. There's also plenty of British meat, game and fish but prepared in an Italian way, with top notch Italian accompaniments. The cooking covers many regions, with daily specials; one or two side dishes are needed for the main course and these, together with the bread, may bump the bill up. The room has a bright, fresh feel; all the furniture is imported from Italy.

Medcalf 😊

K1

British 🍴

40 Exmouth Mkt. ✉ EC1R 4QE
℘ (020) 7833 3533
e-mail mail@medcalfbar.co.uk
www.medcalfbar.co.uk

⊖ Farringdon
Closed 24 December-1 January,
Sunday dinner and bank holidays –
booking essential

Carte £26/37

There is something very 'proper' about Medcalf: maybe that's the no-frills décor that celebrates the original butcher's shop that was here from 1912 (the lights are held up by meat hooks); maybe it's the loud and buzzy pub-like atmosphere, with the good range of draught beers, wines by the glass and assorted snacks or maybe it's the fresh, appealing and very seasonal British cooking, with dishes like Barnsley chop or Calves liver, which has a satisfyingly robust, masculine feel to it. Whatever it is, it works as the restaurant gets very busy, very quickly. Those who think jellies and foams should only be found at children's playtime rather than on a dinner plate will find much to celebrate here at Medcalf.

The Mercer

 **Modern European** XX

M3

34 Threadneedle St ✉ EC2R 8AY   ⊖ Bank
☏ (020) 7628 0001   Closed 24 December-2 January,
e-mail info@themercer.co.uk   Saturday, Sunday and
www.themercer.co.uk   bank holidays

Carte £28/42

The credit crunch means it's even less likely that a restaurant will ever be converted into a bank so, at the moment, the trend remains from bank to restaurant; here at The Mercer you can even see where the tellers used to sit. The high ceilings and windows let in plenty of light and the place has a pleasingly animated brasserie feel, with service that is slick and well paced. Open from breakfast, the kitchen concentrates on familiar flavours and comforting classics. While the cooking may not always live up to the promise of the menu, it is nonetheless satisfying. Scottish beef features in the Grill section and there are daily specials which could be corned beef hash or a fish pie. There's a huge choice of wines by the glass or carafe.

Mint Leaf Lounge

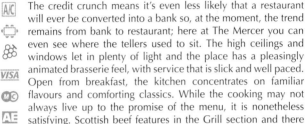 **Indian** XX

M3

12 Angel Ct., Lothbury ✉ EC2R 7HB   ⊖ Bank
☏ (020) 7600 0992   Closed 25-26 December, Saturday,
e-mail reservations@mintleaflounge.com   Sunday and bank holidays
www.mintleaflounge.com

Menu £18 (lunch) – Carte £30/45

This was formerly NatWest's HQ and has been turned into a stylish and slick Indian restaurant. The bar is bigger and the dining area smaller than the original branch in St James's, but with the stock market the way it's been, you can't blame them for that. The menu cleverly allows for flexibility in that many of the dishes are available in both starter and main course size and the presentation on the plate is quite contemporary. The majority of influences come from the more southerly parts of India and dishes demonstrate genuine care in preparation. Fish, meat or vegetarian platters are available and there's a good value set lunch menu. Knowledgeable staff in ubiquitous black provide nicely paced service.

The Modern Pantry

K1

International ✗

47-48 St John's Sq. ✉ EC1V 4JJ
✆ (020) 7553 9210
e-mail enquiries@themodernpantry.co.uk
www.themodernpantry.co.uk

⊖ Farringdon
Closed 25-26 December –
booking advisable

Carte £27/40

This Georgian building has been everything from a foundry to a carpentry workshop but these days plays host to New Zealander Anna Hansen's fusion restaurant. The smart glass doors lead into a simple, crisp space; there's an upstairs too, split between two rooms, which offers a little more intimacy but lacks the buzz of downstairs. The kitchen's peregrinations are reflected in a menu that has few boundaries. You'll probably need to ask for an explanation of at least one ingredient but the staff are clued up, which is no mean feat since menus change daily as ingredients come in. Despite all that's happening on the plate, flavours are well-judged and complementary. Most dishes also come with thoughtfully suggested wine matches.

Morito

K1

Spanish ✗

32 Exmouth Market ✉ EC1R 4QE
✆ (020) 7278 7007

⊖ Farringdon
Closed Sunday and
Monday lunch

Carte £20/25

Morito may not seduce you with its looks but once you start eating you'll find it hard to tear yourself away. This authentic tapas bar comes courtesy of the owners of next door Moro and shares their passion for Moorish cuisine. It's modestly kitted out but endearingly so, with a two-tone formica counter and half a dozen small tables; just turn up and if they haven't got space they'll take your number and you can have a drink in Exmouth Market while you wait. Seven or eight dishes between two should be enough but at these prices you can never overspend. Highlights of the immensely appealing menu include jamon and chicken croquetas and succulent lamb chops with cumin and paprika, all served in authentic earthenware dishes.

Moro

Mediterranean ✗

34-36 Exmouth Market ✉ EC1R 4QE   ⊖ Farringdon
☎ (020) 7833 8336   Closed Christmas and New Year,
e-mail info@moro.co.uk   Easter and bank holidays –
www.moro.co.uk   booking essential

Carte £28/40

A/C

☀

VISA

M©

AE

O

Despite being a feature of Exmouth market for over a decade, Moro remains one of the busiest restaurants around, but anyone left frustrated by not getting a table should consider just pitching up and sitting at the zinc-topped bar: it's a great spot for tapas and some wonderful sherries, you'll get the full benefit of the wondrous aromas from the open kitchen and be able to watch the chefs in action. Moorish cooking is the draw which means Spain and the Muslim Mediterranean. The wood-burning oven and charcoal grill provide the smokiness and charring to improve and enhance the poultry, meat and sourdough bread. The cooking is colourful and invigorating and the menu changes fully every two weeks.

1901

M2

French

Liverpool St. ✉ EC2M 7QN   ⊖ Liverpool Street
☎ (020) 7618 7000   Closed Saturday lunch, Sunday and
e-mail london.restres@andaz.com   bank holidays
www.andaz.com

Menu £22 – Carte £36/47

A/C

⊡

VISA

M©

AE

O

1901 is the redecorated, rebranded and relaunched version of what was previously called Aurora. It's one of several restaurants within the Andaz hotel and is very much their flagship. This is a hugely impressive room, which they've painted white to make the eye-catching cupola even more striking. A cocktail bar has been added, along with a cheese and wine room; the cheeses being of predominantly British provenance. The cooking is mostly French in preparation and technique but stoutly British in terms of the ingredients it uses. A refined and delicate touch is evident in dishes such as poached halibut with saffron potatoes and the smoked haddock boudin. There is an army of staff on hand who are well-practised but also friendly.

Oxo Tower

K4

Modern European 𝔛𝔛𝔛

Oxo Tower Wharf (8th floor),
Barge House St. ⊠ SE1 9PH
☏ (020) 7803 3888
e-mail oxo.reservations@harveynichols.com
www.harveynichols.com

⊖ Southwark

Menu £35 (lunch) – Carte £46/64

The Oxo Tower Restaurant is the smarter, more serious and ambitious sibling to the next door brasserie but both share terrific views and wonderful terraces from their location on the 8th floor of the iconic former Oxo riverside factory. The restaurant appears to be permanently busy and this means staff are sometimes a little too eager to tell you what time you have to vacate your table rather than making you feel welcome. The place is roomy, bright and open, with plenty of bustle; the cooking is contemporary and mostly European in influence while the kitchen uses plenty of top-end ingredients. Those views really are great but, on a clear day, you can see plenty of more reasonably priced restaurants.

Oxo Tower Brasserie

K4

Modern European 𝔛

Oxo Tower Wharf (8th floor),
Barge House St. ⊠ SE1 9PH
☏ (020) 7803 3888
e-mail oxo.reservations@harveynichols.com
www.harveynichols.com

⊖ Southwark

Carte £37/57

If you've never asked for a window table before, then now is the time to start. Better still, ask for the terrace and face east towards St Paul's for the best views. The light-filled, glass-encased brasserie on the eighth floor of the iconic Oxo Tower makes much of its riverside location but that's not to say that this is just a spot for a summer's day. The bold, zingy flavours and influences from around the globe ensure that the cooking is bright and sunny even when it's dull outside. Staff do their bit by being a responsive bunch and the place really rocks in the evenings when there's live music and the open kitchen becomes more of a feature. It's much more fun than the restaurant and the prices are friendlier too.

Paternoster Chop House

British 🍴

L3

Warwick Ct., Paternoster Sq. ✉ EC4M 7DX   ⊖ St Paul's

📞 (020) 7029 9400

e-mail paternosterr@dandlondon.com

www.paternosterchophouse.com

Closed 24 December-1 January,
Saturday, Sunday dinner
and bank holidays

Menu £27 – Carte £29/45

If you could make just one restaurant legally obliged to serve British food then it would probably be the one that lies in the shadow of St Paul's Cathedral, one of Britain's most symbolic landmarks. Fortunately, Paternoster Chop House negates the need of a bye-law by offering classics from all parts of these isles. The first thing you see on the neatly laid out menu is the comfortingly patriotic sight of a 'Beer of the Day'. Their livestock comes from small farms, their fish from day boats in the south west and all the old favourites are present and correct: native oysters, cottage pie, potted hough, liver and bacon, and apple crumble. The dining room is large and open; you might have to fight your way through the busy bar.

Peasant

Gastropub 🍺

L1

240 St John St ✉ EC1V 4PH   ⊖ Farringdon.

📞 (020) 7336 7726

e-mail eat@thepeasant.co.uk

www.thepeasant.co.uk

Closed 25 December to 2 January
– booking essential

Menu £35 – Carte £18/38

Come along too early in the evening and you'll find the bar four deep with city boys having a quick pint on the way home. However, things do quieten down later and, when they do, you'll notice what a characterful spot this is. Most of the eating gets done upstairs in the dining room with its dimmed chandeliers, open fire and circus-themed posters. The cooking has been simplified and returned to a core of British dishes accompanied by the occasional Mediterranean note. The result is that it is far more satisfying and the well-judged dishes –whether braised rib of beef with horseradish mash or roast pollock with shrimps – all largely deliver on flavour. You will need a side dish or two with your main course, which can push up the final bill.

Le Pont de la Tour

French 𝕏𝕏𝕏

N4

36d Shad Thames,
Butlers Wharf ⊠ SE1 2YE
☏ (020) 7403 8403
e-mail lepontres@danddlondon.com
www.lepontdelatour.co.uk

⊖ London Bridge

Menu £32/43

The regeneration of the River and Butlers Wharf were there for all to see in 1991 when Le Pont de la Tour opened and its glamorous reputation was done no harm when Tony Blair entertained Bill Clinton here in 1997. The elegant room provides diners with terrific views of Tower Bridge and the activity on the river, especially from the delightful terrace, while the menu offers a comprehensive selection of dishes that borrow heavily from France, all served by a well-drilled team. For those after less formal surroundings then head for the Bar & Grill which specialises in crustaceans and fruits de mer while those wanting something to take home are catered for by an impressive array of produce in the adjacent food store.

Portal

Mediterranean 𝕏𝕏

L1

88 St John St. ⊠ EC1M 4EH
☏ (020) 7253 6950
e-mail reservations@portalrestaurant.com
www.portalrestaurant.com

⊖ Farringdon
Closed Christmas, Easter,
Saturday lunch,
Sunday and bank holidays

Carte £33/49

You may be tempted to stay in the front bar, where they serve an appealing array of petiscos or Portuguese tapas, but once through the throng you'll find yourself in pleasant, semi-industrial surroundings with neatly dressed tables. The service is enthusiastic and helpful, as one would expect from somewhere family owned and run. It is to Southern Europe and particularly Portugal where the kitchen seeks inspiration, so head for the fish, shellfish and pork specialities, like bacalhau or bisaro; if you're in a big group think of pre-ordering the suckling pig. The kitchen commendably concentrates more on flavours rather than presentation. Portugal also features heavily on the wine list and there's an impressive selection of port by the glass.

Restaurant at St Paul's Cathedral

British ❌

St Paul's Churchyard ✉ EC4M 8AD   ⊖ St. Paul's
📞 (020) 7248 2469   Booking advisable – (lunch only)
e-mail enquiries@restaurantatstpauls.co.uk
www.restaurantatstpauls.co.uk

Menu £24

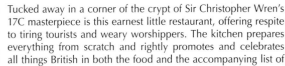

Tucked away in a corner of the crypt of Sir Christopher Wren's 17C masterpiece is this earnest little restaurant, offering respite to tiring tourists and weary worshippers. The kitchen prepares everything from scratch and rightly promotes and celebrates all things British in both the food and the accompanying list of drinks – even the back of the menu is graced with a collection of interesting local food facts. Start by sharing some nibbles such as wild boar salami or potted shrimp; move on to corned beef hash or a shepherd's pie and finish with a comforting Bakewell tart or some Neal's Yard cheeses. Service is done on the run but the staff are a friendly bunch and if you stay put for long enough, they'll start serving afternoon tea.

Roast

British ❌❌

The Floral Hall, Borough Mkt. ✉ SE1 1TL   ⊖ London Bridge
📞 (0845) 034 7300   Closed 26 and 31 December,
e-mail info@roast-restaurant.com   1 January and Sunday dinner –
www.roast-restaurant.com   booking essential

Menu £26 (lunch) – Carte £39/54

It's in the one place where you don't look when you find yourself in the deliciously enticing surroundings of Borough Market – up. Jump into the lift and upstairs you'll be greeted and led into a vast room; the best seats are in the raised section beyond the bar. The place is always busy and the young team are a friendly bunch, although they can sometimes appear to be a man down. The food is all about being British and proud of it, reflecting the values of the market below and the importance of provenance. Start with the cocktail of the week, move on to Cornish herring or Arbroath smokie followed by roast lamb or steak and onion pudding and finish with a Bakewell tart or rhubarb crumble. You'll leave whistling 'Land of Hope and Glory'.

Rhodes Twenty Four ✿

M3

British 🍴🍴🍴

24th floor, Tower 42, 25 Old Broad St.
✉ EC2N 1HQ
✆ (020) 7877 7703
e-mail reservations@rhodes24.co.uk
www.rhodes24.co.uk

⊖ **Liverpool Street**
Closed 24 December-
4 January, Saturday,
Sunday and bank holidays

Carte £37/61

Rhodes Twenty Four

You will need to factor in a little extra time to allow for the security checks on the ground floor of Tower 42, and for catching the lift up to the 24th floor of what is still the City's tallest building. But once inside the restaurant, provided you've asked for a window table, you'll be rewarded with great views of the city skyline. The unmistakeable signature of Gary Rhodes is writ large on the menu: dishes of a pleasingly British persuasion and the reassuring sight of words like 'pudding', 'pie' and 'crumble'. This being the City, where the male form of the species appear to remain largely in the ascendancy, means that the menu also has a stoutness to it, so, even in summer you'll be able to start with the oxtail cottage pie with a red wine sauce and finish with a bread and butter pudding. What all dishes also have is a look of comparative simplicity, which often belies the depth of flavour and the skill that has gone into them. As with most restaurants, service gels better when it's busier, which usually means at lunch.

First Course

- Sardines on toast with tomato and cucumber dressing.
- Oxtail cottage pie with red wine gravy.

Main Course

- Steamed mutton and onion suet pudding with carrots.
- Sea trout with asparagus and new potatoes.

Dessert

- Bread and butter pudding.
- Rhubarb crumble cheesecake with ginger ice cream.

St John ✿

St John

British ☠

L2

26 St John St. ⊠ EC1M 4AY
☎ (020) 7251 0848
e-mail reservations@stjohnrestaurant.com
www.stjohnrestaurant.com

Carte £28/53

⊖ Barbican
Closed Christmas-New Year,
Easter, Saturday lunch,
Sunday dinner and bank holidays,
– booking essential

The walls, painted in a shade of detention centre white, add to the utilitarian feel of the room which was once a smokehouse in the 19C. There's no standing on ceremony; indeed no ceremony at all, and that makes dining at St John such a joyful experience as the focus is entirely directed at the food. You can play it safe and go for some crab and then roast beef but this is the place to try new flavours, whether that's the cuttlefish or the ox tongue. Game is a real favourite and the only gravy will be the blood of the bird – this is natural, 'proper' food. Seasonality is at its core – the menu is rewritten for each service – and nothing sums up the philosophy more than the potatoes and greens: they are always on the menu but the varieties and types change regularly. The waiters all dress in chef's jackets and spend some time in the kitchen so they know what they're talking about. There are dishes for two as well as magnums of wine for real trenchermen – and be sure to order a dozen warm madeleines to take home.

First Course
- Potted beef with pickled beetroot.
- Smoked eel and potted prunes.

Main Course
- Poached rabbit with carrots and borlotti beans.
- Plaice with fennel and green sauce.

Dessert
- Damson jelly with shortbread.
- Apricot crumble and vanilla ice cream.

CITY OF LONDON, CLERKENWELL, FINSBURY & SOUTHWARK ▶ PLANS VIII-IX-X

Sauterelle

French ✗✗

M3

The Royal Exchange ✉ EC3V 3LR   ⊖ Bank
☎ (020) 7618 2483   Closed Christmas-New Year,
www.restaurantsauterelle.com   Saturday, Sunday and bank holidays

Menu £24 – Carte £31/54

A/C
⟨⚬⟩
VISA
MC
AE
OD

Sauterelle enjoys a hugely impressive setting on the mezzanine floor of The Royal Exchange and looks down over the Grand Café below which was the original trading floor. This City landmark was rebuilt in 1844, but its layout remains largely true to Sir Thomas Gresham's 1565 original. The striking ceiling and ornate arches add to the already comfortable feel of the restaurant. The menu is largely French, but more contemporary than classic which means the addition of the occasional Italian note. The kitchen certainly doesn't skimp on luxury ingredients: foie gras, turbot, Anjou pigeon and Pyrenean lamb make regular appearances and are appreciated by big spending customers for whom the credit crunch is but a distant memory.

Skylon

Modern European ✗✗✗

J4

1 Southbank Centre, Belvedere Rd   ⊖ Waterloo
✉ SE1 8XX   Closed 25 December and
☎ (020) 7654 7800   Sunday dinner
e-mail skylonreservations@danddlondon.com
www.skylonrestaurant.co.uk

Menu £28/45

⟨
A/C
⅗⅘
VISA
MC
AE
OD

The original Skylon was a steel structure built for the Festival of Britain in 1951 to promote better quality design. Its name now lives on as the restaurant within the Royal Festival Hall, which was built just yards from where this 'vertical feature' once stood. The South Bank is now a much appreciated area of London and the restaurant offers wonderful river views. It's a large space, with a busy central cocktail bar, a formally laid out restaurant on one side and a simpler grill-style operation on the other. The latter serves fishcakes, burgers, steaks and the like; the restaurant uses more expensive ingredients and puts a modern spin on classic combinations. Be sure to ask for a window table.

Tapas Brindisa

18-20 Southwark St., Borough Market ⊖ London Bridge
✉ SE1 1TJ   Closed 25-28 December and
☎ (020) 7357 8880   1 January –
e-mail office@tapasbrindisa.com   (bookings not accepted)
www.brindisatapaskitchens.com

Carte £19/27

As in Spain, you have the option of standing or sitting for your tapas. The bar is a great place for a glass of Fino while you watch the acorn-fed Iberian charcuterie being sliced, and the list of hot and cold tapas is extensive, from cured fish and speciality cheeses to grilled chorizo and sautéed chicken livers. It all happens on the edge of Borough Market in what was once a potato warehouse; the owners spent years importing Spanish produce so they know what they're talking about. With its tightly packed tables and convivial atmosphere, it does get very busy and as they don't take reservations, be prepared to wait; if they are full then ask nicely and you can put your name down and then wander around the market.

Tate Modern (Restaurant)

Tate Modern (7th floor), Bankside ⊖ Southwark
✉ SE1 9TG   Closed 24-26 December –
☎ (020) 7887 8888   (lunch only and dinner
e-mail tate.modernrestaurant@tate.org.uk   Friday-Saturday)
www.tate.org.uk/modern/eatanddrink

Carte £30/36

Floor to ceiling windows on two sides and a large mural on a third allow light and colour to fill this large restaurant on the 7th floor of the Tate Modern and balance all that black. Even if you don't get a window table you'll still get a great view of St. Paul's. There's seating for 145 but they stop taking reservations when they get to 100 to allow for the impulse diner. Lunch starts at 11.30 and ends at 3pm so there's every possibility of getting in but waiting at the bar is no hardship. The menu is an appealing mix of light, seasonal, fresh and zesty dishes, with a daily fish from Newlyn. The influences are mostly British, with the occasional Italian note. There's a good choice of wines by the glass and carafe as well as interesting soft drinks.

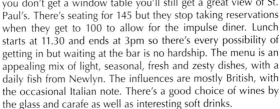

CITY OF LONDON, CLERKENWELL, FINSBURY & SOUTHWARK ▶ PLANS VIII-IX-X

Terranostra

Italian 🍴

L3

27 Old Bailey ✉ EC4M 7HS
✆ (020) 3201 0077
e-mail info@terranostrafood.co.uk
www.terranostrafood.co.uk

⊖ St Paul's
Closed Saturday lunch and Sunday
– booking advisable at lunch

Carte £23/30

VISA
MC
AE

The City, and especially the area around the Old Bailey, is an area not exactly known for its cheery spirit and bonhomie. So praise be for Terranostra because its informal, relaxed style and sweet-natured service could brighten up anyone's day. The food is honest, light and fresh and comes in generous sizes. The menu is nicely balanced and has appealing Sardinian leanings, which means malloreddus and fregola pastas, the sausage known as salsiccia sarda, rich and golden bottarga and plenty of moreish, crisp bread. On sunny days the French doors open onto the pavement terrace and those on a celebratory lunch from the courtrooms virtually opposite might find added resonance in D.H. Lawrence's view that Sardinia was "like freedom itself".

28°-50° 😊

French 🍴

K3

140 Fetter Ln ✉ EC4A 1BT
✆ (020) 7242 8877
e-mail info@2850.co.uk
www.2850.co.uk

⊖ Temple
Closed Christmas-New Year,
Saturday and Sunday

Menu £22 (lunch) – Carte £28/35

Despite the lack of a displayed menu, an unprepossessing entrance and a long staircase down, you'll find this subterranean spot almost always heaving with customers. For their second project, the owners of Texture opted for this 'wine workshop and kitchen', named after the latitudes between which most wines are produced, and with a cellar effect enhanced by brick walls and oenological accessories. A bar menu of charcuterie, rillettes and cheese is there to accompany a choice of over 30 wines by the glass. Beyond is the simple restaurant with a concise menu of robust, mostly French dishes such as bouillabaisse, onglet of beef and baba au rhum, which shouldn't break the bank – unless you have an unquenchable thirst for 1989 Hermitage.

Vanilla Black

Vegetarian

17-18 Tooks Ct. ✉ EC4A 1LB   ⊖ Chancery Lane
✆ (020) 7242 2622
www.vanillablack.co.uk

Closed Christmas and New Year,
Saturday lunch, Sunday and
bank holidays except Good Friday

Menu £23/30

Those who think vegetarian food is all nut cutlets and knitted muesli should get along to Vanilla Black. Run by a Teesside couple who had a restaurant of the same name in York, they prove that vegetarian food can be varied, flavoursome and filling. The room is neat but quite stark and crisp in its decoration; sufficient warmth comes from the owner and her team of waiting staff. The set priced menu represents fair value and the cooking displays sufficient originality and imagination. Certainly no one leaves hungry as the flavoursome dishes use liberal amounts of cheese and potato. This is a proper restaurant that could heal the wounds of any carnivore scarred in their youth by an unpleasant vegetarian experience.

Village East

Modern European

171-173 Bermondsey St. ✉ SE1 3UW   ⊖ London Bridge
✆ (020) 7357 6082
e-mail info@villageeast.co.uk

Closed 25-26 December

Carte £29/37

Clever name - sounds a bit downtown Manhattan. But while Bermondsey may not be London's East Village, what Village East does is give this part of town a bit more 'neighbour' and a little less 'hood'. It's tricky to find so look for the glass façade and you'll find yourself in one of the bars, still wondering if you've come to the right place. Once, though, you've seen the open kitchen you know the dining area's not far away. Wood, brick, vents and large circular lamps give it that warehouse aesthetic. The menu is laid out a little confusingly but what you get is ample portions of familiar bistro style food, as well as some interesting combinations. The separately priced side dishes are not really needed and can push the bill up.

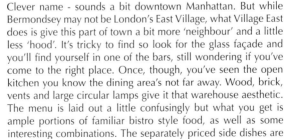

CITY OF LONDON, CLERKENWELL, FINSBURY & SOUTHWARK ▶ PLANS VIII-IX-X

205

Vinoteca

L2

Modern European ✗

7 St John St. ✉ EC1M 4AA ⊖ Farringdon
✆ (020) 7253 8786 Closed 24 December-1 January and Sunday
e-mail enquiries@vinoteca.co.uk
www.vinoteca.co.uk

Carte £21/31

Vinoteca, a self-styled 'bar and wine shop', comes divided into two tiny rooms and is always so busy that you'll almost certainly have to wait for a table. But what makes this frenetic place so special is the young and very passionate team who run it so well. The wine list is thrilling: it is constantly evolving and covers all regions, including less familiar territories along with the organic and the biodynamic. In circumstances such as these, the food can often be an afterthought but here it isn't. Alongside the cheeses and the cured meats that are available all day are classic dishes like pear, chicory and Roquefort salad; potted shrimps; bavette steak and panna cotta; all fresh tasting, well-timed and enjoyable.

Vivat Bacchus

K2

Traditional ✗✗

(basement) 47 Farringdon St ✉ EC4A 4LL ⊖ Farringdon
✆ (020) 7353 2648 Closed 24 December-5 January, Saturday
e-mail info@vivatbacchus.co.uk and Sunday
www.vivatbacchus.co.uk

Menu £15/18 – Carte £20/42

The wine list is just a teaser: they actually have 750 labels, 20,000 bottles and five cellars. Glory to the god of wine indeed. And few things complement wine better than red meat and cheese – the two other specialities here. The large premises are mostly taken up with the wine bar and deli, with an appealing selection of platters, cheeseboards and tapas. For a more intimate experience head to the basement for a menu of two halves: one modern European, the other specialising in meats. Côte de boeuf is for two brave people with similar appetites while the presence of Springbok, and the huge number of South African wines, reveals the nationality of the owner. Customers are welcome to tour the cellars and the impressive cheese room.

Vivat Bacchus London Bridge

Traditional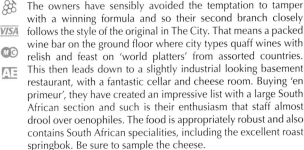

4 Hays Ln. ✉ SE1 2HB   ⊖ London Bridge
✆ (0207) 234 0891   Closed 24 December-3 January, bank
e-mail londonbridge@vivatbacchus.co.uk   holidays and Sunday
www.vivatbacchus.co.uk

Menu £12/20 – Carte £26/36

The owners have sensibly avoided the temptation to tamper with a winning formula and so their second branch closely follows the style of the original in The City. That means a packed wine bar on the ground floor where city types quaff wines with relish and feast on 'world platters' from assorted countries. This then leads down to a slightly industrial looking basement restaurant, with a fantastic cellar and cheese room. Buying 'en primeur', they have created an impressive list with a large South African section and such is their enthusiasm that staff almost drool over oenophiles. The food is appropriately robust and also contains South African specialities, including the excellent roast springbok. Be sure to sample the cheese.

Well

Gastropub

180 St John St ✉ EC1V 4JY   ⊖ Farringdon.
✆ (020) 7251 9363
e-mail james@downthewell.co.uk
www.downthewell.com

Carte £30/60

The Well is perhaps more of a locals' pub than many others found around these parts. It's all quite small inside but, thanks to some huge sliding glass windows, has a surprisingly light and airy feel, and the wooden floorboards and exposed brick walls add to the atmosphere of a committed metropolitan pub. Monthly changing menus offer modern dishes ranging from potted shrimps, to foie gras and chicken liver parfait, or sea trout and samphire, as well as classic English puddings like Eton Mess and some particularly good cheeses. The downstairs bar with its seductive lighting and fish tank is only available for private hire; check out the picture of a parched desert and a well which follows the curve of the wall on your way down.

The White Swan

K2

108 Fetter Lane ✉ EC4A 1ES
℘ (020) 7242 9696
e-mail info@thewhiteswanlondon.com
www.thewhiteswanlondon.com

⊖ Chancery Lane
Closed 25-26 December

Carte £30/40

A/C

☼

VISA

M⊙

AE

You'll find something akin to an assault course at the White Swan because to get to the first floor restaurant you have to fight your way through the drinkers in the ground floor bar and, at lunch time, this is more challenging than you think. Once upstairs, you'll find a small but neat room and service that is polite and friendly but also well paced and professional. The mirrored ceiling and large windows add plenty of light, although the closeness of the tables can make private conversation tricky. However, the cooking is good enough to induce the odd contented silence. It is classical in its base but with the occasional contemporary tweak and dishes display a certain refinement. Pricing is also fair when one considers the location.

Wright Brothers

M4

11 Stoney St., Borough Market ✉ SE1 9AD
℘ (020) 7403 9554
e-mail info@wrightbrothersoysterhouse.com
www.wrightbrothers.co.uk

⊖ London Bridge
Closed Christmas-New Year and
bank holidays –
booking advisable

Carte £23/40

☼

VISA

M⊙

AE

If you want to take a breather from the hordes at Borough Market then nip into Wright Brothers, but do it early as it quickly fills. Their motto is 'Not just oysters' but then they do excel in them – hardly surprising when you consider that this small place started as an oyster wholesaler. Grab a table and enjoy them raw or cooked, by candlelight, along with the perfect accompaniment – a glass of porter – or else share a bench or the counter, opt for a platter of fruits de mer and order a bottle of chilled Muscadet. If the bivalve is not your thing, then there are daily specials such as skate knobs, as well as pies and, for dessert, either chocolate truffles or crème brûlée. An air of contentment reigns.

Zucca

M5

184 Bermondsey St ✉ SE1 3TQ
✆ (020) 7378 6809
www.zuccalondon.com

⊖ Borough
Closed 24 December-10 January, Sunday dinner and Monday – booking essential at dinner

Carte £18/24

A/C
🐾
VISA
MC
AE
①

The suitably fresh faced young chef-owner seems to have got it all pretty spot-on: the simple but informed Italian cooking is driven by the ingredients, the prices are more than generous, the room is bright and crisp and the service, sweet and responsive. The antipasti forms the largest part of the weekly changing menu and the hard part – especially if you're sharing – is knowing when to stop ordering; but do always include the zucca fritti – the pumpkin speciality. The kitchen team are an unflustered group, largely because they don't fiddle with the food and know that less equals more. The freshly baked breads come with Planeta olive oil; there are usually two pasta dishes and the aromas that fill the room make it hard to leave.

Remember, stars (❀❀❀...❀) are awarded for cuisine only! Elements such as service and décor are not a factor.

Chelsea · Earl's Court · Hyde Park · Knightsbridge · South Kensington

Though its days of unbridled hedonism are long gone - and its 'alternative' tag is more closely aligned to property prices than counter-culture - there's still a hip feel to **Chelsea.** The place that put the Swinging into London has grown grey, distinguished and rather placid over the years, but tourists still throng to the **King's Road,** albeit to shop at the chain stores which have steadily muscled out SW3's chi-chi boutiques. It's not so easy now to imagine the heady mix of clans that used to sashay along here, from Sixties mods and models to Seventies punks, but for practically a quarter of a century, from the moment in 1955 when Mary Quant opened her trend-setting Bazaar, this was the pavement to parade down.

Chelsea's most cutting-edge destination these days is probably the gallery of modern art that bears the name of Margaret Thatcher's former favourite, Charles Saatchi. Which isn't the only irony, as Saatchi's outlandishly modish exhibits are housed in a one-time military barracks, the Duke of York's headquarters. Nearby, the traffic careers round **Sloane Square,** but it's almost possible to distance yourself from the fumes by sitting amongst the shady bowers in the centre of the square, or watching the world go by from a prime position in one of many cafés. Having said that, *the* place to get away from it all, and yet still be within striking distance of the King's Road, is the delightful **Physic Garden,** down by the river. Famous for its healing herbs for over 300 years, it's England's second oldest botanic garden.

Mind you, if the size of a green space is more important to you than its medicinal qualities, then you need to head up to **Hyde Park,** the city's biggest. Expansive enough to accommodate trotting horses on Rotten Row, swimmers and rowers in the Serpentine, up-to-the-minute art exhibitions at the Serpentine Gallery, and ranting individualists at Speakers' Corner, the park has also held within its borders thousands of rock fans for concerts by the likes of the Rolling Stones, Simon and Garfunkel and Pink Floyd.

Just across from its southern border stands one of London's most imperious sights, The **Royal Albert Hall,** gateway to the cultural hotspot that is South Kensington. Given its wings after the 1851 Great Exhibition, the area round **Cromwell Road** invested heavily in culture and learning, in the shape of three world famous museums and three heavyweight colleges. But one of its most intriguing museums is little known to visitors, even though it's only a few metres east of the Albert Hall: the Sikorski is, by turns, a moving and spectacular showpiece for all things Polish.

No one would claim to be moved by the exhibits on show in nearby **Knightsbridge,** but there are certainly spectacular credit card transactions made here. The twin retail shrines of Harvey Nichols and Harrods are the proverbial honey-pots to the tourist bee, where a 'credit crunch' means you've accidentally trodden on your visa. Between them, in **Sloane Street,** the world's most famous retail names line up like an A-lister's who's who. At the western end of Knightsbridge is the rich person's Catholic church of choice, the Brompton Oratory, an unerringly lavish concoction in a baroque Italianate style. Behind it is the enchanting Ennismore Gardens Mews, a lovely thoroughfare that dovetails rather well with the Oratory.

Further west along Old Brompton Road is **Earl's Court,** an area of grand old houses turned into bedsits and spartan hotels. An oddly bewitching contrast sits side by side here, the old resting alongside the new. The old in this case is Brompton Cemetery, an enchanting wilderness of monuments wherein lie the likes of Samuel Cunard and Emmeline Pankhurst. At its southwest corner, incongruously, sits the new, insomuch as it's the home of a regular influx of newcomers from abroad, who are young, gifted and possessed of vast incomes: the players of Chelsea FC.

C. Eymenier/MICHELIN

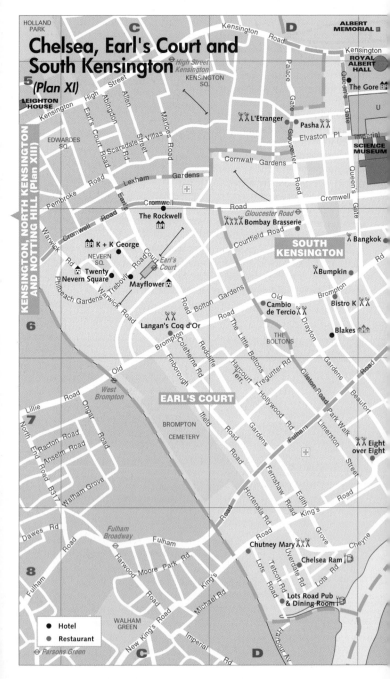

Chelsea, Earl's Court and South Kensington
(Plan XI)

HOLLAND PARK

LEIGHTON HOUSE

EDWARDES SQ.

ALBERT MEMORIAL

Kensington Road

ROYAL ALBERT HALL

The Gore

High Street Kensington

KENSINGTON SQ.

L'Etranger

Pasha

Elvaston Pl.

Imperial SCIENCE MUSEUM

Cornwall Gardens

Cromwell

The Rockwell

Gloucester Road

Bombay Brasserie

Courtfield Road

SOUTH KENSINGTON

Bangkok

K + K George

NEVERN SQ.

Twenty Nevern Square

Earl's Court

Mayflower

Bumpkin

Old Brompton

Cambio de Tercio

Bistro K

Blakes

Langan's Coq d'Or

Bolton Gardens

The Little Boltons

THE BOLTONS

Old

West Brompton

EARL'S COURT

BROMPTON CEMETERY

Eight over Eight

Fulham Broadway

Chutney Mary

Chelsea Ram

WALHAM GREEN

Lots Road Pub & Dining Room

- ● Hotel
- ● Restaurant

Parsons Green

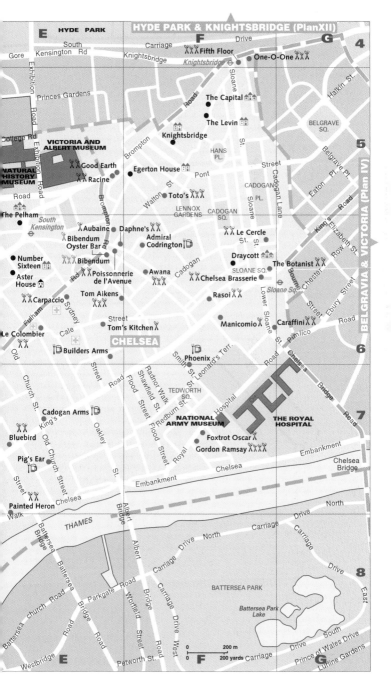

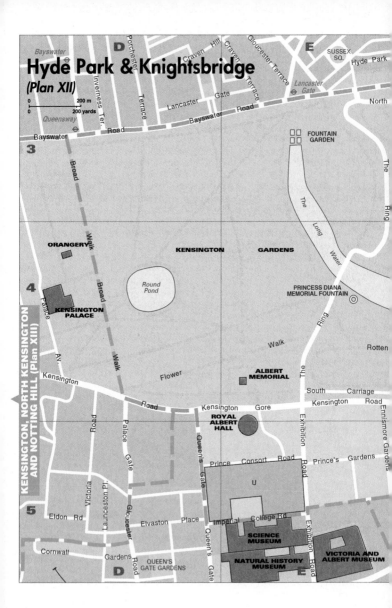

Hyde Park & Knightsbridge
(Plan XII)

0   200 m
0   200 yards

Bayswater

Queensway

Bayswater

Porchester

Inverness Ter.

Terrace

Lancaster Gate

Broad

Road

Bayswater Road

Craven Hill

Craven Terrace

Gloucester Terrace

Lancaster Gate

SUSSEX SQ.

Hyde Park

North

FOUNTAIN GARDEN

3

The Ring

The Long Water

ORANGERY

Walk

Broad

KENSINGTON   GARDENS

PRINCESS DIANA MEMORIAL FOUNTAIN

4

Round Pond

KENSINGTON PALACE

Palace

Av.

Kensington

Walk

Flower

Walk

ALBERT MEMORIAL

The Ring

Rotten

South   Carriage

Kensington   Road

Road

Palace Gate

Victoria

Launceston Pl.

Gloucester

Kensington   Road

Queen's Gate

Kensington   Gore

ROYAL ALBERT HALL

Prince   Consort   Road

Exhibition

Prince's   Gardens

Ennismore Gardens

5

Eldon Rd

Elvaston   Place

Imperial   College Rd

U

Road

Prince's

Cornwall

Gardens

QUEEN'S GATE GARDENS

Queen's Gate

SCIENCE MUSEUM

NATURAL HISTORY MUSEUM

Exhibition Rd

VICTORIA AND ALBERT MUSEUM

KENSINGTON, NORTH KENSINGTON AND NOTTING HILL (Plan XIII)

D   E

214

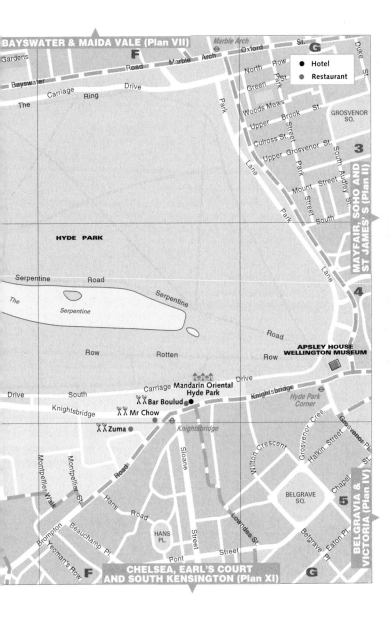

Admiral Codrington

F6

Gastropub

17 Mossop St ✉ SW3 2LY   ⊖ South Kensington.
☎ (020) 7581 0005
e-mail theadmiralcodrington@333holdingsltd.com
www.theadmiralcodrington.com

Carte £24/30

The Admiral Codrington is a smart, dependable affair as befits an establishment named after a hero of the Battles of Trafalgar and Navarino. What was once the HQ of the Sloane Ranger movement is now known for the quality of its food, although it still attracts a well turned-out crowd. The main bar and terrace are quite subdued during the day but get busy in the evening when all the eating is done in the neat, comfortable restaurant with its sliding glass roof. The menu can't quite decide whether this is a pub or a restaurant and so covers all bases from chilli salt squid to roast beef and coq au vin to fish and chips, with baguettes available at lunch. Service can sometimes lack a little personality but the young team do get the job done.

Aubaine

E6

French

260-262 Brompton Rd. ✉ SW3 2AS   ⊖ South Kensington
☎ (020) 7052 0100   Closed 25 December
e-mail francesco.manzari@aubaine.co.uk
www.aubaine.co.uk

Carte £22/44

This was the first of the bourgeoning Aubaine brand and it is easy to understand the appeal. A country-style aesthetic is coupled with functionality and flexibility, so that a brisk morning coffee trade is followed by brunch, then a more structured lunch and dinner. Influences are European but the kitchen has its feet firmly set in France. Highlights include well-timed scallops and a decent rib-eye. Desserts are presented on a tray, to remind you this is also a place where one can pick up bread and pastries for home. The midday lunching ladies give way to a more mixed crowd in the evenings and service is young and eager. If you've got an appetite, then you may find it pricier than you expected but it's an easy place to like.

Awana

F6

Malaysian XXX

85 Sloane Ave. ⊠ SW3 3DX
☏ (020) 7584 8880
e-mail info@awana.co.uk
www.awana.co.uk

⊖ South Kensington
Closed 25 December and 1 January
– booking essential

Menu £15 (lunch) – Carte £27/54

AC
☼
VISA
MC
AE
DC

The rich culinary diversity of Malaysia is presented here at Awana; a restaurant which manages the trick of looking smart and stylish, while staying relaxed and informal. It has also proved to be quite a hit with the Chelsea locals so it's worth booking in advance. Service does depend somewhat on the enthusiasm of your particular waiter, but if you choose to sit at the Satay Bar at the end of the room, you'll find the chef behind the counter takes very good care of you. To fully experience all the different cultures that influence Malaysian cooking, consider ordering the 'Malaysian Journey' menu, which comes with wine pairings; the highlights are the satay, roti canai, beef rendang and the prawn and chicken wonton soup.

Bangkok

E6

Thai X

9 Bute St ⊠ SW7 3EY
☏ (020) 7584 8529
www.bankokrestaurant.co.uk

⊖ South Kensington
Closed Christmas-New Year and Sunday

Carte £22/29

AC
VISA
MC

Bangkok has been going strong for years and, for that, we should all be grateful. It is an honest, unpretentious neighbourhood restaurant and one of the first in the capital to offer Londoners a taste of Thailand in the days before gap years, package holidays and our discovery of woks. The menu's not overlong; starters include quite a few soups but the beef and chicken satay are particularly good. Main courses are helpfully divided into beef, pork and chicken; highlights include the beef with crispy Thai basil, while the noodles are very light and moreish. The prices are decidedly unKensington-like and the ladies go about their service with organised efficiency. The multitudinous following ensures there's always a bubbly atmosphere.

Bar Boulud

F4

66 Knightsbridge ⊠ SW1X 7LA
☏ (020) 7201 3899
e-mail barboulud@mohg.com
www.barboulud.com/barbouludlondon

⊖ Knightsbridge

Menu £20 (lunch and early dinner) – Carte £29/48

[A/C]
[❄]
[🎭]
[☼]
[VISA]
[MC]
[AE]
[①]

Lyon-born Daniel Boulud built his considerable reputation in New York and these two cities now inform the menu here at his London outpost. Order a plate of excellent charcuterie while you look at the menu; sausages are a highlight and there are plenty of classic French dishes, from fruits de mer to coq au vin, but it's the burgers that steal the show. Designed by Adam Tihany, the restaurant makes the best of its basement location which was previously used by the Mandarin Oriental Hotel as a storeroom. Don't think you'll be in exile if they lead you to a table around the corner: it's a good spot and you'll be facing the open kitchen. Service is fast and furious; prices are sensible and the place is noisy, fashionable and fun.

Bibendum

E6

Michelin House, 81 Fulham Rd.
⊠ SW3 6RD
☏ (020) 7581 5817
e-mail reservations@bibendum.co.uk
www.bibendum.co.uk

⊖ South Kensington
Closed 24-26 December and 1 January

Menu £30 – Carte £40/61

[A/C]
[❄]
[☼]
[VISA]
[MC]
[AE]

Bibendum is now well into its twenties but very little has changed over those years, which is why it remains a favourite restaurant for so many. Matthew Harris' cooking continues to produce the sort of food that Elizabeth David would adore – it's mostly French but with a subtle British point of view. The set lunch menu has now been joined by a small à la carte selection; evening menus are handwritten and the roast chicken with tarragon for two remains a perennial presence. Side dishes can bump the final bill up further than expected but the food is easy to eat and satisfying. The striking character of Michelin's former HQ, dating from 1911, is perhaps best appreciated at lunch when the sun lights up the glass Bibendum - the Michelin Man.

Bibendum Oyster Bar

E6

Michelin House, 81 Fulham Rd.

✉ SW3 6RD

✆ (020) 7589 1480

e-mail reservations@bibendum.co.uk

www.bibendum.co.uk

⊖ South Kensington

Closed 24-26 December and 1 January
– (bookings not accepted)

Carte £20/33

The plateau de fruits de mer, for two, is the house speciality here. It includes crab, langoustines, prawns, oysters, winkles and whelks and will leave anyone being satisfied and, when the sun is shining, pleased with the world in general. You'll find other satisfying classics, from potted shrimps to egg mayonnaise, assorted salads and, predictably enough, a selection of oysters. The accessible wine list includes 460ml pots. It is all served in a relaxed continental-style café, with a mosaic floor and colourful ceramic tiles depicting the early days of French motoring – as befits any establishment located in the former foyer of Michelin House. The crustacea stall and florist at the front of the building attract plenty of passers-by.

Bistro K

D6

117-119 Old Brompton Rd. ✉ SW7 3RN

✆ (020) 7373 7774

e-mail info@bistro-k.co.uk

www.bistro-k.co.uk

⊖ Gloucester Road

Closed Christmas and New Year, 2 weeks
August, Monday and bank holidays

Menu £15/25 (early dinner) – Carte £29/44

They call themselves a 'restaurant and lounge bar', so why use the word 'bistro' in their name? Perhaps they intended to distance themselves from the overtly ceremonial Ambassade de L'Ile, which previously occupied this spot, although it does suggest a level of informality that isn't entirely the case here: there are plenty of suited managers and the cooking is surprisingly delicate. The kitchen is clearly a skilled one and the cooking is underpinned by sound French techniques but is unafraid of adding the odd twist. The 'lounge bar' part of their name is represented by the type of music they play; a fact mildly baffling to their more mature customers, who don't realise that the restaurant is trying to target a younger crowd.

Bluebird

E7

350 King's Rd. ✉ SW3 5UU   ⊖ Sloane Square
☎ (020) 7559 1000
e-mail enquiries@bluebird-restaurant.co.uk
www.bluebirdchelsea.com

Menu £21 – Carte £26/73

The last refurbishment may have softened the huge space a little but Bluebird still delivers the atmosphere and excitement one expects from such a large industrial space. A former garage built in 1923; it houses everything from a wine store and café to a food shop and private members club, with the restaurant as the centrepiece. The kitchen champions British produce and highlights their provenance, be it Herdwick mutton, Cumbrian beef or Goosnargh chicken. It also features British cheeses along with seasonal fruit and veg. That being said, not all the dishes are so Anglo-centric: there are assorted pasta choices and the occasional French classic. Sunday roasts and a children's menu ensure that all bases are covered.

Bombay Brasserie

D6

Courtfield Rd. ✉ SW7 4QH   ⊖ Gloucester Road
☎ (020) 7370 4040   Closed 25-26 December – booking
e-mail bombay1brasserie@aol.com   advisable at dinner
www.bombaybrasserielondon.com

Menu £22 (weekday lunch buffet) – Carte £31/43

Going strong since 1982, The Bombay Brasserie has always been one of the smartest Indian restaurants around but it began 2009 with a brand new look which revitalised the whole place. Plushness abounds, from the deep carpet and huge chandeliers of the large main room to the show kitchen of the conservatory and the very smart bar. The staff also got a new look with their burgundy waistcoats, but they continue to offer very charming and professional service. The menu wasn't forgotten either and was overhauled by Hemant Oberoi. They replaced the predictable with the more creative, while at the same time respecting traditional philosophies; influences are a combination of Bori, Parsi, Maharashtrian and Goan cuisine.

The Botanist

F6

7 Sloane Sq ✉ SW1W 8EE

𝒞 (020) 7730 0077

e-mail info@thebotanistonsloanesquare.com

www.thebotanistonsloanesquare.com

⊖ Sloane Square

Closed 25-26 December,
Saturday, Sunday and
bank holidays

Menu £29 – Carte £26/33

Unlike say New Yorkers, Londoners seemingly prefer their bars separate from their restaurants, which is a shame as The Botanist demonstrates how well the two can coexist. You enter first into the bar and, by osmosis, its general bustle adds to the convivial atmosphere of the adjoining bright and warm restaurant. The place always appears full of people who 'get' what a restaurant should feel and sound like. The menu mixes cheffy descriptions like 'escabeche' with more prosaic words like 'pie' so expect a choice that includes terrines, fish from Billingsgate or more ambitious numbers like pigeon with Puy lentils. Dishes are unfussy in appearance – always a sign of a confident kitchen – and deliver on flavour.

Builders Arms

E6

13 Britten St ✉ SW3 3TY

𝒞 (020) 7349 9040

e-mail buildersarms@geronimo-inns.co.uk

www.geronimo-inns.co.uk

⊖ South Kensington.

Closed 25-26 December –
(bookings not accepted)

Carte £25/30

The Builders Arms is very much like a packed village local - the only difference being that, in this instance, the village is Chelsea. They adopt a simple but effective approach to cooking – there's an easy to read menu, supplemented by a daily specials blackboard, which always includes a soup and fresh fish. Dishes range from devilled kidney on toast to herb-crusted lamb; others, such as the corn-fed peri-peri chicken are designed for sharing. Presentation has an appealingly rustic edge; portions are appropriately pub-size and prices are kept realistic. There's a weekly Bordeaux selection as well as regular wine promotions. Bookings are only taken for larger parties but just tell the staff that you're here to eat and they'll sort you out.

Bumpkin

D6

102 Old Brompton Rd ✉ SW7 3RD   ⊖ Gloucester Road
✆ (020) 7341 0802
e-mail skreservations@bumpkinuk.com
www.bumpkinuk.com

Carte £28/40

[A/C]
[:::]
[☼]
[VISA]
[MC]
[AE]

The slogan is "for city folk who like a little country living",
which is exactly the reason why many of the moneyed in this
prosperous neighbourhood bought weekend retreats. This
Bumpkin follows the success of the Notting Hill branch and
they've largely repeated the formula by creating a restaurant
with a pub-like informality that champions British produce. The
rear room, with its large open-plan kitchen, is the more fun of
the two and service is spirited and friendly. Quarterly printed
menus double as placemats, with additional daily specials on
the board. Expect lots of pies, burgers using Welsh Black beef
and hot pots, with the simpler dishes often being the best ones.
Weekend brunches and Sunday roasts are very popular.

Cadogan Arms

E7

298 King's Rd ✉ SW3 5UG   ⊖ South Kensington.
✆ (020) 7352 6500   Closed 25-26 December –
e-mail nadia@etmgroup.co.uk   booking advisable at dinner
www.thecadoganarmschelsea.com

Carte £24/37

[A/C]
[☼]
[VISA]
[MC]
[AE]

The Martin brothers seem to have the King's Road covered, with
The Botanist dominating the Sloane Square end and The Cadogan
Arms doing its thing at the other. The tiled entrance step reads
'Luncheon, bar and billiards' which sounds appealingly like a
lost afternoon and it is clear that this is still a proper, blokey
pub. The upstairs billiard tables are available by the hour and,
while you eat, you'll feel the beady eyes of the various stuffed
and mounted animals on the walls staring at you. The cooking
is appropriately gutsy. Juicy Aberdeen Angus rib-eye, golden-
fried haddock, Dexter Beef and Welsh lamb are all staples of
the menu. Starters and desserts are a little showier – perhaps
something for the ladies? Staff catch the mood just so.

Cambio de Tercio

Spanish XX

163 Old Brompton Rd ✉ SW5 0LJ   ⊖ Gloucester Road
✆ (020) 7244 8970
e-mail alusa@btconnect.com
www.cambiodetercio.co.uk

Carte £30/54

The concept works well: choose 3 or 4 tapas each from the left side of the menu and they'll arrive in an orderly fashion so that sharing can be done at a leisurely pace. But if you feel that the tapas size just doesn't hit the spot or you haven't liked sharing since childhood then the dishes on the right hand side are pretty much the same except they come in regular main course size. Definitely start with Iberica ham and include the spicy patatas bravas and the sticky and rich oxtail in red wine. The chef uses his toys to good effect with the more contemporary desserts. Lots of vintages from Vega Sicilia and Pingus wines feature, along with Alion and Roda. Service gets better the more you visit. They also own the tapas bar across the road.

Caraffini

Italian XX

61-63 Lower Sloane St. ✉ SW1W 8DH   ⊖ Sloane Square
✆ (020) 7259 0235   Closed 25 December, Easter, Sunday and
e-mail info@caraffini.co.uk   bank holidays – booking essential
www.caraffini.co.uk

Carte £23/41

One doesn't have to look far to see why Paolo Caraffini's restaurant is always so busy: it has a wonderfully genial host, smooth service, reliably good Italian food and a highly hospitable atmosphere. Just watching the number of regulars Paolo greets as friends, from Chelsea art dealers to King's Road shoppers, will make you want to become a part of the club. Warm and cosy in winter, bright and sunny in summer with pavement tables for alfresco dining, this really is a place for all seasons. Daily specials supplement the already balanced menu that covers many regions of Italy and any requests to veer off-menu are satisfied without fuss or fanfare. Caraffini is proof that good hospitality is very much alive and kicking.

CHELSEA, SOUTH KENSINGTON, EARL'S COURT, HYDE PARK & KNIGHTSBRIDGE ▶ PLANS XI-XII

Carpaccio

E6

4 Sydney St. ⊠ SW3 6PP
✆ (020) 7352 3435
e-mail guicat156@aol.com
www.carpacciorestaurant.co.uk

⊖ **South Kensington**
Closed Christmas, Sunday,
Monday lunch and bank holidays

Carte £26/42

Ladies-who-lunch may have colonised much of Chelsea but, here at Carpaccio, the decoration is far more blokey: there are stills from assorted James Bond films and, reflecting the owner's passion for all things related to Formula 1, the cockpit of an Ayrton Senna racing car. It's a lively place with animated service from an all-Italian crew and it attracts a wide range of customer; the best seats are at the back under a large skylight. Pizzas have been added to the menu, and they are done well and the daily specials are always worth considering – as are the varied veal dishes. Aptly enough, carpaccio of meat and fish is a speciality and Sunday lunches are real family affairs. The wine list is exclusively Italian, with a fair choice by the glass.

Le Cercle

F6

1 Wilbraham Pl ⊠ SW1X 9AE
✆ (020) 7901 9999
e-mail info@lecercle.co.uk
www.lecercle.co.uk

⊖ **Sloane Square**
Closed Christmas - New Year,
Sunday and Monday

Carte £20/35

Knowing this is owned by the same team as Club Gascon may lead to the raising of false hopes, as this is an altogether different operation. Le Cercle positions itself as a fashionable stop on the celebrity circuit and has the unsmiling receptionist and the managers with Secret Service ear pieces to prove it. Lunch sees a bewildering mix of business types and senior local ladies but what is certain is that it all comes alive at dinner; and its drapes and high ceiling do give it a fairly striking look. Where it does follow the same theme as its City sister is in the menu format, whereby you order three or four small dishes per person from the various sections. Dishes are nicely balanced and the French flavours pronounced.

Chelsea Brasserie

French ✗✗

7-12 Sloane Sq. ✉ SW1W 8EG
℘ (020) 7896 9988
e-mail rob@chelsea-brasserie.co.uk
www.sloanesquarehotel.co.uk

⊖ Sloane Square
Closed Christmas and
Sunday dinner

Menu £25 (weekday dinner) – Carte £34/40

AC

VISA

MC

If you're not going on to either the Royal Court or Cadogan Hall theatres then it may be best to alert your waiter; they are clearly so used to getting their customers fed and watered before curtain up that they sometimes find it hard to shift down a gear later on. It's no surprise that it is so busy early evening because their theatre menus represent excellent value. The menus, like the waiters, are mostly French born with some intercontinental experience. Vegetarians get plenty of choice and carnivores should be satisfied with the selection from the grill. The cooking has a breezy confidence and hits the spot. The front section of the restaurant attached to the bar is more fun, while tables at the back are quieter.

Chelsea Ram

Gastropub 🍺

32 Burnaby St ✉ SW10 0PL
℘ (020) 7351 4008
e-mail bookings@chelsearam.co.uk

⊖ Fulham Broadway.
Closed Sunday dinner

Carte £18/30

AC

VISA

MC

It's easy to see why the Chelsea Ram is such a successful neighbourhood pub: it's somewhat secreted position means there are few casual passers-by to upset the peace, the locals appreciate the relaxed and warm feel of the place and the pub provides them with just the sort of food they want. That means proper pub grub, with highlights being things on toast, like chicken livers or mushrooms, and the constant presence of favourites like The Ram burger or haddock and leek fishcake; prices are fair and portions large. They do take bookings but somewhat reluctantly, as they always want to keep a table or two for that spontaneous visit. The Chelsea Ram's winning formula is that it's comfortable just being what it is – a friendly, reliable local.

Chutney Mary

D8

535 King's Rd. ✉ SW10 0SZ
✆ (020) 7351 3113
e-mail chutneymary@realindianfood.com
www.realindianfood.com

⊖ Fulham Broadway
Closed dinner 25 December –
(dinner only and
lunch Saturday-Sunday)

Menu £22 – Carte £37/47

If you can't find it, ask a cabbie, as the precise location of Chutney Mary is reputed to form part of 'The Knowledge'. This long-standing Indian restaurant has always been more West End sophisticate than local eatery and was at the vanguard when Indian restaurants came of age in London. Silk wall hangings from Jaipur are the latest addition to the decoration which gets regularly refreshed, while the conservatory remains a favoured spot. The cooking has become slightly lighter recently and the flavours more subtle. Newer dishes include dabba gosht made with lamb, halibut in a mustard sauce and steamed bream in a banana leaf, but kebabs and tandoor and grilled dishes remain popular. Wine from the glass-fronted cave plays a large part.

Le Colombier

E6

145 Dovehouse St. ✉ SW3 6LB
✆ (020) 7351 1155
e-mail lecolombier1998@aol.com
www.le-colombier-restaurant.co.uk

⊖ South Kensington

Menu £26 (lunch) – Carte £31/50

Le Colombier is as warm and welcoming as it is honest and reliable and thereby offers proof that being a good neighbourhood restaurant takes more than just being in a good neighbourhood. French influences abound, from the accents of the staff and the menu content to the inordinate amount of double cheek kissing that occurs – most of the customers appear to know one another or feel they should like to know one another. In summer, when the full-length windows fold back, the terrace is the place to sit although the under-floor heating ensures the place is equally welcoming in winter. Oysters, game in season, veal in various forms and regional cheeses are the highlights, as are the classic desserts from crêpe Suzette to crème brûlée.

Daphne's

E6

Italian ✗✗

112 Draycott Ave. ✉ SW3 3AE
℘ (020) 7589 4257
e-mail reservations@daphnes-restaurant.co.uk
www.daphnes-restaurant.co.uk

⊖ South Kensington
Closed 25-26 December and
1 January –
booking essential

**Menu £19 (lunch and early dinner) –
Carte £29/48**

A/C

📺

🕐

☼

VISA

💳

AE

One wonders if theatrical agent Daphne Rye opened her eponymous restaurant as a means of keeping her resting actors busy. Forty years on and Daphne's is a chic Chelsea institution; there's even a branch in Barbados for those who can't live without their vongole on holiday. The narrow room is Tuscan in its look and the best seats are those at the front by the large windows. The many regulars clearly like the reassurance of familiarity so the kitchen sticks largely to a tried and tested assortment of Italian classics but prepared with greater care than one usually expects in an Italian restaurant with a 'celebrity' following. The lunch menu is good value and the occasional new dish, like salt-baked sea bass, gets in under the radar.

Eight over Eight

E7

Asian ✗✗

392 King's Rd ✉ SW3 5UZ
℘ (020) 7349 9934
e-mail eightovereight@rickerrstaurants.com
www.rickerrestaurants.com

⊖ Gloucester Road
Closed Sunday lunch

Menu £17 – Carte £28/39

A/C

📺

VISA

💳

AE

A major fire at the back end of 2009 meant that Eight over Eight stayed shut for most of 2010, but anyone who missed it too much during this period needed only to nip up to Notting Hill to find another one of Will Ricker's fashionable Asian restaurants. From the day it reopened it has been full, so maybe its customers are more loyal than anyone thought; they are certainly a handsome bunch and many of them seem to know one another. The restaurant is largely unchanged; it just feels a little plusher and is better lit. Wisely, they didn't change the menu either; its influences stretch across a number of countries in South East Asia and dishes are designed for sharing. Highlights are the creamy curries and anything that's crispy.

CHELSEA, SOUTH KENSINGTON, EARL'S COURT, HYDE PARK & KNIGHTSBRIDGE ▶ PLANS XI-XII

L'Etranger

D5

Innovative ✕✕

36 Gloucester Rd. ✉ SW7 4QT
✆ (020) 7584 1118
e-mail etranger@etranger.co.uk
www.circagroupltd.co.uk

⊖ Gloucester Road
Closed Saturday lunch –
booking essential

Menu £20 (lunch) – Carte £32/101

[A/C]
When free from the tyranny of traditional recipes, French émigrés are generally more open to the idea of culinary experimentation. Add to the mix the French colony of South Kensington and you end up with a restaurant like L'Etranger: a French restaurant which incorporates influences from Japanese cuisine. The fact that it works owes much to the respect the kitchen has for the ingredients, cooking techniques and flavours of both cultures. The various menus demand detailed examination and include a champagne and fish menu for those really indulging themselves. Finish off, but not literally, with their 'Death by Chocolate'. Silks and lilacs create a stylish, atmospheric space; ask for one of the corner tables. The wine and sake list is impressive.

Fifth Floor

F4

Modern European ✕✕✕

109-125 Knightsbridge ✉ SW1X 7RJ
✆ (020) 7235 5250
e-mail reception@harveynichols.com
www.harveynichols.com

⊖ Knightsbridge
Closed Sunday dinner

Menu £25/40

[A/C]
If there is one thing that's never lacking on the Fifth Floor at Harvey Nicks, it's atmosphere. From the busy shop to the stylish bar and here in the elegant restaurant with its tent-like ceiling, there's seemingly plenty of fun to be had and lots of dressing up to do. The food is your standard modern European with the occasional Asian fling and, while fish appears to be a strength, the kitchen does have a tendency to occasionally add an unnecessary extra flavour that detracts from the overall dish. It's a shame too that service can sometimes be a little too swift for its own good, as you can feel as though staff are more concerned with the time of your departure than in ensuring that you're having a good time.

Foxtrot Oscar

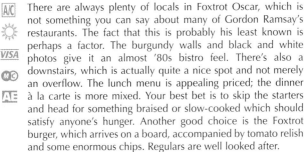

Traditional 🍴

79 Royal Hospital Rd. ✉ SW3 4HN
📞 (020) 7352 4448
e-mail foxtrotoscar@gordonramsay.com
www.gordonramsay.com

⊖ Sloane Square
Closed 25 December –
booking essential

Menu £22 (lunch) – Carte £25/37

There are always plenty of locals in Foxtrot Oscar, which is not something you can say about many of Gordon Ramsay's restaurants. The fact that this is probably his least known is perhaps a factor. The burgundy walls and black and white photos give it an almost '80s bistro feel. There's also a downstairs, which is actually quite a nice spot and not merely an overflow. The lunch menu is appealing priced; the dinner à la carte is more mixed. Your best bet is to skip the starters and head for something braised or slow-cooked which should satisfy anyone's hunger. Another good choice is the Foxtrot burger, which arrives on a board, accompanied by tomato relish and some enormous chips. Regulars are well looked after.

Good Earth

Chinese

233 Brompton Rd. ✉ SW3 2EP
📞 (020) 7584 3658
e-mail chris@goodearthgroup.co.uk
www.goodearthgroup.co.uk

⊖ Knightsbridge
Closed 23-31 December

Menu £14/30 – Carte £28/37

The Brompton Road branch of this small chain has been a reliable constant for many a year and is suitably authentic on all levels: the service is brisk, the menu lengthy, cooking is dependable and desserts are not worth bothering with. There is no particular bias, save for a few Sichuan dishes, but they do use plenty of higher-end ingredients like scallops and Dover sole. Included among the set menus is the Lobster Dinner, a reminder of the restaurant's location and target market. More unusual dishes are often introduced but it's the old favourites and classic combinations that sell. Unlike most restaurants spread over two floors, here the basement level is actually the busier and more popular choice than the ground floor.

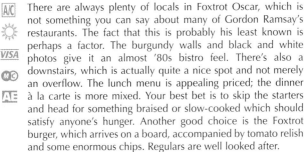

CHELSEA, SOUTH KENSINGTON, EARL'S COURT, HYDE PARK & KNIGHTSBRIDGE ▶ PLANS XI-XII

229

Gordon Ramsay ✿✿✿

French 🗡🗡🗡🗡

F7

68-69 Royal Hospital Rd. ✉ SW3 4HP
☎ (020) 7352 4441
e-mail royalhospitalroad@gordonramsay.com
www.gordonramsay.com

⊖ **Sloane Square**
Closed Christmas,
Saturday and Sunday –
booking essential

Menu £45/90

[A/C]
[🍇]
[VISA]
[MC]
[AE]
[◐]

Gordon Ramsay Holdings

Head Chef Clare Smyth's influence appears to stretch beyond the kitchen: it was her idea to add orchids to the room and this has given it a lighter, fresher look, although the David Collins interior still exudes calm. This composure is essential as the restaurant is as busy as ever, which means securing a reservation can still be a fairly tortuous experience; bookings are taken three months in advance but it is worth trying your luck at the last minute. Clare Smyth has a challenging task because, along with showcasing her lighter style of cooking in the 'seasonal inspiration' menu, she also has to deliver on the Gordon Ramsay classics, such as the ravioli of lobster and langoustine, the braised pig's trotter and the best end of lamb – and these are the dishes that many of the regulars order time and time again. Fortunately, she succeeds and her instinctive feel for and understanding of harmonious flavours is evident. Jean-Claude is a constant presence in the room and if you're a returning guest then he will probably remember you.

First Course

- Butter poached lobster with morels, asparagus and wild garlic.
- Foie gras and calves sweetbreads with almond velouté.

Main Course

- Pigeon with polenta, shallots, beetroot and date sauce.
- Turbot with langoustine, linguine and wild mushrooms.

Dessert

- Strawberry and lemon balm Eton mess with vanilla ice cream wafer.
- Bitter chocolate cylinder with coffee granité and ginger mousse.

Langan's Coq d'Or

C6

254-260 Old Brompton Rd. ⊠ SW5 9HR   ⊖ Earl's Court
☎ (020) 7259 2599   Closed 25-26 December
e-mail admin@langansrestaurant.co.uk
www.langansrestaurants.co.uk

Menu £27

The glass-enclosed front section really comes into its own in summer when it opens out onto the street. But on colder days the best place to sit is in the warm, yellow-hued main room whose walls are covered with an assortment of paintings and cartoons, along with photographs of all the good and the great who have graced one of the Langan's restaurants over the years. The only incongruous note is the presence of a large TV in the bar. The classic brasserie food is prepared with care and dishes come in generous proportions. The set price menu has something for everyone, whether that's a burger, eggs Benedict, coq au vin or some grilled sea bass, along with other more home-grown classics like bangers and mash.

Lots Road Pub & Dining Room

D8

114 Lots Rd ⊠ SW10 0RJ   ⊖ Fulham Broadway.
☎ (020) 7352 6645
e-mail lotsroad@foodandfuel.co.uk
www.lotsroadpub.com

Carte £20/31

Lots Road and its customers are clearly happy with one another as the pub has introduced a customer loyalty scheme, whereby anyone making their fifth visit is rewarded with a discount. Lunch is geared more towards those just grabbing a quick bite but dinner sees a choice that could include oysters, mussels or a savoury tart of the day; the Perthshire côte de boeuf is the house speciality. There are also pies and casseroles, in appropriate pub-like sizes, and even salads for those after something light. Service remains bright and cheery, even on those frantic Thursday nights when the pub offers 'Thursday Treats' with wine tasting and nibbles. The only disappointment is the somewhat ordinary bread for which they make a not insubstantial charge.

Manicomio

Italian ✗

F6

85 Duke of York Sq., King's Rd. ⊠ SW3 4LY   ⊖ Sloane Square
✆ (020) 7730 3366   Closed 25-26 December and 1 January
e-mail info@manicomio.co.uk
www.manicomio.co.uk

Carte £34/40

If anywhere encapsulates King's Road's journey from counterculture hub to retail playground it is Duke of York Square and its outlets. Among these is Manicomio, a glossy Italian restaurant which doesn't need to rely solely on weary shoppers as it also draws visitors from the Saatchi Gallery next door, a fact that shows just what an inspired location this was. Its success is also helped by an accessible menu, offering a greatest hits of easy-to-eat Italian food. Cooking is undertaken with care and the simplest dishes are the best ones, although prices do reflect the Chelsea postcode. Service remains sufficiently perky for one to forgive occasional moments of forgetfulness. The terrific front terrace fills quickly in nearly all seasons.

Marco

Traditional ✗✗

T2

Stamford Bridge, Fulham Rd.   ⊖ Fulham Broadway
⊠ SW6 1HS   Closed 24 July-8 August,
✆ (020) 7915 2929   Sunday and Monday except
e-mail info@marcorestaurant.org   match days – (dinner only)
www.marcorestaurant.org

Menu £22/45 – Carte £35/59

A section of Manchester United fans was once derided as being prawn sandwich eaters; London expectations being what they are, at Chelsea's ground you get a restaurant from Marco Pierre White. Some will inevitably cry foul and shed a tear for football's working class roots; others will cheer for this evidence of our growing culinary maturity. Both sides, though, should applaud the menu, which offers British classics and 'bloke' food galore, from classically prepared liver and bacon to fish and chips and rib-eyes with assorted accompaniments. This being a polyglot club means other nationalities are also represented, in this case a bit of Italy and France, and more sophisticated fare such as foie gras terrine or duck confit is also available.

Mr Chow

Chinese 🍴🍴

151 Knightsbridge ✉ SW1X 7PA
☎ (020) 7589 7347
e-mail mrchowuk@aol.com
www.mrchow.com

⊖ Knightsbridge
Closed 24-26 December,
1 January and Monday lunch

Carte £39/63

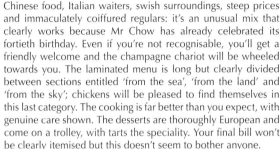

Chinese food, Italian waiters, swish surroundings, steep prices and immaculately coiffured regulars: it's an unusual mix that clearly works because Mr Chow has already celebrated its fortieth birthday. Even if you're not recognisable, you'll get a friendly welcome and the champagne chariot will be wheeled towards you. The laminated menu is long but clearly divided between sections entitled 'from the sea', 'from the land' and 'from the sky'; chickens will be pleased to find themselves in this last category. The cooking is far better than you expect, with genuine care shown. The desserts are thoroughly European and come on a trolley, with tarts the speciality. Your final bill won't be clearly itemised but this doesn't seem to bother anyone.

One-O-One

Seafood 🍴🍴🍴

101 Knightsbridge ✉ SW1X 7RN
☎ (020) 7290 7101
e-mail oneoone@luxurycollection.com
www.oneoonerestaurant.com

⊖ Knightsbridge

Menu £19/42 – Carte £50/66

Walking past the Sheraton Park Tower hotel, one of London's less majestic buildings, you'd never know there was a restaurant behind those heavy net curtains, and a rather good one to boot. Granted, the room size and shape mean an animated atmosphere remains elusive and staff, pleasant though they are, have little presence. But the food is good and that food is mostly fish. They've found a balance between offering a traditional à la carte menu and a list of 'petits plats', 6 of which, taken together, will satisfy the fiercest of appetites. Much of the produce comes from Brittany and Norway; the latter gives us the King crab legs which are the stars of the show. The kitchen is not afraid of adding a little playfulness to its classical base.

233

Painted Heron

Indian

112 Cheyne Walk ⊠ SW10 0DJ
☏ (020) 7351 5232
www.thepaintedheron.com

Menu £35 (dinner) – Carte £31/42

⊖ **Gloucester Road**
Closed 25 December, 1 January –
(dinner only and l
unch Saturday-Sunday)

They call their style "modern Indian" which, in essence, means the kitchen's influences come from across the land; from Kashmir and Rajasthan to Kerala and Goa. Fish, largely from Hastings, is handled dextrously and much is made of seasonal game, whether that's the tandoor pigeon breasts, the partridge with red chilli paste or grouse in a southern stew. Flavours tend to be well-defined and balanced. The room is bigger than you think and has quite a formal feel, thanks largely to the style of service from the young team, but it's broken up into nooks and crannies and hence quite intimate. The open courtyard is an attractive feature and, despite its tiny entrance and tucked away location, the restaurant always appears to be busy.

Pasha

Moroccan

1 Gloucester Rd ⊠ SW7 4PP
☏ (020) 7589 7969
e-mail reservations@pasha-restaurant.co.uk
www.pasha-restaurant.co.uk

Menu £15/30 – Carte £26/32

⊖ **Gloucester Road**
Closed 24-25 December

If the prosaic surroundings of Gloucester Road leave you in need of more colourful fillip to your love-life then try buying into the whole Pasha experience: the exotic scent of incense and the rich, romantic and velvety décor should be enough to arouse anyone's ardour. Downstairs is the place to be, in one of the semi-private booths in particular, where rose petals are strewn seductively over the tables and service is appropriately sweet-natured. Choose from one of the 'feast' menus and the food will keep on coming, including kemia (Moroccan small plates), tagines and sweet pastries. By the end your more corpulent figure may leave you feeling less romantically inclined so be thankful to the belly dancers for buying you some time.

Phoenix

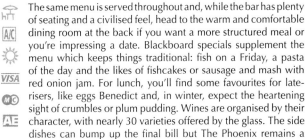

F6/7

23 Smith St ⊠ SW3 4EE
☎ (020) 7730 9182
e-mail thephoenix@geronimo-inns.co.uk
www.geronimo-inns.co.uk

⊖ Sloane Square.
Plan XI
Closed 25-26 December

Carte £23/30

The same menu is served throughout and, while the bar has plenty of seating and a civilised feel, head to the warm and comfortable dining room at the back if you want a more structured meal or you're impressing a date. Blackboard specials supplement the menu which keeps things traditional: fish on a Friday, a pasta of the day and the likes of fishcakes or sausage and mash with red onion jam. For lunch, you'll find some favourites for late-risers, like eggs Benedict and, in winter, expect the heartening sight of crumbles or plum pudding. Wines are organised by their character, with nearly 30 varieties offered by the glass. The side dishes can bump up the final bill but The Phoenix remains a friendly and conscientiously run Chelsea local.

Pig's Ear

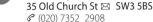

Gastropub

E7

35 Old Church St ⊠ SW3 5BS
☎ (020) 7352 2908
e-mail thepigsear@hotmail.co.uk
www.thepigsear.com

⊖ Sloane Square.
Closed 2 weeks at Christmas and
Sunday dinner

Carte £22/35

This Chelsea pub may not look much like a foodie spot from the outside, or indeed from the inside, but it does have a refreshing honesty to it. Lunch is in the rough-and-ready ground floor bar, decorated with everything from 'Tintin' pictures to covers of 'Sounds' newspaper. There's a decent choice of 5-6 main courses and a wine list on a blackboard. With its wood panelling and dressed tables, the upstairs dining room provides quite a contrast, but the atmosphere is still far from starchy. Here the menu displays a little more ambition but cooking remains similarly earthy and the wine list has plenty of bottles under £30. The kitchen knows its way around an animal: slow-cooked dishes such as pork cheeks are done particularly well.

Poissonnerie de l'Avenue

Seafood XX

E6

82 Sloane Ave. ✉ SW3 3DZ
✆ (020) 7589 2457
e-mail peterr@poissonerle.co.uk
www.poissonneriedelavenue.com

⊖ South Kensington
Closed 24-26 December

Menu £28 (lunch) – Carte £25/39

There is something heartening about dining in a restaurant that is older than its waiters. Poissonnerie de l'Avenue began life in 1946 but the owner is still to be found greeting his customers – many of whom look as though they've been coming since the doors first opened – as old friends, as indeed many are. This is a restaurant all about traditional hospitality and it's easy to understand its longevity. The wood-panelled room has an air of luxury; service is well-organised and the cooking is done 'properly'. The menu is a large affair: expect about 18 starters with everything from oysters to smoked salmon and the same number of seafood and fish main courses. The well-groomed clientele hardly blink when handed the inevitably large bill.

Racine

French XX

E5

239 Brompton Rd ✉ SW3 2EP
✆ (020) 7584 4477
e-mail jon@racine-restaurant.com
www.racine-restaurant.com

⊖ South Kensington
Closed 25 December

Menu £18/20 – Carte £28/44

Racine is as authentic a French brasserie as you can get at this end of the tunnel. The accents are thick; the baguettes are fresh and the room's wood and leather have that reassuring lived-in look. Some of the clientele, who are a mature and confident bunch, give the impression that they come here on a weekly basis and it's easy to understand why: along with the authentically prepared classics, such as steak tartare, tête de veau or fruits de mer, are plenty of other dishes that hit the spot, along with well priced lunch and early evening menus. Try to avoid the tables in the middle of the room because, on windier days, you'll find yourself assailed by the occasional gust of wind, whenever somebody opens the front door.

Rasoi ✿

F6

Indian ✕✕

10 Lincoln St. ✉ SW3 2TS
✆ (020) 7225 1881
e-mail info@rasoirestaurant.co.uk
www.rasoirestaurant.co.uk

⊖ **Sloane Square**
Closed Saturday lunch

Menu £26 (lunch) – Carte £58/83

Rasoi

Part of the appeal of Vineet Bhatia's Rasoi is that it's found in an archetypal Chelsea townhouse and that the atmosphere inside is usually far warmer and more intimate than anything one usually experiences in an Indian restaurant. This is often despite, rather than because of, the staff, who bring a mix of nationalities and varying degrees of competency to the operation. Proof that most people are really here for the food comes in the fact that the 'gourmand' menu is by far the most popular choice. It has been reduced from an unwieldy nine courses to a more manageable seven. The cooking is inventive and the kitchen proves that Indian food can be just as open to interpretation as other cuisines. But what makes it all work is the quality of the ingredients used and the deft, controlled spicing. Tea drinkers will find much to savour in the range and the ritual. Sit in the bigger room at the back which has more personality than the one at the front. Larger parties should consider one of the more opulent private rooms upstairs.

First Course

- Seafood medley with soft-shell crab and gun powder prawn.
- Spice dusted foie gras with wild mushroom naan, spiced fennel salad.

Main Course

- Charcoal roasted lamb chops with chilli and roasted peanut khichdi.
- Grilled ginger and chilli lobster, curry leaf and broccoli.

Dessert

- Spiced caramelised pineapple.
- Cumin chocolate fondant and rose petal jam.

Tom Aikens ❀

E6

43 Elystan St. ⊠ SW3 3NT
✆ (020) 7584 2003
e-mail info@tomaikens.co.uk
www.tomaikens.co.uk

⊖ **South Kensington**
Closed 24-29 December,
1-3 January, Saturday lunch,
Sunday and bank holidays

Carte £53/89

Tom Aikens

Tom Aikens has experienced a challenging couple of years but Chelsea diners are a forgiving and loyal bunch and continue to support his endeavours. This, his principal restaurant, has changed little in appearance over that time and remains a good looking and fairly formal room but one where the customers can create an atmosphere without too much trouble. What change has occurred is in the menu which now includes a section called 'Tom's Classics'; these are slightly less intricate dishes and are all the better for it. There is no doubt that Aikens is a talented chef but the more innovative he tries to be, the less convincing are the results. Gone are the excessive quantities of complimentary extras which added up to something of a culinary overload by the end of the meal. Service is still formally structured but the team are now encouraged to exhibit a little more of their personalities, which makes a difference to what is, in effect, a neighbourhood restaurant, albeit one in a pretty smart neighbourhood.

First Course

- Sheep's cheese gazpacho with chervil cannelloni and honey.
- Foie gras terrine with turnips and pickled radish.

Main Course

- Lamb with aligot potato and anchovy beignet.
- Turbot with thyme and lemon gnocchi.

Dessert

- Truffle and vanilla panna cotta with black pepper.
- Honeycomb with confit lemon and poppy seed ice cream.

Tom's Kitchen

E6

27 Cale St. ✉ SW3 3QP
℘ (020) 7349 0202
e-mail info@tomskitchen.co.uk
www.tomskitchen.co.uk

⊖ South Kensington
Closed 25-26 December

Carte £34/60

The locals may not have taken to his fish and chip shop but they do seem to like his kitchen. This is a restaurant with a thoroughly sound plan: it's open from early in the morning until late at night and offers satisfying comfort food in relaxed surroundings. The tiled walls and open kitchen work well and there's an upstairs room for the overspill. With its shepherd's pie, sausage and mash, and belly of pork, the menu wouldn't look out of place in a pub; although, as the eponymous Tom is Tom Aikens, a few luxury ingredients like foie gras do sneak in. Bread, olives and side dishes can push up the final bill but it's a friendly place with a stress-free atmosphere. There's a less convincing second branch in Somerset House.

Toto's

F5

Walton House, Walton St ✉ SW3 2JH
℘ (020) 7589 0075

⊖ Knightsbridge
Closed 25-27 December –
booking essential at dinner

Menu £27 (lunch) – Carte £33/51

Toto's has been a Chelsea landmark around these parts for donkey's years. Its somewhat hidden location and old school service make you feel part of a club and you'll be dining with plenty of locals – lots of smartly dressed people of a certain age displaying varying degrees of tonsorial ingenuity. The room is not as big as one thinks as there's a mirrored wall at one end but there is also a gallery. The menu is familiar and despite the odd unseasonal ingredient, the cooking is very satisfying. The pasta course, such as black spaghetti with squid and clams, will be a highlight while main courses such as the lamb cutlets with pecorino also hit the spot. It ain't cheap but, if you're concerned about price, then you're in the wrong place.

Zuma

Japanese ✕✕

5 Raphael St ✉ SW7 1DL
☏ (020) 7584 1010
e-mail info@zumarestaurant.com
www.zumarestaurant.com

⊖ **Knightsbridge**
Closed 25-26 December-1 January

Carte £60/90

Japanese food meets contemporary Japanese food at this stylish Knightsbridge restaurant, popular with the glittering and the glitterati and ideally located for those seeking a little respite from the strain of shopping or being photographed doing so. The place is certainly catching in its design, with a plethora of granite, stone, marble and wood creating a restaurant that successfully blends east with west. Choose from a variety of seating options, from the bustle of the main dining area to the theatre afforded by the sushi counter. The menu offers up an intriguing mix of the traditional with the ultra modern, all expertly crafted and delicately presented. Lovers of sake will find over thirty varieties available.

Do not confuse ✕ with ✿ ! ✕ defines comfort, while ✿ are awarded for the best cuisine. Stars are awarded across all categories of comfort.

Kensington · North Kensington · Notting Hill

It was the choking air of 17C London that helped put **Kensington** on the map: the little village lying to the west of the city became the favoured retreat of the asthmatic King William III who had Sir Christopher Wren build **Kensington Palace** for him. Where the king leads, the titled follow, and the area soon became a fashionable location for the rich. For over 300 years, it's had no problem holding onto its cachet, though a stroll down Kensington High Street is these days a more egalitarian odyssey than some more upmarket residents might approve of.

The shops here mix the everyday with the flamboyant, but for a real taste of the exotic you have to take the lift to the top of the Art Deco Barkers building and arrive at the Kensington Roof Gardens, which are open to all as long as they're not in use for a corporate bash. The gardens are now over seventy years old, yet still remain a 'charming secret'. Those who do make it up to the sixth floor discover a delightful woodland garden and gurgling stream, complete with pools, bridges and trees. There are flamingos, too, adding a dash of vibrant colour.

Back down on earth, Kensington boasts another hidden attraction in **Leighton House** on its western boundaries. The Victorian redbrick façade looks a bit forbidding as you make your approach, but step inside and things take a dramatic turn, courtesy of the extraordinary Arab Hall, with its oriental mosaics and tinkling fountain creating a scene like something from *The Arabian Knights.* Elsewhere in the building, the Pre-Raphaelite paintings of Lord Leighton, Burne-Jones and Alma-Tadema are much to the fore. Mind you, famous names have always had a hankering for W8, with a particular preponderance to dally in enchanting **Kensington Square,** where there are almost as many blue plaques as buildings upon which to secure them. William Thackeray, John Stuart Mill and Edward Burne-Jones were all residents.

One of the London's most enjoyable green retreats is **Holland Park,** just north of the High Street. It boasts the 400 year-old Holland House, which is a fashionable focal point for summer-time al fresco theatre and opera. Holland Walk runs along the eastern fringe of the park, and provides a lovely sojourn down to the shops; at the Kyoto Garden, koi carp reach hungrily for the surface of their pool, while elsewhere peacocks strut around as if they own the place.

Another world beckons just north of here – the seedy-cum-glitzy environs of **Notting Hill.** The main drag itself, Notting Hill Gate, is little more than a one-dimensional thoroughfare only enlivened by second hand record shops, but to its south are charming cottages with pastel shades in leafy streets, while to the north the appealing **Pembridge Road** evolves into

S. Ollivier / MICHELIN

the boutiques of Westbourne Grove. Most people heading in this direction are making for the legendary Portobello Road market – particularly on Saturdays, which are manic. The market stretches on for more than a mile, with a chameleon-like ability to change colour and character on the way: there are antiques at the Notting Hill end, followed further up by food stalls, and then designer and vintage clothes as you reach the Westway. Those who don't fancy the madding crowds of the market can nip into the Electric Cinema and watch a movie in supreme comfort: it boasts two-seater sofas and leather armchairs. Nearby there are another two film-houses putting the hip into the Hill – the Gate, and the Coronet, widely recognised as one of London's most charming 'locals'.

Hidden in a mews just north of **Westbourne Grove** is a fascinating destination: the Museum of Brands, Packaging and Advertising, which does pretty much what it says on the label. It's both nostalgic and evocative, featuring thousands of items like childhood toys, teenage magazines…and HP sauce bottles.

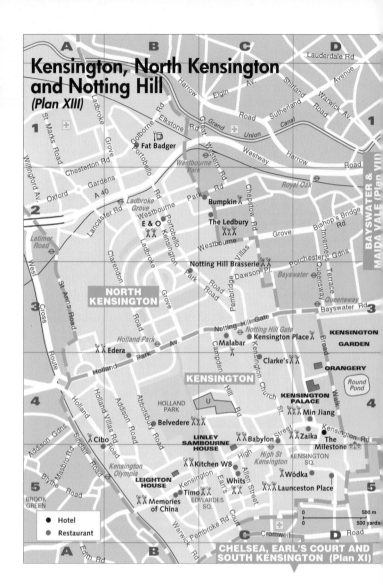

Kensington, North Kensington and Notting Hill
(Plan XIII)

A   **B**   **C**   **D**

Lauderdale Rd

Harrow   Elgin   Av.   Shirland   Avenue

St. Marks Road   Ladbroke   Colborne   Elkstone Rd   Great   Road   Sutherland   Warwick Av.   Road

1

Willingford Av.   Chesterton Rd   Colborne   Portobello   Grove   Western   Union   Westway   Harrow   Road

Fat Badger

Westbourne Park

Oxford   Gardens   A 40   Ladbroke   Grove   Westbourne   Park   Rd   Royal Oak

2

Lancaster Rd   Bumpkin

Latimer Road   Clarendon   Ladbroke   Portobello   Kensington   E & O   The Ledbury   Chepstow Rd   Bishop's Bridge Rd   Inverness   Terrace

West   St. Anns Road   Cross   Route   Ladbroke   Grove   Park   Westbourne   Villas   Grove   Porchester Gdns.   Queensway

Notting Hill Brasserie

Dawson Pl.   Bayswater

NORTH KENSINGTON

Pembridge   Road   Queensway

3

Bayswater Rd

Holland Park   Notting Hill Gate   Notting Hill Gate   **KENSINGTON GARDEN**

Edera   Malabar   Kensington Place

Holland   Park   Av.   Campden   Clarke's   **ORANGERY**

Holland   Kensington Church   Round Pond

KENSINGTON

4

Holland Villas Rd   Addison Road   Abbotsbury Road   **HOLLAND PARK**   U   Hill   **KENSINGTON PALACE**   St.   Min Jiang

Belvedere   Kensington Rd

Addison Gdns   Cibo   **LINLEY SAMBOURNE HOUSE**   Babylon   Zaika   The Milestone

Sinclair   Road   High   High St Kensington   **KENSINGTON SQ.**

Blythe   Road   Kensington   Olympia   **LEIGHTON HOUSE**   Kitchen W8   Allen Street   Wódka

BROOK GREEN   Earl's   Whits   Launceston Place

5

Timo   Memories of China   **EDWARDES SQ.**   Court

0   500 m
0   500 yards

● Hotel
● Restaurant

Warwick   Pembroke Rd   Cromwell   Road

A   **B**   **C**   **D**

Egth Rd

CHELSEA, EARL'S COURT AND SOUTH KENSINGTON (Plan XI)

BAYSWATER & MAIDA VALE (Plan VIII)

Babylon

C4

Modern European 𝗫𝗫

99 Kensington High St
(entrance on Derry St) ✉ W8 5SA
✆ (020) 7368 3993
e-mail babylon@roofgardens.virgin.com
www.roofgardens.virgin.com

⊖ High Street Kensington
Closed 25-30 December and
Sunday dinner

Menu £22 (lunch) – Carte £44/56

The challenge is to find the entrance which is secreted on the right as you walk down Derry Street; then it's the lift up to the 7th floor and suddenly you're surrounded by trees. There's no doubting that this is quite a spot and while the gardens just below may not be 'hanging' they are an understandably appealing place for a party. The restaurant is a long, narrow affair whose contemporary décor reflects the leafy outdoors and the terrace takes some beating in summer. Influences on the menu remain largely within Europe and the cooking shows a degree of perkiness and ambition. The lunch time set menu is priced to appeal to local businesses while the à la carte can get a little expensive. The wine list plants its flag firmly in the New World.

Belvedere

B4

French 𝗫𝗫𝗫

Holland House, off Abbotsbury Rd.
✉ W8 6LU
✆ (020) 7602 1238
e-mail info@belvedererestaurant.co.uk
www.belvedererestaurant.co.uk

⊖ Holland Park
Closed 1 January

Menu £20 (lunch) – Carte £28/44

Built in 17C as the summer ballroom to the Jacobean Holland House, The Belvedere sits in a stunning position in Holland Park. It's hard to believe you're still in London but check the location first as signposts within the park are a little elusive. The ground floor is the more glittery, with mirrors, glass balls and a small bar area. Upstairs is more traditional in style and leads out onto the charming terrace which is well worth booking in summer. Service remains decidedly formal. The menu covers all bases from eggs Benedict to even the occasional Thai offering, but it's worth sticking to the more classical, French influenced dishes as these are kitchen's strength. Produce is well sourced and dishes nicely balanced. France dominates the wine list.

Bumpkin

C2

B r i t i s h 🍴

209 Westbourne Park Rd ✉ W11 1EA
☎ (020) 7243 9818
e-mail reservations@bumpkinuk.com
www.bumpkinuk.com

⊖ **Westbourne Park**
Closed 1 January, 29 August
and 25-26 December

Carte £28/40

How refreshing to find a restaurant's name that sums up its spirit instead of merely repeating its street number or using the name of an obscure vegetable. Bumpkin, whose slogan is 'for city folk who like a little country living', champions British produce in quasi-rustic surroundings with a pub-like informality. Young, keen staff run around with 'Country Girl' or 'Country Boy' emblazoned on their T shirts and the noisy open kitchen adds to the fun. The menu avoids being too earnest and focuses on using first rate ingredients sensibly; the best dishes are the simplest ones, such as a Cow Pie of which Desperate Dan would surely approve. Be sure to sit in the main room, rather than in the corridor of uncertainty between it and the front bar.

Cibo

A5

I t a l i a n 🍴

3 Russell Gdns ✉ W14 8EZ
☎ (020) 7371 6271
e-mail ciborestaurant@aol.com
www.ciborestaurant.net

⊖ **Kensington Olympia**
Closed 1 week Christmas, Sunday dinner
and bank holidays

Carte £23/37

Cibo has long been a familiar landmark in Holland Park and its constituency appears to be mostly regulars whom the owner greets effusively, although any event at nearby Olympia will bring in a few interlopers. It's always felt a little claustrophobic inside, the décor is now looking a little weary and service can be a little distracted if the boss is away but the food still merits attention. Start with some great bresaola with goat's cheese, followed by the huge grilled seafood and shellfish platter – it may be expensive but does include everything from clams and prawns to squid and swordfish and will satisfy the biggest appetite. The best part of the dessert menu is the selection of interesting and original ice creams.

Clarke's

M o d e r n   E u r o p e a n ✗✗

C4

124 Kensington Church St.
✉ W8 4BH
✆ (020) 7221 9225
e-mail restaurant@sallyclarke.com
www.sallyclarke.com

⊖ **Notting Hill Gate**
Closed Christmas, Sunday dinner
and bank holidays

Menu £40 (dinner) – Carte £37/41

Sally Clarke spent a few years in California and those who know Alice Waters' Chez Panisse will recognise the concept: crisp, seasonal produce, a minimal amount of interference from the kitchen and clean, fresh flavours. As the restaurant approaches its quarter of a century it's clear that it doesn't have to be warm and sunny outside to appreciate this type of cooking. The only significant change happened a few years back when customers were given a choice at dinner: for many years there had been a set menu with no alternative. The downstairs is a good spot to watch the kitchen in action; upstairs is more intimate. The long-standing manager keeps things rolling along nicely and knows his regulars. There's bounty galore in the shop next door.

E&O

A s i a n ✗✗

B2

14 Blenheim Cres. ✉ W11 1NN
✆ (020) 7229 5454
e-mail eando@rickerrestaurants.com
www.rickerrestaurants.com

⊖ **Ladbroke Grove**
Closed 25-26 December and
August bank holiday

Menu £19 (weekday lunch) – Carte £27/50

Once you've sidestepped the full-on bar of this Notting Hill favourite, a step from Portobello Road, you'll find yourself in a moodily sophisticated restaurant packed with the beautiful and the hopeful. The room is understatedly urbane, with slatted walls, large circular lamps and leather banquettes, while noise levels are at the party end of the auditory index. Waiting staff are obliging, pleasant and often among the prettiest people in the room. E&O stands for Eastern and Oriental and the menu journeys across numerous Asian countries, dividing itself into assorted headings which include dim sum, salads, tempura, curries and roasts. Individual dishes vary in size and price so sharing, as in life, is often the best option.

247

Edera

B4

148 Holland Park Ave. ✉ W11 4UE
✆ (020) 7221 6090
e-mail roberto@edera.co.uk
www.londonfinedininggroup.com

⊖ **Holland Park**
Closed Christmas and Easter

Carte £36/46

A/C
⌁
☼
VISA
MC
AE

The last makeover made Edera warmer and more comfortable and, while it actually holds up to 75 people, it still manages to feel quite intimate. On a typical night it seems as though the vast majority of customers have been before, that they know one another and probably walked here. In comparison, the staff are a youthful bunch, but they are well marshalled and quietly efficient. The menu is quite broad and portions are on the generous side so if you're having a pasta dish you may struggle with a fourth course. The list of daily specials is wisely printed so you don't have to try to memorise the waiter's recital; there is a Sardinian element to the cooking, with bottarga omnipresent, and the ingredients are first rate.

Fat Badger

B1

310 Portobello Rd ✉ W10 5TA
✆ (020) 8969 4500
e-mail helen@thefatbadger.com
www.thefatbadger.com

⊖ **Ladbroke Grove.**

Menu £25 (lunch) – Carte £20/29

☼
VISA
MC
AE

The Fat Badger treads the line between being worn in and worn out. Stuffing sprouts from sofas and chips and scuffs abound but the locals seem to like the general raggedness. Use of the upstairs restaurant is largely dependent on enough punters requesting it and, besides, the same menu is served in the bar. The one decorative element that really stands out is the patterned wallpaper which only reveals its true nature on close inspection. Service can be hit and miss as not all members of staff share the same attitude towards customer service. But the food is good: the kitchen doesn't try to reinvent anything but also displays a light touch, whether in the crisp cuttlefish and chorizo, the roast chicken breast or the panna cotta.

Kensington Place

C3

Modern European ✗

201-209 Kensington Church St. ⊖ Notting Hill Gate
✉ W8 7LX
✆ (020) 7727 3184
e-mail kpr-res-adm@danddlondon.com
www.kensingtonplace-restaurant.co.uk

Menu £19/23

A/C

It must have been quite difficult for the D&D group to re-establish Kensington Place, especially as Rowley Leigh, its well known former chef, now operates in nearby Bayswater. One thing they have got right is the menu; they dispensed with an à la carte and in its place introduced a competitively priced set menu which offers plenty of choice. There are some supplements for the few dishes using pricier ingredients but these can be easily avoided. The cooking is modern and quite dainty at times; desserts are done well. Service is still speedy and copes well with the numbers when it needs to. The addition of cushions has succeeded in softening the acoustics so it's also easier to have a conversation these days.

VISA

MC

AE

①

Launceston Place

D5

Modern European ✗✗✗

1a Launceston Pl. ✉ W8 5RL ⊖ Gloucester Road
✆ (020) 7937 6912 Closed 25 December, 1 January,
e-mail lpr_res@danddlondon.com Monday lunch and
www.launcestonplace-restaurant.co.uk bank holidays

Menu £20/48

A/C

Launceston Place forms part of the D&D group and is largely unrecognisable from its former days. The last, much needed reincarnation made the walls darker, the lighting moodier and the ambition more evident but the best thing it that the appealing neighbourhood feel has not been lost, even with service that takes itself seriously. Tristan Welch, who previously worked with Marcus Wareing, is the confident young chef at the helm and his cooking is original but also well grounded and balanced. He's also a keen champion of home-grown produce: about 80% of the ingredients come from within the British Isles and he's planning to increase this figure further. Try the Tasting Menu which is priced not far north of the à la carte.

VISA

MC

AE

Kitchen W8 ✵

Modern European ✗✗

C5

11-13 Abingdon Rd. ✉ W8 6AH   ⊖ High Street Kensington
✆ (020) 7937 0120   Closed bank holidays
e-mail reservations@kitchenw8.com
www.kitchenw8.com

Menu £20 (lunch) – Carte £32/41

A/C

☼

VISA

MC

AE

Kitchen W8

Rebecca Mascarenhas, doyenne of south west London's restaurant scene, and Philip Howard, luminary chef of The Square, joined forces and considerable amounts of experience to open Kitchen W8 in a Kensington side street. Perhaps the only thing they didn't get quite right is the name as it implies a level of casualness that is just not present – this is quite a smart and comfortable restaurant with structured and relatively formal service. However, it does have a palpable neighbourhood feel and it helps that Abingdon Road has always played host to a good smattering of restaurants. Prices too are relatively restrained, particularly when one considers the quality of the ingredients and what equivalent restaurants with a W1 postcode would charge. Dishes appear relatively simple on the plate and are refreshingly free of showiness, but the flavours do have depth and it is clear that this is a kitchen with skill and ambition. It displays a lightness of touch when one is required but also knows when to add a little oomph.

First Course

- Smoked eel and mackerel with sweet mustard dressing.
- Ravioli of wild mushrooms and melted onions.

Main Course

- Cod with Parmesan gnocchi and girolles.
- Roast pigeon with foie gras baked potato and celeriac.

Dessert

- Salted chocolate parfait with honeycomb ice cream.
- Rice pudding with prunes and sherry.

The Ledbury ✿✿

French 🍴🍴🍴

127 Ledbury Rd. ✉ W11 2AQ
✆ (020) 7792 9090
e-mail info@theledbury.com
www.theledbury.com

⊖ **Notting Hill Gate**
Closed 24-26 December, August bank
holiday and Monday lunch

Menu £28/65

The Ledbury

The Ledbury has been quietly going about its business, getting better and better. The Australian head chef, Brett Graham, is one of the more intelligent chefs around and his passion for quality ingredients really shines through. He is constantly on the lookout for new supplies and suppliers and knows what to do when he gets them. Hebridean lambs arrive whole and are then butchered, with every part of the beast used; game is also one of the kitchen's strengths – Brett is a keen shot. The kitchen is also firmly grounded in technique so that whenever a slightly unusual flavour or a little tease is introduced, it is done merely to enhance the dish. This is bravado cooking but without affectation. Even though Brett also has an involvement in The Harwood Arms, he does so without ever taking his eye off the ball here. Along with The Ashes, let's hope he realises he belongs on this side of the world. The room is elegant without being overdressed and the serving team are well organised and professional but they never forget that fundamentally this is a neighbourhood restaurant.

First Course

- Scallop ceviche with seaweed and horseradish.
- Chicken wings with milk skin, carrots and girolles.

Main Course

- Roe deer baked in Douglas Fir with beetroot and bone marrow.
- Turbot, liquorice, mussels and elderflower.

Dessert

- Honey and gingerbread soufflé with thyme ice cream.
- Crème caramel with apricot and jasmine.

Malabar ⊛

C3

27 Uxbridge St. ✉ W8 7TQ   ⊖ Notting Hill Gate
✆ (020) 7727 8800   Closed 24-27 December – (buffet lunch
e-mail feedback@malabar-restaurant.co.uk   Sunday)
www.malabar-restaurant.co.uk

Menu £23 s – Carte £19/33 s

AIC
🕐
☼
VISA
MC
AE

One of the reasons why Malabar has been going strong since 1983 is that it keeps on top of its appearance, as, it seems, do most of its Notting Hill customers. These days the front has a sleek, understated look; the interior is fashionable grey and the staff do their bit by dressing in black. What doesn't change is the quality of the food, from the fabulous breads to the piping hot thalis. The favourites remain but the seafood section has been beefed up with the addition of a monkfish curry and a whole gilt-head bream; and just because the tandoori dishes sit beside the starters on the menu, don't assume they come in starter sizes. The excellent value Sunday buffet lunch, when children under 12 eat for free, still packs them in.

Memories of China

B5

353 Kensington High St   ⊖ High Street Kensington
✉ W8 6NW   Closed 25-26 December and
✆ (020) 7603 6951   1 January – booking essential
e-mail mocken@londonfinedininggroup.com
www.memoriesofchinaken.co.uk

Menu £20 – Carte £32/59

AIC
☼
VISA
MC
AE

Memories of China is a well established Chinese restaurant which pulls in both the locals, many of whom will never have a bad word said about the place, and those staying in one of the surrounding hotels. As such, it's always busy so it's well worth coming secure in the knowledge that you've made a reservation. The menu, rather like the room, is relatively compact and keeps things on the straight and narrow by focusing on classic Cantonese and Szechuan cooking. Set menus are available for groups or those who prefer others to make their decisions for them. The glass façade of this corner restaurant chimes with the bright and modern décor of the interior with Chinese themed murals and calligraphy.

Min Jiang

D4

Chinese 𝕏𝕏𝕏

Royal Garden Hotel,
10th Floor, 2-24 Kensington High St.
✉ W8 4PT
☎ (020) 7361 1988
e-mail reservations@minjiang.co.uk
www.minjiang.co.uk

⊖ High Street Kensington

Menu £15/48 – Carte £34/119

Named after the Min River in Sichuan province, this restaurant on the 10th floor of the Royal Garden hotel is an offshoot of the original in Singapore. The speciality is Beijing duck; its glistening skin is carved at the table and one then has the difficult task of choosing how to have the second serving from the six options available. The cuisine covers all provinces, most of which have representatives in the chef's ranks. Other signature dishes include prawns Gong Bao with plenty of chillies and braised pork belly with Chinese buns. The room is a stylish one, with vases influenced by the Ming Dynasty and photos of assorted Chinese scenes. Tables 11 and 16 offer the best views of Kensington Palace and Gardens below.

Notting Hill Brasserie

B3

French 𝕏𝕏

92 Kensington Park Rd ✉ W11 2PN
☎ (020) 7229 4481
e-mail enquiries@nottinghillbrasserie.com
www.nottinghillbrasserie.com

⊖ Notting Hill Gate

Menu £24/27 – Carte £40/53

The lighting is flatteringly dim and there's always a good smattering of locals but this restaurant, housed within an Edwardian townhouse, is hardly what one expects from somewhere calling itself a brasserie. It's got a large bar, where the jazz musos perch themselves each evening and the dining room is divided up between smaller rooms, each with their own individual character and this adds to the intimacy. Service is a real strength and the staff are all generally clued-up. The menu reads very well, with each dish headlined by the single main component and influences stretch across the Mediterranean. When those dishes arrive they look very appealing, although flavours can sometimes be a little timid.

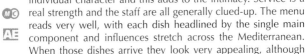

253

Timo

B5

Italian ✗✗

343 Kensington High St.
✉ W8 6NW
✆ (020) 7603 3888
e-mail timorestaurant@fsmail.net
www.timorestaurant.net

⊖ High Street Kensington
Closed Christmas,
Sunday and bank holidays

Menu £14 (lunch and early dinner) – Carte £30/44

At the Olympia end of Kensington High Street sits this warm and inviting Italian restaurant. The colours of cream and beige, matched with summery paintings of garden landscapes, lend a sunny feel, whatever the season outside. The tables are as smartly dressed as the waiters, who provide conscientious service and the suited owner does the rounds and knows his regulars. The set menu comes divided into the typically Italian four courses, although the impressive looking bread basket will test your powers of self-restraint. Daily specials to supplement the menu are temptingly described and the desserts merit particular investigation. This is a solidly reliable neighbourhood restaurant which sensibly doesn't try to reinvent anything.

Whits

C5

Modern European ✗✗

21 Abingdon Rd. ✉ W8 6AH
✆ (020) 7938 1122
e-mail info@whits.co.uk
www.whits.co.uk

⊖ High Street Kensington
Closed Christmas, New Year,
Sunday and Monday

Menu £19/24 – Carte dinner £31/39

Privately-owned restaurants with a couple at the helm are becoming something of a rarity but there is a certain kind of service one only gets from an owner of a restaurant; it is usually a combination of concern, confidence, pride and sincerity. Eva at Whits is a case in point – she's one of life's natural hosts who puts all customers at ease and the relaxed atmosphere is the restaurant's great strength. Her partner Steve's cooking certainly doesn't pull any punches; combinations are tried and tested, techniques are classic and flavours bold and upfront. The presentation on the plate is somewhat elaborate but diners all leave eminently satisfied, thanks to some generous portioning. There's a good value set menu alongside the à la carte.

Wódka

Polish ✗

12 St Albans Grove ✉ W8 5PN ⊖ High Street Kensington
✆ (020) 7937 6513 (dinner only and lunch Wednesday-Friday)
e-mail info@wodka.co.uk
www.wodka.co.uk

Menu £18 (lunch and early dinner) – Carte £23/33

Once through the velvet curtain you'll be struck instantly by the warmth of both the restaurant itself and the charming young Polish ladies who run it so well. It's divided into two rooms – the one furthest from the bar is the more intimate – and has a unpretentious, local feel. The enticing menu is full of Eastern European promise and the kitchen delivers with its full-bodied and gutsy cooking. There's plenty of game on show in season alongside the heartening soups, as well as favourites like blinis with salmon through to caviar. But the kitchen can do more than just put hairs on your chest: desserts such as an excellent pear tart reveal an unexpected lightness of touch. There are chilled or warm vodkas galore, along with Polish beers.

Zaika

Indian ✗✗

1 Kensington High St ✉ W8 5NP ⊖ High Street Kensington
✆ (020) 7795 6533 Closed 25-26 December, 1-2 January
e-mail zaika@btconnect.com and Monday lunch
www.zaika-restaurant.co.uk

Menu £25 (lunch) – Carte £31/48

Chef Sanjay Dwivedi is making his mark here at Zaika and choosing from his menu can take time as there are plenty of things on it that sound different and interesting. His judicious use of spicing ensures that the main ingredient of each dish is never overwhelmed and while his cooking has a refined and sophisticated quality that's a far cry from most Indian restaurants, those dishes still arrive in generous proportions. To see what the kitchen can really do, try one of the tasting menus. Perhaps to disguise its previous incarnation as a bank, the room has been decorated in a theatrical and flamboyant way, with plenty of drapes and lots of colour. The bar is a fun spot for drinks and service is unobtrusive and efficient.

KENSINGTON, NORTH KENSINGTON & NOTTING HILL ▶ PLAN XIII

Greater London

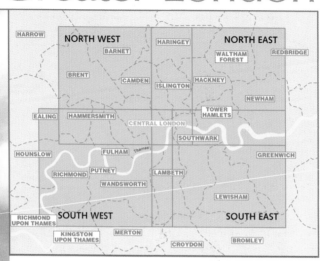

D. Chapuis/MICHELIN

257

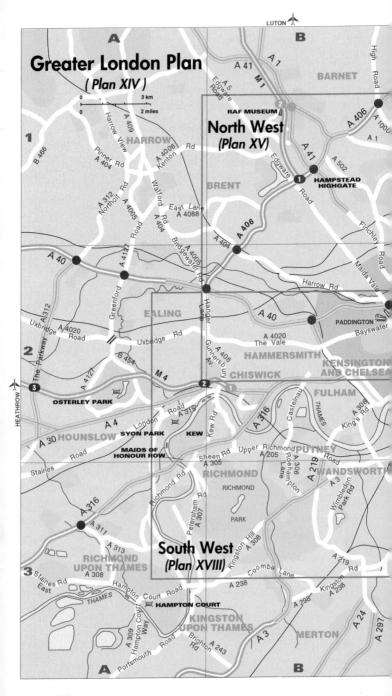

Greater London Plan
(Plan XIV)

LUTON

A

B

BARNET

A 41 A 1

A 41

M 1

A 5
Edgware
Road

High Road

0   3 km
0   2 miles

Harrow View

B 466

A 409

HARROW

Kenton Rd

A 4006

RAF MUSEUM

North West
(Plan XV)

A 406
A 1000

A 1

A 502

1

Pinner Rd
A 404

A 312

Northolt Rd
A 4005

Watford Rd
A 404

East Lane A 4088

BRENT

Edgware
Road

1 HAMPSTEAD
HIGHGATE

Finchley
Road

Maida Vale

A 406

A 404

Bridgewater Rd
A 4005

A 40

A 4127

Greenford

A 4127

The Parkway
A 312

A 4020
Uxbridge Road

B 454

Uxbridge Rd

Hanger Lane

EALING

Gunnersbury Av.

A 406

Harrow Rd

A 40

A 4020
The Vale

HAMMERSMITH

PADDINGTON

Bayswater

KENSINGTON
AND CHELSEA

2

HEATHROW

3

M 4

2

CHISWICK

FULHAM

Castelnau

THAMES

King's Rd

A 308

OSTERLEY PARK

A 4

London Road

A 315

A 30 HOUNSLOW

SYON PARK

Staines Road

MAIDS OF
HONOUR ROW

Staines

KEW

Yew Rd

A 316

A 316

Sheen Rd Upper Richmond
A 305   A 205   Roehampton Lane

A 306

PUTNEY

A 219

Road

WANDSWORTH

A 3

Wimbledon
Park Rd

RICHMOND

Richmond Rd

RICHMOND

PARK

Petersham Rd
A 307

Kingston Hill
A 308

A 316

A 311

A 313

RICHMOND
UPON THAMES

A 308

3

Staines Rd
East

THAMES

Hampton Court Road

HAMPTON COURT

A 309

Hampton Court
Way

Portsmouth Road

Coombe Lane

A 238

A 219
Rd

Kingston
A 238

A 298

A 3

South West
(Plan XVIII)

KINGSTON
UPON THAMES

Brighton Rd
A 243

A 3

MERTON

A 24

A 297

A

B

258

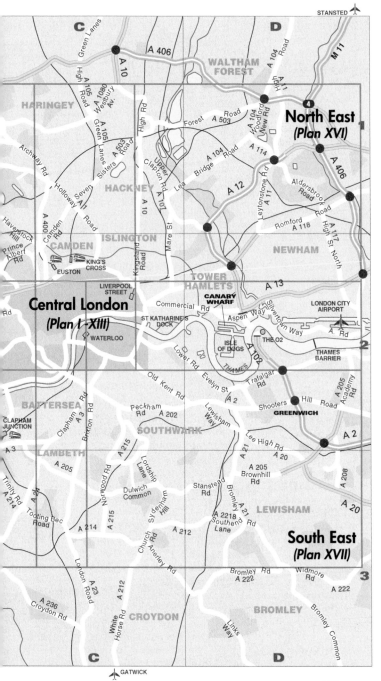

North-West London

Heading north from London Zoo and Regent's Park, the green baton is passed to two of the city's most popular and well-known locations: Hampstead Heath and Highgate Wood. In close proximity, they offer a favoured pair of lungs to travellers emerging from the murky depths of the Northern Line. Two centuries ago, they would have been just another part of the area's undeveloped high ground and pastureland, but since the building boom of the nineteenth century, both have become prized assets in this part of the metropolis.

People came to seek shelter in **Hampstead** in times of plague, and it's retained its bucolic air to this day. Famous names have always enjoyed its charms: Constable and Keats rested their brush and pen here, while the sculptors Henry Moore and Barbara Hepworth were residents in more recent times. Many are drawn to such delightful places as Church Row, which boasts a lovely Georgian Terrace. You know you're up high because the thoroughfares bear names like Holly Mount and Mount Vernon. The Heath is full of rolling woodlands and meadows; it's a great place for rambling, particularly to the crest of **Parliament Hill** and its superb city views. There are three bathing ponds here, one mixed, and one each for male and female swimmers, while up on the Heath's northern fringes, **Kenwood House,**

along with its famous al fresco summer concerts, also boasts great art by the likes of Vermeer and Rembrandt. And besides all that, there's an ivy tunnel leading to a terrace with idyllic pond views.

Highgate Wood is an ancient woodland and conservation area, containing a leafy walk that meanders enchantingly along a former railway line to **Crouch End,** home to a band of thespians. Down the road at Highgate Cemetery, the likes of Karl Marx, George Eliot, Christina Rossetti and Michael Faraday rest in a great entanglement of breathtaking Victorian over-decoration. The cemetery is still in use – most recent notable to be buried here is Alexander Litvinenko, the Russian dissident.

Next door you'll find **Waterlow Park,** another fine green space, which, apart from its super views, also includes decorative ponds on three levels. Lauderdale House is here, too, a 16C pile which is now an arts centre; more famously, Charles II handed over its keys to Nell Gwynn for her to use as her North London residence. Head back south from here, and **Primrose Hill** continues the theme of glorious green space: its surrounding terraces are populated by media darlings, while its vertiginous mass is another to boast a famously enviable vista.

Of a different hue altogether is **Camden Town** with its buzzy edge, courtesy of a renowned in-

S. Ollivier/ MICHELIN

die music scene, goths, punks, and six earthy markets selling everything from tat to exotica. Charles Dickens grew up here, and he was none too complimentary; the area still relishes its seamy underside. A scenic route out is the **Regent's Canal,** which cuts its way through the market and ambles to the east and west of the city. Up the road, the legendary Roundhouse re-opened its arty front doors in 2006, expanding further the wide range of Camden's alt scene.

One of the music world's most legendary destinations, the **Abbey Road** studios, is also in this area and, yes, it's possible to join other tourists making their way over that zebra crossing. Not far away, in Maresfield Gardens, stands a very different kind of attraction. The Freud Museum is one of the very few buildings in London to have two blue plaques. It was home to Sigmund during the last year of his life and it's where he lived with his daughter Anna (her plaque commemorates her work in child psychiatry). Inside, there's a fabulous library and his working desk. But the pivotal part of the whole house is in another corner of the study – the psychiatrist's couch!

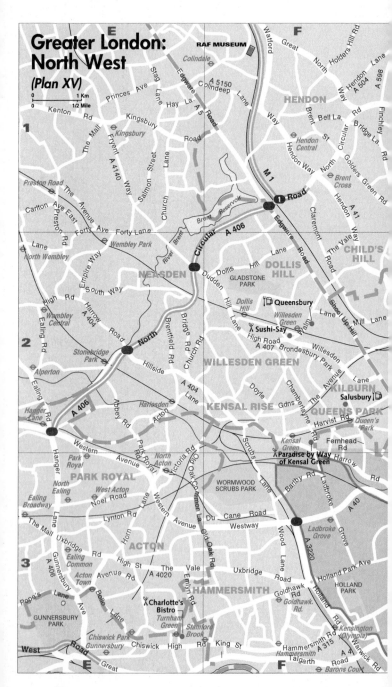

Greater London: North West
(Plan XV)

E **F**

RAF MUSEUM

0 ——— 1 Km
0 ——— 1/2 Mile

Colindale

Great

Watford

North Holders Hill Rd

Hendon Lane

A 504

Finchley

A 598

Colindeep Lane

A 5150

Princes Ave

Stag Lane

Edgware Road A 5

Hay La. A 5

HENDON

Way

Brent

Bell La.

St

North Circular Rd

Bridge La.

Golders Green Rd

Rd

Kenton Rd

Kingsbury

The Mall

Fryent

A 4140 Way

Kingsbury

Salmon Street

Church Lane

Road

Hendon Central

Hendon Way

M 1

Brent Cross

Hendon

A 41

Claremont Road

The Vale

CHILD'S HILL

Preston Road The

Avenue

Carlton Ave East

A 1140

Preston Rd

Forty Ave

Forty Lane

Wembley Park

Brent Reservoir

North Circular A 406

Edgware Road

1 Road

Lane

Lane Hill

DOLLIS HILL

Sheet Up Hill Lane

Lane

North Wembley Lane

Empire Way

South Way

River Brent

NEASDEN

Dudden Hill Lane

GLADSTONE PARK

Dollis Hill

Queensbury

Willesden Green

Watling

Wembley Central

High Rd

Harrow A 404 Road

Stonebridge Park

Hillside

Bridge Rd

Church Rd

Brentfield Rd

Sushi-Say

High Road A 407

Brondesbury Park

WILLESDEN GREEN

Willesden Lane

The Avenue

KILBURN

Salusbury

QUEENS PARK

Alperton

Ealing Rd

A 406

Abbey Rd

Harlesden

Acton Lane

A 404 Lane

Doyle

Chamberlayne Rd

KENSAL RISE

Gdns

Harvist Rd

Queen's Park

Hanger Lane

Western Park Royal Avenue

North Acton

Victoria Rd

Old Oak Common La.

Scrubs Lane

Kensal Green

Paradise by Way of Kensal Green

Fernhead Rd

Harrow Rd

Rd

Barlby Rd

Ladbroke

Ladbroke Grove

A 40

PARK ROYAL

North Ealing

West Acton

Noel Road

Lynton Rd

Western Avenue

WORMWOOD SCRUBS PARK

Du Cane Road

Westway

Wood Lane

A 3220

Ladbroke Grove

HOLLAND PARK

Ealing Broadway

The Mall

Uxbridge Rd

Horn Lane

ACTON

High St

The Vale

A 4020

Emlyn Rd

Uxbridge Road

Holland Park Ave

Holland Rd

Gunnersbury A 406

Ealing Common

Acton Town

Avenue Rd

Bollo Lane

Pope's Lane

Gunnersbury Ave

HAMMERSMITH

Charlotte's Bistro

Turnham Green

Goldhawk Rd

Goldhawk. Rd.

Kensington (Olympia)

A 315

GUNNERSBURY PARK

Chiswick Park

Gunnersbury

Chiswick High Rd

Stamford Brook

King St

Hammersmith Rd

Hammersmith

Talgarth

A 4

Warwick Rd

West

Road

Great

Barons Court

E **F**

262

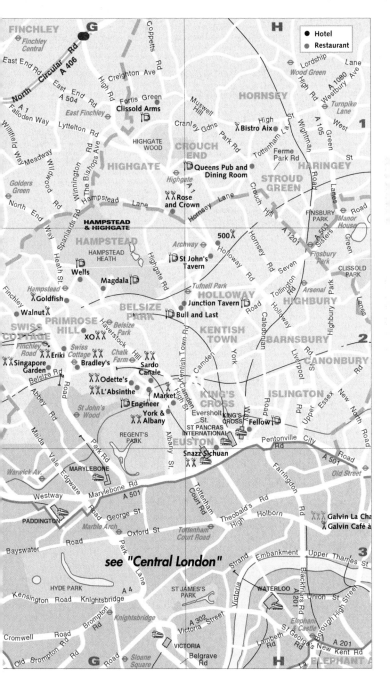

500

Archway
782 Holloway Rd ⊠ **N19 3JH**
✆ (020) 7272 3406
e-mail contact@500restaurant.co.uk
www.500restaurant.co.uk

⊖ Archway
Closed first 2 weeks in August, 21-31
December, Sunday lunch
and Monday – booking essential

Carte £20/25

Named after the cute little Fiat and that couldn't be more appropriate because here is a restaurant that is small, fun, well-priced and ideal for London. The owner is an ebullient fellow who takes an active role in the service, as does the chef who likes to see the look of satisfaction on his customers' faces. Their shared passion is evident in the cooking: homemade breads and pastas are very good; the fluffy gnocchi with sausage ragu delivers a kick; the tender veal chop is a winner and the rabbit is the house special. The menu, which has occasional Sardinian leanings, changes regularly and the sheet of daily specials includes great little snacks to have with a drink. Black and white photos of old Holloway are the only incongruity.

St John's Tavern

Gastropub 🍺

Archway
91 Junction Rd ⊠ **N19 5QU**
✆ (020) 7272 1587
www.stjohnstavern.com

⊖ Archway.
Closed 25-26 December and lunch
Monday-Thursday

Carte £23/30

Too many diners arrived expecting Clerkenwell's St John restaurant – hence the addition of 'tavern' to the name of this pub, which has long been a beacon of hope on drab old Junction Road. The dark colours and fireplace in the dining room may make it look like somewhere for a winter's night but staff keep things light and perky throughout the year. The menu changes daily and the open kitchen puts some thought into the vegetarian choices, be they the courgette and cheddar tart or the squash and halloumi parcels; but they also know how to fire up the heat when cooking a pork chop or rib-eye. The wine list is sensibly priced, with enough carafes to make up for the 125ml glasses, although Black Sheep bitter is a popular alternative.

XO

Asian ✗✗

Belsize Park

29 Belsize Ln. ✉ NW3 5AS

✆ (020) 7433 0888

e-mail xo@rickerrestaurants.com

www.rickerrestaurants.com/xo

⊖ **Belsize Park**

Closed 25-26 December
and 1 January

Menu £15 (lunch) – Carte £23/44

Who knew Belsize Park was so trendy? Apart from estate agents, obviously. This branch of Will Ricker's small chain of glossy pan-Asian restaurants may not be quite as frenetic as the others but it still attracts plenty of shiny happy people, many of whom are holding hands. It follows the same theme as the others: a busy front bar that serves decent cocktails, behind which is the slick, uncluttered restaurant in shades of lime. The menu trawls through most of Asia; start with some warm edamame while reading through it. Highlights include the ever-popular crispy squid and the tender and tasty Indonesian lamb rendang curry but tempura is done with too heavy a hand. Sharing is the key, especially as those who come in large parties get the booths.

Market

British ✗

Camden Town

43 Parkway ✉ NW1 7PN

✆ (020) 7267 9700

www.marketrestaurant.co.uk

⊖ **Camden Town**

Closed Christmas and New Year, Sunday
dinner and bank holidays –
booking essential

Carte £23/30

The name is spot on because this is all about market fresh produce, seasonality and cooking that is refreshingly matter of fact, with big, bold flavour and John Bull Britishness. Dishes come as advertised, with no pointless ornamentation, and you can expect to find the likes of brawn, ox tongue fritters and devilled kidneys alongside stews and shepherd's pie in winter, followed by proper puddings, not desserts. But be sure to have lamb or beef dripping on toast as a pre-starter – it'll leave you licking your lips for the next few hours. The exposed brick walls, zinc-topped tables and old school chairs work very well and the atmosphere is fun without ever becoming too excitable. The terrific prices entice in plenty of passers-by.

York & Albany

Modern European ✗✗

G2

Camden Town
127-129 Parkway ✉ NW1 7PS
☎ (020) 7388 3344
e-mail yorkandalbany@gordonramsay.com
www.gordonramsay.com/yorkandalbany

⊖ Camden Town
Booking essential

Menu £21 (lunch and early dinner) – Carte £36/52

Hard to believe that this 1820s John Nash coaching inn lay virtually derelict before Gordon Ramsay Holdings resuscitated and relaunched it. The terrific front bar offers a more civilised environment than is usually the case in Camden and leads into the restaurant at the back. Don't come expecting pub grub: the cooking here is quite neat and refined in its makeup, but without being fussy, and is designed to be enjoyed as three courses. The menu is not overly long and keeps its influences mostly within Europe. If you want to watch how it's all done then ask for a table in the basement level where you'll find the open kitchen. Service can still be a little hit and miss but the overall atmosphere and look of the place add extra appeal.

Bistro Aix

French ✗

H1

Crouch End
54 Topsfield Par, Tottenham Ln. ✉ N8 8PT
☎ (020) 8340 6346
e-mail bistroaix@hotmail.co.uk
www.bistroaix.co.uk

Closed 26 December, 1 January and
Monday

Menu £15 (weekday dinner) – Carte £20/34

Contemporary artwork, antique dressers and glass-filled cabinets lend an authentic Gallic edge to this local bistro whose subtle lighting and warm atmosphere also clearly appeal to Crouch Enders of a romantic disposition. The American owner runs a popular place and offers a big menu whose highlights are the more traditional French choices such as onion soup and steak frites. Desserts are also done well and the individual Tarte Tatins are a constant presence. Those willing to venture out at the beginning of the week are rewarded with a good value early evening set menu. Service is earnest but can become slightly distracted during busier times; ask for a table at the back to avoid a bracing draft whenever the front door opens.

Queens Pub and Dining Room

H1

Crouch End
26 Broadway Par ⊠ N8 9DE
☎ (020) 8340 2031
e-mail queens@foodandfuel.co.uk
www.thequeenscrouchend.co.uk

Carte approx. approx. £25

It would be hard to find a more striking example of Victoriana than The Queens Pub and Dining Room. From the original mahogany panelling to the beautiful stained glass windows and ornate ceiling, this pub has it all. The dining room is particularly stunning – ask for tables 105 or 106 on the raised section. The open kitchen recognises that some will only want classic pub food in this environment – so you'll find beef and mushroom pie, rib-eye, plaice goujons and various sausages – while others want something slightly more ambitious, hence the likes of risotto, plates of smoked meats, sea bass and assorted choices of a more Mediterranean persuasion. Selected dishes are highlighted to form part of the affordable 'This week we love…' menu.

Bull and Last

G2

Dartmouth Park
168 Highgate Rd ⊠ NW5 1QS
☎ (020) 7267 3641
e-mail info@thebullandlast.co.uk
www.thebullandlast.co.uk

⊖ Tufnell Park
Closed 25 December –
booking essential

Carte £25/32

You'll be thankful that Parliament Hill is so close because you'll need the exercise – portions at the reinvigorated Bull and Last are man-sized and that man was clearly hungry. It was taken over in 2008 by the team behind Putney's Prince of Wales and they've kept plenty of character. It's bright and breezy and hugely popular so book first. Suppliers are name-checked on boards behind the bar which tells you they take their food seriously. Animals are taken whole and butchered accordingly so expect lots of terrines and homemade charcuterie, along with everything from oysters to smoked eel; the menu can change twice a day depending on available produce. There's an upstairs room used at weekends that's like a taxidermist's showroom.

Snazz Sichuan

Chinese 🍴🍴

H2/3

Euston   ⊖ Euston
37 Chalton St ✉ NW1 1JD
✆ (020) 7388 0808
www.newchinaclub.co.uk

Carte £10/40

If you want Chinese food but something a little different, then Snazz Sichuan should fit the bill. If forms part of the New China Club, set up by an émigré from Sichuan, which includes a members' club, an art gallery and this, the restaurant. If you didn't already know that Sichuan cooking is hot then you soon will. To be honest, the clue is in the name of some of the dishes, like 'hot and numbing beef jerky'— so you can't say you weren't warned. And don't be fooled into thinking that a cold dish will be any less fiery. The ingredients are also a little different: stir-fry kidney, pig's blood mix, fried intestines and pig's ear in chilli oil. Service is sweet natured and this feels more like a local than its location would suggest.

Clissold Arms

Gastropub 🍴🍺

G1

Fortis Green   ⊖ East Finchley.
115 Fortis Green ✉ N2 9HR   Closed 1 January
✆ (020) 8444 4224

Carte £22/35

Such is the growing reputation of The Clissold Arms that it may soon be better known for the quality of its cooking than its more longstanding claim to fame – that of having played host to The Kinks' first gig. Come at lunch and the menu and atmosphere make you feel you're in a proper pub where you can expect classics like fishcakes or steak sandwiches. At dinner it all looks more like a restaurant, with loftier prices and slightly more ambitious, but still carefully prepared, dishes. The place is a lot bigger than you expect and, while staff could do with a little more guidance, it's often busy with locals grateful to have somewhere other than chain restaurants in their neighbourhood. The decked terrace has recently been extended.

Goldfish

Hampstead
82 Hampstead High St. ☒ NW3 1RE
✆ (020) 7794 6666
www.goldfish-restaurant.co.uk

⊖ Hampstead
Closed 24-25 December

Carte £20/28

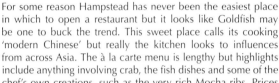

For some reason Hampstead has never been the easiest place in which to open a restaurant but it looks like Goldfish may be one to buck the trend. This sweet place calls its cooking 'modern Chinese' but really the kitchen looks to influences from across Asia. The à la carte menu is lengthy but highlights include anything involving crab, the fish dishes and some of the chef's own creations, such as the very rich Mocha ribs. Prices at lunch are very reasonable, especially the dim sum which pulls in plenty of punters at weekends. The place is divided into three little rooms which all have their own style. Staff have their hearts in the right place and they remember their regulars, of whom there are growing numbers.

Magdala

Hampstead
2A South Hill Park ☒ NW3 2SB
✆ (020) 7435 2503
e-mail themagdala@hotmail.co.uk
www.the-magdala.com

⊖ Belsize Park.

Carte £19/28

The Magdala is divided into three: on the right-hand side is the locals bar – you can eat here but not many do as it's a little dark and you'll feel like an impostor. Just go left, grab a seat anywhere and you'll be served. The third part of the operation is the upstairs, used as an extension at weekends or for hosting the monthly comedy club or fortnightly quiz. There's nothing on the menu to frighten the horses: there are burgers, sausages, paella and charcuterie plates or meze to share. However, the cooking is undertaken with greater care than you expect and you end up feeling as though you're in a country pub miles from the city. The owner certainly found a novel solution to the problem of keeping her chef – Reader, she married him.

Wells

Hampstead
30 Well Walk ⊠ NW3 1BX
✆ (020) 7794 3785
e-mail info@thewellshampstead.co.uk
www.thewellshampstead.co.uk

⊖ Hampstead.

Carte £28/38

London pubs can be loud, hysterical affairs but The Wells is a more sober beast, as one would expect from a pub in the middle of Hampstead village. Being so near the Heath makes it feel like a country pub but, then again, it's equally close to the High Street which adds a dose of urban poise. Downstairs is usually pretty busy but head up to the neat, first floor dining room that's divided into three, with the brightest - the blue room - looking down over the spring blossom. The cooking reflects the pub: it's hearty but with a sophisticated finish. You'll find duck confit or rump of lamb, scallops and wood pigeon but also veggie shepherd's pie and Sunday roasts. Puddings are big and they do a good apple and rhubarb crumble.

Rose and Crown

Highgate
86 Highgate High St. ⊠ N6 5HX
✆ (020) 8340 0770
e-mail info@roseandcrownhighate.co.uk
www.roseandcrownhighgate.co.uk

⊖ Archway
Closed 2-7 January,
Sunday dinner and
Monday lunch

Carte £27/36

An attractive white façade, illuminated at night, highlights what was once a pub but is now most definitely a restaurant. There's some 18C cornicing still there but the theme is now contemporary and all black and white. The bar remains but is now where you sit deliberating over the menu and the dining tables are smartly laid with linen. This may all give the impression of a formal restaurant but in fact the atmosphere is relaxed and inclusive, thanks largely to the confident and genial staff. The influences on the kitchen are mostly European, although the original touches are not quite as daring as they suggest. Overall the cooking is soundly executed and the prices more than fair, especially on the weekly changing set menu.

Paradise by way of Kensal Green

Kensal Green
19 Kilburn Ln ✉ W10 4AE
✆ (020) 8969 0098
e-mail caroline@thecolumbogroup.com
www.theparadise.co.uk

⊖ Kensal Green.

Menu £25/30 – Carte £28/40

Their slogan is 'They love to party at Paradise' and, frankly, who can blame them? This is so much more than just a pub, it's a veritable fun palace – upstairs plays host to everything from comedy nights to film clubs and you can even 'host your own roast' with friends in a private room. If you're coming in to eat then grab a squashy sofa in the Reading room off the bar and share some of the terrific snacks; or sit in the dining room where the French-influenced cooking is showy but satisfyingly robust. Whether it's potted meats, terrines, chateaubriand or poached turbot, it's clear that this is a very capable kitchen. The atmosphere throughout is great and helped along in no small way by a clued-up team who know their food.

L'Absinthe

Primrose Hill
40 Chalcot Rd ✉ NW1 8LS
✆ (020) 7483 4848
e-mail info@labsinthe.co.uk

⊖ Chalk Farm
Closed 1 week Christmas
and Monday

Menu £13 (lunch) – Carte £19/29

L'Absinthe has succeeded on a site where so many tried and failed because it gives the locals exactly what they have clearly always wanted: a classic French bistro run with integrity and enthusiasm. It offers the sort of food that really hits the spot at the end of a working day: beef bourguignon, duck confit, steak frites or some fresh skate, with a crème brûlée to follow. The place has an authentic air too, with its Belle Époque posters and staff who are either French or can at least do a convincing accent. Don't be put off if they give you a table downstairs – even if you are the first down there, it'll soon fill up with regulars. The other great strength is the wine list: the owner merely charges corkage on the retail price.

Engineer

Primrose Hill　　　　　　　　　　　⊖ Chalk Farm.
65 Gloucester Ave ✉ NW1 8JH
✆ (020) 7722 0950
e-mail info@the-engineer.com
www.the-engineer.com

Carte £24/32

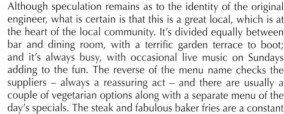

Although speculation remains as to the identity of the original engineer, what is certain is that this is a great local, which is at the heart of the local community. It's divided equally between bar and dining room, with a terrific garden terrace to boot; and it's always busy, with occasional live music on Sundays adding to the fun. The reverse of the menu name checks the suppliers – always a reassuring act – and there are usually a couple of vegetarian options along with a separate menu of the day's specials. The steak and fabulous baker fries are a constant and cooking is wholesome and generally gutsy. The wine list is printed within old cartoon annuals; wines are decently priced and divided up according to their character.

Odette's

Primrose Hill　　　　　　　　　　　⊖ Chalk Farm
130 Regent's Park Rd. ✉ NW1 8XL　Closed Christmas and Monday
✆ (020) 7586 8569
e-mail info@odettesprimrosehill.com
www.odettesprimrosehill.com

Menu £20 (lunch and early dinner) – Carte £31/44

It's amazing what a window can do: they've installed a big one at the front of the restaurant and it seems to open up the whole place and makes it feel far more welcoming. Locals used to regard Odette's as being a little bit standoffish but service is now a lot chattier and the atmosphere more relaxed, which in turn makes it feel more a part of the community. The cooking is also a little less complicated than it was and is all the better for it, although there is still a depth and balance to the dishes. Flavours are robust and braised dishes are a highlight. The lunch and early evening menus are a steal and change every fortnight, while there are also tasting and vegetarian menus alongside the à la carte.

Sardo Canale

G2

Italian XX

Primrose Hill
42 Gloucester Ave. ✉ NW1 8JD
✆ (020) 7722 2800
e-mail info@sardocanale.com
www.sardocanale.com

⊖ Chalk Farm
Closed 25 December and Monday

Menu £13 (lunch) – Carte £25/34

It may be beside Regent's Canal but the gates and security camera spoil the image somewhat. That being said, this good-looking restaurant beneath a red-bricked building is still a bright spot in which to spend a summer's evening and is not bad either for the other seasons. It comes divided into different areas; the most interesting being the vaulted brick section which was once a canal access tunnel. This being the sister to Sardo in Bloomsbury means Sardinian specialities, from golden hued spaghetti alla bottarga to pastas like malloreddus, culurgiones and fregola. The cooking is nicely balanced and has a zingy freshness to it. The wine list is fairly priced and promotes exploration of Vermentino and other Sardinian wines.

Salusbury

F2

Gastropub 🍺

Queen's Park
50-52 Salusbury Rd ✉ NW6 6NN
✆ (020) 7328 3286
e-mail thesalusburypub@btconnect.com

⊖ Queen's Park.
Closed 25-26 December, 1 January
and Monday lunch

Menu £22/25

The Salusbury is a pleasingly down-to-earth pub; one side is for drinking, the other hosts a laid-back dining room. The Italian menu is a model of understatement and it's not until the food arrives that one realises how seriously this pub takes its cooking. There's plenty of choice, including about five pasta dishes that can be taken as starters or main courses. Dishes are as generous in size as they are in flavour. The crisp Sardinian guttiau bread comes with aubergine and pecorino and is a great way of starting proceedings; the pappardelle with the tender duck ragu is very tasty; an impressive array of fish go into the fritto misto and the tiramisu would shame many a smart Italian restaurant. The wine list offers plenty for under £20.

Bradley's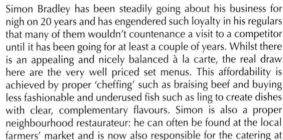

Modern European ✕✕

Swiss Cottage
25 Winchester Rd. ⊠ NW3 3NR
✆ (020) 7722 3457
e-mail bradleysnw3@btinternet.com
www.bradleysnw3.co.uk

⊖ **Swiss Cottage**
Closed Christmas, Saturday lunch
and Sunday dinner

Menu £17/24 – Carte £30/40

[A/C]
😊
VISA
M C
AE

Simon Bradley has been steadily going about his business for nigh on 20 years and has engendered such loyalty in his regulars that many of them wouldn't countenance a visit to a competitor until it has been going for at least a couple of years. Whilst there is an appealing and nicely balanced à la carte, the real draw here are the very well priced set menus. This affordability is achieved by proper 'cheffing' such as braising beef and buying less fashionable and underused fish such as ling to create dishes with clear, complementary flavours. Simon is also a proper neighbourhood restaurateur: he can often be found at the local farmers' market and is now also responsible for the catering at the splendid Hampstead theatre around the corner.

Eriki

Indian ✕✕

Swiss Cottage
4-6 Northways Par., Finchley Rd. ⊠ NW3 5EN
✆ (020) 7722 0606
e-mail info@eriki.co.uk
www.eriki.co.uk

⊖ **Swiss Cottage**
Closed Christmas,
1 January and Saturday

Menu £11/20 – Carte £23/34

[A/C]

VISA

M C
AE

Eriki eschews tired old standards and instead offers a diverse and contrasting gastronomic tour around all parts of India, from Goan curries to Punjabi-style prawns, Hariyali scallops to Lucknowi lamb. The cooking is fresh and invigorating; vegetarians will be in clover and the breads are good. The cutlery is imported from Rajasthan and the carved tables and heavy chairs add a sense of permanence. The staff are a pleasant bunch, although this vibrantly coloured restaurant can go from quiet to full in a matter of moments so get your order in quickly. Eriki is so much more than your typical neighbourhood Indian restaurant, a fact not lost on its many regulars. The only negative is the less than inspiring view of drab old Finchley Road.

Singapore Garden

Asian XX

G2

Swiss Cottage
83 Fairfax Rd. ⊠ NW6 4DY
✆ (020) 7328 5314
e-mail info@singaporegarden.co.uk
www.singaporegarden.co.uk

⊖ Swiss Cottage
Closed Christmas

Menu £20/30 – Carte £30/45

[A/C]
[◌]
[☼]
[VISA]
[MC]
[AE]

Avoid the more generic dishes on the menu at this longstanding Swiss Cottage favourite and head instead to the back page of Singaporean and Malaysian specialities or to the separate list of seasonal dishes such as the 'grandma pork belly'. Squid blachan with sugar snap peas and plenty of chilli is a fresh and fiery number; Chiew Yim soft shell crab is full of flavour and Daging curry of tender beef and coconut is satisfying and filling. The staff are a happy and helpful lot; its female members wear traditional costumes, their male counterparts, bowties. The room is comfortable and the clientele are a smart and mature bunch. The moped-riders keeping warm outside testify to its popularity in the local home delivery market too.

Junction Tavern

Gastropub

G2

Tufnell Park
101 Fortess Rd ⊠ NW5 1AG
✆ (020) 7485 9400
www.junctiontavern.co.uk

⊖ Tufnell Park.
Closed 24-26 December
and 1 January

Carte £23/30

[☂]
[☼]
[VISA]
[MC]

Over the years, Tufnell Park has appealed to young urban professionals because, along with its pretty Victorian terraces, it has a belligerent edge to add a little credibility. The Junction Tavern fits in well. The menu changes daily and portion size has been slightly reduced to give more balance to the menu as a whole; the cooking remains unfussy and relies on good flavours. There's plenty of choice, from light summer dishes such as grilled sardines and seared tuna to the more robust rib-eye and pork belly. Staff are a chatty bunch who know their beers – they offer weekly changing guest beers and hold a popular beer festival; the 'pie and a pint' choice remains a favourite. Commendably, they also offer tap water without being prompted.

Walnut

G2

Traditional ✗

West Hampstead
280 West End Ln., Fortune Grn. ✉ NW6 1LJ
✆ (020) 7794 7772
e-mail info@walnutwalnut.com
www.walnutwalnut.com

⊖ West Hampstead
Closed Monday –
(dinner only)

Carte £23/34

| A/C |
| ☼ |
| VISA |
| MC |
| AE |
| ⓪ |

'Local. Seasonal. Sustainable' proclaims the menu at this convivial local restaurant. This is no empty slogan: the chef-owner also outlines in print the 'Walnut ethos' which includes working with good-practice suppliers, recycling and energy-saving – even the staff all walk or cycle to work. More importantly, he understands what people want from a local restaurant: at least some part of the menu changes daily and his classical background and honest approach means that the emphasis is on flavours rather than presentation; fish and game are handled particularly well and the crusty breads are homemade. The well-meaning service can sometimes struggle to keep up but the warmth and integrity of the place make one surprisingly forgiving.

Queensbury

F2

Gastropub 🍺

Willesden Green
110 Walm Ln ✉ NW2 4RS
✆ (020) 8452 0171
e-mail info@thequeensbury.net
www.thequeensbury.net

⊖ Willesden Green.

Carte £20/30

The Conservative Club of Willesden Green have displayed a questionable lack of fiscal foresight because it's hard to sell off your building to a property developer when you've already offloaded the half that housed your snooker room and seen it turned into a pub. The inside hasn't changed much from when this was called The Green: a long narrow bar leading into a bright and open dining room, complete with antique mirrors. The blackboard menu blends pub numbers like pies and jerk chicken burgers with the more adventurous pork belly with chorizo; Parma ham with celeriac remoulade comes on a wooden board and desserts appear to be a strength of the kitchen. There's brunch at weekends and further snacky choices available in the bar.

Sushi-Say

Willesden Green
33B Walm Ln. ✉ NW2 5SH
☎ (020) 8459 2971

Menu £19/40 – Carte £17/43

⊖ Willesden Green
Closed 21 February-8 March, 2 weeks
August, 25-26 December, 1 January,
Monday and Tuesday – (dinner only and
lunch Saturday-Sunday)

VISA
MC

One of the delights of Willesden Green must surely be this long-standing Japanese restaurant which has never looked back since being revamped back in 2007 and which is nearly always full. As the name suggests, sushi is the reason why many come and a seat at the counter, watching owner Mr Shimizu's expertise with his knife, is the place to be; if you're tempted to supplement your selection with some creamy uni or rich, warmed unagi then just ask him and he'll oblige. If you prefer other styles of Japanese cookery then you'll find plenty of choice; it's often worth considering the monthly specials menu; the yakitori is particularly good and there's a well-priced selection of sake and shochu. Mrs Shimizu leads her team with alacrity and efficiency.

Look out for **red** symbols,
indicating a particularly
pleasant ambiance.

North-East London

If northwest London is renowned for its leafy acres, then the area to its immediate east has a more urban, brick-built appeal. Which has meant, over the last decade or so, a wholesale rebranding exercise for some of its traditionally shady localities. A generation ago it would have been beyond the remit of even the most inventive estate agent to sell the charms of Islington, Hackney or Bethnal Green. But then along came Damien Hirst, Tracey Emin et al, and before you could say 'cow in formaldehyde' the area's cachet had rocketed.

Shoreditch and **Hoxton** are the pivotal points of the region's hip makeover. Their cobbled brick streets and shabby industrial remnants were like heavenly manna to the artists and designers who started to colonise the old warehouses twenty years ago. A fashionable crowd soon followed in their footsteps, and nowadays the area around **Hoxton Square** positively teems with clubs, bars and galleries. Latest must-see space is Rivington Place, a terrific gallery that highlights visual arts from around the world. Nearby are Deluxe (digital installations), AOP (photographic shows) and Hales (Spencer Tunick's acres of gooseflesh… etc).

Before the area was ever trendy, there was the Geffrye Museum. A short stroll up Hoxton's **Kingsland Road,** it's a jewel of a place, set in elegant 18C almshouses, and depicting English middle-class interiors from 1600 to the present day. Right behind it is St. Mary's Secret Garden, a little oasis that manages to include much diversity including a separate woodland and herb area, all in less than an acre. At the southern end of the area, in Folgate Street, Dennis Severs' House is an original Huguenot home that recreates 18 and 19C life in an original way – cooking smells linger, hearth and candles burn, giving you the impression the owners have only just left the place. Upstairs the beds remain unmade: did a certain local artist pick up any ideas here?

When the Regent's Canal was built in the early 19C, **Islington's** fortunes nose-dived, for it was accompanied by the arrival of slums and over-crowding. But the once-idyllic village managed to hold onto its Georgian squares and handsome Victorian terraces through the rough times, and when these were gentrified a few years ago, the area ushered in a revival. **Camden Passage** has long been famed for its quirky antique emporiums, while the slinky Business Design Centre is a flagship of the modern Islington. Cultural icons established themselves around the Upper Street area and these have gone from strength to strength. The **Almeida** Theatre has a habit of hitting the production jackpot with its history of world premieres, while the King's Head has earned itself a

reputation for raucous scene-stealing; set up in the seventies, it's also London's very first theatre-pub. Nearby, the Screen on the Green boasts a wonderful old-fashioned neon billboard.

Even in the 'bad old days', Islington drew in famous names, and at Regency smart **Canonbury Square** are the one-time homes of Evelyn Waugh (no.17A) and George Orwell (no.27). These days it houses the Estorick Collection of Modern Italian Art; come here to see fine futuristic paintings in a Georgian villa. To put the history of the area in a proper context, head to St. John Street, south of the City Road, where the Islington Museum's shiny new headquarters tells the story of a colourful and multi-layered past.

Further up the A10, you come to **Dalston,** a bit like the Islington of old but with the buzzy Ridley Road market and a vibrant all-night scene including the blistering Vortex Jazz Club just off Kingsland Road. A little further north is **Stoke Newington,** referred to, a bit unkindly, as the poor man's Islington. Its pride and joy is Church Street, which not only features some characterful bookshops and eye-catching boutiques, but also lays claim to Abney Park Cemetery, an enchanting old place with a wildlife-rich nature reserve.

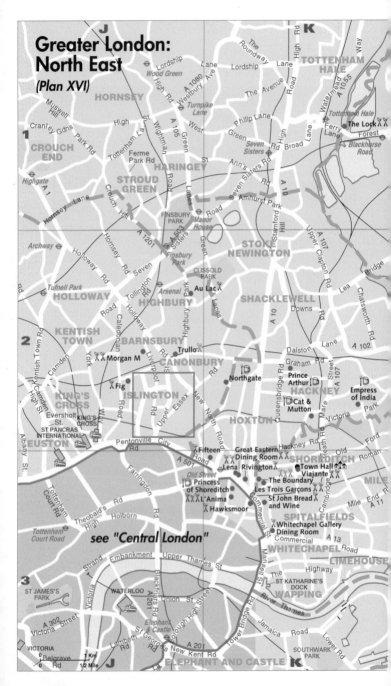

Greater London: North East

(Plan XVI)

J **K**

The Roundway

High Road

K Way

TOTTENHAM HALE

Lordship
Wood Green

Lordship Lane

Lane

A 1080 Westbury Ave

Watermead Way

A 1055

HORNSEY

The Avenue

Tottenham Hale

Muswell Hill

Turnpike Lane

Philip Lane

Ferry Lane

The Lock ✗✗

Cranley Gdns

Park Rd

High St

West

Green

Seven Sisters Rd

Broad

Forest

Blackhorse Road

1

CROUCH END

Tottenham La

Ferme Park Rd

A 105

Wightman

St

Ann's Rd

High

Seven Sisters Rd

A 10

Highgate

HARINGEY

A 1

STROUD GREEN

Crouch Hill

Hornsey Lane

Road

FINSBURY PARK

A 1201

Seven Sisters

A 503

Road

Manor House

Amhurst Park

Stamford Hill

Upper Clapton Rd

A 107

Bridge

Lea

Archway

Holloway

Hornsey Rd

Finsbury Park

Green

STOKE NEWINGTON

Chatsworth Rd

Tufnell Park

Tollington Rd

Seven

CLISSOLD PARK

Rd

Caledonian

Arsenal

Au Lac ✗

SHACKLEWELL

HOLLOWAY

HIGHBURY

Downs

A 10

Road

Holloway Rd

Highbury

Lanes

Dalston

Lane

A 102

KENTISH TOWN

Kentish Town Rd

2

BARNSBURY

York ✗✗ Morgan M

Liverpool Rd

Trullo ✗

CANONBURY

Rd

Graham Rd

Prince Arthur

Mare Street

A 107

HACKNEY

Camden

Rd

Northgate

Empress of India

Camden High St

✗ Fig

ISLINGTON

Upper

Essex

New North Road

Cat & Mutton

Victoria

Park

KING'S CROSS

Eversholt St.

ST PANCRAS INTERNATIONAL

KING'S CROSS

Way

Rd

HOXTON

Queensbridge Rd

Hackney Rd

Ford

EUSTON

Albany St.

Pentonville

Rd

City Road

✗ Fifteen

Great Eastern Dining Room ✗✗

Old

Roman

MILE

Farringdon

A 501

Old Street

Lena ✗ Rivington ✗

Town Hall

Viajante ✗✗

SHOREDITCH

Heath St

Cambridge

Mile End Rd

Princess of Shoreditch

The Boundary

Les Trois Garçons ✗✗

Commercial

Mile

Tottenham Court Rd

Theobald's Rd

High

Holborn

✗✗✗ L'Anima

✗ Hawksmoor

St John Bread and Wine ✗

SPITALFIELDS

A 13

Road

Tottenham Court Road

see "Central London"

Strand

Embankment

Upper Thames St

✗ Whitechapel Gallery Dining Room

Commercial

WHITECHAPEL

LIMEHOUSE

3

Blackfriars Rd

A 201

Waterloo

ST JAMES'S PARK

WATERLOO

Union St

The Highway

ST KATHARINE'S DOCK

WAPPING

River Thames

Victoria

A 302

A 201

Elephant & Castle

Borough Rd

Tower Bridge Rd

Jamaica Road

Lower Rd

SOUTHWARK PARK

VICTORIA

Belgrave Rd

Lambeth Rd

St George's Rd

New Kent Rd

A 201

J ELEPHANT AND CASTLE **K**

0 — 1 Km

0 — 1/2 Mile

280

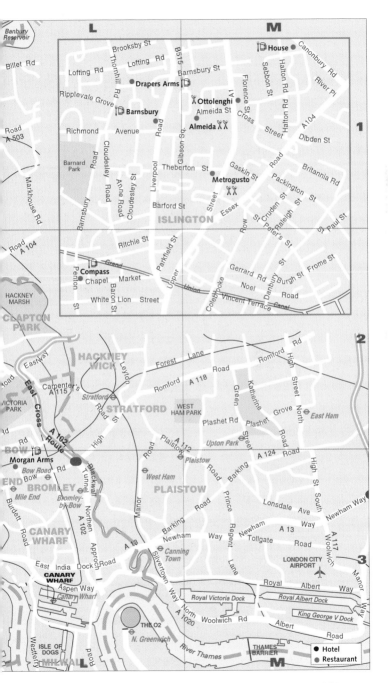

Fig

J2

Modern European ✗

Barnsbury
169 Hemingford Rd. ✉ N1 1DA
✆ (020) 7609 3009
e-mail figrestaurant@btconnect.com
www.fig-restaurant.co.uk

⊖ **Caledonian Road**
Closed 23 December-6 January
and Sunday – (dinner only)

Carte £31/36

If anyone is ever in doubt about the true meaning of a 'neighbourhood' restaurant they should get along to Fig. This is a warm, cosy and inviting little bistro, with enthusiastic owners and possessive local followers. It's quaint without being twee and intimate without being stifling. The chef-owner is Danish and the Scandinavian influence on his cooking is palpable: the ingredients are first rate, there's a lightness of touch in their preparation and some twists in flavour combinations. This kitchen has also travelled extensively and is not averse to using other cuisines to add an extra dimension. The simple A4 printed menu changes monthly and is seasonally pertinent. Service is friendly and gets on with the job in hand.

Morgan M

French ✗✗

Barnsbury
489 Liverpool Rd. ✉ N7 8NS
✆ (020) 7609 3560
e-mail morganmeunier@btconnect.com
www.morganm.com

⊖ **Highbury and Islington**
Closed 24-30 December, Sunday dinner,
Monday and lunch Tuesday and Saturday

Menu £28/41

Bold patterned wallpaper and retro lighting have added some warmth to this converted pub which has firmly established itself in this corner of Islington. The M stands for Meunier, a proud Frenchman from the Champagne region, and his classic, full flavoured cooking continues to appeal to a refreshingly varied group of customers. The menu can appear a little bewildering at first, as it offers à la carte, seasonal and Garden choices, with some overlap, but portions are generous and all come with plenty of extra little dishes. The predominantly French wine list is accessibly priced. A little more personality from the suited managers wouldn't go amiss, especially during the early evening while the restaurant is still filling up.

Morgan Arms

Gastropub

L3

Bow ⊖ Bow Road.
43 Morgan St ⊠ **E3 5AA** Closed 25-26 December –
✆ (020) 8980 6389 (bookings not accepted)
e-mail themorgan@geronimo-inns.co.uk
www.geronimo-inns.co.uk

Carte £19/35

This former boozer's clever makeover respects its heritage while simultaneously bringing it up to date. The bar's always busy while the dining area is more subdued. You'll find the kitchen keeps its influences mostly within Europe but also understands just what sort of food works well in a pub. The daily-changing menu usually features pasta in some form and staples like whitebait - which come devilled in this instance - assorted tarts and the perennial favourite, fishcakes accompanied by a poached egg. What's more, prices are kept at realistic levels which, together with their policy of not taking bookings, makes this pub appealing to those who live nearby and who like a little spontaneity in their lives.

House

Gastropub

M1

Canonbury ⊖ Highbury and Islington.
63-69 Canonbury Rd ⊠ **N1 2DG** Closed Monday lunch
✆ (020) 7704 7410
e-mail info@inthehouse.biz
www.thehouse.islington.com

Menu £18 (lunch) – Carte £26/35

The House is one of the smarter pubs around; indeed, with its attractive terrace it can look more like a restaurant from the outside but step inside and you'll find sufficient numbers of regulars relaxing around the bar exuding a general sense of localness. Even the eating area towards the rear has that reassuringly hotchpotch feel and, while the service is clearly on the button, it is also friendly and chatty. The menu covers all corners, from the classics like shepherd's pie and apple crumble to other more elaborate choices such as sea bass with artichoke purée and peppered venison with spiced red cabbage. Cooking is clean, crisp and confident and there's an emphasis on good quality, organic ingredients.

Trullo

Italian ✗

Canonbury
300-302 St Paul's Rd. ✉ N1 2LH
✆ (020) 7226 2733
e-mail bookings@trullorestaurant.com
www.trullorestaurant.com

⊖ Highbury and Islington
Closed Sunday dinner and Monday
– booking essential – (dinner only and
lunch Saturday and Sunday)

Menu £25 (lunch) – Carte £14/34

The owners' CVs read like a checklist of eateries known for their relaxed atmospheres and uncomplicated cooking, including Moro, St John, and the River Café, so it is no surprise to find delicious Italian cooking here in this friendly restaurant, filled every day with noisily contented diners. The menu, small in size and content, changes daily so don't be surprised when something runs out, but expect great antipasti, such as pumpkin and chilli fritti, as well as flavoursome dishes cooked on the charcoal grill – and all at terrific prices. Trullo is named after the conically shaped buildings of southern Italy, used primarily by farm workers for meeting and eating, which seems most appropriate for somewhere exuding such contentment.

Cat & Mutton

British 🍺

Hackney
76 Broadway Mkt ✉ E8 4QJ
✆ (020) 7254 5599
e-mail catandmutton@yahoo.co.uk
www.catandmutton.co.uk

⊖ Bethnal Green.
Closed 25-26 December

Carte £20/31

Four sets of doors provide your first challenge at this Victorian corner pub (clue: it's the smallest that allows access). Inside, the high counter means the bar staff tower over you when you're ordering a drink and the place has a worn and slightly scruffy feel that seemingly appeals to a young crowd, many of whom are often accompanied by their dogs and/or laptops. The relatively concise menu changes weekly; the cooking is straightforward but is also undertaken with more care than you'd expect. So you'll find the dishes deliver on flavour, whether it's a pie, crumble, pan-fried fish or something on toast. Quiz nights and art classes in an upstairs room, reached via the spiral staircase, add to the neighbourhood feel.

Empress of India

Hackney
130 Lauriston Rd, Victoria Park ✉ E9 7LH
✆ (020) 8533 5123
e-mail info@theempressofindia.com
www.theempressofindia.com

⊖ **Mile End.**
Closed 25 December

Carte £24/35

Built in the 1880s, The Empress of India has enjoyed a variety of incarnations over the years, including time as a nightclub and print works. In 2006, it was restored by the Martin brothers and now it's hard to imagine the place being anything other than this family-friendly pub with a stoutly British menu. As well as restoring the pub's original name, they have kitted it out with mosaics, murals and photos commemorating Queen Victoria and the British Raj – just beware the Bengal tiger. The menu triumphs the British provenance of its meats, poultry and game, many of which are spit-roasted. Hams are cured in-house and while some dishes don't always deliver on the promise of the menu, the more robust choices won't disappoint.

Lena

Hackney
66 Great Eastern St. ✉ EC2A 3JT
✆ (020) 7739 5714
e-mail reception@lenarestaurant.com
www.lenarestaurant.com

⊖ **Old Street**
Closed 26-29 December
and Sunday

Menu £14 (weekdays) – Carte £30/45

If you want customers to know that your new Italian restaurant is authentic, then naming it after your mother is a good start. Eclectically decorated to befit its fashionable Shoreditch postcode, it uses leather, plastic, woods and ceramics to create the sort of high-maintenance shiny interior that one instantly either loves or hates. Jazz enthusiasts will find much to enjoy here, particularly the live weekend jazz in the stylish bar downstairs. The cooking looks to more southerly regions of Italy for influences, more especially around Naples and the Amalfi coast. Dishes have a bracing freshness to them, although the dessert selection is a little more predictable. Breads, pastas and ice creams are all homemade.

Prince Arthur

Gastropub 🍺

K2

Hackney
95 Forest Rd ✉ E8 3BH
📞 (020) 7249 9996
e-mail info@theprincearthurlondonfields.com
www.theprincearthurlondonfields.com

⊖ **Bethnal Green.**
Closed 25 December and
Monday-Thursday lunch

Carte £22/32

Those who judge by first impressions will probably walk on by as this slightly scruffy corner pub would struggle to entice anyone on looks alone. To be honest, the inside isn't much keener on the eye, apart from the stuffed animals and the postcard collection, but then this isn't about appearances, more about good food and convivial company. Sit anywhere in the U-shaped room and the amiable staff will be quick to come over. The menu reads appealingly: smoked salmon, terrines, fish and chips, sausage and mash – but the cooking is done with unexpected care and more than a little skill; fish from Billingsgate is handled particularly deftly. Just thinking about the deep-fried jam or cherry sandwich for dessert will be enough to seal an artery.

Au Lac

Vietnamese 🍴

J2

Highbury
82 Highbury Park ✉ N5 2XE
📞 (020) 7704 9187

⊖ **Arsenal**
(dinner only and
lunch Thursday and Friday)

Carte £8/21

Au Lac may look a little ordinary from the outside, but that just adds to its appeal. Run enthusiastically by two brothers – one's in the kitchen, the other's out front – it provides proof of why Vietnamese cooking is considered one of Asia's healthiest cuisines: it involved lots of quick stir-frying, uses plenty of fresh herbs like mint and basil and keeps vegetables crisp. Specialities here include 'Pho' noodle soup with rare beef and chargrilled sea bass with banana leaves but they also regularly introduce new dishes on the menu. Portions are on the more-than-generous side so sharing is necessary and, while there are a few Chinese dishes on the menu to attract the less adventurous, it's best to stick to what they do best.

Fifteen London

Hoxton
13 Westland Pl ✉ N1 7LP
✆ (0871) 3301 515
www.fifteen.net

⊖ **Old Street**
Booking essential

NORTH-EAST ▶ PLAN XVI

Menu £28 (weekday lunch)/60 – Carte £36/42

A/C

VISA

M/C

AE

This is the original branch of Jamie Oliver's charitable 'Fifteen' restaurants and it's already on its ninth intake of trainees. Their programme lasts for 18 months and they receive schooling in all departments of the restaurant while being closely monitored by the experienced full-time staff. There are two operations here: the buzzy ground floor trattoria and a slightly more formal basement restaurant. The Italian cooking bears the unmistakeable signature of Jamie Oliver and the students are clearly being taught that most valuable of lessons: buy the best quality, seasonal ingredients and don't mess them about too much. This laudable project makes worrying about the occasional lapse seem somewhat mean-spirited.

Great Eastern Dining Room

Hoxton
54 Great Eastern St. ✉ EC2A 3QR
✆ (020) 7613 4545
e-mail greateastern@rickerrestaurants.com
www.rickerrestaurants.com

⊖ **Old Street**
Closed Saturday lunch,
Sunday and bank holidays

Menu £15 (lunch and early dinner) – Carte £17/38

A/C

VISA

M/C

AE

Will Ricker's flourishing group of hip restaurants came into its own here in Great Eastern Street and coincided with Hoxton's own emergence onto the fashion radar. The format here is similar to the others in the group: the bar, given equal billing as the restaurant, occupies most of the front section and it's usually so packed even a sardine would think twice. The noise spills into the restaurant, adding a lively vibe to the place. It's all great fun. The kitchen's influences spill across South East Asia, with dim sum, curries, roasts and tempura all carefully prepared. Helpfully, the reverse of the menu carries a glossary of Asian culinary terms. The serving team are a sassy and well-informed bunch.

Almeida

M1

Islington
30 Almeida St. ✉ **N1 1AD**
✆ (020) 7354 4777
e-mail almeidareservations@danddlondon.com
www.almeida-restaurant.co.uk

⊖ **Angel**
Closed 26 December, 1 January, Sunday
dinner and Monday lunch

Menu £16/33 – Carte lunch £21/37

If you're not here for a pre-theatre bite before going to the Almeida theatre opposite then try not to arrive around 7-7.30pm as you'll find yourself in the midst of an almighty exodus which leaves the restaurant in a degree of disarray and the waiters looking shell-shocked. They then dim the lights and take a deep breath but it's usually a while before the atmosphere builds again. Prices at this crisply decorated restaurant are more realistic these days, especially at lunch when the room really benefits from the two large new windows. The menu's French influence is a little less pronounced but dishes still use intelligent combinations, like venison with pumpkin and lamb with artichoke. Look out for some interesting French regional wines.

Barnsbury

L1

Islington
209-211 Liverpool Rd ✉ **N1 1LX**
✆ (020) 7607 5519
e-mail info@thebarnsbury.co.uk
www.thebarnsbury.co.uk

⊖ **Highbury and Islington.**
Closed 24-26 December,
1 January and Monday lunch

Carte £25/35

The young new owner may have a background in some of London's more fashionable dining establishments, but he's keen to turn The Barnsbury back into a proper local pub as he felt it had become too much like a restaurant. That being said, the food is still done well and the menu is appealing, with tarts, salads, potted shrimps and mussels jostling for attention alongside Toulouse sausages, risottos and steaks served with the ubiquitous triple-cooked chips; the homemade puds are especially good. Lunch trade is not big in these parts so the midday menu is more limited. Chandeliers fashioned from wine glasses are dotted around the place and add character; but do sit in the more atmospheric front bar rather than in the dining area at the back.

Compass

Gastropub

Islington
58 Penton St ✉ N1 9PZ
✆ (020) 7837 3891
e-mail info@thecompassn1.co.uk
www.thecompassn1.co.uk

⊖ Angel.
Closed lunch Monday and Tuesday

Carte £22/30

The Compass is another Victorian pub that has been rescued from a life of seedy anonymity and turned into a lively local known for the quality of its food. Most of the original features remain, such as the tiling, floorboards and ceiling lights, but the fact that the chefs are also on display gives a clue as to where the emphasis now lies. Decent olives and homemade bread kick things off and recognisable favourites from the gastropub canon, such as fishcakes, rib-eye and rump of lamb are combined with other dishes of more European provenance. Lighter classics and a good value set menu feature at lunch and the cooking is accurate and clearly confident. The wine list is concise but offers a good few choices by the glass and carafe.

The Drapers Arms 😊

British

Islington
44 Barnsbury St ✉ N1 1ER
✆ (020) 7619 0348
e-mail info@thedrapersarms.com
www.thedrapersarms.com

⊖ Highbury and Islington.

Carte £22/29

This handsome Georgian pub was rescued, revived and reopened a couple of years ago by new owners, one of whom is the son of restaurant critic Fay Maschler. The chef is an alumnus of St John but, while his experience informs his cooking, that doesn't make it a facsimile. It does place the same emphasis on seasonality, on unfussy 'proper' British cooking and on the use of less familiar cuts, but there's also an acknowledgement that this is a local pub first and foremost. Reservations are only taken for the somewhat starkly decorated upstairs dining room but you'll find the same menu in the bar, where it's more fun, with its shelves of Penguin Classics and board games as well as a further menu of dishes such as oysters, devils on horseback and whelks.

Metrogusto 😊

Italian ✗✗

Islington
13 Theberton St ✉ N1 0QY
✆ (020) 7226 9400
e-mail ambroianeselli@btconnect.com
www.metrogusto.co.uk

⊖ **Angel**
Closed 25 December,
1 January, Monday and bank holidays
– (dinner only and
lunch Saturday-Sunday)

Menu £19 – Carte £24/33

[A/C]
[🍇]
[🎭]
[VISA]
[MC]
[AE]

Ambro Ianselli is not only one of the most charming restaurateurs around but his Metrogusto restaurant leads the struggle against the inexorable and inexplicable rise of the chain restaurant in Islington. So, instead of blandly inoffensive, corporately-inspired decoration, you get walls covered with bold, thought-provoking and regularly changing art; and, in place of androidenal service and lacklustre cooking, you get warm hospitality and carefully prepared Italian food. Even on price this independently owned restaurant comes up trumps as it offers some very competitively priced set menus alongside its à la carte and regular visitors will never get bored thanks to the daily changing pasta, risotto, 'catch of the day' and 'butcher's cut'.

Northgate

Gastropub 🍺

Islington
113 Southgate Rd ✉ N1 3JS
✆ (020) 7359 7392
e-mail jspt@hotmail.co.uk

⊖ **Dalston Kingsland (rail).**
Closed 25 December
– (dinner only and lunch
Saturday and Sunday)

Carte £20/27

[☂]
[☀]
[VISA]
[MC]
[①]

The Northgate is decked out in the usual gastropub aesthetic of mismatched furniture and local artists' work for sale on the walls; at the back you'll find tables laid up for dining and an open kitchen. You'll also find an extraction fan that's so strong you can feel its tug. Staff are pretty laid back, at times almost to the point of somnolence; go with a similarly relaxed frame of mind to avoid irritation. Where the pub scores is in the food: there's a strong Mediterranean influence on the vast blackboard. You'll find merguez and chorizo sausages, assorted pastas, a bit of Greek and some French – all in generously sized proportions with the emphasis on flavour. Finish with something a little closer to home like treacle tart.

Ottolenghi

M1

Islington
287 Upper St. ✉ N1 2TZ
✆ (020) 7288 1454
e-mail upper@ottolenghi.co.uk
www.ottolenghi.co.uk

⊖ **Highbury and Islington**
Closed 25-26 December, 1 January and
Sunday dinner – booking essential

Carte £20/35

Coming with friends and sharing is the key at Ottolenghi. It's primarily a deli, with tempting piles of meringues and salads in its window, but morphs into a little restaurant at night, with communal tables, speedy but sociable service and a fun atmosphere. Dishes come either 'from the counter', where a waitress will go and dish up for you – so be nice – or 'from the kitchen' which involves some heating up. The menu changes daily and influences come from all parts of the wider Mediterranean: this is all about good fresh ingredients yielding plenty of flavour – and Veggies will be in clover. Three dishes per person are too many, yet two are not enough, so sharing is the key. The desserts are especially good and if you think you know salad, think again.

Fellow

H2

King's Cross
24 York Way ✉ N1 9AA
✆ (020) 7833 4395
e-mail info@thefellow.co.uk
www.thefellow.co.uk

⊖ **King's Cross.**
Plan XV
Closed Sunday dinner

Carte £27/32

It was just a matter of time before a few decent pubs opened around the rapidly developing area of King's Cross. The Fellow is one of the busiest, attracting a youthful and local clientele; it also manages to give the impression it's been here for years. Eating happens on the dark and atmospheric ground floor, with drinkers heading upstairs to the even more boisterous cocktail bar. The menu is quite a sophisticated little number but the kitchen is up to the task. Start with ham hock terrine or potted crab, followed by roast rump of lamb or grilled haddock with champ. Desserts such as apple tart display a lightness of touch. The serving team are a bright, capable bunch. There is an outdoor terrace but you'll be surrounded by smokers.

L'Anima

Italian XXX

Shoreditch
1 Snowden St. ✉ EC2A 2DQ
✆ (0207) 422 7000
e-mail info@lanima.co.uk
www.lanima.co.uk

⊖ **Liverpool Street**
Closed Saturday lunch, Sunday and bank
holidays – booking essential

Menu £29 (lunch) – Carte £29/48

A/C
iⓄ
VISA
Ⓜ Ⓒ
AE

L'Anima is an extremely handsome restaurant that looks as though it should be located somewhere slightly more glamorous than the edge of The City. A glass wall separates the bar from the restaurant, where you find limestone walls, impeccably laid tables, white leather chairs and clever lighting; ask for one of the tables on the raised section at the back. The mood is sophisticated and the look smart and stylish. The chef may come from Calabria but his team have arrived from all parts of Italy. His menu is appealing and balanced, offering a mix of classic and less familiar dishes; and there's a helpful glossary of terms for the unfamiliar. The emphasis is on flavour and most dishes deliver that in spades. Service is smooth but also personable.

Boundary

French XXX

Shoreditch
2-4 Boundary St. ✉ E2 7DD
✆ (020) 7729 1051
e-mail info@theboundary.co.uk
www.theboundary.co.uk

⊖ **Old Street**
Closed Sunday dinner,
lunch Monday and Saturday

Menu £25 (lunch) – Carte £33/54

A/C
✿
iⓄ
VISA
Ⓜ Ⓒ
AE
Ⓞ

When the management team took over his restaurant group, many thought Sir Terence Conran's days of opening restaurants were over. Not a bit of it, because he was soon back with a bang with Boundary. As is his way, he has taken an interesting building, in this case a large warehouse and former printworks, and turned it into a veritable house of fun. From the top, you have a roof terrace with an open fire; Albion is a ground floor 'caff' alongside a shop and bakery and Boundary is the French-inspired 'main' restaurant below it. The room is stylish, good-looking and works well, while the kitchen serves up reassuringly familiar cross-Channel treats, including fruits de mer. The fourth part of the equation are the comfy, individually designed bedrooms.

Princess of Shoreditch

K3

Shoreditch

76-78 Paul St ✉ EC2A 4NE

✆ (020) 7729 9270

e-mail info@theprincessofshoreditch.com

www.theprincessofshoreditch.com

⊖ Old Street.

Closed 25-26 December

Menu £20 – Carte £25/35

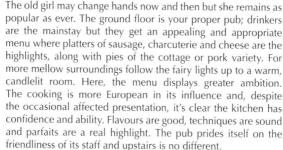

The old girl may change hands now and then but she remains as popular as ever. The ground floor is your proper pub; drinkers are the mainstay but they get an appealing and appropriate menu where platters of sausage, charcuterie and cheese are the highlights, along with pies of the cottage or pork variety. For more mellow surroundings follow the fairy lights up to a warm, candlelit room. Here, the menu displays greater ambition. The cooking is more European in its influence and, despite the occasional affected presentation, it's clear the kitchen has confidence and ability. Flavours are good, techniques are sound and parfaits are a real highlight. The pub prides itself on the friendliness of its staff and upstairs is no different.

Rivington Grill

K3

Shoreditch

28-30 Rivington St. ✉ EC2A 3DZ

✆ (020) 7729 7053

e-mail shoreditch@rivingtongrill.co.uk

www.rivingtongrill.co.uk

⊖ Old Street

Closed 24-26 December
and 1 January

Menu £19 (weekend lunch) – Carte £25/49

A converted warehouse surrounded by design studios, galleries and printing premises means not only that this place is popular with artistically inclined types but that it also shows work itself, including a Tracey Emin neon "Life without you, never". However, it is also close to The City so head left when you enter as larger groups tend to occupy the tables on the right. The British menu will fill you with patriotic fervour – if this was what John Major had meant when he referred to 'back-to basics' there wouldn't have been such derision. There's a section 'on toast' and oysters are a speciality; there are pies, chops and faggots, even fish fingers and bubble and squeak. There are also plenty of bottles under £30 and special offers for weekend lunches.

NORTH-EAST ▶ PLAN XVI

Lock

K1

Tottenham
Heron House, Hale Wharf, Ferry Ln.
✉ N17 9NF
✆ (020) 8885 2829
e-mail thelock06@btconnect.com
www.thelockrestaurant.com

⊖ **Tottenham Hale**
Closed 26 December-
4 January and Monday

Menu £17 (lunch) – Carte dinner £22/48

A stark looking restaurant next to an ugly office development in the outer reaches of Tottenham doesn't sound like much of a sure thing but The Lock is proving to be stayer. This has been achieved by adhering to the aphorism of our time: the prices represent value for money. The chef-owner's food is artistically presented and comes with a certain Mediterranean élan, with a few twists thrown in for good measure. There is a tendency towards over-elaboration but the ingredients are good and the execution sound. Service is affable and friendly and also makes up for a lack of character to the room. The local corporate trade, grateful they don't have to hack into the West End for a decent meal, are taken with The Lock.

Remember, stars
(❀❀❀...❀) are awarded
for cuisine only! Elements
such as service and décor
are not a factor.

South-East London

Once considered not only the wrong side of the tracks, but also most definitely the wrong side of the river, London's southeastern chunk has thrived in recent times courtesy of the Docklands Effect. As the gleaming glass peninsula of **Canary Wharf** (ironically, just north of the Thames) sprouted a personality of its own – with bars, restaurants, slinky bridges and an enviable view, not to mention moneyed residents actually putting down roots – the city's bottom right hand zone began to achieve destination status on a par with other parts of London. You only have to stroll around the glossy and quite vast **Limehouse Basin** – a slick marina that was once a hard-grafting East End dock – to really see what's happened here.

Not that the area hasn't always boasted some true gems in the capital's treasure chest. **Greenwich,** with fabulous views across the water to the docklands from its delightfully sloping park, has long been a favourite of kings and queens: Henry VIII and Elizabeth I resided here. The village itself bustles along with its market and plush picturehouse, but most visitors make their way to the standout attractions, of which there are many. The **Royal Observatory** and the Meridian Line draw stargazers and hemisphere striders in equal number, while the palatial Old Royal Naval College is a star turn for lovers of Wren, who designed it as London's answer to Versailles. On the northern edge of Greenwich Park, the **National Maritime Museum** has three floors of sea-faring wonders; down by the pier, the real thing exists in the rather sorry-looking shape of the **Cutty Sark,** devastated by fire in 2007. Up on the peninsula, the O2 Arena's distinctive shape has become an unmistakable landmark, but if you fancy a contrast to all things watery, the Fan Museum on Crooms Hill has more handheld fans (over 3,000 of them) than anywhere else on earth. Strolling south from Greenwich park you reach **Blackheath,** an alluring suburban village, whose most striking feature is the towering All Saints' Church, standing proud away from the chic shops and restaurants.

Of slightly less spectacular charms, but a real crowd-pleaser nevertheless, is **Dulwich Village,** hidden deeper in the southeastern enclaves. It's a leafy oasis in this part of the world, with a delightful park that boasts at its western end, next to the original buildings of the old public school, the Dulwich Picture Gallery. This will soon reach its 200th birthday, and its pedigree is evident in works by the likes of Rembrandt, Rubens, Van Dyck and Canaletto. Half an hour's walk away across the park is the brilliant Horniman Museum, full of natural history and world culture delights – as well as a massive aquarium that seems to take up much of southeast London.

GREENWICH MARKET

ERECTED· MDCCCXXXI·

A bit further east along the South Circular, there's the unexpected gem of Eltham Palace, originally the childhood home of Henry VIII with a magnificent (and still visible) Great Hall. What makes it unique is the adjacent Art Deco mansion built for millionaires in the 1930s in Ocean Liner style. It's the closest you'll ever get to a setting fit for hog roast and champagne. Heading back towards London, a lifestyle of bubbly and banquets has never really been **Peckham**'s thing, but it boasts a couple of corkers in the shape of the South London Gallery with its zeitgeist-setting art shows, and the Peckham Library, a giant inverted 'L' that after a decade still looks like a lot of fun to go into.

Back in the luxury flat-lands of the **Docklands, Wapping** has become an interesting port of call, its new-build architecture mixing in with a still Dickensian feel, in the shape of glowering Victorian warehouses and Wapping New Stairs, where the bodies of pirates were hanged from a gibbet until seven tides had showered their limp bodies. You can catch a fascinating history of the whole area in the nearby Museum in Docklands.

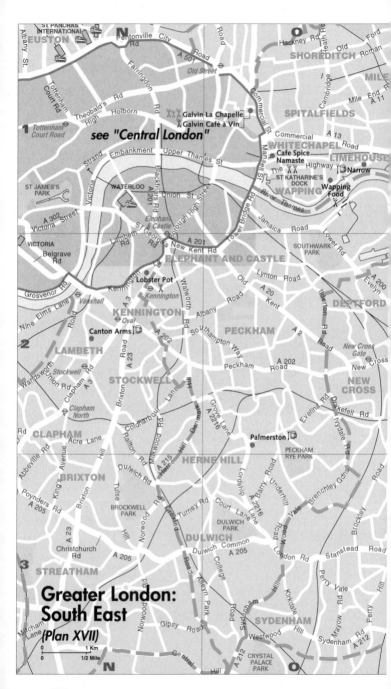

N

ALBANY St.

ST PANCHAS
INTERNATIONAL
EUSTON

Pentonville

City

Road

Hackney Rd

Old

Roman

Ford

SHOREDITCH

MILE

Mile End Rd

A 11

A 501

Old Street

Tottenham
Court Rd

Theobald's
High

Holborn

Farringdon

Road

Commercial St

SPITALFIELDS

Commercial

A 13

Road

WHITECHAPEL

LIMEHOUSE

Mansell St

XXX Galvin La Chapelle
X Galvin Café à Vin

see "Central London"

Strand

Embankment

Upper Thames St

Cafe Spice
Namaste

Highway

ST KATHARINE'S
DOCK

Narrow

Tottenham
Court Road

1

ST JAMES'S
PARK

WATERLOO

A 302

Victoria Street

VICTORIA

Belgrave
Rd

Grosvenor Rd

Victoria

Blackfriars Rd

A 201

Union St

Borough High Street

Elephant
& Castle

Lambeth
Rd

St George's
Rd

New Kent Rd

A 201

ELEPHANT AND CASTLE

The

WAPPING

Wapping
Food

River Thames

Jamaica Road

Lower Rd

SOUTHWARK
PARK

A 200

Evelyn

DEPTFORD

Lobster Pot

Kennington

Walworth

Old

Lynton Road

Kent

A 20

Ilderton Rd

Road

Nine Elms Lane

Vauxhall

A 3

KENNINGTON

Oval

Canton Arms

A 202

Albany Road

Southampton Way

PECKHAM

A 2

New Cross
Gate

New Cross

2

LAMBETH

Wandsworth

Union Rd

Stockwell

Clapham Rd

A 3

Clapham
North

STOCKWELL

Brixton Road

A 23

Coldharbour

Railton Rd

Milkwood

Rd

Peckham

A 202

Road

Grove Lane

A 2216

Denmark Hill

Palmerston

Evelina Rd

NEW
CROSS

Drakefell Rd

Nydale Rd

Road

Rd

CLAPHAM

Acre Lane

Abbeville Rd

King's Avenue

Poynders Rd

A 205

BRIXTON

Brixton

Hill

Tulse

Dulwich Rd

A 215

Herne Hill

HERNE HILL

Lordship Lane

Barry Road

Underhill Rd

A 2216

PECKHAM
RYE PARK

Brenchley Gdns

Brockley

Road

A 23

Christchurch
Rd

A 205

BROCKWELL
PARK

Norwood

Rd

Croxted Rd

Turney Rd

Court Lane

DULWICH
PARK

London Rd

Vale

Stanstead

Road

STREATHAM

3

DULWICH

Dulwich Common

A 205

College

Alleyn Park

Perry Vale

Kirkdale

Perry Hill

**Greater London:
South East**

(Plan XVII)

Mitcham
Lane

Norwood

Road

Gipsy

Road

Sydenham

Central

Hill

Westwood

Hill

A 212

CRYSTAL
PALACE
PARK

SYDENHAM

Sydenham Rd

A 212

Mayow Rd

0   1 Km
0   1/2 Mile

N

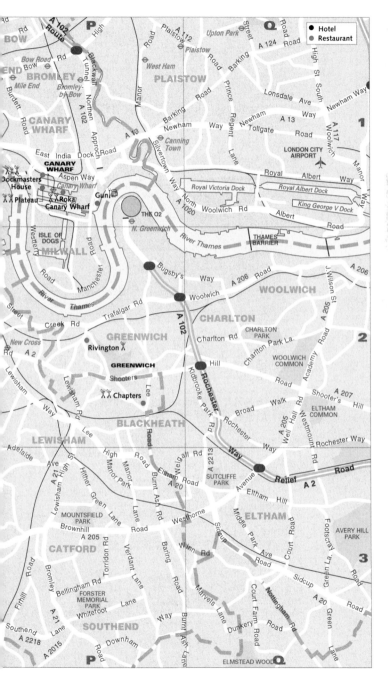

Legend:
- ● Hotel
- ● Restaurant

BOW
Rd
A 102
Route
Bow Road
Bow
Rd
High
Road
Plaistow
A 112
Plaistow
Road
Upton Park
Street
Road
A 124
Road
High
St
END
Mile End
BROMLEY
Bromley-by-Bow
Northern
Approach
West Ham
Manor
PLAISTOW
Barking
Road
Prince
Regent
Lonsdale
Ave
South
Newham Way
A 117
Woolwich
Manor

Burdett
Road
CANARY
WHARF
A 102
East India Dock Road
A 13
Newham
Way
Canning
Town
Silvertown
Way
Newham
Way
Tollgate
A 13
Road
LONDON CITY
AIRPORT

CANARY
WHARF
Aspen Way
Canary Wharf
Dockmasters
House
Plateau
Roka
Canary Wharf
Gun
North
Woolwich Rd
A 1020
Royal
Royal Victoria Dock
Royal Albert Dock
Albert
Way
Road
King George V Dock
Albert
Road
Way

ISLE OF
DOGS
Westferry
Road
MILLWALL
Manchester
Road
THE O2
N. Greenwich
River Thames
THAMES
BARRIER
A 206

River
Thames
Bugsby's
Way
A 206
Road
WOOLWICH
J. Wilson St
A 205

New Cross
Rd
A 2
Creek Rd
Trafalgar Rd
A 102
Woolwich
Road
CHARLTON
Charlton Rd
CHARLTON
PARK
Charlton Park La.
A 205
Academy
Road
A 206

Lewisham
Lewisham
Rd
GREENWICH
Rivington
GREENWICH
Shooters
Chapters
Lee
Hill
Kidbrooke Park Rd
Rochester
Way
WOOLWICH
COMMON
Road
Walk
Broad
A 205
Well Hall Rd
Westmount
Shooter's
A 207
Hill
ELTHAM
COMMON
Rochester Way

LEWISHAM
Lee
Road
BLACKHEATH
Rochester
Adelaide
Ave
A 21
Lewisham High
Hither Green Lane
High
Manor Park
Road
Manor
Burnt Ash Rd
Eltham
Road
A 20
Wricall Rd
A 2213
SUTCLIFFE
PARK
Avenue
Eltham
Hill
Relief
A 2
Road
Rd

MOUNTSFIELD
PARK
Brownhill
A 205
Lane
Road
Westhorne
Middle
Park
Ave
Road
Court Road
ELTHAM
AVERY HILL
PARK
Footscray
Rd

CATFORD
Bromley
Torridon Rd
Verdant Lane
Baring
Road
Winn
Rd
Sidcup
Road
Court Farm
Road
Sidcup
A 20
Green
Lane
Road

Firhill
Road
Bellingham Rd
A 21
FORSTER
MEMORIAL
PARK
Whitefoot
Lane
SOUTHEND
Lane
Burnt Ash Lane
Way
Marvels Lane
Dunkery Road
Nottingham Rd
A 20

Southend
A 2218
Lane
A 2015
Downham
Way
ELMSTEAD WOOD

299

Viajante ✿

K3

Bethnal Green
Patriot Sq.
(entrance on Cambridge Heath Rd) ⊠ E2 9NF
☎ (020) 7871 0461
e-mail info@viajante.co.uk
www.viajante.co.uk

⊖ Bethnal Green
Plan XVI
Booking essential

Menu £25/60

Viajante

Bethnal Green's converted Victorian town hall is the unlikely setting for Portuguese chef Nuno Mendes' highly innovative style of cooking. Despite the presence of large, looming lampshades, there's still a whiff of civic functionality about the restaurant – although the chairs are comfier than they look. But it's all about the food here and the sight of chefs working away with tweezers in the very open kitchen tells you it'll be a little different. Don't be entirely fooled by their swan-like serenity, however: there's another kitchen downstairs where the donkey work is done. The choice is between 6, 9 or 12 courses; so, if you haven't got the time, don't bother. Each delicate and diminutive course provides a blast of flavour and textures are enjoyably contrasting. Dishes are highly inventive and sometimes playful in their make-up and presentation, but ingredients match and there's no recourse to using unusual combinations. Inevitably, some dishes work better than others, but when taken as a whole, one cannot fail to be impressed.

First Course

- Scallop, pickled cucumber and celery juice.
- Braised salmon skin and aubergine.

Main Course

- Iberico pig neck, langoustine and broth.
- Octopus with pimentón potatoes, chorizo and eggs.

Dessert

- Panna cotta ice cream with basil and apple.
- Crumbled polenta with lemon paste and strawberries.

Chapters ⊛

Modern European ✕✕

P2

Blackheath
43-45 Montpelier Vale ✉ SE3 0TJ
✆ (020) 8333 2666
e-mail chapters@chaptersrestaurants.com
www.chaptersrestaurants.com

Carte £18/45

Down at Chapters it appears to be the '80s all over again: the champagne flows, the cocktails are shaken and everyone knows everyone else. If ever there was a change of concept that worked it was here: out went the serious, in came just the sort of place you'd want to come to after a hard day's work. The bar is always packed; the restaurant has an ersatz industrial feel and the menu is reassuringly familiar with a roll-call of classics that include fish and chips and belly of pork. The most expensive dishes are also the most popular – the assorted meats cooked over charcoal in the Josper oven. It's an all-day operation and they take as much care with breakfast as they do with dinner, while service is ably performed by a nimble team.

Dockmaster's House

Indian ✕✕✕

P1

Canary Wharf
1 Hertsmere Rd ✉ E14 8JJ
✆ (020) 7345 0345
e-mail reservations@dockmastershouse.com
www.dockmastershouse.com

⊖ Canary Wharf
Closed 25 December-1 January, Saturday lunch and Sunday – booking advisable

Menu £19 (lunch and early dinner) – Carte £29/39

On the edge of Canary Wharf and in the shadow of its skyscrapers sits this striking three-storey Georgian house which has been given a contemporary overhaul. There are two contrasting dining rooms: one in the original part of the house with all the period features; the other more modern and shiny and encased in a glass extension. There's a funky basement bar, plus rooms upstairs and a garden for private parties. The Indian food adds modern twists to its conventional foundations. The menu is more seasonally based than many but it is also more expensive. The saffron prawns are good, the grilled section is worth exploring and there are interesting teas; but a little less pretentiousness all round wouldn't be a bad thing.

Gun

P1

Canary Wharf
27 Coldharbour ⊠ E14 9NS
℘ (020) 7515 5222
e-mail info@thegundocklands.com
www.thegundocklands.com

⊖ Blackwall (DLR).
Closed 25 December

Carte £21/30

The 18C Gun may have had a 21C makeover but that doesn't mean it has forgotten its roots: its association with Admiral Lord Nelson, links to smugglers and ties to the river are all celebrated in its oil paintings and displays of assorted weaponry. The dining room and the style of service are both fairly smart and ceremonial, yet The Gun is a pub where this level of formality seems appropriate. Dockers have now been replaced by bankers, the majority of whom rarely venture beyond the 35-day aged steak. This is a shame as the menu cleverly combines relatively ambitious dishes such as game or John Dory with more traditional local specialities like eel and oysters. Even the dessert menu offers a mix, from soufflés to stewed plums.

Plateau

P1

Canary Wharf
Canada Place (4th floor),
Canada Square ⊠ E14 5ER
℘ (020) 7715 7100
e-mail plateau@danddlondon.com
www.plateaurestaurant.co.uk

⊖ Canary Wharf
Closed 25-26 December,
1 January, Saturday,
Sunday and Bank Holidays

Menu £18/27 – Carte £35/44

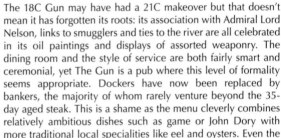

In a building that wouldn't look out of place in Manhattan is a restaurant that harks back to a time when bankers ruled the world. It is still, though, an impressive open-plan space and the dramatic glass walls and ceilings make the surrounding monolithic office blocks look strangely appealing. The striking 1970s retro design also seems to fit perfectly. There are two choices: the Grill where, as the name suggests, the choice is from rotisserie meats and classic grilled dishes, or the formal restaurant beyond with its comfortable surroundings. Here, the range is more eclectic and dishes are constructed with more global influences. They also come in ample sizes, though, so ignore the enthusiastic selling of the side dishes.

Quadrato

Canary Wharf   ⊖ Canary Wharf

Westferry Circus ✉ E14 8RS

✆ (020) 7510 1999

e-mail reservations.caw@fourseasons.com

www.fourseasons.com/canarywharf

Carte £33/53

Grumbling that a restaurant within a Four Seasons Hotel in Canary Wharf is a little too corporate in its look is like protesting about all the grockles in a Torquay tearoom. Granted, most customers are tied and jacketed, but it is still a comfortable, well run room whose size is made more manageable by its subdivision into four smaller sections – but do ask for a table either facing the exposed glass-fronted kitchen or overlooking the terrace and river. The kitchen helps itself to plenty of luxury ingredients and uses them in dishes that reflect styles and flavours from all parts of Italy; portions are generous and clearly much care goes into the preparation. Sunday brunches draw in the crowds from an easterly direction.

Roka Canary Wharf

Canary Wharf   ⊖ Canary Wharf

Ist Floor,4 Park Pavilion ✉ E14 5FW

✆ (020) 7636 5228

e-mail info@rokarestaurant.com

www.rokarestaurant.com

Closed 25 December, 1 January, Sunday and bank holidays – booking essential

Carte approx. £38

London's second Roka restaurant sits in the shadow of Canary Wharf Tower, still the UK's tallest building, and the first thing to hit you, once you've actually found the entrance, is a wall of sound. This is a big, open and perennially busy affair, with tightly packed tables which are usually occupied by large groups of City folk – and is not somewhere for a quiet dinner à deux. The menu follows the format of the Charlotte Street branch by offering a wide selection of mostly contemporary Japanese dishes. The easiest option is to head straight for one of the tasting menus which offer a balanced picture of what the food is all about. The robata grill is the centrepiece of the kitchen's operation – the lamb chops are particularly good.

Palmerston

02

East Dulwich
91 Lordship Ln ✉ SE22 8EP
✆ (020) 8693 1629
e-mail info@thepalmerston.net
www.thepalmerston.net

⊖ East Dulwich (rail)

Menu £15 (lunch) – Carte £22/29

It's not just for the locals – those passing through for a visit to the Horniman Museum or Dulwich Picture Gallery must also be pleased to have somewhere so welcoming in which to extend their stay in SE22. You can sit anywhere, although there is a section at the back with wood panelling and a mosaic floor which they call 'the dining room'. The menus tend to evolve on a monthly basis, with influences ranging from the Med to Asia. The bread is good, which usually augurs well and, refreshingly, the dishes come with just the ingredients described on the menu. Add a well-priced weekday menu and a host of engaging young staff and it's little wonder the pub attracts such a wide range of ages, which in turn creates a pleasant atmosphere.

Rivington Grill

P2

Greenwich
178 Greenwich High Rd.
✉ SE10 8NN
✆ (020) 8293 9270
e-mail greenwich@rivingtongrill.co.uk
www.rivingtongreenwich.co.uk

⊖ Greenwich (DLR)
Closed 25 December, Monday and lunch
Tuesday and Wednesday

Carte £21/39

It's open from breakfast until late and the menu changes every two weeks so they can introduce seasonal specials; the 'on toast' section is a local favourite and includes Welsh rarebit and devilled kidneys. Steaks are from Scotland; the prosperous can upgrade their fish and chips to lobster and chips and the puds are rich and satisfying. The wine list is sensibly priced and includes beers and Somerset brandies. It's spread over two floors, with the ground floor being the more casual; it attracts a younger, hipper crowd than the Shoreditch branch and has a more local feel; and it gets swamped with look-alikes whenever there's a pop siren playing the O2 arena. Tables of up to four people can get a discount at the next door cinema.

Lobster Pot

 N2

French

Kennington
3 Kennington Ln. ✉ SE11 4RG
✆ (020) 7582 5556
www.lobsterpotrestaurant.co.uk

⊖ Kennington
Closed 25 December-4 January,
Sunday and Monday

Carte £38/50

A/C

VISA

M©

AE

Ignore the fairly shabby exterior, dive straight in and you'll think you've stumbled onto a French film set. Fish tanks, portholes, the cries of seagulls and the hoots of ferries…the place has the lot and it's hard to avoid getting caught up in the exuberance of it all. It's no surprise that it's also all about fish. The chef-owner, from Vannes in Brittany, goes to Billingsgate each morning and he knows what he's doing: his menu is classical and appetising, with fruits de mer, plenty of oysters, a lobster section and daily specials on the blackboard. Be sure to make room for the crêpes, which are great. It's not cheap but it is an experience. Underlining the family nature of the business, the son has opened a brasserie next door.

Narrow

 O1

Gastropub

Limehouse
44 Narrow St ✉ E14 8DP
✆ (020) 7592 7950
e-mail thenarrow@gordonramsay.com
www.gordonramsay.com

⊖ Limehouse (DLR).
Booking essential

 Menu £22 – Carte £21/27

Despite receiving some negative publicity a while back, when it was revealed that certain dishes in Gordon Ramsay's pubs are prepared in a central kitchen, The Narrow does not seem to be any less frenetic. This 'logistical cooking', as they describe it, is used for dishes requiring a lengthy cooking process, such as the slow-roasted pork belly or beef braised in Guinness. However it gets there, the food on the plate is tasty, seasonal and laudably British, be it devilled kidneys, Morecambe Bay brown shrimps, a chicken pie or a sherry trifle. What is also certain is that no other London pub has better views, as one would expect from a converted dockmaster's house; just be sure to request a table in the semi-permanent conservatory.

Galvin Café a Vin 🐶

01

Spitalfields
35 Spital Sq.
(entrance on Bishops Sq.) ✉ E1 6DY
☎ (020) 7299 0404
e-mail info@galvinrestaurants.com
www.galvinrestaurants.com

⊖ Liverpool Street
Closed 25-26 December
and 1 January

Menu £15 (lunch) – Carte £23/33

In the same building as La Chapelle, but with a separate entrance around the corner, is this simpler but no less professionally run operation from the Galvin brothers. The room may not have the grandeur of next door but what is does offer is classic French bistro food at very appealing prices. Snails, confit of duck and rum baba are all here — tasty and satisfying dishes to evoke memories of French holidays and have you reaching for the Gauloises. So, if you want the fillet or the loin, go next door; if you're happy with the leg or bavette then come here. The place is loud, fun and friendly, and the atmosphere is helped along by a cheerful team and a thoughtfully compiled wine list which is also well priced.

Hawksmoor

K3

Spitalfields
157 Commercial St. ✉ E1 6BJ
☎ (020) 7247 7392
e-mail info@thehawksmoor.com
www.thehawksmoor.com

⊖ Shoreditch
Plan XVI
Closed Christmas, Sunday dinner and
bank holidays – booking advisable

Carte £34/51

Hawksmoor was a 17C architect and student of Sir Christopher Wren so you could expect this steakhouse to be housed in a building of note rather than in this modern edifice of little aesthetic value. Inside is equally unremarkable but no matter because this place is all about beef and, more specifically, British beef which has been hung for 35 days. It comes from Longhorn cattle raised by Ginger Pig in the heart of the North Yorkshire Moors and the quality and depth of flavour is exceptional. Just choose your preferred weight – go for 400g if you're hungry. Starters and puds don't come close in quality but again, no matter, because when you've got some fantastic red meat in front of you, all you need is a mate and a bottle of red wine.

Galvin La Chapelle ✿

French 🍴🍴🍴

01

Spitalfields
35 Spital Sq. ✉ E1 6DY
📞 (020) 7299 0400
e-mail info@galvinrestaurants.com
www.galvinrestaurants.com

⊖ **Liverpool Street**
Closed 25-26 December and 1 January

Menu £25 (lunch)/29 (early dinner) – Carte £37/56

VISA

MC

AE

Galvin La Chapelle

These days, it is rare to walk into a restaurant in London and be taken back with the grandeur and sheer scale of a room. However, the latest venture from the Galvin Brothers, who have already proved themselves expert restaurateurs, is one that will dazzle the most jaded of diner. The Victorian splendour of St. Botolph's Hall, with its vaulted ceiling, arched windows and marble pillars, lends itself effortlessly to its new role as a glamorous restaurant. There are tables in booths, in the wings or in the middle of the action and those who like some comfort with their food will not be disappointed. It is also a fitting backdrop to the food, which is, in essence, bourgeois French but with a sophisticated edge, which means it is immensely satisfying. There are no unnecessary fripperies, just three courses of reassuringly familiar combinations with the emphasis on bold, clear flavours. Add in a service team who are a well-drilled, well-versed outfit and you have somewhere that will be part of the restaurant landscape for years to come.

First Course	*Main Course*	*Dessert*
• Lasagne of crab with velouté of girolles.	• Tagine of pigeon with aubergine purée and harissa sauce.	• Tarte tatin with crème fraîche.
• Ballottine of foie gras with peaches and pain d'épices.	• Red mullet 'boulangère' with fennel and olives.	• Rum baba with crème Chantilly.

St John Bread and Wine

British 🍴

K3

Spitalfields
94-96 Commercial St ✉ E1 6LZ
☎ (020) 7251 0848
e-mail reservations@stjohnbreadandwine.com
www.stjohnbreadandwine.com

⊖ Shoreditch
Plan XVI
Closed Christmas-New Year
and bank holidays

Carte £24/27

Ⓐ/Ⓒ
☼
𝗩𝗜𝗦𝗔
Ⓜ/Ⓒ
ⒶⒺ

Less famous but by no means less loved than its sibling, this English version of a classic comptoir is the sort of place we would all like to have at the end of our road. Just the aroma as you enter is enough to get the appetite going. As the name suggests, this is a wine shop and a bakery but also a local restaurant. The menu changes twice a day and depends on what's in season; the Britishness of its ingredients and its promotion of forgotten recipes will enthuse everyone, not just culinary genealogists. But it's not all man-food like roast pig spleen or 'raw Angus'; there are lighter dishes such as plaice with samphire; and the Eccles cakes are a must. From breakfast to supper, certain dishes are only ready at certain times, so do check first.

Les Trois Garcons

French 🍴🍴

K3

Spitalfields
1 Club Row ✉ E1 6JX
☎ (020) 7613 1924
e-mail info@lestroisgarcons.com
www.lestroisgarcons.com

⊖ Shoreditch
Plan XVI
Closed 16-31 August, 23 December-
10 January, Sunday and Bank Holidays
– (dinner only and lunch in December)

Menu £46

Ⓐ/Ⓒ

🖼
𝗩𝗜𝗦𝗔
Ⓜ/Ⓒ
ⒶⒺ

The surrounding streets may be somewhat drab but the three friends (hence the name) who own this former pub are also antique dealers (hence the eccentric and exuberant decoration that resembles a theatrical props department). There are stuffed animals, beads, handbags and assorted objets d'art; heavy velvet curtains ensure that the lighting is dim and atmospheric. The kitchen, on the other hand, uses fairly classical French cooking techniques and flavour combinations, although the majority of ingredients are British. The menus change seasonally and presentation on the plate is neat and appetising. The early-in-the-week set menu is good value; the à la carte somewhat expensive. Service can occasionally veer from the efficient to the over-confident.

Canton Arms

Gastropub

Stockwell   ⊖ Stockwell.

177 South Lambeth Rd   Closed 25-26 December, 31 December,
✉ SW8 1XP   1 January, Monday lunch, Sunday dinner
✆ (020) 7582 8710   and bank holidays
e-mail thecantonarms@googlemail.com
www.cantonarms.com

Carte £20/26

Its appreciative audience prove that the demand for fresh, honest, seasonal food is not just limited to smart squares in Chelsea or Islington. The oval-shaped bar dominates the room, with the front half busy with drinkers and the back laid up for diners, although it's all very relaxed and you can eat where you want. The kitchen's experience in places like the Anchor & Hope and Great Queen Street is obvious on their menu which features rustic, earthy British food, of the sort that suits this environment so well. Lunch could be a kipper or tripe and chips; even a reinvented toasted sandwich. Dinner sees a short, no-nonsense menu offering perhaps braised venison or grilled haddock, with daily specials like steak and kidney pie for two.

Wapping Food

Modern European

Wapping   ⊖ Wapping

Wapping Wall ✉ E1W 3SG   Closed 24 December-3 January,
✆ (020) 7680 2080   Sunday dinner and bank holidays
www.thewappingproject.com

Carte £30/54

What does a former theatre director with a passion for food do when looking for a change? She buys a disused Victorian former hydraulic power station, spends two years doing it up and then opens it as the Wapping Project, a bringing together of a restaurant and an art gallery. The two functions marry perfectly: you sit among the old turbines and enjoy robust dishes fashioned from what suppliers have brought in that day. This could be mackerel with fennel, a ham hock terrine, Brecon lamb shank or a panna cotta; all served by an enthusiastic team who know their onions. To make the most of your visit, be sure to take in the artwork before or after your meal; it could take the form of an installation, an exhibition or a performance.

Cafe Spice Namaste 🐦

Indian ✕✕

O1

Whitechapel
16 Prescot St. ✉ E1 8AZ
✆ (020) 7488 9242
e-mail info@cafespice.co.uk
www.cafespice.co.uk

⊖ **Tower Hill**
Closed Saturday lunch,
Sunday and bank holidays

Menu £30/65 – Carte £23/29

AC
VISA
MC
AE
①

Cyrus Todiwala's contribution to Indian cuisine and the hospitality industry were recognised in 2010 when he was appointed an OBE. Café Spice Namaste opened back in 1995 and was where the dining public first became aware of his ability. The bright decoration of this former magistrate's court may not be quite so effervescent these days but the food remains just as fresh and vibrant. Many of the ingredients used are from within the British Isles and the cooking influences are spread across India; the Parsee specialities are particularly memorable. There's a plethora of menus to look through but don't hesitate to ask Cyrus' wife Pervin for guidance; she's a charming hostess who runs a tight ship and keeps an eye on everything.

Whitechapel Gallery Dining Room

Mediterranean ✕

K3

Whitechapel
77-82 Whitechapel High St. ✉ E1 7QX
✆ (020) 7522 7896
e-mail info@whitechapelgallery.org
www.whitechapelgallery.com

⊖ **Aldgate East**
Plan XVI
Closed Christmas and New Year,
Monday and dinner Sunday
and Tuesday – booking advisable

Menu £23 (lunch) – Carte (dinner) £27/34

VISA
MC
AE

The Whitechapel Gallery, founded in 1901 and best known for exhibiting Picasso's 'Guernica', underwent a major refit and expansion in 2009 into the former library next door. Not only did this double the available space but it also allowed for the creation of this very sweet restaurant. It's a bright, well-lit room, with tightly packed tables and lots of wood and mirrors. The seasonal British ingredients are invigorated with Mediterranean flavours and influences, so that pork belly comes with shaved fennel and a tomato salad, while sea bass is joined by squid, chilli and oregano. For dessert, great things are done with plums. The menu changes often and is refreshingly short; the four starters and main courses include a veggie option.

South-West London

Meandering like a silver snake, **The Thames** coils serenely through south-west London, adding definition to the area's much-heralded middle-class enclaves and leafy suburbs. It's the focal point to the annual **university boat race** from **Putney** to **Mortlake,** and it serves as the giant glass pond attractively backing countless bank-side pubs. This area has long been regarded as the cosy bourgeois side of town, though within its postcode prowls the lively and eclectic **Brixton,** whose buzzing street markets and lauded music venues such as the Academy and the Fridge add an urban lustre and vibrant edge.

In most people's minds, though, south-west London finds its true colours in the beautiful terrace view from the top of **Richmond Hill,** as the river bends majestically through the meadows below. Or in the smart **Wimbledon Village,** its independent boutiques ranged prettily along its own hill, with the open spaces of the Common for a back garden. Or, again, in the Italianate architecture that makes **Chiswick House** and grounds a little corner of the Mediterranean close to the Great West Road.

Green space is almost as prolific in this zone as the streets of Victorian and Edwardian villas. **Richmond Park** is the largest royal park in the whole of London and teems with kite flyers, cyclists and deer – though not necessarily in that order. From here, round a southerly bend in the river, delightful grounds surround **Ham House,** which celebrated its 400th birthday in 2010, although not so excessively as during the seventeenth century when it was home to Restoration court life. Head slightly north to **Kew Gardens** and its world famous 300 acres can now be viewed from above – the treetop walkway, opened in 2008, takes you 60 feet up to offer some breath-taking views. Just across the river from here is another from the historical hit-list: **Syon Park,** which boasts water meadows still grazed by cattle, giving it a distinctly rural aspect. Syon House is considered one of architect Robert Adam's finest works; it certainly appealed to Queen Victoria, who spent much of her young life here. Up the road in bourgeoning Brentford, two unique museums bring in hordes of the curious: the Musical Museum includes a huge Wurlitzer theatre organ (get lucky and watch it being played), while almost next door, the Kew Bridge Steam Museum shows off all things steamy on a grand scale, including massive beam engines which pumped London's water for over a century.

Hammersmith may be known for its bustling Broadway and flyover, but five minutes' walk from here is the Upper Mall, which has iconic riverside pubs and Kelmscott House, the last home of artistic visionary William Morris: down in the basement and coach house are

impressive memorabilia related to his life plus changing exhibitions of designs and drawings. From here, it's just a quick jaunt across **Hammersmith Bridge** and down the arrow-straight Castelnau to the Wetland Centre in Barnes, which for ten years has lured wildlife to within screeching distance of the West End. **Barnes** has always revelled in its village-like identity – it juts up like an isolated peninsula into the Thames and boasts yummy boutiques and well-known restaurants. The Bulls Head pub in Lonsdale Road has featured some of the best jazz in London for half a century.

In a more easterly direction, the urbanised areas of **Clapham** and **Battersea** have re-established themselves as desirable places to live over the last decade. **Clapham Common** is considered prime southwest London turf, to the extent that its summer music festivals are highly prized. It's ringed by good pubs and restaurants, too. Battersea used to be famous for its funfair, but now the peace pagoda in the park lends it a more serene light. And if you're after serenity on a hot day, then a cool dip in the wondrous **Tooting** Lido is just the thing.

313

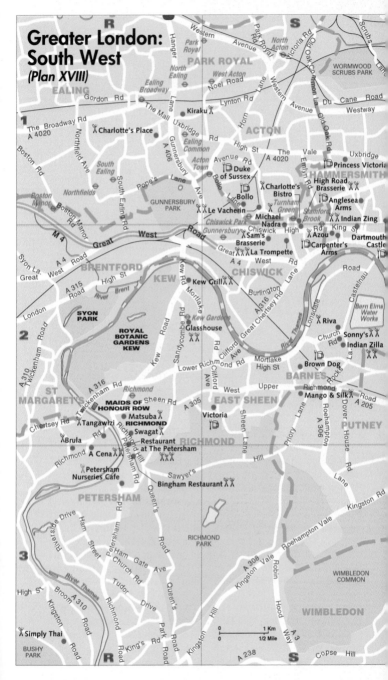

Greater London: South West
(Plan XVIII)

R

S

Western Avenue

Hanger

Park Royal

North Acton

Victoria Rd

Old Oak Co

Scrubs

PARK ROYAL

WORMWOOD SCRUBS PARK

North Ealing

West Acton

Noel Road

Western Avenue

Du Cane Road

Westway

EALING

Ealing Broadway

Gordon Rd

The Mall

Uxbridge

Lynton Rd

Horn Lane

High St

ACTON

The Vale

A 4020

Emlyn Rd

Uxbridge

Old Oak Rd

Anson Lane

X Kiraku

1

The Broadway Rd
A 4020

X Charlotte's Place

Northfield Ave

Boston Rd

Gunnersbury Rd
A 406

Ealing Common

Acton Town

Avenue Rd

Bollo Lane

Princess Victoria

HAMMERSMITH

High Road Brasserie XX

South Ealing

Pope's Lane

South Ealing Lane

Duke of Sussex

X Charlotte's Bistro

Anglesea Arms

X Indian Zing

Northfields

Boston Manor

Boston Manor Rd

GUNNERSBURY PARK

X Le Vacherin

Bollo

Chiswick Park

Turnham Green

Michael Nadra

Stamford Brook

M 4

Great

West

Road

Gunnersbury

X Sam's Brasserie

Chiswick High Rd

King St

X Azou

Carpenter's Arms

Dartmouth Castle

Syon La.

A 4

Great West Road

Great XXX La Trompette

A 4

West Road

CHISWICK

Road

Castelnau

BRENTFORD

A 315

High St

River Brent

Kew Rd

X Kew Grill X

Burlington Lane

A 316

Great Chertsey Rd

Lonsdale Rd

KEW

London Rd

A 310 Twickenham Road

SYON PARK

ROYAL BOTANIC GARDENS KEW

Sandycombe Rd

Kew Gardens Rd

X Glasshouse

Mortlake Rd

Clifford Ave

Lower Richmond Rd

Clifford Ave

West

Mortlake High St

Brown Dog

BARNES

Bern Elms Water Works

X Riva

Church Rd

Sonny's X

Indian Zilla XX

Rocks La.

2

ST MARGARET'S

A 316

Richmond Rd

Twickenham Rd

MAIDS OF HONOUR ROW

Matsuba

X Tangawizi

RICHMOND

Swagat

A 305

Sheen Rd

Victoria

EAST SHEEN

Upper Richmond Rd A 205

Mango & Silk X

Dover House Rd

PUTNEY

X Brula

A Cena XX

Richmond Rd

Richmond Hill

Petersham Rd

Restaurant at The Petersham XXX

RICHMOND

Sheen Lane

Priory Lane

Roehampton Lane A 306

X Petersham Nurseries Cafe

Sawyer's

Bingham Restaurant XX

Queen's Road

Hill

PETERSHAM

River's Drive

Ham Street

Petersham Rd

Ham Gate Ave

Church Rd

RICHMOND PARK

Kingston Vale

Roehampton Vale

Kingston Rd

3

River Thames

High St

A 310

Broom Road

Kingston

King's Road

Park Road

Queen's Road

Kingston Hill

Robin Hood Way

A 3

WIMBLEDON COMMON

WIMBLEDON

X Simply Thai

BUSHY PARK

0   1 Km

0   1/2 Mile

A 238

Copse Hill

R

S

314

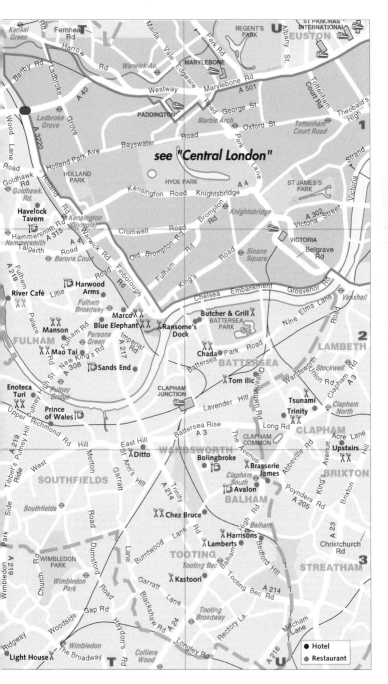

Kensal
Green
Fernhea
Rd
Harrow
Rd
Barlby Rd
Ladbroke
A 40
Maida Vale
Edgware
Warwick Av.
MARYLEBONE
Westway
Marylebone Rd A 501
George St
REGENT'S
PARK
Park Rd
Albany
St.
Tottenham
Court Rd
ST PANCRAS
INTERNATIONAL
EUSTON
Theobald's
High
Strand
1
Wood
Lane
Road
A 3220
Ladbroke
Grove
PADDINGTON
Marble Arch
Oxford St
Tottenham
Court Road
Holland Park Ave
Bayswater
Road
see "Central London"
Goldhawk
Rd
Goldhawk
Rd.
HOLLAND
PARK
HYDE PARK
A 4
ST JAMES'S
PARK
Victoria
Havelock
Tavern
Kensington
(Olympia)
Hammersmith Rd
Kensington Road
Knightsbridge
Knightsbridge
Brompton
Rd
A 302
Victoria Street
Hammersmith
Talgarth
A 4
Road
Warwick Rd
Cromwell
Road
Old Brompton
Rd
Fulham
Road
King's
Road
Sloane
Square
VICTORIA
Belgrave
Rd
Barons Court
Finborough Rd
Fulham
A 219
River Café
Lillie
Harwood
Arms
Fulham
Broadway
Marco
Blue Elephant
Ransome's
Dock
Chelsea Embankment
Grosvenor Rd
Butcher & Grill
BATTERSEA
PARK
Nine Elms Lane
Vauxhall
2
LAMBETH
Manson
Mao Tai
Palace
Fulham Rd
Parsons
Green
Imperial
Rd
A 217
New King's Rd
A 308
Sands End
High St
Chada
Park
Road
Battersea
BATTERSEA
Wandsworth
Stockwell
Union Rd
A 3
Clapham Rd
Enoteca
Turi
Putney
Prince
of Wales
Bridge
Richmond
Rd
Putney Hill
Upper
Hill
A 219
Tibbet's
Ride
West
CLAPHAM
JUNCTION
Tom Ilic
Queenstown Rd
Lavender Hill
Tsunami
Trinity
Clapham
North
Long Rd
CLAPHAM
Acre Lane
East Hill
St Ann's Hill
Battersea Rise
A 3
WANDSWORTH
Ditto
Bolingbroke
Merton
Garratt
SOUTHFIELDS
Southfields
CLAPHAM
COMMON
The Avenue
Brasserie
James
Clapham
South
Avalon
BALHAM
Abbeville Rd
Upstairs
BRIXTON
King's Avenue
Poynders
A 205
Brixton
Chez Bruce
Trinity
A 214
Clapham
Rd
Burntwood Lane
Balham
High Rd
Balham
Harrisons
Lamberts
Bedford Hill
A 23
Christchurch
Rd
STREATHAM
3
Park
Side
A 219
WIMBLEDON
PARK
Wimbledon
Park
Church Rd
Durnsford
Road
TOOTING
Tooting Bec
Kastoori
Garratt
Lane
Blackshaw Rd A 24
Tooting Bec Rd
A 214
Tooting
Broadway
Rectory La.
Mitcham
Lane
Wimbledon Park
Ridgway
Light House
Wimbledon
The Broadway
Woodside
Gap Rd
Haydon's
Rd
Colliers
Wood
Longley Rd
A 216

● Hotel
● Restaurant

315

Bollo

S1

Acton Green   ⊖ Chiswick Park.
13-15 Bollo Ln ✉ W4 5LR
✆ (020) 8994 6037
e-mail thebollohouse@btconnect.com
www.thebollohouse.co.uk

Carte £20/30

The Bollo is a large, handsome Victorian pub whose glass cupola and oak panelling give it some substance and personality in this age of the generic pub makeover. Tables and sofas are scattered around in a relaxed, sit-where-you-want way. The menu changes as ingredients come and go; the kitchen appeals to its core voters by always including sufficient numbers of pub classics be they the Bollo Burger, the haddock or the fishcakes. But there is also a discernible southern Mediterranean influence to the menu, with regular appearances from the likes of chorizo, tzatziki, bruschetta and hummus. This is a pub where there's always either a promotion or an activity, whether that's the '50% off a main course' Monday or the Wednesday quiz nights.

Duke of Sussex

S1

Acton Green   ⊖ Chiswick Park.
75 South Par ✉ W4 5LF   Closed Monday lunch
✆ (020) 8742 8801
e-mail thedukeofsussex@realpubs.co.uk

Carte £20/28

This grand old Victorian Duke has been given a new lease of life by an enthusiastic pair of gastropub specialists. They've done it all up and, most importantly, introduced some very appealing menus. The best place to eat is in the back room, which was once a variety theatre and comes complete with proscenium arch and chandeliers. The menu is printed daily and the Spanish influence highlights where the chef's passions lie. Rustic and satisfying stews, whether fish or fabada, suit the place perfectly, as does a plate of cured meats or a tortilla; there are often dishes designed for sharing and on some evenings the kitchen will roast a boar or suckling pig. The wine list is short but affordable, with plenty available by the glass or carafe.

Le Vacherin

S1

Acton Green
76-77 South Par. ✉ W4 5LF
✆ (020) 8742 2121
e-mail info@levacherin.com
www.levacherin.com

⊖ Chiswick Park
Closed Monday lunch and bank holidays

Menu £17/33 – Carte dinner £34/43

A/C

☼

VISA

MC

AE

Le Vacherin calls itself a bistro but, with its brown leather banquette seating, mirrors and belle époque prints, it feels more like a brasserie, and quite a smart one at that. The most important element of the operation is the appealing menu of French classics which rarely changes, largely because they don't need to but also because the regulars wouldn't allow it. The check list includes oeufs en cocotte, escargots, confit of duck and crème brûlée. Beef is something of a speciality, whether that's the côte de boeuf, the rib-eye or the chateaubriand. Portions are sensible, flavours distinct and ingredients good. The only thing missing in terms of authenticity are some insouciant French staff and a little Piaf playing in the background.

Avalon

U3

Balham
16 Balham Hill ✉ SW12 9EB
✆ (020) 8675 8613
e-mail info@theavalonlondon.com
www.theavalonlondon.com

⊖ Clapham South.
Booking advisable

Menu £18 – Carte £20/25

A/C

⊡

☼

VISA

MC

AE

A full renovation has turned The George into a slick and imaginatively styled pub, where Sir Edward Coley Burne-Jones prints add a suitably mythical edge to the aesthetic. The rear dining room's walls are covered in cream tiles but any resemblance to a morgue is thankfully undone by the general bustle and those eye-catching chandeliers. The menu combines British and Mediterranean influences, sometimes, as in the case of the kedgeree risotto, in the same dish. Expect roasted veal marrow bones, crab linguine, venison carpaccio, lamb cutlets and crème brûlée, but also crumble, appropriately of the apple variety. The concise wine list is appealingly priced and there's beer aplenty. Those locals still can't quite believe that Avalon really exists.

Brasserie James

Modern European ✗

 Balham
47 Balham Hill ✉ SW12 9DR
☎ (020) 8772 0057
e-mail info@brasseriejames.com
www.brasseriejames.com

⊖ **Clapham South**
Closed 23-31 December

Menu £15/17 – Carte £26/36

If you have the courage to open your own restaurant, especially in times of economic anxiety, then no one will begrudge your naming it eponymously. Craig James is a former chef in the Conran/D&D empire and he has brought his experience to bear in the more relaxed environs of a neighbourhood joint. It's on a site previously home to a Pakistani restaurant that was itself quite a local institution and he's given it a top-to-toe revamp. There's something for everyone on the menu, from seasonal oysters and the popular moules à la crème, to daily fish from the market, quality meats, pasta and good old-fashioned puds. There are good value set price menus; brunch at weekends and sensibly priced wines by the bottle, glass or carafe.

Harrison's

Mediterranean ✗

 Balham
15-19 Bedford Hill ✉ SW12 9EX
☎ (020) 8675 6900
e-mail info@harrisonsbalham.co.uk
www.harrisonsbalham.co.uk

⊖ **Balham**
Closed 25-26 December

Menu £16/18 (weekdays) – Carte £22/36

Following the success of Sam's Brasserie in Chiswick, owner Sam Harrison took over what was Soho House Bar and Grill and turned it into another all-day brasserie. It provides a lesson for all neighbourhood restaurants in the importance of being a focal point for the local community: it is open from breakfast until late and is as welcoming to those just in for a coffee as those wanting a three course meal. The food is uncomplicated, fresh and satisfying, whether that's a cheeseburger, tuna Niçoise, Cumberland sausages or a fishcake. Brunch is served at weekends; they offer a kids' menu, as well as a good value weekday set menu, and there's a decent wine selection. It's hardly surprisingly the locals have embraced the place.

Lamberts

U3

Balham   ⊖ Balham
2 Station Par. ⊠ SW12 9AZ   Closed Sunday dinner and Monday
✆ (020) 8675 2233   – (dinner only and lunch Saturday-Sunday)
e-mail bookings@lambertsrestaurant.com
www.lambertsrestaurant.com

Menu £20/30

A/C

VISA

Mr Lambert and his eponymous restaurant have succeeded by offering the locals exactly what they want: relaxed surroundings, hospitable service and tasty, seasonal food. The menu is updated each month and small suppliers have been sought out. The cooking is quite British in style and has a satisfying wholesomeness to it; Sunday's ribs of Galloway beef or legs of Salt Marsh lamb are hugely popular. Equal thought and passion has gone into the commendably priced wine list, which includes some favourites offered in 300ml decanters. Other nice touches include filtered water delivered gratis and velvety truffles brought with the coffee. The owner's enthusiasm has rubbed off on his team, for whom nothing is too much trouble.

Brown Dog

S2

Barnes   ⊖ Barnes Bridge (Rail).
28 Cross St ⊠ SW13 0AP   Closed 25-26 December
✆ (020) 8392 2200
www.thebrowndog.co.uk

Carte £20/30

VISA

Thankfully, changes of ownership don't appear to mean much here – perhaps you really can't teach an old dog new tricks – because The Brown Dog remains a terrific neighbourhood pub and the locals clearly love it just the way it is. Mind you, this pretty Victorian pub is so well hidden in the maze of residential streets that it's a wonder any new customers ever find it anyway. The look fuses the traditional with the modern and service is bubbly and enthusiastic. Jugs of iced water arrive without prompting and the cleverly concise menu changes regularly. A lightly spiced crab salad or pint of prawns could be followed by a succulent rump of lamb, while puddings not only display a terrific lightness of touch but are also very commendably priced.

Indian Zilla

Indian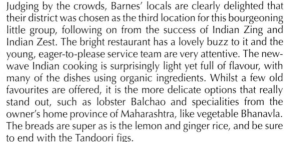

S2

Barnes
2-3 Rocks Ln. ✉ SW13 0DB
✆ (020) 8878 3989
e-mail info@indianzilla.co.uk
www.indianzilla.co.uk

Menu £15 (lunch) – Carte £19/35

Judging by the crowds, Barnes' locals are clearly delighted that their district was chosen as the third location for this bourgeoning little group, following on from the success of Indian Zing and Indian Zest. The bright restaurant has a lovely buzz to it and the young, eager-to-please service team are very attentive. The new-wave Indian cooking is surprisingly light yet full of flavour, with many of the dishes using organic ingredients. Whilst a few old favourites are offered, it is the more delicate options that really stand out, such as lobster Balchao and specialities from the owner's home province of Maharashtra, like vegetable Bhanavla. The breads are super as is the lemon and ginger rice, and be sure to end with the Tandoori figs.

Riva

Italian

S2

Barnes
169 Church Rd. ✉ SW13 9HR
✆ (020) 8748 0434
e-mail rivarestaurants@btconnect.com

Closed Christmas and New Year, 3 weeks August, 1 week Easter, Saturday lunch and bank holidays

Carte £31/47 s

Customer loyalty is the sine qua non of any successful restaurant; those seeking guidance on how to build it should get down to Barnes and learn from Andrea Riva. His secret is to shower so much attention on his regulars that all other diners sit imagining the day when they will be treated in the same way – when he will tell them what he's going to cook especially for them. That could be some milk-fed lamb, game, suckling pig or some risotto; all expertly rendered using tip-top, seasonal ingredients. While you wait for graduation, you'll be served by a friendly young female team and still get to enjoy some gutsy, flavoursome food. Andrea is also a keen wine collector so if you can talk oenology it could improve your chances of joining the club.

Sonny's

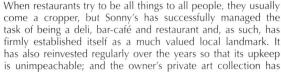

Modern European

S2

Barnes Closed Sunday dinner and bank holidays

94 Church Rd ✉ SW13 0DQ

✆ (020) 8748 0393

e-mail manager@sonnys.co.uk

www.sonnys.co.uk

Menu £16/19 – Carte £28/32

When restaurants try to be all things to all people, they usually come a cropper, but Sonny's has successfully managed the task of being a deli, bar-café and restaurant and, as such, has firmly established itself as a much valued local landmark. It has also reinvested regularly over the years so that its upkeep is unimpeachable; and the owner's private art collection has added to its personality. The restaurant menu is full of seasonal goodness, like pot-roasted pheasant to warm the bones in winter or tortellini of crab for lighter months. This being Not-the-West-End means portions are generously sized and there's a very smartly priced set menu for midweek. Meanwhile, staff display a warmth and confidence that belie their youthful looks.

Bolingbroke

Gastropub

U3

Battersea ⊖ Clapham Junction (Rail).

174 Northcote Rd ✉ SW11 6RE

✆ (020) 7228 4040

e-mail thebolingbrokepub@renaissancepubs.co.uk

www.thebolingbroke.com

Menu £19 – Carte £25/33

The influx of professionals with young families is such that this end of Northcote Road is now known as 'Nappy Valley'. A Cath Kidston shop? Check. Artisan food markets? Check. Antique emphoria? Check. Now it's time for a decent pub and here's where The Bolingbroke comes in. Its glass roof makes the fairly small dining room feel bigger, although the romantically inclined should ask for the table under the stairs. The menus change weekly, with more choice at dinner. British influences lead the way, from the asparagus and cheddar tart, to the lamb shoulder and apple crumble. Steaks and burgers are perennials but you'll also find additional Euro stars like ravioli and a niçoise salad. Unsurprisingly, there's also a children's menu.

Butcher & Grill

U2

Traditional

Battersea
39-41 Parkgate Rd ✉ SW11 4NP
✆ (020) 7924 3999
e-mail info@thebutcherandgrill.com
www.thebutcherandgrill.com

Closed 25-26 December, dinner Sunday and bank holidays

Menu £15 (weekdays) – Carte £17/43

There are times when only steak and chips will do and, for those times, there is The Butcher and Grill. This butcher's-cum-food emporium-cum-steakhouse has a touch of Manhattan's Meatpacking district about it, what with its former warehouse surroundings and general all-day buzz. Fortuitously, one of the owners has a farm in East Sussex from whence much of the produce comes. The meat counter tenders an impressive array, from homemade bangers to pig's trotters and fore ribs. Choose the grills on the menu: they range from lamb burgers to rib-eye, T-bone to pork chops; the chips are good and there are none of those irksome additional charges made for sauces. And there's no let-up with desserts: one chocolate brownie will feed two.

Chada

U2

Thai ✗✗

Battersea
208-210 Battersea Park Rd. ✉ SW11 4ND
✆ (020) 7622 2209
e-mail enquiry@chadathai.com
www.chadathai.com

Closed bank holidays and Sunday – (dinner only)

Carte £19/47

Chada, whose positively resplendent façade marks it out on Battersea Park Road, is still going strong after 20 years, although it doesn't face huge competition. A striking carved Buddha dominates the simply dressed room but check out the owner's gilded headdress, displayed in a cabinet, which she uses for festivals. This may never be the busiest restaurant around but the welcome is always warm, the service polite and endearing and the Thai cooking satisfying and keenly priced. The menu is still a very long affair but it's easy to navigate through and the seafood selection is an undoubted highlight. Several dishes can be made with a choice of chicken, duck, prawn or vegetables; portions are generous and presentation is appealing.

Ransome's Dock

British 🍴

Battersea

35-37 Parkgate Rd. ✉ SW11 4NP

✆ (020) 7223 1611

e-mail chef@ransomesdock.co.uk

www.ransomesdock.co.uk

Closed 25-26 December, August bank holiday and Sunday dinner

Carte £23/38

It's not just honest cooking and a great wine list that are responsible for the impending 20 year anniversary: owners Martin and Vanessa Lam's passion and palpable enjoyment have also contributed to the success. Their menu is underpinned by seasonality and careful sourcing: duck is from Devon; lamb from Elwy Valley; beef from Cornwall and fish from Essex day boats. They also know their butchery and have most beasts delivered whole, so you may find gutsy dishes like braised shin on the lunch menu. Martin is equally passionate about wine; not only is his wine list far-reaching and well-priced but he also hosts winemaker dinners. The converted warehouse has a relaxed feel; the terrace overlooking the canal is a great spot in summer.

Tom Ilić

Traditional 🍴

Battersea

123 Queenstown Rd. ✉ SW8 3RH

✆ (020) 7622 0555

e-mail info@tomilic.com

www.tomilic.com

Closed Christmas, 1 week August, dinner Sunday, lunch Tuesday and Monday – booking essential

Menu £17/22 – Carte £27/36

Serbian Tom Ilić came to the UK 20 years ago, took a job as a dish washer before a planned career in engineering, developed an interest in food and now has his own restaurant. He's chosen the site formerly occupied by The Food Room, which is an unpretentious, neighbourly place with closely set tables and a semi-open kitchen. It's also in an area of Battersea that's played host to a few famous restaurants in its day. His menu is written in a refreshingly straightforward way. There's plenty of offal featured as well as lots of pork, something of a beloved national dish for Serbs. Flavours are far from shy but his cooking also displays a certain graft and clear respect for the ingredients; prices are kept realistic.

Upstairs

U2

Brixton
89b Acre Ln. ⊠ SW2 5TN
📞 (020) 7733 8855
e-mail contact@upstairslondon.com
www.upstairslondon.com

⊖ **Clapham North**
Closed 24 December-7 January,
17-26 April, 14-30 August, Sunday and
Monday – (dinner only)

Menu £30

VISA
MC
AE

At the risk of upsetting the locals who clearly like the idea of having a hard-to-find, and thus almost secret, restaurant in their neighbourhood, you'll need to look for the buzzer on the side door next to the Opus coffee shop if you want to go Upstairs. You'll still be a little unsure as you climb the dark staircase, at least until you're greeted by the hospitable manager who'll offer you a drink in the bar; dining is then done on the next floor up. The set menu is a short affair, with just three choices per course plus the occasional special, but its price is fair. As one would expect from an alumni of Chez Bruce, the food is prepared with understanding and seasonal relevance; it is easy to eat, uncomplicated and flavoursome.

Charlotte's Bistro

S1

Chiswick
6 Turnham Green Terr. ⊠ W4 1QP
📞 (020) 8742 3590
e-mail bistro@charlottes.co.uk
www.charlottes.co.uk

⊖ **Turnham Green**
Closed 26 December
– booking advisable

Menu £15 – Carte £22/28

A/C
☀
VISA
MC

Unlike many desirable London neighbourhoods, Chiswick has always had plenty of restaurants, so locals never feel the need to venture too far from home for dinner. This little sister to nearby Ealing's Charlotte's Place provides them with another pleasantly unpretentious option. A large bar takes up most of the front section and then it's a few steps up to the bright dining room with a glass roof. The menu changes regularly and has a European accent, with such dishes as crab and celeriac tian, cod brandade, pan-fried halloumi, rolled leg of lamb and fishcakes. There's also a nice little cheese menu. Wines are listed by character and include bottles from some small producers. Service and prices are equally friendly.

High Road Brasserie

Traditional 🍴

S2

Chiswick
162 Chiswick High Rd ✉ W4 1PR
☎ (020) 8742 7474
e-mail reservations@highroadhouse.co.uk
www.highroadhouse.co.uk

⊖ **Turnham Green**
Booking essential

Carte £21/42

It's usually so busy you'll have trouble getting in the door – quite literally sometimes, as the entrance is often crowded with evening drinkers or lunchtime pushchairs. This modern take on the brasserie certainly has the look, with its mirrors, panelling and art deco lighting; turn right for the more comfy seating. Staff are used to being busy and get the job done, although without much time for pleasantries. What is surprising is that, despite the volume of customers, the kitchen is able to deliver a good standard of accurately cooked classics including steak frites, duck confit, grilled lobster or whole sea bass, along with salads and sandwiches. The bill can rise quickly as sides are required, but there's a good value daytime menu.

Michael Nadra

Modern European 🍴🍴

S1/2

Chiswick
6-8 Elliott Rd. ✉ W4 1PE
☎ (020) 8742 0766
e-mail info@restaurant-michaelnadra.co.uk
www.restaurant-michaelnadra.co.uk

⊖ **Turnham Green**

Menu £16 (lunch) – Carte £32/40

Tucked away from the more excitable restaurants on the High Street, Michael Nadra has been quietly and steadily going about the business of creating a very good restaurant. The result is that there are enough regulars now appreciating his cooking for him to have the confidence to finally put his own name above the door. Seafood remains an important part of his repertoire – crab tempura and monkfish with salmon mousse remain perennial favourites – but he now offers more meat dishes and there's a greater degree of sophistication to his cooking. Along with the fixed price menu is a very reasonable 7 course tasting menu, with suggested wine pairings. The restaurant has an intimate, local feel which is helped along by friendly staff.

Sam's Brasserie

S2

M e d i t e r r a n e a n ✗

Chiswick
11 Barley Mow Passage ✉ W4 4PH
✆ (020) 8987 0555
e-mail info@samsbrasserie.co.uk
www.samsbrasserie.co.uk

⊖ Turnham Green
Closed 24-28 December

Menu £18 – Carte £29/39

A/C
☀
VISA
MC
AE

In challenging financial times restaurateurs can either just sit and wonder where everyone's gone or they can take some action. Sam Harrison does the latter by sending out chatty monthly newsletters about wine or whisky tastings, bridge afternoons or book signings and by making sure his brasserie is fun. The building was once a Sanderson wallpaper mill and the industrial feel works well. Dining is on two levels; the mezzanine is the quieter one while the larger room looks into the kitchen and has plenty of bustle. Menus are seasonal and lean towards the Med; the food is fresh and flavoursome and service is young and keen. Puds are done well and most of the wine list is under £30. A jazz band plays every other Sunday. It is certainly fun.

Trinity

U2

I n n o v a t i v e ✗✗

Clapham
4 The Polygon ✉ SW4 0JG
✆ (020) 7622 1199
e-mail dine@trinityrestaurant.co.uk
www.trinityrestaurant.co.uk

⊖ Clapham Common
Closed 23-29 December, 2 January,
Monday lunch and Sunday dinner

Menu £25 (weekdays) – Carte dinner £28/51

A/C
VISA
MC
AE

Trinity is smarter and a little more formal than your average neighbourhood restaurant and residents of Clapham Old Town have clearly taken to it, especially as it means they don't have to schlep up to the West End for a 'proper' night out. The cooking is suitably sophisticated, with the kitchen adding some innovative combinations to what is a fairly classical base. Offal dishes are often the highlight and the pig's trotter on toasted sourdough has become a signature dish. The lunch menu is simpler in style and content but is priced very appealingly. To underline its neighbourhood credentials, the restaurant also offers cookery classes. In summer, ask for a table by the windows, which open up to add a little continental colour.

La Trompette ❀

Modern European

Chiswick
5-7 Devonshire Rd ✉ W4 2EU
✆ (020) 8747 1836
e-mail reception@latrompette.co.uk
www.latrompette.co.uk

⊖ Turnham Green
Closed 24-25 December and 1 January
– booking essential

Menu £24/40

La Trompette

Chiswick now makes regular appearances in those 'Don't you wish you lived here?' features that bulk up the weekend papers, thanks largely to its impressive number of restaurants and cafés. Chief among them is La Trompette, although many of its local regulars presumably hope its reputation doesn't spread too far, otherwise they'll never get a table. The interior is stylish and comfortable but also warm and relaxing, and there's usually a buzzy atmosphere. The menu may be a single sheet of A4 but everyone will find something on it that appeals. Dishes come and go as the seasons pass and, while there's a clear classic base, there are also other European influences exerted. Sauces are clearly a strength of the kitchen and there's refreshing lack of frippery to the dishes when they arrive at the table. The wine list is a weighty, leather-bound tome which offers a remarkably varied selection in both geography and price. The serving team's competence and friendliness enhances the experience still further.

First Course	*Main Course*	*Dessert*
• Pithiviers of quail and mushroom with sauce Soubise.	• Cod with shrimp vol-au-vent, celery and chives.	• White chocolate tart with raspberries and honeycomb.
• Mackerel with potato, bacon and mustard.	• Rump of beef with fondant potato, carrot and horseradish.	• Bramley apple crumble tart.

Tsunami

U2

Japanese %

Clapham
Unit 3, 5-7 Voltaire Rd
✉ SW4 6DQ
☎ (020) 7978 1610
e-mail clapham@tsunamirestaurant.co.uk
www.tsunamirestaurant.co.uk

⊖ Clapham North
Closed 24-26 December and 1 January
– (dinner only and lunch Saturday-Sunday)

Menu £11 (lunch) – Carte £18/41

A/C

☼

VISA

MC

Tsunami has always allowed Clapham residents to boast that they don't have to journey 'up west' if they want to eat modern Japanese food in stylish surroundings. After successfully opening a second branch in Charlotte Street – to perhaps prove that you can now find friendly neighbourhood restaurants in the West End too – the owners refurbished this, their original HQ, in 2009 so now it's even slicker and sexier than ever but also just as lively. The menu's focus is on modern, fusion food but there is an extensive nigiri and sashimi section. Sharing is positively encouraged and, as enticing aromas float through the room and the majority of dishes are visually appealing, you could find yourself diving in with Pavlovian enthusiasm.

Charlotte's Place

R1

Modern European %

Ealing
16 St Matthew's Rd. ✉ W5 3JT
☎ (020) 8567 7541
e-mail restaurant@charlottes.co.uk
www.charlottes.co.uk

⊖ Ealing Common
Closed 26 December-4 January

Menu £15 (weekday lunch) – Carte £24/34

It's been a sweet shop, a transport café and a private drinking club but has found its niche as an honest and warmly run local restaurant. The ground floor offers views over the Common so is popular at lunch; downstairs is more intimate and ideal for couples who only have eyes for each other. The à la carte offers ample choice and the cooking is largely British, with smoked fish, traditional Sunday lunches and homely puddings done well; there are also one or two Mediterranean influences and the beef onglet is a constant. There is a small cover charge but in this case it covers bread and unlimited supplies of filtered water, rather than being an accountant's wheeze for squeezing more money out of the customers.

Kiraku

Japanese

R1

Ealing
8 Station Par., Uxbridge Rd.
✉ W5 3LD
✆ (020) 8992 2848
e-mail mail@kiraku.co.uk
www.kiraku.co.uk

⊖ **Ealing Common**
Closed Christmas and New Year, 10 days
August, Tuesday following bank holidays
and Monday

Carte £15/33

The name means 'relax and enjoy' and it's hard not to. Ayumi and Erica became so frustrated with the lack of a decent local Japanese restaurant that they decided to open one themselves; and now it is not just the bourgeoning Japanese community who flock to this cute little place. It's modestly styled and enthusiastically lit, but service is very charming. The choice is extensive and there are photos for the uninitiated. Zensai, or starters, include the popular Agedashi dofu; these can then be followed by assorted skewers, noodles and rice dishes. Fish is purchased daily and there's a large selection of sushi; Bara Chirashi is the house speciality. There are further specials on the board and assorted bargain lunch menus.

Mango & Silk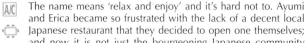

Indian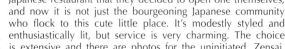

S2

East Sheen
199 Upper Richmond Rd. West ✉ SW14 8 QT
✆ (020) 8876 6220
www.mangoandsilk.co.uk

Closed Monday –
(dinner only and
Sunday lunch)

Carte £18/23

Mango and Silk welcomes you to "the mystic and exotica of classic Indian dining in a serene and peaceful surrounding" and you can't argue with that. Owner Radhika Jerath is a natural and charming hostess but, more importantly, she has persuaded Udit Sarkhel back to the stove. His reputation was sealed from the day he opened his eponymous restaurant in Southfields and his menu provides an exhilarating culinary tour of India. His cooking displays a lightness of touch, expert spicing and a respect for ingredients; the Hyderabadi Chicken Sixers are a speciality. That window on the kitchen works both ways: he likes to see his customers enjoying themselves. The prices are terrific and those are his paintings on the wall.

Victoria

British

S2

East Sheen
10 West Temple Sheen ✉ SW14 7RT
✆ (020) 8876 4238
e-mail bookings@thevictoria.net
www.thevictoria.net

⊖ Mortlake (Rail).
Closed 2 days between
Christmas and New Year

Carte £25/35

Many pubs claim to be genuine locals – The Victoria is the real deal: it sponsors local clubs and the chef is patron of the local food festival and holds cookery workshops at the school next door. This is a beautifully decorated pub, with a restored bar with a wood burning stove and plenty of nooks and crannies; a few steps down and you're in the more formal conservatory overlooking the terrace. The cooking is modern British with the odd international note. Warm homemade bread could be followed by Scotch egg with roast beetroot, cod with a white bean stew and, to finish, blood oranges with rhubarb sorbet. Produce is local where possible: veg is from Surrey and honey from Richmond. Service is engaging and there are simple bedrooms available.

Blue Elephant

Thai

T2

Fulham
4-6 Fulham Broadway ✉ SW6 1AA
✆ (020) 7385 6595
e-mail london@blueelephant.com
www.blueelephant.com

⊖ Fulham Broadway
Closed 25 December
and 1 January – booking essential

Menu £15/35 – Carte £32/50

This London institution shows what imagination and unrestrained ambition can lead to. There are plants and streams, pergolas and bridges and the place is about the size of a film set with a healthy budget - you half expect Indiana Jones to come through the undergrowth, machete in hand. It's sensibly divided into smaller sections so you'll have just as good a time if you're a table of two or have come with nine friends. Granted, the service can get stretched but the staff are a pleasant bunch. Dishes are a mix of classics from across Thailand and contemporary creations. The ingredients are good and the curries a strength. There's a cabinet by reception selling their own branded goods and recipes to remind you this is now a global chain.

Harwood Arms ✿

T2

Fulham
Walham Grove ✉ SW6 1QP
✆ (020) 7386 1847
e-mail admin@harwoodarms.com
www.harwoodarms.com

⊖ **Fulham Broadway.**
Closed 24-28 December, 1 January
and Monday lunch

Carte £28/32

Michelin

More chefs should eat here so they can see that great food doesn't always have to be served in lavish surroundings by formally dressed staff to whispering diners. The Harwood Arms is a proper, noisy pub and is just as welcoming to drinkers as it is to diners – it's just that the food is the sine qua non of the operation. While not wholly traditional pub food, it does provide appropriately robust flavours in reassuringly recognisable combinations. There are usually a couple of sharing dishes, such as shoulder of cider-braised Roe deer on the bone, and good use is made of great seasonal produce like Jersey Royals, Herefordshire snails and Berkshire pheasant. You'll also find it hard to resist the warm little doughnuts at the end. Prices are pleasingly down to earth when one considers the quality of the cooking; service is chatty and chummy and the place is as refreshingly uncomplicated as it looks from the outside. Even the bar snacks are thoughtfully prepared. Come on a Tuesday for Quiz Night.

First Course

- Herefordshire snails with oxtail and stout.
- Beer battered fillets of red mullet with peas, lettuce and shrimps.

Main Course

- Braised beef cheeks and celeriac purée.
- Sea bream with carrots, crab and chervil.

Dessert

- Camp coffee ice cream.
- Brown sugar baked custard with blood orange sorbet.

Manson

T2

Fulham
676 Fulham Rd. ✉ SW6 5FA
✆ (020) 7384 9559
e-mail enquiries@mansonrestaurant.co.uk
www.mansonrestaurant.co.uk

⊖ **Parsons Green**
Booking advisable

Menu £16 (lunch) – Carte £29/38

Manson is the second project from the team who brought us The Sands End. This time they have created a restaurant rather than a pub, but it too appears to have been an instant hit with the locals. Smoked mirrors and 1930s French street lamps give it a slightly lived-in, Left Bank aesthetic and the breezy service keeps things moving along nicely. However, there is a slight disparity between the relaxed look and feel of the place and the sophistication of its cooking. That's not to say the food is fussy or overblown, but is does display more ambition and creativity than one usually finds in Fulham. Excellent homemade breads kick things off and along with the refined dishes are a few more straightforward offerings like côte de boeuf.

Mao Tai

T2

Fulham
58 New Kings Rd.,
Parsons Green ✉ SW6 4LS
✆ (020) 7731 2520
e-mail mark.maotai@googlemail.com
www.maotai.co.uk

⊖ **Parsons Green**
Closed 25-27 December –
(dinner only and Sunday lunch)

Carte £38/54

Fulham residents clearly expect a certain standard from their local Chinese restaurant as they've remained loyal to Mao Tai for years. The modern menu uses influences from across China, ranging from Shanghai dumplings to Sichuan duck. Dim sum is also served at dinner and other Asian countries get a look-in too; the cooking is crisp and the natural flavours of the ingredients are apparent. It's not just the food that's a cut above the average: the restaurant is divided into two stylish rooms, with the front section being a little more animated as that's where the cocktail bar is found. Be aware of over-ordering as the final bill can easily mount up, but that's probably not too much of a concern for the locals.

Sands End

 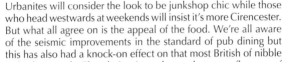

Gastropub

Fulham
135-137 Stephendale Rd ✉ SW6 2PR
☎ (020) 7731 7823
e-mail thesandsend@hotmail.co.uk
www.thesandsend.co.uk

⊖ Fulham Broadway.
Booking advisable

Menu £13 (lunch) – Carte £24/30

Urbanites will consider the look to be junkshop chic while those who head westwards at weekends will insist it's more Cirencester. But what all agree on is the appeal of the food. We're all aware of the seismic improvements in the standard of pub dining but this has also had a knock-on effect on that most British of nibble – the bar snack. The choice is no longer between flavours of crisps: here drinkers are offered homemade sausage rolls, Scotch eggs and Welsh rarebit soldiers. Those who prefer sitting when eating will also find much to savour from the concise menu. Snails come in garlic butter or as an accompaniment to rib-eye; steak and kidney pie sits alongside guinea fowl, and rice pudding competes for your attention with panna cotta.

Anglesea Arms

Gastropub

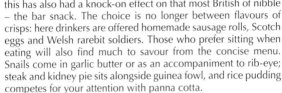

Hammersmith
35 Wingate Rd ✉ W6 0UR
☎ (020) 8749 1291
e-mail anglesea.events@gmail.com
www.anglesea-arms.com

⊖ Ravenscourt Park.
Closed 25 December –
(bookings not accepted)

Carte £17/46

Anglesea Arms proves that you can update a pub while still respecting its heritage. Its windows are etched with the inviting words 'Pies and Hams' and 'Stout and Oysters' and above the door is 'Mon Mam Cymru', Mother of Wales, as the Isle of Anglesey is known. The wood-floored, wood-panelled bar has a cluttered, lived-in feel and gets very crowded, so if you're in for eating head for the brighter rear dining room, with its part-glass ceiling and exposed kitchen. The blackboard menu might change between services and can be a little unbalanced with lots of starters, fewer mains and a limited number of puddings but the cooking is robust and has a strong British bias, with the likes of pig's head terrine, smoked eel and game featuring.

Azou

S2

Hammersmith
375 King St. ✉ W6 9NJ
✆ (020) 8563 7266
e-mail info@azou.co.uk
www.azou.co.uk

⊖ **Stamford Brook**
Closed 25-26 December – (dinner only)

Menu £15 – Carte £20/32

You'll probably walk past the first time and not notice this unassuming little place but, once visited, you won't walk past again. Inside is all silks, lanterns and rugs but it is also very personally run; the owner will often pop out from his kitchen to offer guidance – and his advice is well worth listening to. The cooking skips across North African countries – order some Algerian olives while you choose from the wide choice of main courses. Understandably, most of the regulars come here for a tajine, especially the Constantine with its tender lamb and triple steamed couscous. Highlights to start include the terrific baba ganoush with homemade bread and fresh briouat. It's the perfect food to share as the dishes come in large portions.

Carpenter's Arms

S2

Hammersmith
91 Black Lion Ln ✉ W6 9BG
✆ (020) 8741 8386
e-mail carpsarm@googlemail.com
www.carpentersarmsw6.co.uk

⊖ **Stamford Brook.**
Booking essential

Menu £16 (lunch) – Carte £30/55

The Carpenter's Arms is a civilised sort of place that doesn't look like much from the outside and indeed inside has made a virtue of its pared down, somewhat plain decorative style. Apart from allowing passers-by to have a good gawp in, the windows let in plenty of light during the day; while at night the gas fires make it cosier. The atmosphere is always convivial, helped along by the efforts made with the service. Despite the relatively compact size of the place, the menu is quite extensive and offers something for all tastes and appetites, from foie gras terrine to a bowl of soup; hotpot to halibut; ice cream to clafoutis. Add game in season and some Mediterranean flavours and you have a pub that knows how to satisfy its customers.

Dartmouth Castle

Gastropub

Hammersmith
26 Glenthorne Rd ⊠ **W6 0LS**
✆ (020) 8748 3614
e-mail dartmouth.castle@btconnect.com
www.thedartmouthcastle.co.uk

⊖ **Hammersmith.**
Closed 24 December to 1 January
and 2nd Monday in August

Carte £18/30

The view one way is of offices, the other, smart Victorian terraced houses, so this pub has to satisfy a wide variety of customers and their differing needs – and it does so with aplomb. Plenty just come in for a drink but you can eat on either of the two floors, although the ground floor has the better atmosphere, despite its somewhat over-enthusiastic lighting; just order at the bar and leave them your credit card. The Mediterranean exerts quite an influence on the large menu, whose prices are more than fair. Pasta dishes appear to come in two sizes – big or even bigger – and the antipasti dish for two is great for sharing over a bottle of wine. Sandwiches use ciabatta, and dishes like tiramisu or panna cotta finish things off nicely.

Havelock Tavern

Gastropub

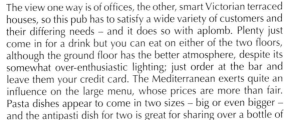

Hammersmith
57 Masbro Rd, Brook Grn
⊠ **W14 0LS**
✆ (020) 7603 5374
e-mail info@thehavelocktavern.co.uk
www.thehavelocktavern.com

⊖ **Kensington Olympia.**
Closed 25 December –
(bookings not accepted)

Carte £21/26

Head straight for the bar where smiley, somewhat dishevelled looking staff will organise a drink, open a tab and add your name to the list of those waiting for a table, which are allocated on a first-come-first-served basis. This actually appears to add to the atmosphere as everyone is forced to rub shoulders in the bar first, where you'll find bowls of pistachios and olives while you wait. The blackboard menu changes with each service and cooking is on the stout side so you're better off sharing a nibble like chipolatas and mustard or pickled quail egg, before choosing a pie or a steak; only if your appetite is really healthy will you have room for crumble and custard. The busier the place gets, the better the service.

335

Indian Zing

S1/2

Indian ✗✗

Hammersmith

236 King St. ✉ W6 0RF

✆ (020) 8748 5959

e-mail indianzing@aol.com

www.indianzing.co.uk

⊖ Ravenscourt Park

Menu £15 (lunch) – Carte £20/30

Many have warmed to Indian Zing and it's easy to see why. Chef-owner Manoj Vasaikar is so keen to see his customers satisfied that he has been known to send out an extra complimentary dish if he feels their order is not sufficiently balanced. He also reinvests everything back into the restaurant and has most recently added outside dining areas. While he is from Bombay, his cooking seeks inspiration from all over India; from sweet fish dishes to drier North Indian dishes or spicier Madras specialities; he is most proud of his 'feasts'. The restaurant is colourfully decorated and the close proximity of tables encourages conversations between customers. The serving team are equally keen but can sometimes appear a little disorganised.

Kew Grill

R2

Beef specialities ✗✗

Kew

10b Kew Grn. ✉ TW9 3BH

✆ (020) 8948 4433

e-mail kewgrill@awtrestaurants.com

www.awtrestaurants.com

⊖ Kew Gardens

Closed 25-26 December and

Monday lunch – booking essential

Menu £15 (lunch) – Carte £25/38

Busy, relaxed and fun are the hallmarks of these Antony Worrall Thompson neighbourhood joints specialising in meats. Top quality steaks come with a choice of a sauce or butter; there are daily specials like shepherd's pie or duck confit and even a section dedicated to AWT's pork. There are seasonal dishes like haunch of venison; fish-eaters and veggies are catered for and children aren't forgotten either. The cooking is heart-warming and unfussy, the aged beef really is excellent and the nursery puds will finish you off. The concise wine list offers a good selection by the carafe. It's all done in quite a narrow room with something of a country feel; the friendly staff help the atmosphere along nicely.

River Café ✿

Hammersmith
Thames Wharf, Rainville Rd
✉ W6 9HA
✆ (020) 7386 4200
e-mail info@rivercafe.co.uk
www.rivercafe.co.uk

Carte £49/78

⊖ **Barons Court**
Closed 25 December-1 January,
Sunday dinner and bank holidays
– booking essential

River Cafe

They should run a shuttle service from local catering colleges to the River Café so that the students can learn the secret of good cooking: good ingredients. There's a renewed vigour to the kitchen here after the last refurbishment and now that it's all opened up and on view there seems to be more of a relationship between cook and customer. The big wood-fired oven really catches the eye and the restaurant seems to attract a wonderfully mixed bunch of customers, united in their appreciation of what makes a restaurant tick. That includes charming service: on looks alone, the team can rival all those glossier, shallower impostors but they break ranks here by actually smiling and caring about their customers. The menu is still written twice a day and head chef Sian Wyn Owen has brought an added sparkle to the cooking. Things taste just the way you want them to taste. Ordering a pasta dish ought to be made compulsory and the Chocolate Nemesis dessert should be a recognised treatment for depression.

First Course

- Wood-roasted langoustines with chilli and lemon.
- Tagliarini with English porcini, thyme cream.

Main Course

- Slow roast veal shin with sage, polenta and Parmesan.
- Wood-roasted turbot with borlotti beans and red wine vinegar.

Dessert

- Panna cotta with grappa and raspberries.
- Pear and almond tart.

337

The Glasshouse ✿

Modern European ✗✗

R2

Kew
14 Station Par. ✉ TW9 3PZ
✆ (020) 8940 6777
e-mail info@glasshouserestaurant.co.uk
www.glasshouserestaurant.co.uk

⊖ **Kew Gardens**
Closed 24-26 December and 1 January

Menu £24/40

The Glasshouse

There are some restaurants where the style of food matches the setting perfectly and The Glasshouse is one such example. Despite opening on the eve of the new millennium, the bright and open interior still feels fresh and contemporary. Meanwhile, the seasonally informed cooking is as crisp and vibrant as ever. A seamless change of head chef has seen no drop in the general standard and the flavours are allowed to shine on each dish. The menu is a lesson in balance and the cooking is predominantly modern European but the kitchen is not averse to slipping in a few tastes of the East. Offal remains something of a highlight and wines are shrewdly recommended and graciously served. The service team are imbued with an unflappable confidence which, in turn, relaxes the room, although most of the customers appear to already have the imperturbable demeanour of those who know their food and recognise a decent restaurant when they see one. Reservations for weekends, when lunches are largely family affairs, need to be made about a month in advance.

First Course

- Ravioli of rabbit with spring greens and thyme.
- Tuna with radish, coriander, soy and sesame.

Main Course

- Monkfish and octopus with fennel and sauce antiboise.
- Poulet noir with gnocchi, leeks and tarragon.

Dessert

- Crème fraîche parfait with strawberry sorbet.
- Homemade yoghurt with cherry compote and madeleines.

Enoteca Turi

T2

Italian 🍴🍴

Putney
28 Putney High St. ⊠ SW15 1SQ
☎ (020) 8785 4449
e-mail enoteca@tiscali.co.uk
www.enotecaturi.com

⊖ **Putney Bridge**
Closed 25-26 December,
1 January, lunch bank holidays
and Sunday

Menu £19/30 – Carte £26/38

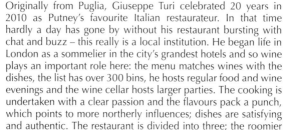

Originally from Puglia, Giuseppe Turi celebrated 20 years in 2010 as Putney's favourite Italian restaurateur. In that time hardly a day has gone by without his restaurant bursting with chat and buzz – this really is a local institution. He began life in London as a sommelier in the city's grandest hotels and so wine plays an important role here: the menu matches wines with the dishes, the list has over 300 bins, he hosts regular food and wine evenings and the wine cellar hosts larger parties. The cooking is undertaken with a clear passion and the flavours pack a punch, which points to more northerly influences; dishes are satisfying and authentic. The restaurant is divided into three; the roomier front section is the best place to sit.

Prince of Wales

T2

British 🍴🍺

Putney
138 Upper Richmond Rd ⊠ SW15 2SP
☎ (020) 8788 1552
e-mail info@princeofwalesputney.co.uk
www.princeofwalesputney.co.uk

⊖ East Putney.

Carte £30/40

You'll feel the warmth as soon as you enter. The bar, whose walls are lined with tankards, is usually packed with a mix of drinkers and diners, perhaps enjoying homemade scotch eggs or fish with triple-cooked chips; you'll feel as though you just want to join in the fun. There is a quieter space behind the bar but if you want something completely different then go down a few steps and you'll find a grand and lavishly kitted out baronial-style dining room. The daily changing menu is full of seasonality and diversity. Oysters, Asian salads or charcuterie can be followed by beef Bourguignon or some terrific game, and there's usually a great selection of ice creams to finish. Sunday lunch is a family affair, with spit-roast chicken a speciality.

Bingham Restaurant ❀

Modern European ✗✗

Richmond
61-63 Petersham Rd. ✉ TW1O 6UT
✆ (020) 8940 0902
e-mail info@thebingham.co.uk
www.thebingham.co.uk

Closed first week January
and Sunday dinner

Menu £23/45

Michelin

Chef Shay Cooper's cooking is assured and bold, but far from brash, and his dishes are prepared with skill and imagination. More importantly, there is nothing on the plate that's surplus to requirements – a sure sign of a chef's confidence in his own ability. If you want the full culinary experience, then go for the 7 course affair; if you're just after a relaxed lunch with friends there's a keenly priced set menu. That's another strength of The Bingham: it feels part of the local community and has lots of supporters and regulars in the neighbourhood who use it for a variety of different occasions. Perhaps its location – within a relatively unremarkable looking building –does it a favour as the restaurant has something of a 'hidden jewel' feel about it. The décor is surprisingly swish but, more importantly, it's comfortable. Come on a warm summer's day and you could find yourself having lunch on the balcony terrace, looking out over a garden and the Thames, and you don't get that everywhere.

First Course

- Calves sweetbreads with caper and raisin vinaigrette.
- Brill with scallop, lemon purée and aubergine compote.

Main Course

- Suckling pig with fennel, apple and pistachio.
- Thornback Ray with squid, glazed beetroot, celery and caper relish.

Dessert

- Passion fruit curd with blood orange sorbet.
- Hazelnut marquis with malt custard and butterscotch sauce.

Matsuba

Japanese

R2

Richmond
10 Red Lion St ✉ TW9 1RW
☎ (020) 8605 3513
e-mail matsuba.restaurant@gmail.com

Closed 25-26 December,
1 January and Sunday

Carte approx. £35

[AC] [VISA] [MC] [AE]

Matsuba is a small, family-run place that is so understated it's easy to miss – look out for the softly lit sign above the narrow façade. The interior is equally compact and low-key, with just a dozen or so tables along with a small counter at the back with room for four more. In fact the biggest thing in the room is the menu, which offers a comprehensive tour through most recognisable points in Japanese cooking. The owners are Korean so you can also expect to see bulgogi, the Korean barbecue dish of marinated meat that comes on a sizzling plate. All the food is fresh and the ingredients are good; lunch sees some very good value set menus. The service is well meaning and it's hard not to come away thinking kind thoughts.

The Restaurant at The Petersham

French XXX

R3

Richmond
Nightingale Ln. ✉ TW10 6UZ
☎ (020) 8940 7471
e-mail enq@petershamhotel.co.uk
www.petershamhotel.co.uk

Closed 24-26 December

Menu £25 (lunch) – Carte dinner £29/45

[AC] [VISA] [MC] [AE] [D]

From its vantage point on Richmond Hill, the Petersham Hotel, built in 1865, offers wonderfully unspoilt vistas of the Thames at its most majestic and, thanks to its large windows, diners at virtually all the tables in its restaurant can enjoy this great view. The advantages of dining within a hotel include the considerable elbow and leg-room: tables are well-spaced for added privacy and there's a comfortable lounge and bar, with its own terrace. Those understandably hesitant about dining within a hotel can rest assured that the room does have its own personality. The cooking displays a classical French education, but will also please those who prefer their culinary ambitions to be a little closer to home.

341

Petersham Nurseries Café

Italian influences ✗

R3

Richmond
Church Ln (off Petersham Rd)
✉ TW10 7AG
☎ (020) 8605 3627
e-mail info@petershamnurseries.com
www.petershamnurseries.com

Closed 23 December-12 January,
Monday and Tuesday – booking
advisable – (lunch only)

Carte £38/46

Michelin

Don't even think about driving – this plot of paradise should only be reached via a stroll along the river and across the fields – and allow time to wander around the nursery, because if you want to really appreciate lunch here then you have to buy into the Sunday supplement loveliness of it all. The Café is a moveable feast: it's on the terrace on summer days and in a greenhouse the rest of the time; the well-meaning service comes from grown-up versions of the Famous Five. Skye Gyngell's kitchen epitomises the 'less is more' maxim of the modern kitchen: it simply works with the best seasonal produce and lets natural flavours shine. Amalfi lemons are used for the jugs of lemonade; a glass of prosecco with rose syrup makes for the perfect aperitif. The menu is not overlong and there is an earthiness to the food that seems so right when you're eating among plants and flowers. It may not come cheap but neither do the ingredients. And don't wear the Manolo Blahniks – unless he's started designing wellies – as there's nothing but soil underfoot.

First Course	*Main Course*	*Dessert*
• Halibut brandade with polenta and basil.	• Beef fillet with white beans, chard and salsa verde.	• Almond tart with roasted peaches.
• Scallops with radicchio and red peppers.	• Sardines with sauce vierge.	• Chocolate mousse with ginger.

Swagat

R2

Richmond

86 Hill Rise ✉ TW10 6UB

☎ (0208) 940 7557

e-mail swagat.india@yahoo.co.uk

www.swagatindiancuisine.co.uk

⊖ Richmond
Closed 25-26 December and 1 January
– (dinner only)

Menu £30 – Carte £22/34

A/C

☀

VISA

MC

Richmond's nascent restaurant scene was given a boost by the arrival of Swagat, which translates as 'welcome'. With just 14 tables, it's best to book otherwise you'll find yourself in a queue with the locals. Its popularity is down to the attentive, very well-meaning service and the likeable menu, which aims to promote healthy eating by using less oil and more subtle spicing. You'll find plenty of classics but try the less recognisable dishes, like chicken Chettinad from southern India. Fortnightly changing specials add further interest, as do the moist breads, fresh chillies and the complimentary poppadoms and chutneys. Prices are also appealing and allow vegetarian dishes to be ordered as main courses or accompaniments.

Princess Victoria

S1

Shepherd's Bush

217 Uxbridge Rd ✉ W12 9DH

☎ (020) 8749 5886

e-mail info@princessvictoria.co.uk

www.princessvictoria.co.uk

⊖ Shepherd's Bush.
Closed 2 weeks at Christmas

Menu £15 (lunch) – Carte £22/32

A/C

🎭

☀

VISA

MC

From tramstop to live music venue, this magnificent Victorian gin palace has seen it all. A chef and a sommelier then took it over, gave it a top-to-toe revamp and the old girl has since had a whole new lease of life. The large dining room is dominated by a grand centre table. The stunning wine list has over 350 bottles, with a focus on Rhône, Pinot Noir and Riesling. Food-wise, it's a mix of classics, with the odd Asian or Mediterranean influence. The Pork Board starter, which includes pig's cheek and Bayonne ham, has become a favourite, and you'll always find the Angus rib-eye. Sausages are homemade and the kitchen knows its butchery. More nostalgia comes courtesy of the pudding menu, with the appearance of coupes and sundaes.

343

Simply Thai

R3

Teddington
196 Kingston Rd. ✉ TW11 9JD
☎ (020) 8943 9747
e-mail simplythai1@yahoo.co.uk
www.simplythai-restaurant.co.uk

Closed 25 December and Monday –
(dinner only)

Menu £25 – Carte £28/33

AC
☼
VISA
MC

The delightful owner, Patria Weerapan, made her television debut in 2010 when Simply Thai was featured in Gordon Ramsay's The F Word'. Her restaurant wasn't exactly quiet beforehand, but now it is positively heaving. Decoratively it's as modest inside as the unassuming façade suggests but everyone comes here for the food and forgives the occasional delay. She cooks everything fresh, from a bewilderingly large menu; dishes themselves are quite small so order one dish more than you think you need, which shouldn't be too difficult as the prices are far from high. Along with the new creations that are often being added to the menu are the favourites like spicy sweet pork, fishcakes, a refreshing trout salad and crisp deep-fried soft shell crab.

Kastoori

U3

Tooting
188 Upper Tooting Rd
✉ SW17 7EJ
☎ (020) 8767 7027
www.kastoorirestaurant.com

↔ Tooting Bec
Closed 25-26 December and
lunch Monday and Tuesday

Carte £14/19

There are plenty of neon lights vying for your attention on this strip and Kastoori doesn't necessarily stand out amongst them in the looks department. However, where it is head and shoulders above its near neighbours is in the originality of its food and the pride taken in its preparation. The Thanki family are originally from Uganda and celebrate their Gujarati heritage through their vegetarian cooking. Start with the Puri, or 'tastebombs' as they describe them, filled with chick peas and spices. The tomato curry remains a favourite, as do many of the 'family specials' and there is always a particularly wide selection of dishes on a Sunday. Staff are always on hand to offer advice or to explain the history of a dish.

A Cena

Twickenham
418 Richmond Rd. ⊠ TW1 2EB
📞 (020) 8288 0108
e-mail acenarichmond@gmail.com
www.acena.co.uk

⊖ **Richmond**
Closed 24-26 December,
1 January, Sunday dinner
and Monday lunch

Carte £19/37

A/C
VISA
MC
AE

Stroll past during the evening and the candlelight from the bar will draw you in. This relaxed but well-run Italian neighbourhood restaurant has a rustic yet quite intimate feel, with large mirrors, scrubbed floorboards and pew seating. The seasonal menus showcase the prime ingredients that the kitchen gets its hands on and dishes, some of which change daily, are vibrant, full of flavour and arrive in generous proportions. Wonderfully moist focaccia starts things off and, in spring for example, can be followed by asparagus and new season lamb with peas. Influences range across the country although they do host a regional evening every couple of months. The menu at lunch is a little lighter and prices are reduced.

Brula

Twickenham
43 Crown Rd., St Margarets ⊠ TW1 3EJ
📞 (020) 8892 0602
e-mail lawrence@brula.co.uk
www.brula.co.uk

Closed Christmas and Sunday dinner
– booking essential

Menu £18 (lunch) – Carte £28/38

VISA

MC
AE

Brula has already enjoyed its tenth birthday and this relative longevity can be put down to a combination of reliable cooking, sensible prices and personable service. This pretty Victorian building has been both a pub and a butcher's shop in the past but now thoroughly suits its role as an authentic looking bistro. France remains at the heart of the cooking but over the past couple of years other influences have started to appear on the menu, which is priced per course rather than per dish. Cooking is also more exact in its execution. The cheeses and the thoughtfully arranged wine list remain exclusively French. The friendly and helpful service also extends to those using one of the private rooms.

Tangawizi

R2

Twickenham
406 Richmond Rd., Richmond Bridge
✉ TW1 2EB
✆ (020) 8891 3737
e-mail tangawizi_richmond@hotmail.com
www.tangawizi.co.uk

⊖ **Richmond**
Closed 25 December –
(dinner only)

Carte £15/30

|A/C|
|☼|
|VISA|
|MC|
|AE|

Rich in colour and vitality, Tangawizi - meaning 'ginger' in Swahili – is another in the new breed of Indian restaurants. That means thoughtful design with clever use of silks and saris, attentive and elegant staff but, above all, cooking that is original, fresh and carefully prepared. North India provides much of the influence and although the à la carte menu offers plenty of 'safe' options, there are gems such as the roasted then stir-fried 'liptey' chicken. Diners should, however, head for the 'specials' section where the ambition of the kitchen is more evident. Lamb is another house speciality and is marinated to ensure it arrives extremely tender. For cooking this good, the prices are more than fair.

Light House

T3

Wimbledon
75-77 Ridgway ✉ SW19 4ST
✆ (020) 8944 6338
e-mail info@lighthousewimbledon.com
www.lighthousewimbledon.com

⊖ **Wimbledon**
Closed 25-26 December, 1 January and
Sunday dinner

Menu £15 (lunch) – Carte £24/34

|VISA|
|MC|
|AE|

The façade may have been smartened up but one's first impression is of being in a branded operation. Fortunately, that notion is quickly dispelled by the quality of the food. While they still have the odd Thai dish, it is in Italy where the majority of the menu and the kitchen's strength lie, with a roll call of favourites that include tagliatelle, gnocchi, saltimbocca and panna cotta. The food is wholesome and confident, with plenty of bold flavours. Prices at lunch and early evening are attractive, which ensures that it is often very busy. The result is that the young team can sometimes struggle to keep up, but they remain admirably calm and cheery. As this was once a shop selling lights and fittings, it is fittingly well lit.

Chez Bruce 🏵

French 🍴🍴

U3

Wandsworth
2 Bellevue Rd ✉ SW17 7EG
✆ (020) 8672 0114
e-mail enquiries@chezbruce.co.uk
www.chezbruce.co.uk

⊖ Tooting Bec
Closed 24-26 December and 1 January
– booking essential

Menu £28 (weekday lunch)/45

A/C
📺
🍇
☀
VISA
MC
AE

Chez Bruce

Not only did Chez Bruce weather the choppy waters of recession better than most but, in 2010, it finally expanded into the old deli next door. What this means for its merry band of dependable followers will hopefully be nothing more than 'business as usual,' as Chez Bruce had had a successful formula for years. That means flavoursome and uncomplicated food, sprightly service, sensible prices and an easy-going atmosphere. Matthew Christmas is the head man in the kitchen, having worked closely with Bruce Poole for over 10 years. His cooking provides an object lesson in the importance of flavours and balance: dishes are never too crowded and natural flavours are to the fore. The base is largely classical French but comes with Mediterranean tones, so expect words like parfait, pastilla, brandade and confit. The menu offers an even-handed selection, with a choice of around seven dishes per course. Cheese is always worth exploring and coffee comes with shortbread at lunch and terrific palmiers at dinner.

First Course	*Main Course*	*Dessert*
• Hake with courgette flower, escabèche of mackerel and coriander. • Chicken wings with snails and sweetbreads.	• Pork with choucroute, crispy belly and boudin blanc. • Sea bream with shellfish, bacon and sourdough crouton.	• Apricot and almond tart with amaretto ice cream. • Strawberry and basil trifle with lemon sorbet.

Where to **stay**

▶ *These 50 recommended hotels are extracted from the Great Britain & Ireland 2011 guide, where you'll find a larger choice of hotels selected by our team of inspectors.*

Andaz Liverpool Street

Liverpool St. ✉ EC2M 7QN   ⊖ Liverpool Street
📞 (020) 7961 1234
e-mail info.londonliv@andaz.com
www.andaz.com

264 rm – †£270/378 ††£300/408, ⌕ **£20 – 3 suites**

Andaz Liverpool Street

The 'Andaz' brand (which apparently means "personal style" in Hindi) belongs to Hyatt, and this former railway hotel, which once went by the less ambiguous name of the Great Eastern, was the London prototype before its export to New York and L.A. The idea is to create luxury hotels with a less structured and more informal feel. In practical terms this mostly means that instead of a reception desk you have staff wandering around the nearest thing they have to a lobby, armed with laptops. The hotel may not be quite as hip as they imagine but it does provide a comfortable and contemporary environment that has a palpable sense of individualism. The crisply dressed bedrooms use a slick red, white and black palette and mod cons are comprehensive and largely concealed. Those wanting to be fed and watered will find themselves almost overwhelmed by the choice: there's the traditional George pub, a cosy Japanese, a lively brasserie, stylish seafood with its own champagne bar and the eye-catching 1901.

The Arch

50 Great Cumberland Pl. ⊠ W1H 7FD ⊖ Marble Arch
✆ (020) 7724 4700
e-mail info@thearchlondon.com
www.thearchlondon.com

80 rm – ⸙£294 ⸙⸙£360/540, ⫰ £18.95 – 2 suites

The Arch

If God is in the detail, then The Arch shows touches of the divine. Fashioned out of a row of seven terrace houses and a couple of mews cottages, the hotel has been thoughtfully put together by people who have clearly stayed in a lot of places and who know what it takes to make them comfortable. For starters, the bedrooms offer an impressive list of extras such as HD TVs and internet radios; beds have oversized duvets so there's no nocturnal wrestling required to secure one's half; there are complimentary soft drinks and coffee; and some of the larger rooms not only have a TV in the bathroom but also have a pillow in the tub to make the watching of it more comfortable. The public areas are relatively compact but are smartly designed. The restaurant, which doubles as a champagne bar and is named after the dialling code from the '50s, has an easy-going menu, with a kitchen that makes good use of its wood fired oven. The Martini bar has discreet call buttons to summon service and interesting pieces of art are scattered liberally around the hotel.

REGENT'S PARK ▶ PLAN V

Aster House

3 Sumner Pl. ✉ SW7 3EE   ⊖ South Kensington
✆ (020) 7581 5888
e-mail asterhouse@btinternet.com
www.asterhouse.com

13 rm ☲ – ♦£96/216 ♦♦£240/300

Michelin

If you made a mathematical calculation to find the best location for a tourist in London, then chances are the X would mark a spot somewhere near Aster House on Sumner Place. You've got all the best museums within strolling distance; Hyde Park mere minutes away; all the famous shops and, above all, you're staying in a charming Victorian house in a typical Kensington street where people actually live rather than in a faceless hotel district. Mr and Mrs Tan keep the house commendably shipshape and are enthusiastic hosts. The bedrooms at the front of the house benefit from larger windows while those at the back are quieter and overlook the garden, but all boast fairly high ceilings and room to breathe. Wi-fi is available without charge in all the rooms, while L'Orangerie, a first floor conservatory looking down over Sumner Place, doubles as the breakfast room and guests' sitting room. Prices are also kept within the parameters of decency so bookings need to be made plenty of time in advance.

Athenaeum

116 Piccadilly ✉ W1J 7BJ   ⊖ Hyde Park Corner
✆ (020) 7499 3464
e-mail buntingc@athenaeumhotel.com
www.athenaeumhotel.com

145 rm – ♦£390 ♦♦£516, ☲ £27 – 11 suites

Athenaeum

The Athenaeum has such a high number of regular guests who treat it as a home from home that before the hotel undertook its radical refurbishment, it conducted a lengthy survey to find out what they wanted. Gone is the country house style of old and in its place has come a refreshing new look which blends all the latest mod cons with pastel shades and floor to ceiling windows. In these days of hidden charges, it's refreshing to find a hotel where the price of the room includes wi-fi, soft drinks from the mini-bar and a daily paper. The restaurant menu is appealingly down-to-earth and offers a decent selection of easy-to-eat classics with an English bent. The bar boasts over 250 bottles of whisky. Another striking feature of the hotel is its 'Living Wall', which is basically a vertical garden; this can be admired from the comfortable lounge, which does a brisk trade in afternoon tea. There are apartments for longer stays and those with children will appreciate the Kids' Concierge who will organise relevant activities.

MAYFAIR ▶ PLAN II

B + B Belgravia

64-66 Ebury St ✉ SW1W 9QD ⊖ Victoria
✆ (020) 7259 8570
e-mail info@bb-belgravia.com
www.bb-belgravia.com

17 rm ⌂ – **†£99 †† £170**

Michelin

It's really more Victoria than Belgravia and is certainly a degree more stylish than your average B&B. But what is certain is that B&B Belgravia provides very good value accommodation in a central location and is just the sort of place that London needs more of. The discreet entrance and key pad entry system make you feel as though you've borrowed a friend's place while the funky lounge comes complete with a complimentary coffee machine and plenty of magazines and DVDs. Breakfast is a buffet, with eggs cooked to order; those not good in the morning may find the staff's sunny demeanour and the room's general brightness akin to a second wake-up call. Rooms are virtually identical in style: they are contemporary in tone with sleek lines, high ceilings and good amenities. 6 of the 17 rooms have baths, the rest just showers. This being Central London, the rooms on the front can get a little noisy so ask for a room overlooking the gravelled garden at the back, such as Room 12. And do the booking in plenty of time as this place is understandably popular.

Berkeley

Wilton Pl. ✉ SW1X 7RL   ⊖ Knightsbridge
☎ (020) 7235 6000
e-mail info@the-berkeley.co.uk
www.the-berkeley.co.uk

189 rm – ♦£588/708 ♦♦£708, ⌂ £29 – **25 suites**

🍴**Marcus Wareing at The Berkeley and Koffmann's**
(See restaurant listing)

The Berkeley

You'd have thought that having Marcus Wareing's luxury restaurant on one side of the hotel would be enough, but the hotel then coaxed Pierre Koffman out of retirement and his restaurant now provides the bookend on the other side. In the middle you have the Blue Bar which is as cool as the name suggests and, on the other side of the lobby, the Caramel Room whose target audience is obvious when you consider that tea is called "Prêt-à-Portea" and the biscuits look like mini handbags. The most unique area of the hotel must be the 7th floor, with its roof-top pool, treatment rooms and personal training services to satisfy the most slavishly health-conscious traveller. By using a number of different designers, bedrooms have been given both personality and a sense of individualism; the most recent have softer, calmer colours and a lighter, more contemporary feel while the classic rooms feel richer, thanks to their deeper, more intense colours. All the rooms are immaculately kept and several of the suites have their own balcony.

BELGRAVIA ▶ PLAN IV

Blakes

D6

33 Roland Gdns. ⊠ SW7 3PF   ⊖ Gloucester Road
✆ (020) 7370 6701
e-mail blakes@blakeshotels.com
www.blakeshotels.com

33 rm – ♦£180/318 ♦♦£390/450, ☕ £25 – 8 suites

Blakes

To see Blakes at its best, one needs to up the financial ante and go for one of the stylish deluxe rooms with their towers of cushions, flowing drapes and luxury bathrooms. Room 5 comes all in white, which means it occupies the housekeeping department more than any other; Room 7 covers such an impressive acreage that entry-level bedrooms can suffer by comparison. The hotel was created by Anouska Hempel in the early '80s and remains a favoured pit-stop for those riding the celebrity circuit. All mod cons are there in the rooms but are just camouflaged and concealed – Anouska was clearly not too fond of TVs and other electronic paraphernalia as they must have got in the way of the overall design effect. Downstairs is a slick and stylish affair, from the dark and mysterious Chinese room and bar to the intimate restaurant with its Asian-influenced menu. There's a charming courtyard at the back and since these days the hotel is a little more welcoming to those who aren't staying, it now offers afternoon tea.

Brown's

Albemarle St. ✉ W1S 4BP   ⊖ Green Park

℘ (020) 7493 6020

e-mail reservations.browns@roccofortecollection.com

www.roccofortecollection.com

105 rm – ♦£312/474 ♦♦£354/540, ☲ £27 – 12 suites

Brown's

Opened in 1837 by James Brown, Lord Byron's butler, Brown's has a long and distinguished history and has been the favoured hotel of many a visiting dignitary: it was here that Alexander Graham Bell first demonstrated his telephone and The Kipling Suite is just one named after a former guest. It reopened in 2005 after a full face-lift, with Olga Polizzi personally overseeing the design and her blending of the traditional with the modern works well. The bedrooms have personality and reflect the character of the hotel, albeit with all of today's required gadgetry. One thing that has remained constant is the popularity of the afternoon teas – the selling point, apart from the pianist, is that the waiter replenishes all stands and pots without extra charge. The wood-panelled restaurant took slightly longer to bed in and now goes by the name of Hix at The Albemarle; the menu features British comfort food. The Donovan Bar is probably the hotel's best feature and celebrates the distinguished work of British photographer Terence Donovan.

MAYFAIR ▶ PLAN II

The Capital

22-24 Basil St. ⊠ SW3 1AT   ⊖ Knightsbridge
℘ (020) 7589 5171
e-mail reservations@capitalhotel.co.uk
www.capitalhotel.co.uk

49 rm – ♥£276/366 ♥♥£366, ⌑ £19.50 – 8 suites

The Capital

Celebrating 40 years in 2011, The Capital is one of London's most enduringly discreet and comfortable hotels and is thoroughly British in its feel. In all this time it has been owned by David Levin and it is this continuity which had lead directly to there only being five head chefs over this period. The restaurant is as elegant as ever, with a menu filled with classic British dishes and an extensive wine list that includes selections from the Levin's own winery in the Loire. Bedrooms remain classically chic and the contemporary embellishments are restrained and in keeping with the general atmosphere. Each floor is slightly different and uses designs from the likes of Mulberry, Ralph Lauren and Nina Campbell. What has always raised The Capital to greater heights than similarly styled hotels has been the depth and detail of the service. No one can walk through the small lobby without being greeted and the concierge is old-school in the best sense of the word and can arrange anything for anyone.

Charlotte Street

15 Charlotte St. ⊠ W1T 1RJ   ⊖ Goodge Street
✆ (020) 7806 2000
e-mail charlotte@firmdale.com
www.firmdalehotels.com

48 rm – ♦£276 ♦♦£384, ☕ £20 – 4 suites

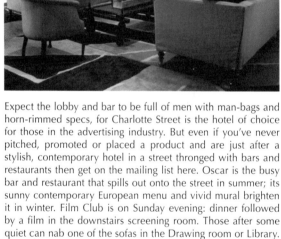

Firmdale

Expect the lobby and bar to be full of men with man-bags and horn-rimmed specs, for Charlotte Street is the hotel of choice for those in the advertising industry. But even if you've never pitched, promoted or placed a product and are just after a stylish, contemporary hotel in a street thronged with bars and restaurants then get on the mailing list here. Oscar is the busy bar and restaurant that spills out onto the street in summer; its sunny contemporary European menu and vivid mural brighten it in winter. Film Club is on Sunday evening: dinner followed by a film in the downstairs screening room. Those after some quiet can nab one of the sofas in the Drawing room or Library. The bedrooms are, as with all hotels in the Firmdale group, exceptionally well looked after. Every year, three or four are fully refurbished and one thing you'll never see is a bit of dodgy grouting or a scuff mark. They are all decorated in an English style but there is nothing chintzy or twee about them. Bathrooms are equally immaculate and the baths now face little flat screen TVs.

Claridge's

G3

Brook St ⊠ W1K 4HR ⊖ Bond Street
☎ (020) 7629 8860
e-mail info@claridges.co.uk
www.claridges.co.uk

143 rm – ♦£732 ♦♦£732, ☄ £29 – 60 suites

🍴**Gordon Ramsay at Claridge's** *(See restaurant listing)*

🍴
⅙
🛗
♿
A/C
((•))
SAT
👤
VISA
MC
AE
①

Claridge's

Stand in the lobby looking bewildered and, before you know it, a liveried member of staff will appear promptly before you to enquire after your well being; Claridge's may have a long and very illustrious history but it recognises that reputations are forged because of service rather than longevity. That being said, no modern, purpose-built hotel could afford the extravagance of having such wide corridors or such ornate decoration. The art deco is perhaps the hotel's most striking decorative feature and it's kept suitably fresh and buffed. Despite its long and glittery past, Claridge's has never been in danger of being a museum piece; the David Collins designed bar attracts a more youthful crowd and The Foyer, with its eye-catching light sculpture, proves that afternoon tea need not be a stuffy or quaint affair. The Gordon Ramsay restaurant continues to pull in the punters and the people-watchers. Further bedrooms and other guest facilities are to be added over the next few years and the challenge will be to make this extension as seamless as possible.

Connaught

Carlos Pl. ⊠ W1K 2AL   ⊖ Bond Street
☏ (020) 7499 7070
e-mail info@the-connaught.co.uk
www.the-connaught.co.uk

95 rm – ♦£660 ♦♦£780, ☲ £30 – 26 suites

🍽**Hélène Darroze at The Connaught** *(See restaurant listing)*

The Connaught

The new bedrooms were the final piece of the renovation jigsaw which has seen The Connaught restored to its original splendour and, no doubt, to a level far beyond. These rooms are more contemporary in style, with wooden floors, leather worked into the soft furnishings and larger marble bathrooms; some overlook a small oriental garden, others some mews houses. All bedrooms offer a full butler service, use linen specially woven in Milan and toiletries from Daylesford, and the Aman spa offers a whole range of treatments. The Coburg Bar honours the hotel's original name and its seats are so deep, it's a wonder anyone ever leaves. In contrast, the Connaught Bar attracts a more youthful and sprightlier clientele than the one hitherto associated with the hotel. Hélène Darroze oversees the main restaurant with her refined French cooking, while Espelette is an all-day venue just off the main lobby that offers a weekly changing list of classic French and British dishes. If you need anything else, just consult one of the hotel's 300 members of staff.

Covent Garden

13

10 Monmouth St. ✉ WC2H 9HB ⊖ Covent Garden
✆ (020) 7806 1000
e-mail covent@firmdale.com
www.firmdalehotels.com

56 rm – †£288 ††£408, ☕ £21 – 2 suites

Firmdale

The Covent Garden Hotel has always been hugely popular with those of a theatrical bent, whether cast or audience member, not least because of its central location, a mere saunter away from the majority of playhouses and productions. The hotel was once a French hospital – the words 'Nouvel hopital et dispensaire francais' are etched into the brickwork – but the style is essentially British. Mannequins, soft fabrics and antique furniture are juxtaposed with crisp lines and contemporary colours to create a very stylish and comfortable environment. The first floor residents-only wood-panelled sitting room is a delight and so is occasionally used by a visiting grandee for a backdrop to an interview; the presence of an honesty bar adds further to the appeal. The Screening Room holds weekend dinner-and-a-film nights, while Brasserie Max feels much more like a proper restaurant than a mere addendum, having been extended in 2008. Its menu is appealingly accessible and afternoon tea is now also provided.

Dorchester

Park Ln. ✉ W1K 1QA   ⊖ Hyde Park Corner
✆ (020) 7629 8888
e-mail reservations@dorchester.collection.com
www.thedorchester.com

196 rm – ♦£258/906 ♦♦£318/906, ☕ £31.50 – 54 suites

🍴**Alain Ducasse at The Dorchester** and **China Tang**
(See restaurant listing)

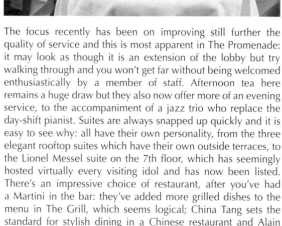

The Dorchester

The focus recently has been on improving still further the quality of service and this is most apparent in The Promenade: it may look as though it is an extension of the lobby but try walking through and you won't get far without being welcomed enthusiastically by a member of staff. Afternoon tea here remains a huge draw but they also now offer more of an evening service, to the accompaniment of a jazz trio who replace the day-shift pianist. Suites are always snapped up quickly and it is easy to see why: all have their own personality, from the three elegant rooftop suites which have their own outside terraces, to the Lionel Messel suite on the 7th floor, which has seemingly hosted virtually every visiting idol and has now been listed. There's an impressive choice of restaurant, after you've had a Martini in the bar: they've added more grilled dishes to the menu in The Grill, which seems logical; China Tang sets the standard for stylish dining in a Chinese restaurant and Alain Ducasse provides luxury surroundings to match the food.

MAYFAIR ▶ PLAN II

Dorset Square

39 Dorset Sq ⊠ NW1 6QN   ⊖ Marylebone
☎ (020) 7723 7874
e-mail reservations@dorsetsquare.co.uk
www.dorsetsquare.co.uk

37 rm – †£120/240 ††£174/336, ☞ £15

Dorset Square

Many die-hard cricket enthusiasts have, no doubt, made pilgrimages over the years to Dorset Square as this small piece of land was where Thomas Lord laid out his original ground in 1787, before it moved up the road in 1814 to what is now Lord's. The Dorset Square hotel overlooking this sacred turf is a pretty Regency house and the cricket link is maintained with assorted memorabilia, along with the occasional MCC member, scattered around the place. There's a pleasant drawing room with its own honesty bar at the front of the house, while the little basement Italian restaurant has a separate street entrance which makes it feel more self-contained. Here you'll find an accessible menu and live jazz on a Friday night. The bedrooms are spread over four floors and vary in size: there are six small single rooms but also two large four-poster rooms. They all share fine country style fabrics and bags of character and their sloping lintels bear testament to the age and character of the house. The pleasant staff add to the charm.

Draycott

26 Cadogan Gdns ⊠ SW3 2RP   ⊖ Sloane Square
☎ (020) 7730 6466
e-mail info@draycotthotel.com
www.draycotthotel.com

35 rm – ♦£156/312 ♦♦£251/312, ☕ £20.95 – 11 suites

Draycott

The sitting room is one of the best things about The Draycott, especially when the light streams in from the garden outside. It also has a well stocked bar and offers guests complimentary tea at 4pm, champagne at 6pm and hot chocolate at 10pm. This is a discreet little townhouse, decorated more like a country house. The bedrooms have plenty of personality themselves; six have fireplaces and all have an Edwardian feel to their decoration. Each is named after an acting legend about whom you'll find a biography or assorted pictures within the room, be it Vivien Leigh or John Gielgud. The breakfast room is called the Peter O'Toole Room; the name was apparently chosen in a staff competition although he's not a man one would necessarily associate with an early morning meal. Not many hotels have individual guest books in each room and write the names of the occupants on cards outside the door, but The Draycott has always done things 'properly' and its sincere hospitality ensures a very healthy number of returning guests.

CHELSEA ▶ PLAN XI

Dukes

H4

35 St James's Pl. ⊠ SW1A 1NY   ⊖ Green Park
℘ (020) 7491 4840
e-mail bookings@dukeshotel.com
www.dukeshotel.com

84 rm – †£234/530 ††£414/689, ☐ £22 – 6 suites

Dukes

As St James's is one of the more traditionally British parts of London, what with all those gentlemen's clubs, wine merchants and tailors, it is no surprise to find that a hotel like Dukes has been a constant presence here for over 100 years. But that is not to say this is some sort of crusty old museum piece: its most recent refurbishment gave it a fresh and brighter feel and introduced more modern elements without losing any of the character. For example, the pretty little sitting room, popular for afternoon tea, opens out into a small Zen-inspired garden. The bar is quite clubby and was apparently one of Ian Fleming's old haunts and the basement dining room, with its international menu, actually looks out at street levels thanks to the vagaries of local topography. Breakfast is served until the thoroughly louche hour of 11am. Bedrooms are comfortable and discreet and bathrooms are kitted out in marble. This is still the sort of hotel where you can leave your shoes outside the door for cleaning. It is also surprisingly peaceful, when you consider the central location.

Egerton House

17-19 Egerton Ter. ⊠ SW3 2BX   ⊖ South Kensington
✆ (020) 7589 2412
e-mail bookeg@rchmail.com
www.egertonhousehotel.com

27 rm – ♦£282/318 ♦♦£306/390, ⊇ £25 – 1 suite

Egerton House

In challenging economic times hotels can either panic and cut staff and slash rates – a course of action which usually ends in ruin – or they can hold their nerve and add greater value to their guests. Anyone wondering what more a hotel can do should get along to Egerton House. This is a hotel whose decorative style is at the lavish end of the scale; the fabrics are of the highest order and the colours neatly coordinated. The ground floor Victoria and Albert Suite comes with its own little decked terrace and a row of filled decanters for company. All the rooms are slightly different; the marble bathrooms are very neat and the hotel has made the best use of limited space – ask for one of the quieter rooms at the back overlooking the little garden. What really makes this little hotel stand out, though, is the service and the eager attitude of the staff. Lots of hotels spout tosh about being 'a home from home' but here they do make a genuine effort to make their guests feel part of things by, for example, arranging complimentary admission to events at the V&A.

CHELSEA ▶ PLAN XI

367

The Gore

D5

190 Queen's Gate ⊠ SW7 5EX   ⊖ Gloucester Road
✆ (020) 7584 6601
e-mail reservations@gorehotel.com
www.gorehotel.com

50 rm – †£207 ††£242, ⌷ £16.95

The Gore

Being the nearest hotel to the Royal Albert Hall makes The Gore a popular choice for performers as well as attendees and the bright, casual bistro is always busier early and late in the evening than it ever is at 8pm. The hotel clearly stands out at the top of Queen's Gate with its fluttering Union flag and gleaming brass plaque and who needs a fitness room when you've got Kensington gardens just yards away. If you were in any doubt that this is the part of London most closely associated with Queen Victoria, then just step through the door because the walls are covered with pictures and paintings relating to her reign. But, despite the plethora of antiques and all that Victoriana, this is a hip little hotel with a large element of fun attached. Rooms like Miss Fanny and Miss Ada are as camp as they sound; the Tudor Room has a secret bathroom and minstrel's gallery and many of the bathrooms give meaning to the expression 'sitting on the throne'. Bend down in the rooms and you might find a card saying "Look, we've cleaned here too".

The Goring

H5

15 Beeston Pl, Grosvenor Gdns ✉ SW1W 0JW   ⊖ Victoria

📞 (020) 7396 9000

e-mail reception@thegoring.com

www.thegoring.com

65 rm – †£492/570 ††£550, ⚏ **£25 – 6 suites**

The Goring

Not only did The Goring celebrate its centenary in 2010, but it is still owned by the family who built it. Jeremy Goring, the great-grandson of the founder, is now at the helm and this lineage is clearly welcomed by the staff – many of whom have been working at the hotel for years – as well as being appreciated by regular guests, who benefit from the excellent service. The hotel still has a pervading sense of Britishness, which designers like Nina Campbell fully respected when they were asked to update its look. There has been a clever introduction of new technology, from the TVs that rise from the desk to the touch panels that control everything but, reassuringly for those less familiar or enamoured with the modern world, one can still get a proper key with which to open one's bedroom door. The ground floor restaurant is a bright, discreet and comfortable affair and its menu celebrates Britain's own culinary heritage; the bar is colonial in its feel and the veranda overlooks the hotel's surprisingly large back garden.

VICTORIA ▶ PLAN IV

Halkin

G5

5 Halkin St ✉ SW1X 7DJ ⊖ Hyde Park Corner
✆ (020) 7333 1000
e-mail res@halkin.como.bz
www.halkin.como.bz

35 rm – †£348/600 ††£348/600, ☕ £27.50 – 6 suites

Nahm *(See restaurant listing)*

A/C SAT VISA AE

Halkin

The Halkin is still looking pretty sharp considering it opened nearly 20 years ago as one of London's first boutique hotels. It's certainly more discreet than its sibling, The Metropolitan, which attracts a livelier and feistier crowd, although guests here can use its spa. Apart from the relatively recent addition of a small gym, there is not much in the way of public areas, save for the small but perfectly formed bar area next to the lobby, and Nahm, the hotel's acclaimed and inventive Thai restaurant. The hotel is really all about the bedrooms, which are neatly set out and cleverly thought through. The touch pad operation makes everything seem so effortless but the technology never reaches baffling proportions. All rooms have silk covered walls and marble bathrooms with lots of natural minerals; the Nahm menu is also available as room service. Staff are in abundance and appear to stay for a long time, which improves standards of service no end and pleases the regulars. They also all wear Armani, so no pressure there, then.

Hart House

F2

51 Gloucester Pl. ✉ W1U 8JF ⊖ Marble Arch
✆ (020) 7935 2288
e-mail reservations@harthouse.co.uk
www.harthouse.co.uk

15 rm ⌷ – ♦£89/135 ♦♦£125/150

Michelin

Hart House has been in the same family for nearly 40 years and while the owner may not spend as much time in the hotel as he used to, he's got enough friendly staff running the place in his absence. Equally importantly, he's also still writing the occasional cheque, as the recent introduction of new LCD TVs would testify. The hotel wouldn't win any design awards but what you get, for a fair price, is clean and tidy accommodation in a late Georgian terrace house that's in a useful central location: it's just a short walk from Oxford Street and Hyde Park and less than a ten minute cab ride from Paddington for those who've taken the Heathrow Express. Gloucester Place may be a fairly busy thoroughfare but the bedrooms on the front have sufficient double glazing; there are family rooms available as well as rooms on the ground floor. Ceilings get lower the higher you climb, reflecting the time when the house's staff had their quarters at the top of the house. The only public area is the small, basement breakfast room but the hotel still manages to have a sociable, international atmosphere.

Haymarket

14

1 Suffolk Pl. ✉ SW1Y 4HX ⊖ Piccadilly Circus
✆ (020) 7470 4000
e-mail haymarket@firmdale.com
www.firmdalehotels.com

47 rm – ♙£396 ♙♙£396, ⌂ **£19.50 – 3 suites**

Firmdale

It's hard to believe that The Haymarket hotel opened back in 2007 – you would think it no more than a few months ago, which is testament to its housekeeping department. The hotel is a stylish, hip place, fashioned out of a grand John Nash Regency building that had been a gentleman's club and office before being gutted by a fire. Art and an eclectic collection of furniture now run through it; the lobby, conservatory and library are immaculately decorated and set the tone. No two rooms are the same but all come with dressed mannequins – the motif of the Kemp's hotels – and custom-made furniture. Those on the front could be used to advertise double-glazing but for extra quiet, ask to overlook the inner decked courtyard. The location couldn't be better: theatre-land is literally just outside – indeed, the hotel adjoins the Haymarket theatre – and all that London offers is a short stroll away. If that isn't enough, there's a very cool swimming pool downstairs, just for residents. Brumus is the spacious restaurant serving easy, Italian food.

Hazlitt's

13

6 Frith St ✉ W1D 3JA ⊖ Tottenham Court Road
✆ (020) 7434 1771
e-mail reservations@hazlitts.co.uk
www.hazlittshotel.com

29 rm – ♦£149/230 ♦♦£169/230 – 3 suites

Hazlitt's

Along with its central Soho location, one of the best features of Hazlitt's has always been its intimate and chummy atmosphere, which even the addition of eight rooms in 2009 failed to disrupt. The building dates from 1718 and was named after the essayist and critic William Hazlitt, whose home it was. Appropriately, it still attracts plenty of writers today, but while there is much character to be found in all the bedrooms, from the wood panelling and busts to the antique beds and Victorian fixtures, you do also get free wi-fi. Duke of Monmouth is the most striking of the newer rooms: it's spread over two floors and has its own terrace with a retractable roof. Madam Dafloz, named after another of Soho's former roguish residents, is also appealing, with a sultry, indulgent feel. The Library, with its 24/7 honesty bar, is the hotel's only communal area and was slightly enlarged when the newer rooms were added. This is also one of the few hotels where breakfast in bed really is the only option – and who is going to object to that?

SOHO ▶ PLAN II

The Hempel

31-35 Craven Hill Gdns. ✉ W2 3EA ⊖ Queensway
𝒞 (020) 7298 9000 Closed 24-28 December
e-mail info@the-hempel.co.uk
www.the-hempel.co.uk

44 rm – 👤£219/334 👥£219/334, ☕ £21.50 – 6 suites

The Hempel

It's no surprise that The Hempel stands out in this part of town – on any given day you can walk past tourists with faces that tell of the disappointment and distress caused by staying in one of the terrible local hotels. This hotel remains true to the principles of its original designer, Anouska Hempel, who, in the late '90s, created a crisp, minimalist environment in a blizzard of white; the maintenance man must get through gallons of white emulsion to keep it looking fresh. Room 107 boasts one of the highest ceilings in London; there's a suspended bed in 110 and those who prefer black should ask for 405. As newer design-led hotels have sprouted up, so everyone has had to raise their game – The Hempel is no exception and these days is not quite so self-satisfied which, in turn, makes it feel more welcoming. The restaurant has also been moved to the ground floor and the menu changed to a more British affair. Its former space downstairs is now used as an art gallery and for private parties.

K + K George

1-15 Templeton Pl. ⊠ SW5 9NB   ⊖ Earl's Court
✆ (020) 7598 8700
e-mail hotelgeorge@kkhotels.co.uk
www.kkhotels.com

154 rm ⚏ – ♦£264 ♦♦£264/336

K&K Hotels

Providing a model lesson on the importance of keeping on top of your product, The K+K hotel spent time during the recent economic turndown refurbishing all its bedrooms; they now boast fast internet, 320 thread count linen, American cherry wood panelling, flat screen TVs, full minibars, and under-floor heating in the bathroom; and the hotel is reaping the rewards. It occupies seven houses of the stucco fronted terrace; its interior in contrast to the period façade, is colourful and contemporary and fresh flowers and bowls of fruit are scattered around the lobby. The unexpectedly large rear garden, for which most hotels would give their eye teeth, has won local horticultural prizes and hosts breakfast on warm summer days. A simple menu is served in the bar but most guests take advantage of the central location and go out to eat. The hotel may be part of an international chain but there are plenty of staff on hand to add a personal touch and it also manages to feel part of the local community.

Knightsbridge

10 Beaufort Gdns ⊠ SW3 1PT   ⊖ Knightsbridge
📞 (020) 7584 6300
e-mail knightsbridge@firmdale.com
www.knightsbridgehotel.com

44 rm – 🚹£204 🚻£372, ⌣ £17.50

Firmdale

Firmdale Hotels all seem so quintessentially British that it'll be interesting to see what New Yorkers make of them now they have one of their own. The Knightsbridge, converted from a row of Victorian terrace houses in an attractive square, is another typical example of what they do so well: it proves style and comfort are not mutually exclusive and that a hotel can be fashionable without being fuzzy. The work of British artists, such as Carol Sinclair's slate stack and Peter Clark's dog collages sets the tone and the bedrooms are constantly being refreshed and rearranged. Those facing the square on the first floor benefit from floor to ceiling windows, while the Knightsbridge Suite stretches from the front to the back of the building. All rooms are so impeccably tidy and colour coordinated it'll make you question your own dress sense. The Library Room differs from many similarly named hotel sitting rooms by actually containing books, along with an honesty bar which holds everything from fruit and champagne to snacks and ice cream.

Lanesborough

G4

Hyde Park Corner ⊠ SW1X 7TA ⊖ Hyde Park Corner
𝄢 (020) 7259 5599
e-mail info@lanesborough.com
www.lanesborough.com

86 rm – ♦£450/594 ♦♦£594, ⌷ £30 – 10 suites

🍴**Apsleys** *(See restaurant listing)*

The Lanesborough

Many of London's luxury hotels boast long and illustrious histories and have names that are recognised the world over. Having opened in relatively recent 1991, The Lanesborough still feels like something of a beginner, but there is no doubt that it deserves its place among the top tier of London hotels. Constructed in 1733 as Viscount Lanesborough's country house, the building was perhaps better known as a hospital before it was converted into a hotel. A series of drawing rooms are smartly kitted out; the clubby library bar offers a vast selection of whiskies and cognacs and the Garden Room provides a hugely popular sanctuary for cigar smokers. Apsleys is their lavishly dressed Italian restaurant with superlative cooking. Bedrooms come in a rich and decorative Regency style and boast a host of extras, including laptops. There's a butler on each floor, on call 24 hours a day, and rooms are tripled-glazed. Ask for a room facing Hyde Park – you may not hear anything of the outside world but you can enjoy some pretty terrific views.

BELGRAVIA ▶ PLAN IV

Langham

H2

1c Portland Pl., Regent St. ✉ W1B 1JA ⊖ Oxford Circus
✆ (020) 7636 1000
e-mail lon.info@langhamhotels.com
www.langhamhotels.com

359 rm – †£192/225 ††£446/675, ☕ £30 – 21 suites

Langham

When it opened in 1865, The Langham was one of Europe's first purpose-built Grand hotels. Over the years it has been owned by all sorts, including at one stage the BBC – they used it as their library and it is also where 'The Goon Show' was recorded. In 2009 it came out of an extensive refurbishment that didn't provide much change from £80million and is now competing with the big boys once again. Pride of place must be the Palm Court, a twinkling ersatz art deco space which is open for light meals and afternoon teas. The Artesian bar is a stylish affair and does interesting things with rum while, next to it, is The Landau restaurant: an impressive looking circular room with a contemporary menu. The bedrooms have personality and, for a change, the furniture is free-standing rather than fitted. The lighting is good and the bathrooms have under-floor heating. The Club rooms are particularly distinctive, with their bold colours and high ceilings. The health and fitness club is impressively kitted out and includes a swimming pool.

The Levin

28 Basil St. ⊠ SW3 1AS   ⊖ Knightsbridge

𝒞 (020) 7589 6286

e-mail reservations@thelevin.co.uk

www.thelevinhotel.co.uk

12 rm ⌇ – **♦£342 ♦♦£438**

The Levin

Its bigger sister, The Capital, is a few strides down the road and may be better known, but The Levin still does the (Levin) family proud. Here you'll find a different decorative style but still the same level of care and enthusiasm in the service. The eye-catching fibre optic chandelier dominates the staircase, while the collection of Penguin paperbacks reminds you that this is a fundamentally British hotel. All 12 bedrooms are light and fresh-feeling; there are subtle nods in the direction of art deco in the styling but these are combined with a cleverly contemporary look which blends in well with the building. The best room is the top floor open-plan suite. Mini-bars are stocked exclusively with champagne - along with some helpful hints on how to prepare an assortment of champagne cocktails. In the basement you'll find Le Metro which provides an appealing, all-day menu with everything from quiche and salads to shepherd's pie and sausage and mash, along with selections from the family estate in the Loire.

CHELSEA ▶ PLAN XI

Mandarin Oriental Hyde Park

F4

66 Knightsbridge ✉ SW1X 7LA   ⊖ Knightsbridge
✆ (020) 7235 2000
e-mail molon-info@mohg.com
www.mandarinoriental.com/london

173 rm – ♦£666/750 ♦♦£666/750, ☕ £29 – **25 suites**

🍴 **Bar Boulud** *(See restaurant listing)*

Mandarin Oriental Hyde Park

The bewilderingly expensive new apartments next door have now been completed so things should quieten down in this part of town for a while. That said, there has also been plenty of work done on the hotel during this period. Bar Boulud, celebrated New York based chef Daniel Boulud's first European venture, opened in what was previously the hotel's housekeeping storeroom and proved a hit from day one; and as we go to print, Heston Blumenthal is expected to open his London operation here too, which should have the phones ringing off their hooks. The hotel's bedrooms are continually being upgraded and all offer every imaginable luxury and extra. They are decorated in a classic English country house style and come in either beige and blue or red and gold – although the TVs do seem to be incongruously large. If evidence were still needed that the hotel is keen to remain one of the most luxurious hotels in the capital, it comes in the fact that in 2010 it spent a mere £1million just on doing up its Royal Suite.

Mayflower

C6

26-28 Trebovir Rd. ⊠ SW5 9NJ   ⊖ Earl's Court

𝄐 (020) 7370 0991

e-mail info@mayflower-group.co.uk

www.mayflowerhotel.co.uk

43 rm – 🛉**£107/144** 🛉🛉**£138/180,** ☕ **£10 – 4 suites**

Mayflower

The Mayflower shares the same ownership as Twenty Nevern Square just around the corner and it too offers good value accommodation. It is also twice the size so chances of actually getting a room are somewhat greater. Some of those bedrooms can be a little tight on space but this is also reflected in the room rates. Rooms 11, 17 and 18 are the best in the house and the general decoration is a blend of the contemporary with some Asian influence; some of the rooms have jet showers and others balconies. But what makes the hotel stand out is that the owner is nearly always on the property and his enthusiasm has been passed to his staff. This may not be a glitzy West End hotel but they really do make an effort to get to know their guests and help in anyway they can. There is no restaurant, but then it doesn't need one: there are plenty of places in which to eat that are no more than a vigorous stroll away. A plentiful breakfast is provided and, on summer days, can even be taken on the small terrace.

Metropolitan

G4

Old Park Ln ✉ W1K 1LB
⊖ Hyde Park Corner
✆ (020) 7447 1000
Closed 25 December and 1 January
e-mail info.lon@metropolitan.como.bz
www.metropolitan.como.bz

147 rm – †£468 ††£468, ☕ £28 – 3 suites

Nobu *(See restaurant listing)*

Metropolitan

The Metropolitan is inextricably linked to its über-cool hang-out, The Met Bar. If you've never managed to blag your way past the doorman at night you can now secure entry by grabbing yourself some 'Afternoon Delight': a healthy version of afternoon tea with low-fat cakes and breadless sandwiches. The Metropolitan Hotel is well over a decade old now; in design terms, there may be more contemporary competitors around but it continues to hold its own in the fashion stakes by letting its guests create their own atmosphere. The bedrooms are neutral in colour and gadgets are discreetly integrated; all get regular licks of paint or, following an overnight stay from the occasional wannabe rock star, a full redecoration. Plenty of rooms overlook the park but the more interesting views are those facing east over the rooftops. The spa promises plenty of holistic treatments while London's original Nobu on the first floor ensures a further sprinkling of stardust. Even better, the staff now provide good service instead of just standing at an angle, looking cool.

The Milestone

D4

1-2 Kensington Ct. ✉ W8 5DL   ⊖ High Street Kensington
☎ (020) 7917 1000
e-mail bookms@rchmail.com
www.milestonehotel.com

57 rm – ♦£282/336 ♦♦£318/372, ☲ £29 – 6 suites

The Milestone

The Milestone proves that it is the service, not the space, which makes a hotel. With 100 members of staff for 57 bedrooms, it's odds-on you'll be well looked after; the hotel prides itself on keeping records of the whims and preferences of their regulars. Plenty of thought has gone into the design and decoration of the bedrooms which are undergoing a refurbishment. It's in the detail where you notice the extra effort: there's a little gift with the turn-down service and the bathrobes are seasonally adjusted so one gets a lighter robe in summer. The suites display greater levels of whimsy than the standard rooms – just check out the art deco inspired Mistinguett Suite, named in honour of the celebrated music hall entertainer, while Johnny Weissmuller would feel more at home in The Safari Suite. The sitting room is a comfy place, with a jaunty looking Noel Coward hanging above the fireplace. The Jockey bar is so named as this was where the horses were stabled in the days when this Victorian building was a private house. The dining room is an intimate, wood-panelled affair.

KENSINGTON ▶ PLAN XIII

Number Sixteen

16 Sumner Pl ⊠ SW7 3EG ⊖ South Kensington
☏ (020) 7589 5232
e-mail sixteen@firmdale.com
www.numbersixteenhotel.co.uk

42 rm – ♦£144 ♦♦£336, ☕ £17.50

Firmdale

Number Sixteen opened back in 2001 and was the first one in Tim and Kit Kemp's Firmdale Group of hotels not to have its own restaurant. This actually suits it because it feels more like a private house than the others and, with repeat business standing at around 55%, they've clearly got it right. Attention to detail underpins the operation, whether in the individual styling of the bedrooms or the twice-daily housekeeping service. Breakfast is in the conservatory overlooking the little garden – don't miss the smoothie of the day – and is served until midday: welcome acknowledgement that not every guest has an early morning meeting. Firmdale also operates its own laundry service which explains how the bed linen retains such crispness. Rooms 2 and 7 have their own private patio terrace and all the first floor rooms benefit from large windows and balconies. The drawing room, with its plump sofa cushions and pretty butterfly theme, is a very charming spot and there's the added bonus of a nearby honesty bar.

One Aldwych

1 Aldwych ⊠ WC2B 4RH   ⊖ Temple

𝒞 (020) 7300 1000

e-mail reservations@onealdwych.com

www.onealdwych.com

93 rm – ♦£468/583 ♦♦£468/583, ⊑ £23 – 12 suites

ⅠⓄ **Axis** *(See restaurant listing)*

One Aldwych

Things have gone all green down at One Aldwych. The hotel is hoping to take a lead within the hospitality industry on matters environmental (without, of course, neglecting its duties as a luxury hotel) and has appointed a 'green team' to oversee and coordinate procedures. The swimming pool is chemical and chlorine free; bath products are organic, and the chocolate on your pillow has been replaced by a book called 'Change the World'. As far as guests are concerned though, it's business as usual, which means extremely comfortable bedrooms and plenty of polished staff. Fruit and flowers are changed daily in the rooms, which are awash with Bang & Olufsen toys and also come with Frette linen; deluxe rooms and corner suites are particularly desirable. There's a choice of restaurant: the first floor Indigo offers a light, easy menu while Axis boasts more personality and greater ambition in its cooking. The lobby of the hotel is perhaps its most well known feature; not only does it double as a bar surprisingly successfully but it also changes its look according to the seasons.

STRAND AND COVENT GARDEN ▶ PLAN Ⅲ

385

The Pelham

E6

15 Cromwell Pl. ✉ SW7 2LA ⊖ South Kensington
✆ (020) 7589 8288
e-mail reservations@pelhamhotel.co.uk
www.pelhamhotel.co.uk

51 rm – 🚹£182 🚹🚹£299/322, ☕ £17.50 – 1 suite

The Pelham

It may no longer be part of the Firmdale group – it is owned by the people who have The Gore in Queensgate – but The Pelham retains that stylish look which comes from juxtaposing the feel of a classic English country house with the contemporary look of a city townhouse. Originally three houses, the hotel has a pleasing lack of conformity in its layout. Bold pastel colours, fine fabrics and a housekeeping department that could satisfy Howard Hughes combine to create bedrooms that are pristine, warm and comfortable. Spend too long in the panelled sitting room or library, with all those cushions, an honesty bar and a fridge full of ice cream and the world outside will seem positively frenzied. Downstairs you'll find Bistro Fifteen, a relaxed all-day affair which becomes a cosy and romantic dinner spot. Its menu is mostly centred on Europe with an extra Gallic element – a nod to the high number of French émigrés in the neighbourhood. There's a genuine helpfulness and an eagerness to please amongst the staff.

The Ritz

150 Piccadilly ✉ W1J 9BR ⊖ Green Park
✆ (020) 7493 8181
e-mail enquire@theritzlondon.com
www.theritzlondon.com

116 rm – ☦£300/954 ☦☦£420/954, ☕ £35 – 17 suites

🍴**The Ritz Restaurant** *(See restaurant listing)*

The Ritz

Henry James considered that, "There are few hours in life more agreeable than the hour dedicated to the ceremony known as afternoon tea". Such is the popularity of Tea at the Ritz, which is served daily in the grand surroundings of the Palm Court, that the ceremony begins at 11.30 am – an hour before lunch is served in their restaurant – and doesn't cease until 7.30pm. Meanwhile, the rest of the hotel, built in 1906 in the style of a French chateau, remains in fine form thanks to constant re-investment by its owners, the Barclay Brothers. The William Kent Room must be the most ornate private dining room in London and the bedrooms are all immaculately kept. The Royal and Prince of Wales Suites both have enormous square footage and are often booked for long stays by those for whom the credit crunch is no more than a mild irritant. The Ritz Restaurant, with its dinner dances, lavish surroundings and brigades of staff, evokes images of a more formal but more glamorous age and the art deco Rivoli bar remains a veritable jewel.

St James's ▶ Plan II

The Rockwell

181-183 Cromwell Rd. ✉ SW5 0SF   ⊖ Earl's Court
☎ (020) 7244 2000
e-mail reservations@therockwell.com
www.therockwell.com

40 rm – ♦£120/165 ♦♦£180/190, ☕ £12.50

The Rockwell

The Rockwell is steadily establishing itself on the London hotel
scene and is building up quite a loyal client base. They certainly
get a lot of things right: the reception is manned 24/7 and staff
are imbued with sufficient self-confidence to make eye-contact
with their guests and offer help when needed; the housekeeping
department also do an evening service of all the rooms. The
lobby is a comfortable space, with its fireplace and generous
scattering of newspapers. The hotel is made up of two Victorian
houses; the best two rooms are the split level 104 and 105
and those on the lower ground floor have their own private
patios. All rooms have showers rather than baths, and come
with top-brand toiletries, mini bars and free internet – you can
even borrow a laptop. Meals are relaxed affairs with plenty of
favourites and decent cocktails. Freshly baked croissants and
homemade breads are a feature of breakfast; sometimes served
on the south-facing garden terrace which is the hotel's most
appealing feature.

The Rookery

L2

12 Peters Lane, Cowcross St ⊠ EC1M 6DS
℘ (020) 7336 0931
e-mail reservations@rookery.co.uk
www.rookeryhotel.com

⊖ Barbican
Closed 24-26 December

32 rm – ♦£210/276 ♦♦£276, ☕ **£10.95 – 1 suite**

The Rookery

The mere fact that the original opening of the hotel was delayed because the owner couldn't find quite the right chimney pots tells you that authenticity is high on the agenda here. Named after the colloquial name for the local area from a time when it had an unruly reputation, the hotel is made up of a series of Georgian houses whose former residents are honoured in the naming of the bedrooms. Its decoration remains true to these Georgian roots, not only in the antique furniture and period features but also in the colours used; all the bedrooms have either half-testers or four-poster beds and bathrooms have roll-top baths. Rook's Nest, the largest room, is often used for fashion shoots. However, with the addition of flat screen TVs and wireless internet access, there is no danger of the hotel becoming a twee museum piece. Breakfast is served in the bedrooms and there is just one small sitting room which leads out onto a little terrace - its mural of the owner herding some cows goes some way towards blocking out the surrounding sights of the 21C.

St James's Hotel and Club

H4

7-8 Park Pl. ✉ SW1A 1LS ⊖ Green Park
✆ (020) 7316 1600
e-mail reservation@stjameshotelandclub.com
www.stjameshotelandclub.com

50 rm – †£282/414 ††£282/522, ☕ £22 – 10 suites

A/C

SAT

VISA

AE

St James's Hotel & Club

Dating from 1892, this building was a private club for many years and the hotel manages to retain something of that clubby spirit. It certainly feels as though it is run for the benefit of its guests, rather than a balance sheet, and staff make genuine efforts to get to know the guests and their individual peculiarities. While the public areas are quite compact, the interior has been sympathetically modernised and features over 200 pieces of art; mostly British and German works from the 1930s and '40s. Bedrooms are well-equipped and have smart, marble bathrooms. A few have small terraces; the Presidential Suite comes with an enormous one that can host up to 60 people. The restaurant is intimate and the cooking and service are undertaken with considerable expertise. The hotel's other great bonus is its location: this is the centre of central London but Park Place is also a cul-de-sac so it's quiet to boot. There's also a cut-through to Green Park where you'll find a pile of towels and water, left by the hotel for those who insist on running round it.

St Martins Lane

13

45 St Martin's Ln ⊠ WC2N 3HX   ⊖ Charing Cross
☏ (020) 7300 5500
e-mail sml@morganshotelgroup.com
www.morganshotelgroup.com

202 rm – †£246/594 ††£246/594, ☕ £25 – 2 suites

St Martin's Lane

If you're uncomfortable with the idea of hotel staff calling you by your first name or have never considered working out in a gym wearing a pair of stilettos then St Martins Lane is probably not the hotel for you; nor you the right guest for them. Philippe Starck's design of the modern juxtaposed with the baroque creates an eye-catching lobby. The bedrooms are decorated in a blizzard of white, although you can change the lighting according to your mood. The views get better the higher you go but all have floor to ceiling windows. Thanks to the paparazzi, readers of London's excitable free evening newspapers will be familiar with Bungalow 8: Anne Sacco's London outpost of her hip New York club is a favoured hang-out for the already-famous, the would-be-famous and the related-to-someone-famous-famous. Asia de Cuba is Scarface meets Dr No: fiery Floridian Cuban mixed with teasing influence from across Asia – dishes are designed for sharing. The Light Bar is sufficiently hip and the Gymbox is a branded gym with a nightclub vibe – what else?

Sanderson

50 Berners St ⊠ W1T 3NG   ⊖ Oxford Circus
📞 (020) 7300 1400
e-mail sanderson@morganshotelgroup.com
www.morganshotelgroup.com

150 rm – 🛏£414/627 🛏🛏£414/627, ☕ £25

🍴

Spa

🚲

🏋

A/C

((•))

SAT

VISA

MC

AE

D

Sanderson

When the doorman greets you with a "How ya doing?" you
know this is not a hotel that stands on ceremony. But the staff
do now smile, something that was all too rare in the early days
when they were mostly recruited from model agencies and
had a somewhat disdainful attitude towards the whole concept
of service. The Sanderson has always worn its exclusivity
with confidence but now there's some substance to it. The
Philippe Starck designed bedrooms still impress, with their
celestial whiteness, sleigh beds in the middle of the room and
idiosyncrasies such as the framed print hung on the ceiling – its
actually the same print in all the rooms, is called 'Pathway to
Heaven' and is designed to encourage heavenly thoughts before
sleep. Some bedrooms have their own treadmills while others
boast small terraces; the top two suites have their own lifts. On
the ground floor the Purple Bar has over 75 different vodkas,
miniature chairs and a selective door policy; the Long Bar is
more accessible and leads into Suka, their modern Malaysian
restaurant.

Savoy

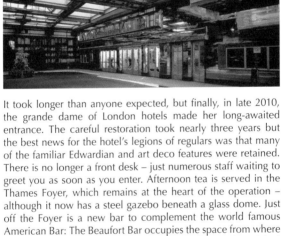
The Savoy

Stand ✉ WC2R 0EU   ⊖ Charing Cross
☎ (020) 7836 4343
e-mail savoy@fairmont.com
www.fairmont.com/savoy

221 rm – ♦£654/714 ♦♦£1,074, ☲ £30 – 47 suites

It took longer than anyone expected, but finally, in late 2010, the grande dame of London hotels made her long-awaited entrance. The careful restoration took nearly three years but the best news for the hotel's legions of regulars was that many of the familiar Edwardian and art deco features were retained. There is no longer a front desk – just numerous staff waiting to greet you as soon as you enter. Afternoon tea is served in the Thames Foyer, which remains at the heart of the operation – although it now has a steel gazebo beneath a glass dome. Just off the Foyer is a new bar to complement the world famous American Bar: The Beaufort Bar occupies the space from where the BBC once broadcast, with a champagne bar on the original stage. The River Room's art deco splendour has been given a contemporary makeover and its windows looking out over the river now open fully in summer. The luxurious bedrooms remain true to the hotel's origins and are split between Edwardian or art deco styles. The Grill had not opened as we went to press.

STRAND AND COVENT GARDEN ▶ PLAN III

Sofitel St James London

14

6 Waterloo Pl. ⊠ SW1Y 4AN   ⊖ Piccadilly Circus
☎ (020) 7747 2200
e-mail H3144@sofitel.com
www.sofitelstjames.com

180 rm ⊑ – †£450/510 ††£528 – 6 suites

🍴○**Brasserie Roux** *(See restaurant listing)*

Sofitel St James London

London's branch of the international Sofitel brand is housed within the impressive Grade II listed former HQ of the Cox and Kings Company. It was built in 1923 when it merged with a bank and is just a few paces away from St James's Park. This is a hotel that has managed the task of appearing quite contemporary to those who like things shiny and new but also sufficiently conservative to those who like things done properly. They also took good care of the basic but important aspects like soundproofing and double-glazing. The bedrooms all have a certain style and logic to their décor and are constantly being refreshed; the lobby is always well-manned and it quickly becomes apparent that service is taken seriously here. The ground floor brasserie is a large French affair and those for whom afternoon tea is a prerequisite of any London visit should get along to the pretty Rose Lounge. The most recent addition to the hotel is the conversion of the former Bank of Nigeria next door into a hugely impressive, state of the art spa.

Soho

4 Richmond Mews ⊠ W1D 3DH   ⊖ Tottenham Court Road

✆ (020) 7559 3000

e-mail soho@firmdale.com

www.sohohotel.com

89 rm – ♦£348 ♦♦£432, ⌷ £19.50 – 2 suites

Firmdale

It's almost as if they wanted to keep it secret. The hotel is on a relatively quiet mews – not something one readily associates with Soho – and, even as you approach, it gives little away. But inside one soon realises that, if it was a secret, it wasn't very well kept as it's always buzzing with people. Their every dietary whim or food mood should find fulfilment in 'Refuel', the restaurant with its own bar as backdrop. Whether your diet is gluten-free, vegetarian, vegan, carnivorous or organic you'll discover something worth ordering and, if you're off out, you'll find the early dinner menu a steal. It's also worth checking out the Film Club for a meal and a movie in the screening room. Upstairs and the bedrooms are almost celestial in their cleanliness. From jazzy orange to bright lime green, from crimsons to bold stripes, the rooms are vibrant in style and immaculate in layout; those on the top floor have balconies and terraces. Add infectiously enthusiastic service and it's little wonder the hotel has so many returning guests. And to think this was once an NCP car park.

Stafford

H4

16-18 St James's Pl. ✉ SW1A 1NJ   ⊖ Green Park
✆ (020) 7493 0111
e-mail information.london@kempinski.com
www.kempinski.com/london

73 rm – ♦£492/528 ♦♦£528, ▭ £25 – 15 suites

Stafford

The new owners of The Stafford plan to inject considerable funds into its refurbishment; an idea which will no doubt terrify many of its loyal and longstanding guests who appear to like things just the way they are. The feel of the hotel has always been that of an English country house in the heart of the city. The dining room keeps things quite formal and is one of the few around still insisting on the wearing of a jacket; its menu is a roll-call of classic British dishes. Perhaps the hotel's most celebrated feature is its American Bar which is festooned with an impressive collection of ties, helmets and pictures and is one of the best in London for those who like their bars with chairs and without music. The hotel is not, however, completely averse to the idea of modernisation: the relatively recently created suites in the Mews House, a converted office block in the rear courtyard of the hotel, are pretty impressive and act as a contrast to the more traditional rooms in the Carriage House.

Twenty Nevern Square

C6

20 Nevern Sq. ⊠ SW5 9PD   ⊖ Earl's Court
𝒞 (020) 7565 9555
e-mail info@twentynevernsquare.co.uk
www.twentynevernsquare.co.uk

20 rm – ♦£119/156 ♦♦£167/215, ☕ £10

Michelin

Booking well in advance is the key here, as this small but friendly hotel, with its quiet and leafy location in the typically Victorian Nevern Square, represents good value for money and gets booked up pretty quickly. The two best rooms are the Pasha and the more recently added Ottoman Suite and both have their own terrace, but all rooms are well looked after and given regular refits. Ten of the rooms overlook the gardens opposite but try to get one of the rooms on the top floor as these have more space. Hand-carved Indonesian furniture is found throughout and, together with the elaborately draped curtains, adds a hint of exoticism. You'll find gratis tea, coffee, water and a pile of daily newspapers laid on in the pleasant lounge beside the lovebirds, Mary and Joseph. Continental breakfast comes included in the room rate; it can be taken in the bedroom or the bright conservatory. The hotel's other great selling point is the genuine sense of neighbourhood one feels. Its sister hotel, the Mayflower, is around the corner.

EARL'S COURT ▶ PLAN XI

Westbury

H3

Bond St. ✉ W1S 2YF
℘ (020) 7629 7755
e-mail enquiries@westburymayfair.com
www.westburymayfair.com

⊖ Bond Street

232 rm – ♦£238/561 ♦♦£298/618, ☕ £26 – 13 suites

Westbury

They spent £25million on The Westbury a few years ago but the owner didn't like the bathrooms so he had them replaced with Italian marble; rather like Premier League football clubs, it helps having an owner who is more concerned with quality than with balance sheets. The hotel was built in the 1950s and caused quite a commotion at the time with its New York sensibilities. Nowadays it benefits from having some of the most famous designer brands just outside the front door while inside it's all very polished and comfortable. The celebrated Polo bar is elegantly decorated in Gucci and Fendi and the restaurant exudes an air of permanence and quiet professionalism. The bedrooms are sleek and comfy, and each floor is decorated with photos from that decade (for example, 1960s style icons adorn the 6th floor). The suites are particularly smart, especially those with art deco styling. The room service menu is also one of the most comprehensive you'll see - there are so many members of staff they have to be kept busy somehow.

Zetter

St John's Sq., 86-88 Clerkenwell Rd. ✉ EC1M 5RJ ⊖ Farringdon
℘ (020) 7324 4444
e-mail info@thezetter.com
www.thezetter.com

59 rm – ♦£222 ♦♦£222, ☕ £9.50

🍴 **Bistrot Bruno Loubet** *(See restaurant listing)*

The Zetter

The Zetter ticks all the boxes for a contemporary hotel - it's a converted Victorian warehouse in a hitherto neglected area of the city that's now having its time and is environmentally aware, with spring water bottled from its building's own well. Its restaurant, thanks to the reputation of chef Bruno Loubet, is busy pulling in the crowds; it has understated bedrooms offering everything from a huge array of music tracks to classic Penguin paperbacks and, to appreciate all these things, it attracts a clientele who know their wiis from their wi-fis. But what makes the place more than just another hip hotel is its friendly and hospitable staff who understand that the principles of hospitality remain the same, regardless of whether the hotel is trendy or traditional, and that coolness need not equate to aloofness. The restaurant has personality and bustle and comes into its own on sunny days thanks to its large windows overlooking St John's Square and the whole hotel has a definable sense of time and place.

You know
the MICHELIN guide

...Do you really
know **MICHELIN?**

- Data 31/12/2009

MICHELIN
A better way forward

The world No.1 in tyres with 16.3% of the market

A business presence in over **170 countries**

A manufacturing footprint
at the heart of markets

In 2009 **72** industrial sites in **19** countries produced:

- **150** million tyres
- **10** million maps and guides

Highly international **teams**

Over **109 200** employees* from all cultures on all continents

including **6 000** people employed in R&D centres in Europe, the US and Asia.

*102 692 full-time equivalent staff

The Michelin Group at a glance

Michelin competes

At the end of 2009

Le Mans 24-hour race
12 consecutive years of victories

Endurance 2009
- 6 victories on 6 stages in Le Mans Series
- 12 victories on 12 stages in American Le Mans Series

Paris-Dakar
Since the beginning of the event, the Michelin group has won in all categories

Moto endurance
2009 World Champion

Trial
Every World Champion title since 1981 (except 1992)

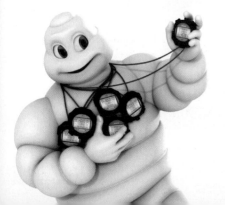

Michelin, established close to its customers

○ **72 plants in 19 countries**

- Algeria
- Brazil
- Canada
- China
- Colombia
- France
- Germany
- Hungary
- Italy
- Japan
- Mexico
- Poland
- Romania
- Russia
- Serbia
- Spain
- Thailand
- UK
- USA

● **A Technology Centre spread over 3 continents**

- Asia
- Europe
- North America

● **Natural rubber plantations**

- Brazil

Our mission

To make a sustainable contribution to progress in the mobility of goods and people by enhancing freedom of movement, safety, efficiency and the pleasure of travelling.

Michelin: committed to environmental-friendliness

Michelin, world leader in low rolling resistance tyres, actively reduces fuel consumption and vehicle gas emission.

For its products, Michelin develops state-of-the-art technologies in order to:
- Reduce fuel consumption, while improving overall tire performance.
- Increase life cycle to reduce the number of tyres to be processed at the end of their useful lives;
- Use raw materials which have a low impact on the environment.

Furthermore, at the end of 2008, 99.5% of tyre production in volume was carried out in ISO 14001* certified plants.

Michelin is committed to implementing recycling channels for end-of-life tyres.

*environmental certification

**Passenger Car
Light Truck**

Truck

Michelin
a key mobility enabler

Earthmover

Aircraft

Agricultural

Two-wheel

Distribution

Partnered with vehicle manufacturers, in tune with users,
active in competition and in all the distribution channels,
Michelin is continually innovating to promote mobility today
and to invent that of tomorrow.

**Maps and
Guides**

ViaMichelin,
travel
assistance
services

**Michelin
Lifestyle,**
for your travel
accessories

MICHELIN
plays on balanced performance

- **Long tyre life**
- **Fuel savings**
- **Safety on the road**

   ... MICHELIN tyres provide you with the best performance,
   without making a single sacrifice.

The MICHELIN tyre pure technology

1 Tread
A thick layer of rubber
provides contact with the ground.
It has to channel water away
and last as long as possible.

2 Crown plies
This double or triple reinforced belt
has both vertical flexibility
and high lateral rigidity.
It provides the steering capacity.

3 Sidewalls
These cover and protect the textile casing
whose role is to attach the tyre tread
to the wheel rim.

4 Bead area for attachment to the rim
Its internal bead wire
clamps the tyre firmly
against the wheel rim.

5 Inner liner
This makes the tyre
almost totally impermeable
and maintains the correct inflation pressure.

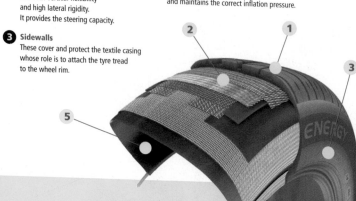

Heed
the MICHELIN Man's advice

To improve safety:

- I drive with the correct tyre pressure
- I check the tyre pressure every month
- I have my car regularly serviced
- I regularly check the appearance
  of my tyres (wear, deformation)
- I am responsive behind the wheel
- I change my tyres according to the season

www.michelin.com
www.michelin.(your country extension – e.g. .fr for France)

🍴🍽 Alphabetical list of Restaurants

A

411

Index **& Maps** ▶ Alphabetical list of Restaurants

413

Index of maps

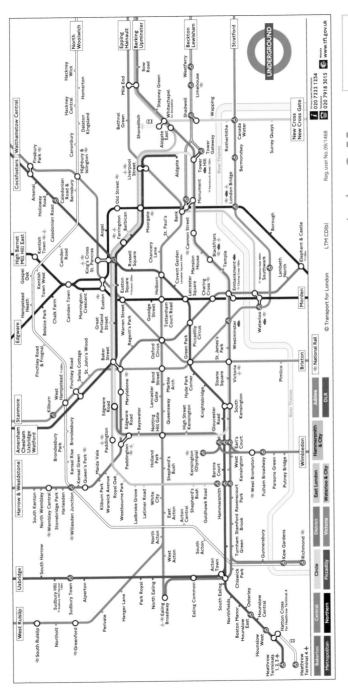

Index & Maps

UNDERGROUND

ℹ 020 7222 1234
✆ 020 7918 3015

www.tfl.gov.uk

Reg. user No./1468   LTM CD(b)   © Transport for London

Great Britain: Based on Ordnance Survey of Great Britain with the permission of the Controller of Her Majesty's Stationery Office, © Crown Copyright 100000247.

Cover photography : Rhodes Twenty Four

Manufacture française des pneumatiques Michelin

Société en commandite par actions au capital de 304 000 000 EUR
Place des Carmes-Déchaux – 63000 Clermont-Ferrand (France)
R.C.S. Clermont-Fd B 855 200 507

© Michelin, Propriétaires-éditeurs

Dépot légal janvier 2011
Printed in Italy : 12-2010
Compogravure : NORD COMPO à Villeneuve-d'Ascq (France)
Impression et brochage : LA TIPOGRAFICA VARESE, Varese (Italia)